EDENS ZERO

WARSHIP OF THE DEMON KING 3

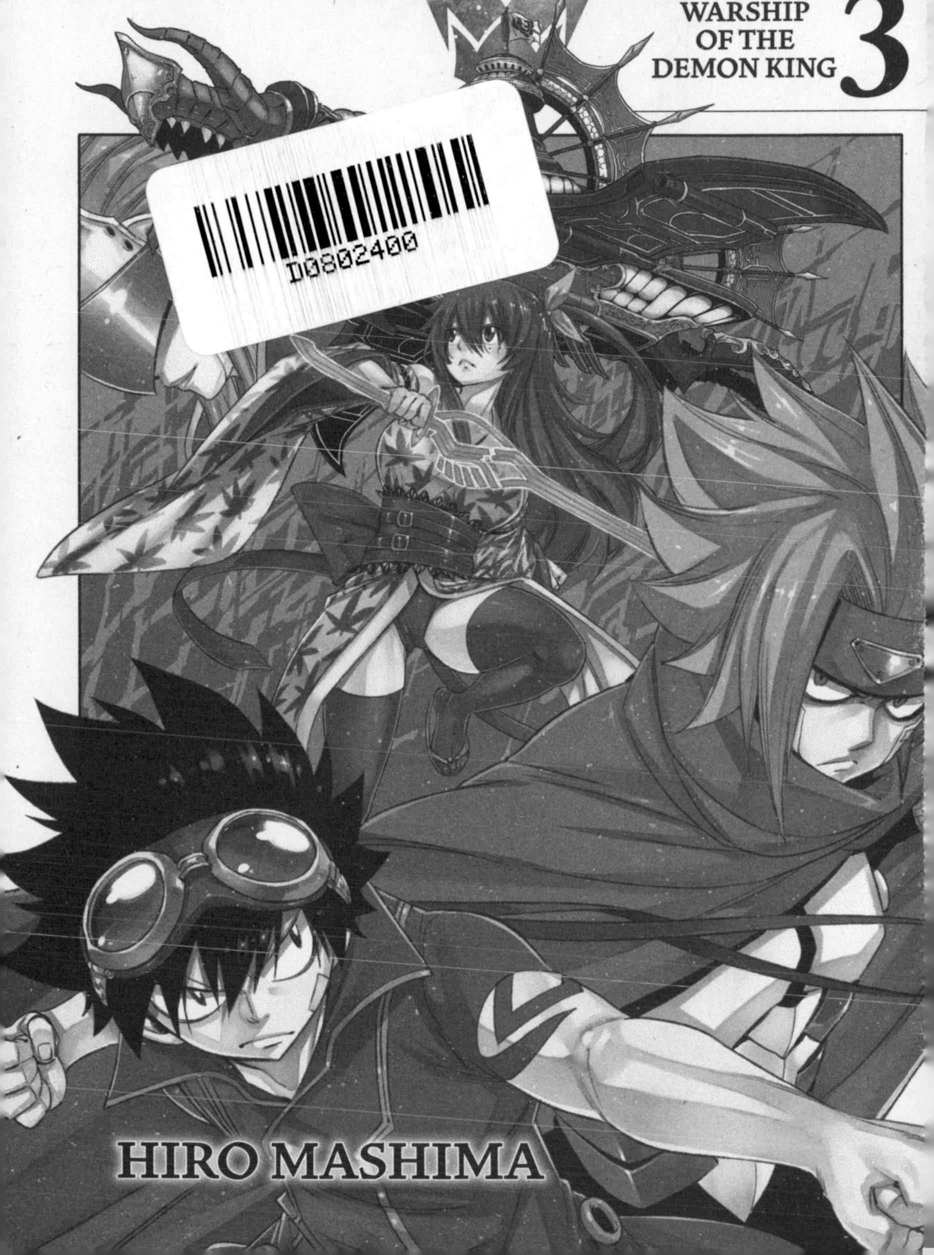

HIRO MASHIMA

EDENS ZERO
3
contents

CHAPTER 15:
WARSHIP OF THE DEMON KING

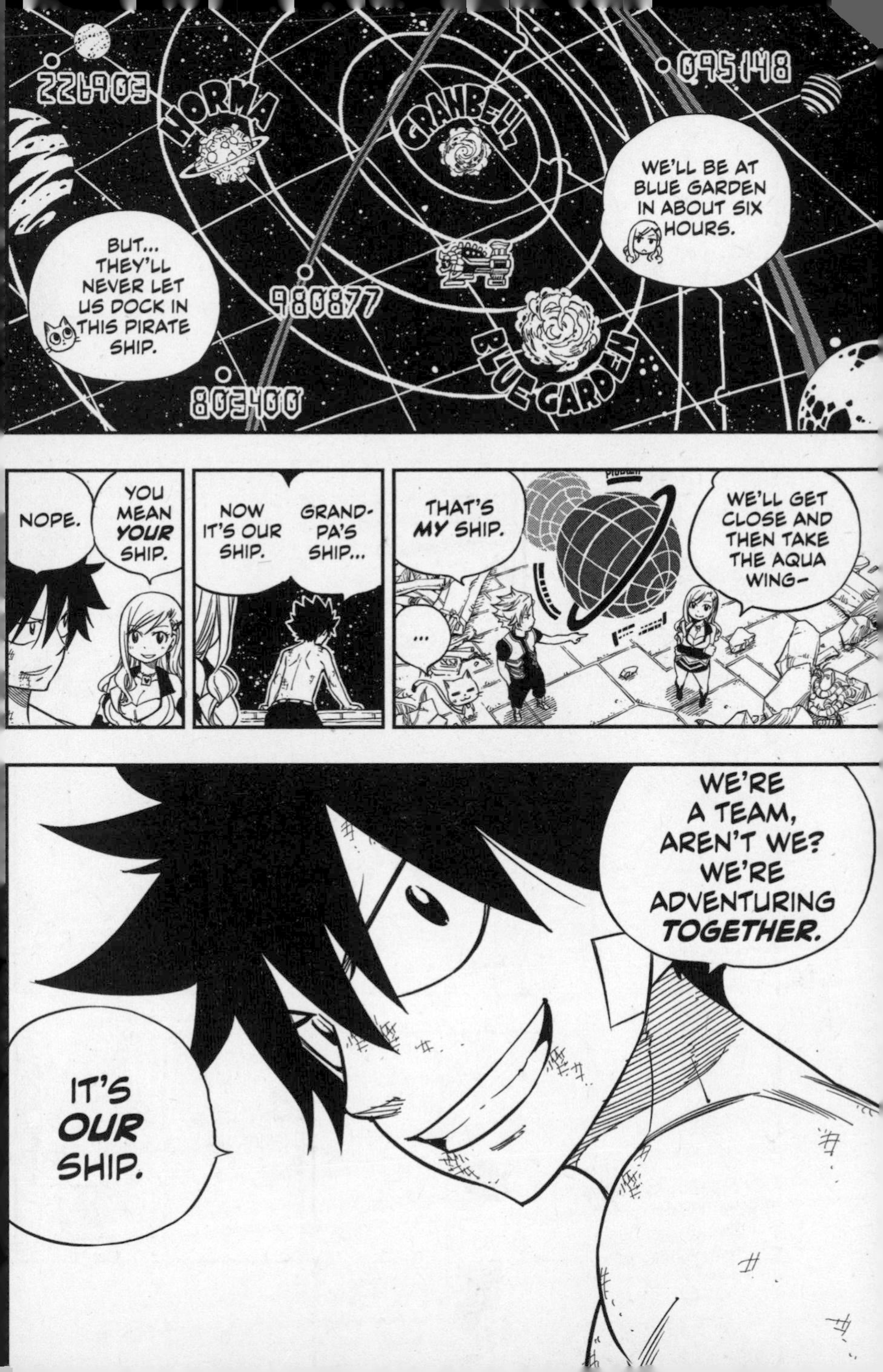

095148
GRANBELL
NORMA
226903
WE'LL BE AT BLUE GARDEN IN ABOUT SIX HOURS.
BUT... THEY'LL NEVER LET US DOCK IN THIS PIRATE SHIP.
980877
BLUE GARDEN
803400
WE'LL GET CLOSE AND THEN TAKE THE AQUA WING-
THAT'S MY SHIP.
...
GRAND-PA'S SHIP...
NOW IT'S OUR SHIP.
YOU MEAN YOUR SHIP.
NOPE.
WE'RE A TEAM, AREN'T WE? WE'RE ADVENTURING TOGETHER.
IT'S OUR SHIP.

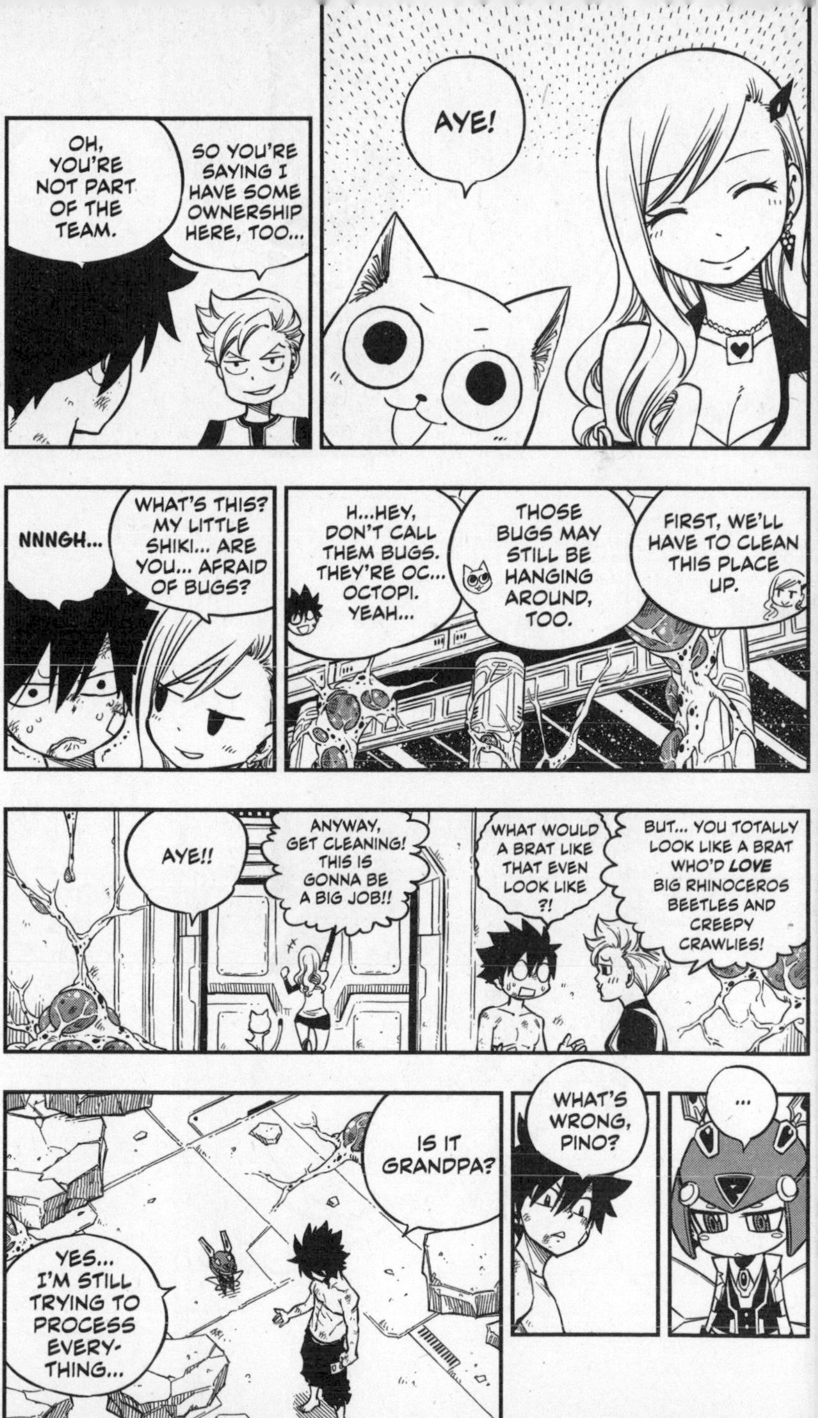
AYE!
SO YOU'RE SAYING I HAVE SOME OWNERSHIP HERE, TOO...
OH, YOU'RE NOT PART OF THE TEAM.
FIRST, WE'LL HAVE TO CLEAN THIS PLACE UP.
THOSE BUGS MAY STILL BE HANGING AROUND, TOO.
H...HEY, DON'T CALL THEM BUGS. THEY'RE OC... OCTOPI. YEAH...
WHAT'S THIS? MY LITTLE SHIKI... ARE YOU... AFRAID OF BUGS?
NNNGH...
BUT... YOU TOTALLY LOOK LIKE A BRAT WHO'D *LOVE* BIG RHINOCEROS BEETLES AND CREEPY CRAWLIES!
WHAT WOULD A BRAT LIKE THAT EVEN LOOK LIKE ?!
ANYWAY, GET CLEANING! THIS IS GONNA BE A BIG JOB!!
AYE!!
...
WHAT'S WRONG, PINO?
IS IT GRANDPA?
YES... I'M STILL TRYING TO PROCESS EVERY-THING...

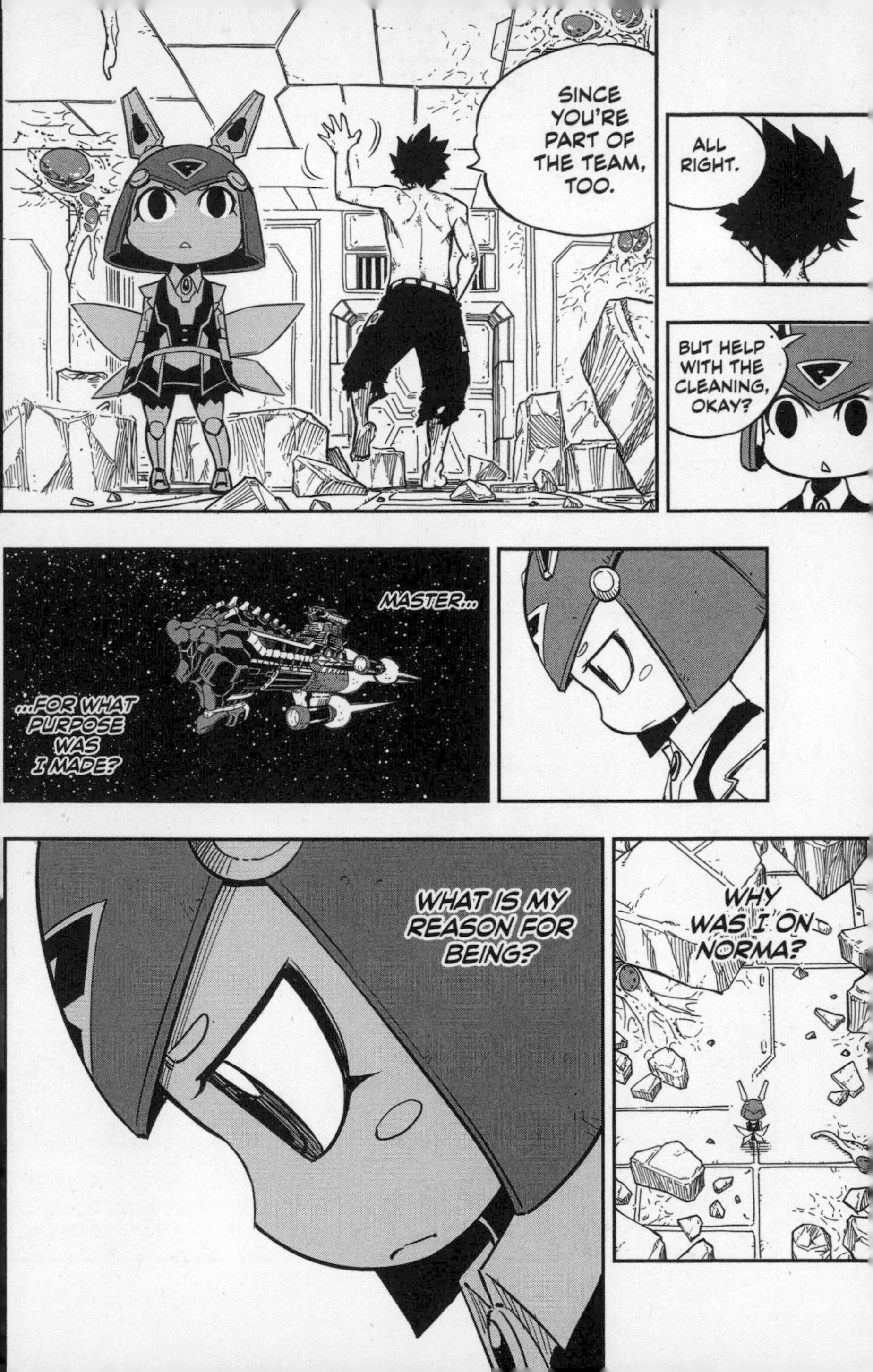
ALL RIGHT.
BUT HELP WITH THE CLEANING, OKAY?
SINCE YOU'RE PART OF THE TEAM, TOO.
MASTER...
...FOR WHAT PURPOSE WAS I MADE?
WHY WAS I ON NORMA?
WHAT IS MY REASON FOR BEING?

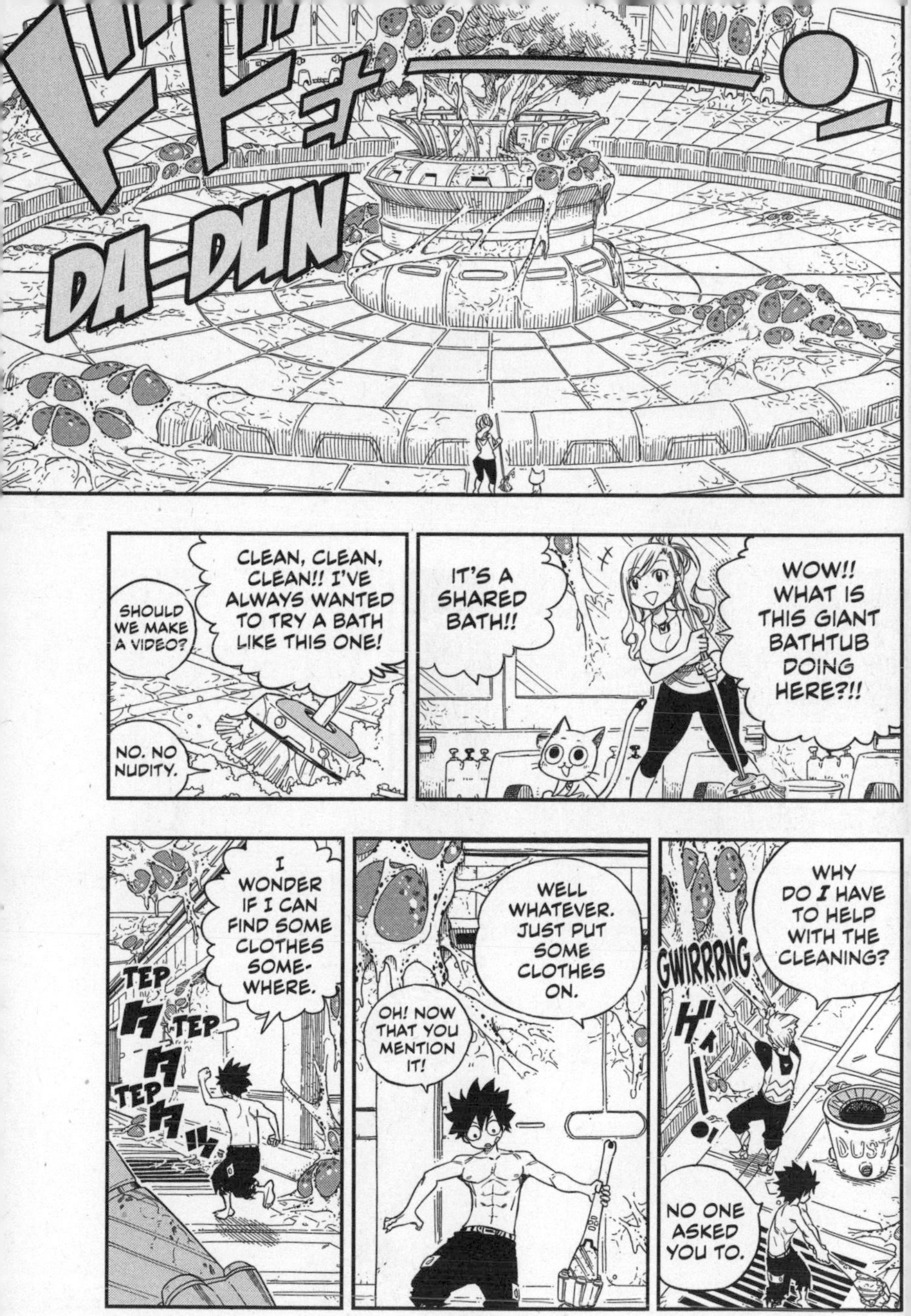
DA-DUN
WOW!! WHAT IS THIS GIANT BATHTUB DOING HERE?!!
IT'S A SHARED BATH!!
CLEAN, CLEAN, CLEAN!! I'VE ALWAYS WANTED TO TRY A BATH LIKE THIS ONE!
SHOULD WE MAKE A VIDEO?
NO. NO NUDITY.
WHY DO *I* HAVE TO HELP WITH THE CLEANING?
GWIRRRNG
DUST
NO ONE ASKED YOU TO.
WELL WHATEVER. JUST PUT SOME CLOTHES ON.
OH! NOW THAT YOU MENTION IT!
I WONDER IF I CAN FIND SOME CLOTHES SOME-WHERE.
TEP
TEP
TEP

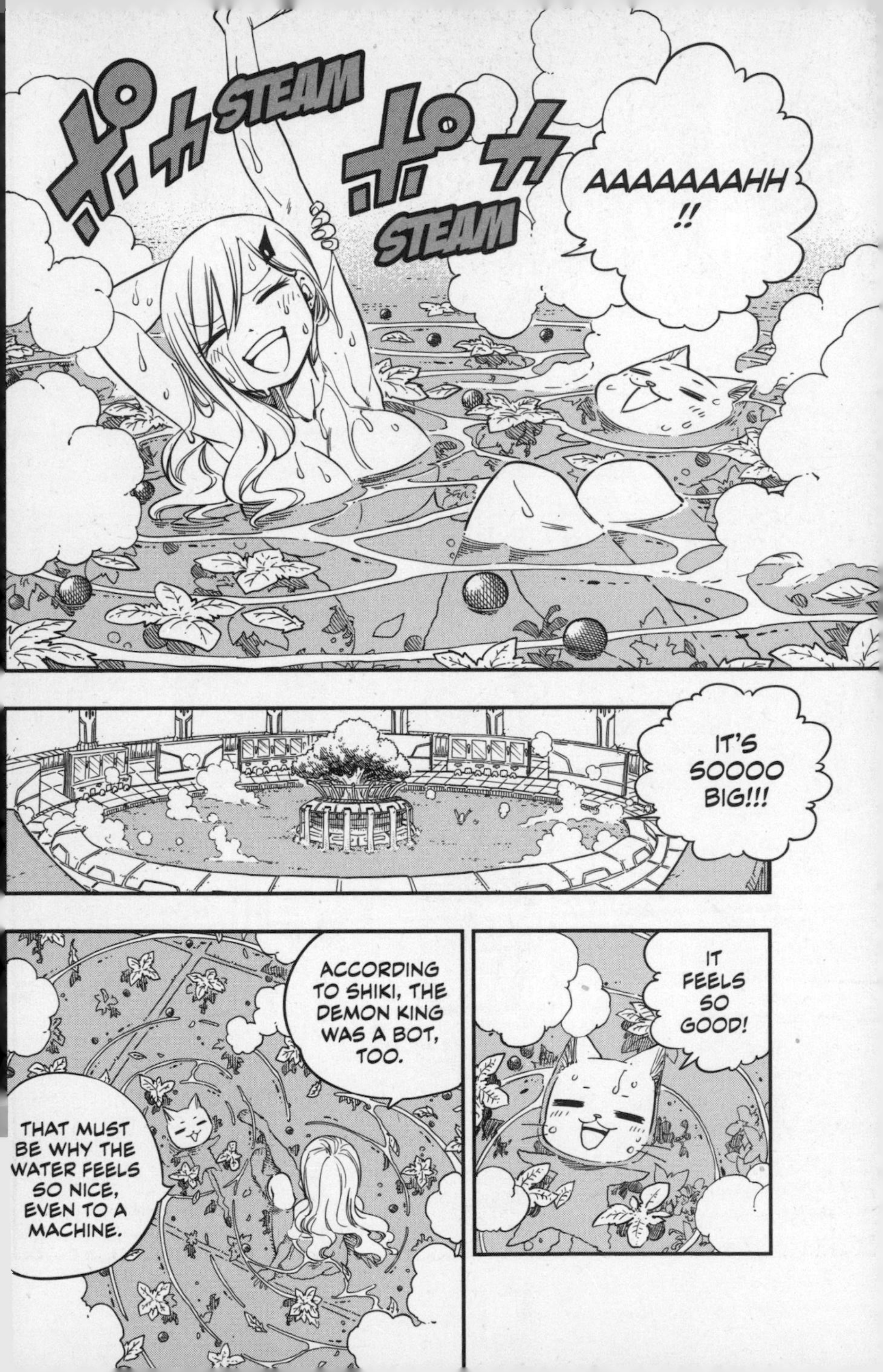
AAAAAAAHH!!
ポカ STEAM
ポカ STEAM
IT'S SOOOO BIG!!!
IT FEELS SO GOOD!
ACCORDING TO SHIKI, THE DEMON KING WAS A BOT, TOO.
THAT MUST BE WHY THE WATER FEELS SO NICE, EVEN TO A MACHINE.

LOOK!! THE STARS ARE SO BEAUTIFUL!

YEAH.

TO THINK, WE USED LIVE IN THE SHADOWS OUTSIDE OF TOWN...

AND NOW HERE WE ARE, ON THIS GIANT SHIP.

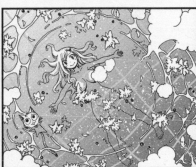

KRIK KRIK KRIK

?

KRIK

REBEC-CA!!

HW'' '' SPLASH

WE CAN!!

GWIP

AND WE WILL!!

DO YOU THINK WE CAN GO EVEN FARTHER?

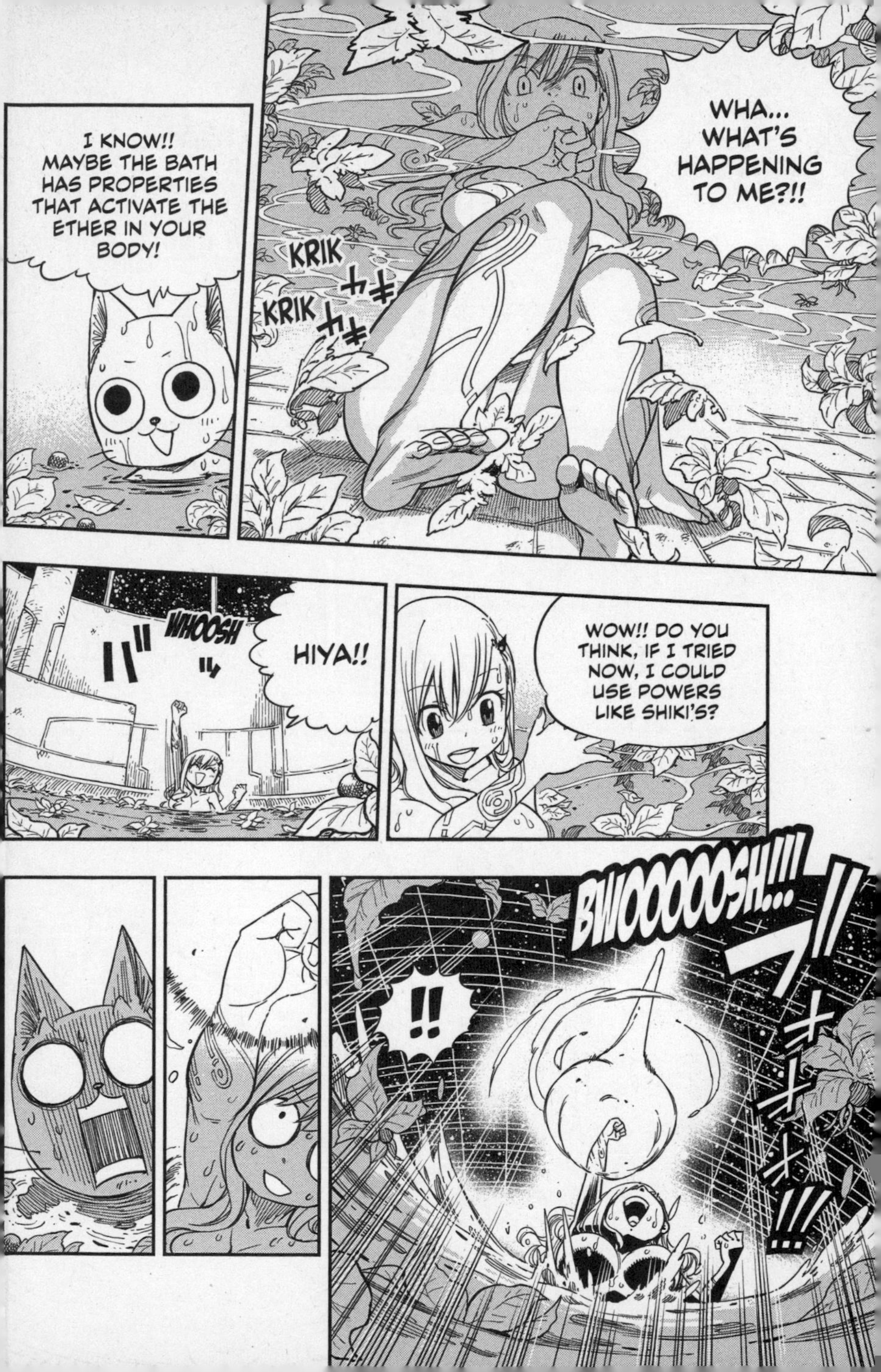
WHA... WHAT'S HAPPENING TO ME?!!
KRIK
KRIK
I KNOW!! MAYBE THE BATH HAS PROPERTIES THAT ACTIVATE THE ETHER IN YOUR BODY!
WOW!! DO YOU THINK, IF I TRIED NOW, I COULD USE POWERS LIKE SHIKI'S?
HIYA!!
WHOOSH
BWIOOOOOSH!!!
!!

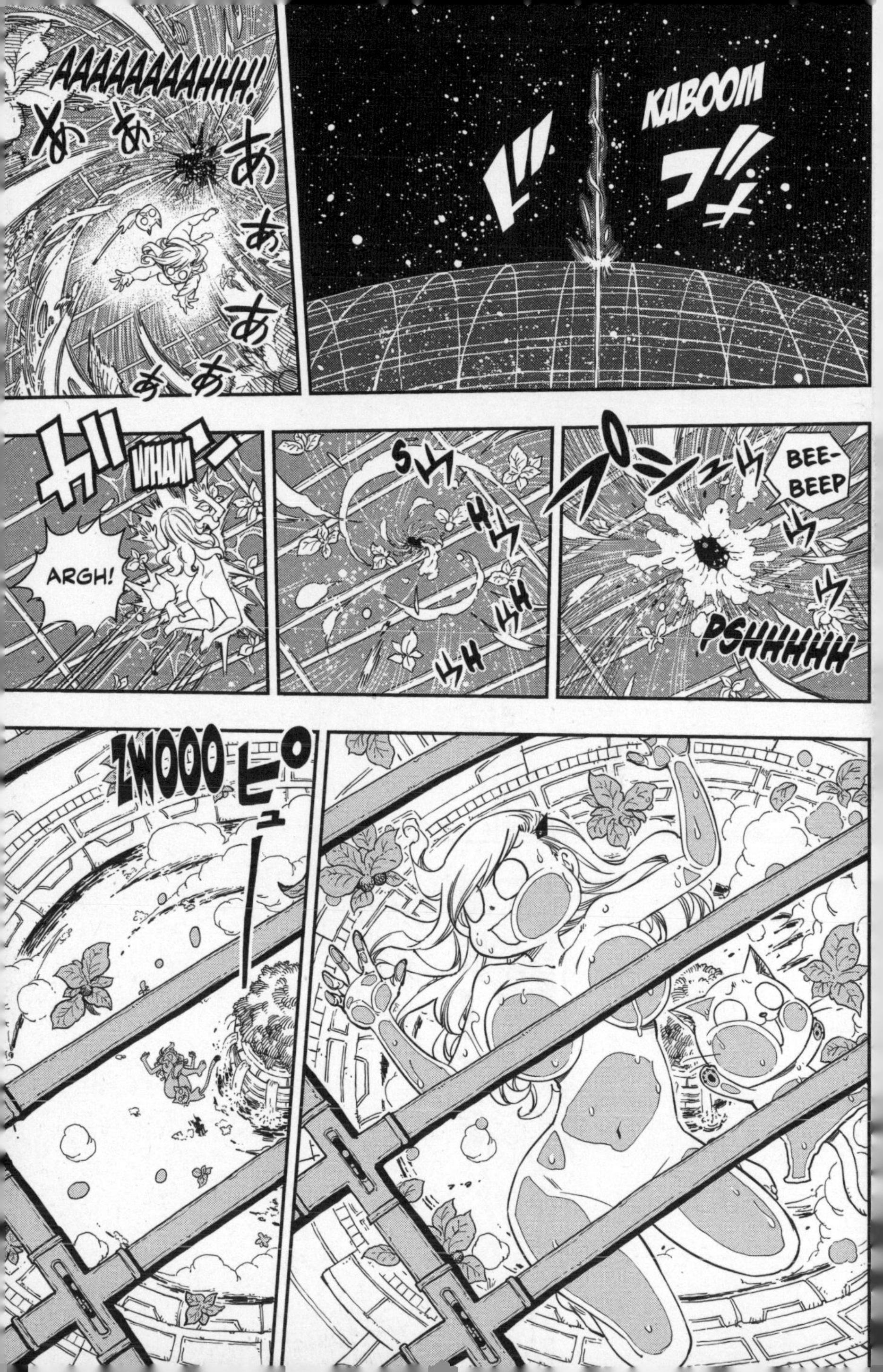

KABOOM
AAAAAAAAAHHH!
BEE-BEEP
PSHHHHHH
SHHHHH
WHAM
ARGH!
ZWOOO

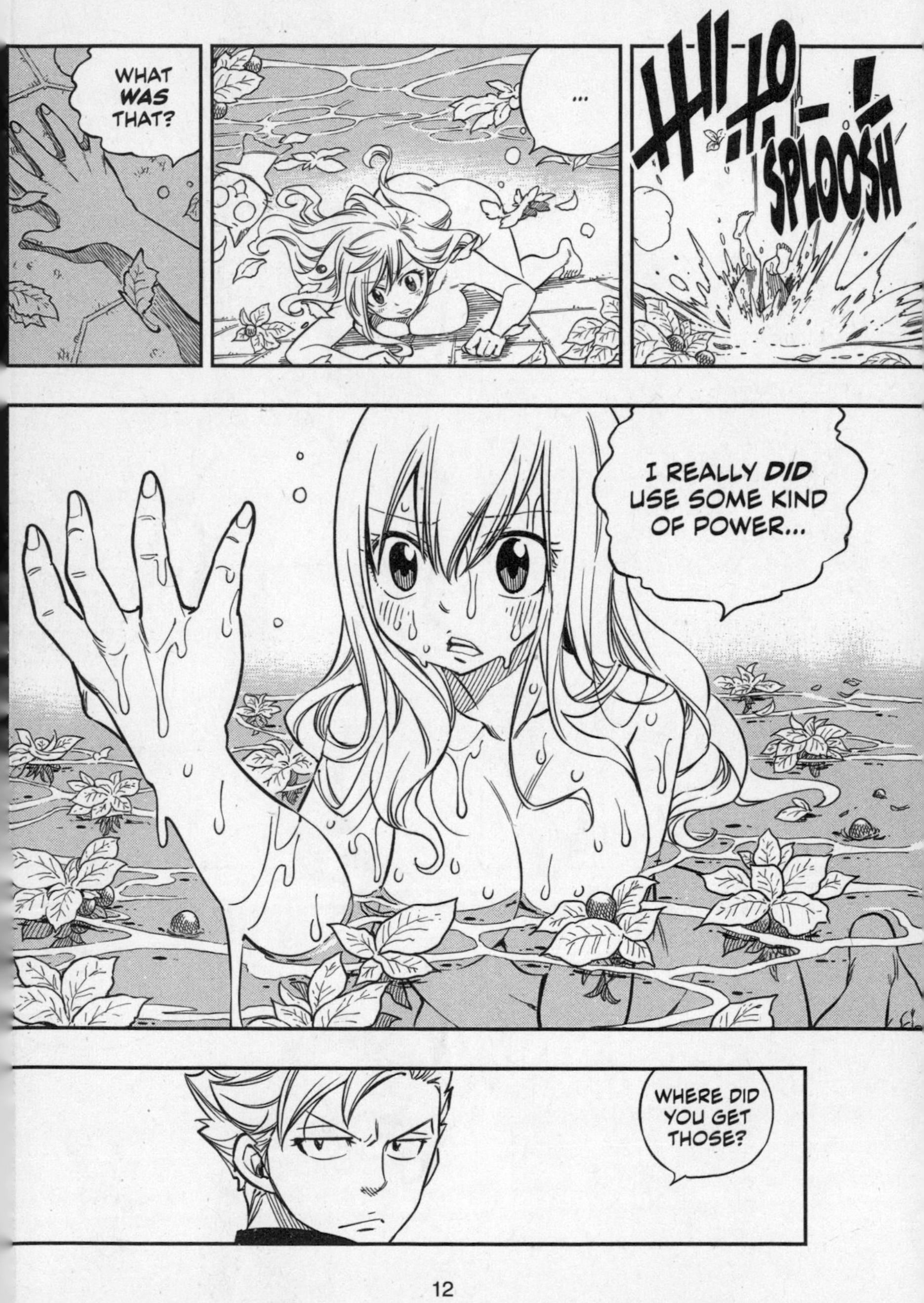
SPLOOSH
...
WHAT WAS THAT?
I REALLY DID USE SOME KIND OF POWER...
WHERE DID YOU GET THOSE?

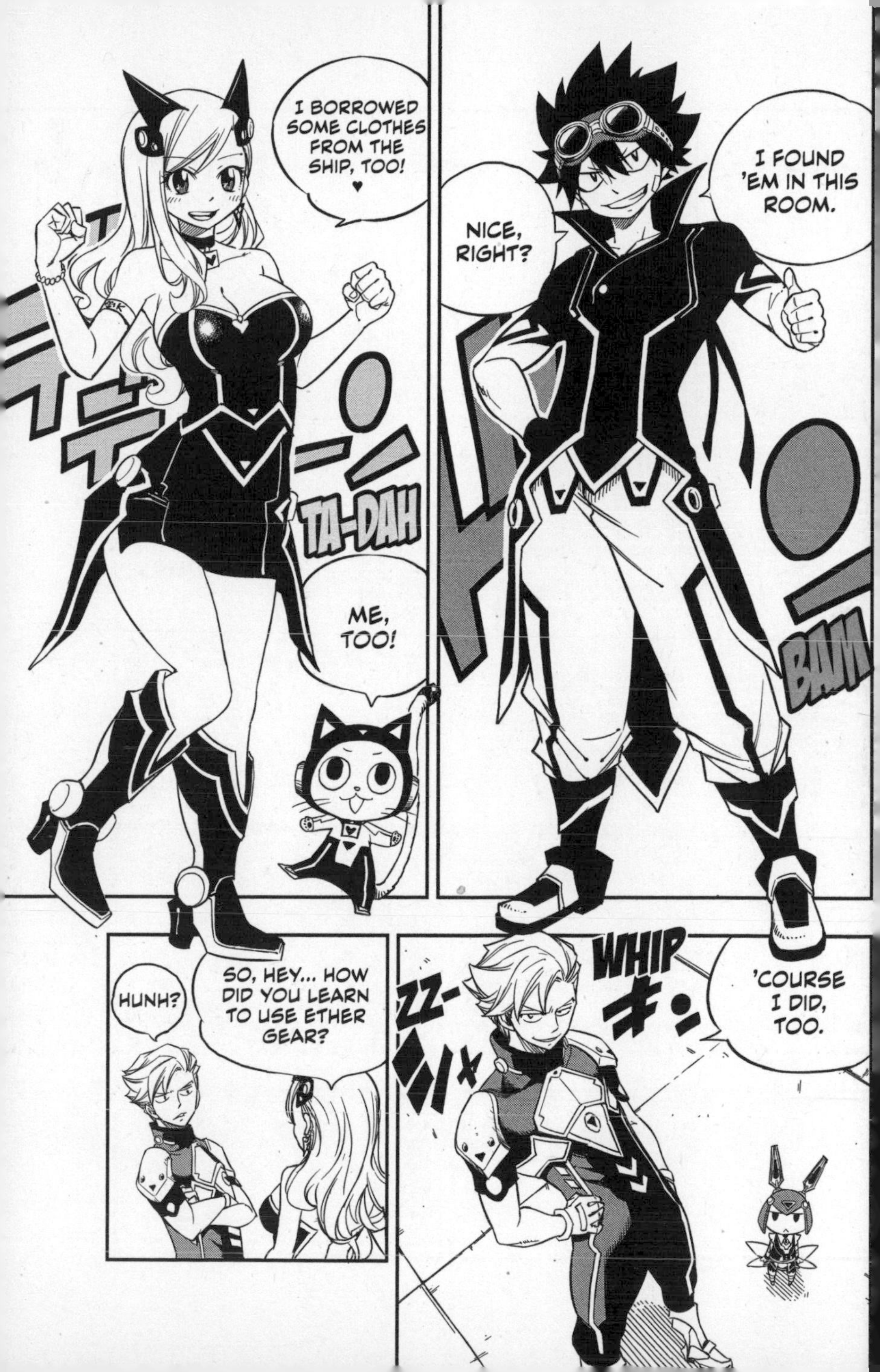
I FOUND 'EM IN THIS ROOM.
NICE, RIGHT?
BAM
I BORROWED SOME CLOTHES FROM THE SHIP, TOO! ♥
TA-DAH
ME, TOO!
'COURSE I DID, TOO.
WHIP
SO, HEY... HOW DID YOU LEARN TO USE ETHER GEAR?
HUNH?

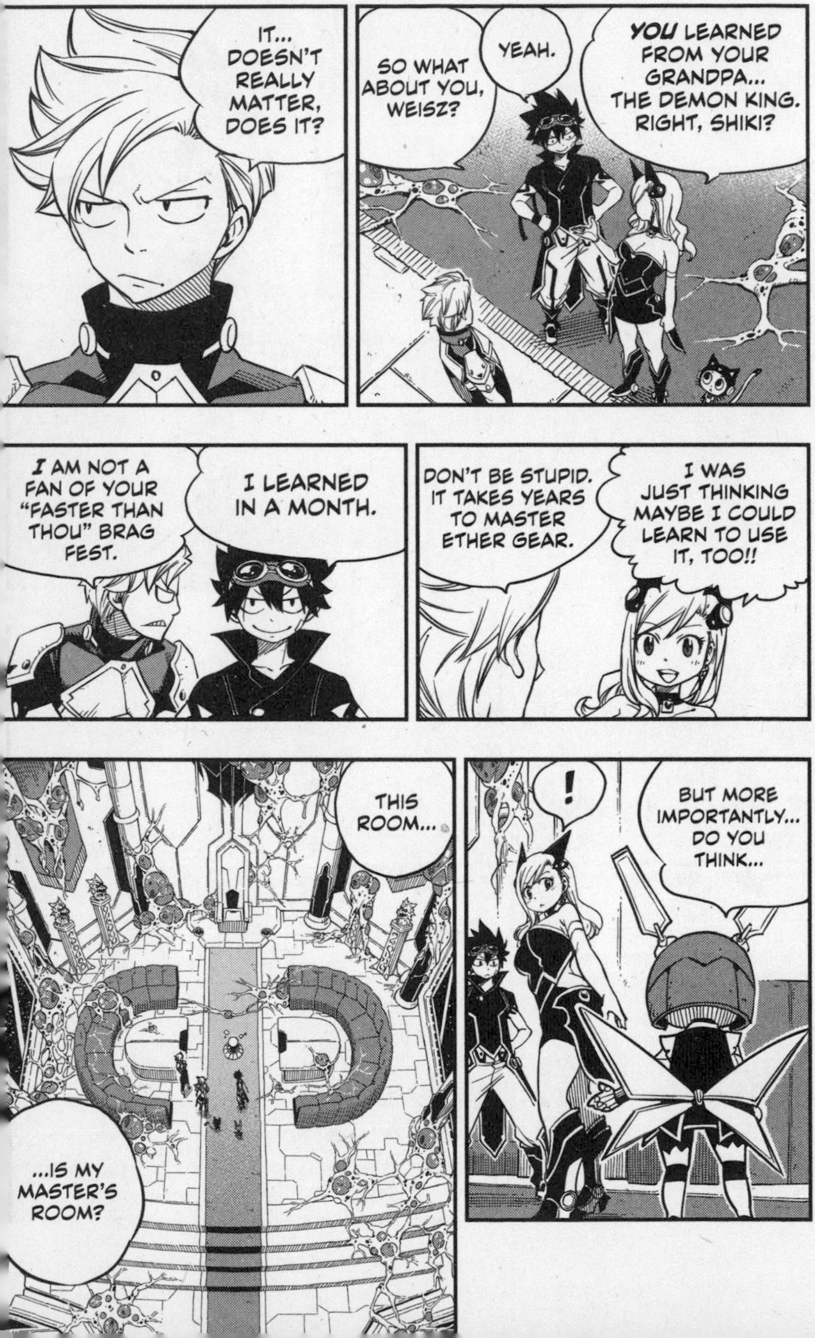
YOU LEARNED FROM YOUR GRANDPA... THE DEMON KING. RIGHT, SHIKI?
YEAH.
SO WHAT ABOUT YOU, WEISZ?
IT... DOESN'T REALLY MATTER, DOES IT?
I WAS JUST THINKING MAYBE I COULD LEARN TO USE IT, TOO!!
DON'T BE STUPID. IT TAKES YEARS TO MASTER ETHER GEAR.
I LEARNED IN A MONTH.
I AM NOT A FAN OF YOUR "FASTER THAN THOU" BRAG FEST.
BUT MORE IMPORTANTLY... DO YOU THINK...
!
THIS ROOM...
...IS MY MASTER'S ROOM?

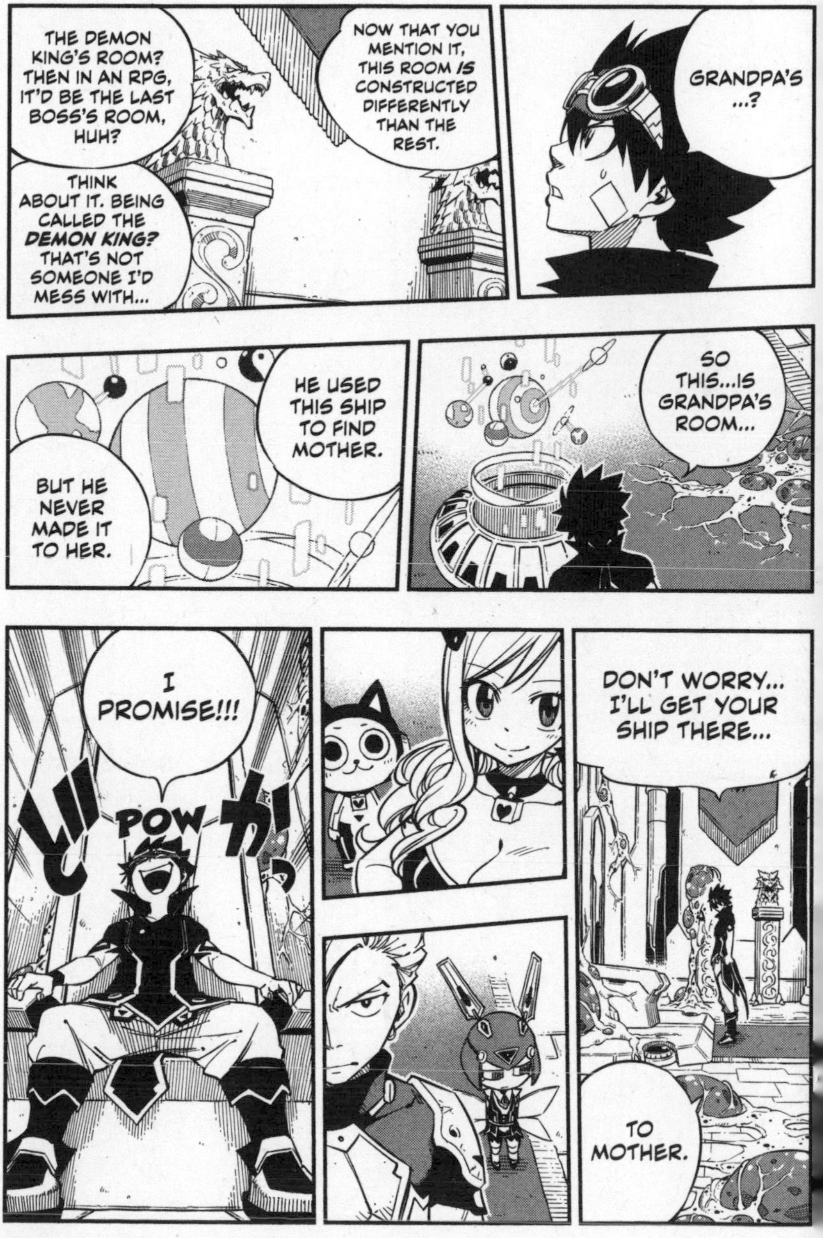
GRANDPA'S ...?
NOW THAT YOU MENTION IT, THIS ROOM *IS* CONSTRUCTED DIFFERENTLY THAN THE REST.
THE DEMON KING'S ROOM? THEN IN AN RPG, IT'D BE THE LAST BOSS'S ROOM, HUH?
THINK ABOUT IT. BEING CALLED THE ***DEMON KING?*** THAT'S NOT SOMEONE I'D MESS WITH...
SO THIS...IS GRANDPA'S ROOM...
HE USED THIS SHIP TO FIND MOTHER.
BUT HE NEVER MADE IT TO HER.
DON'T WORRY... I'LL GET YOUR SHIP THERE...
TO MOTHER.
I PROMISE!!!
POW

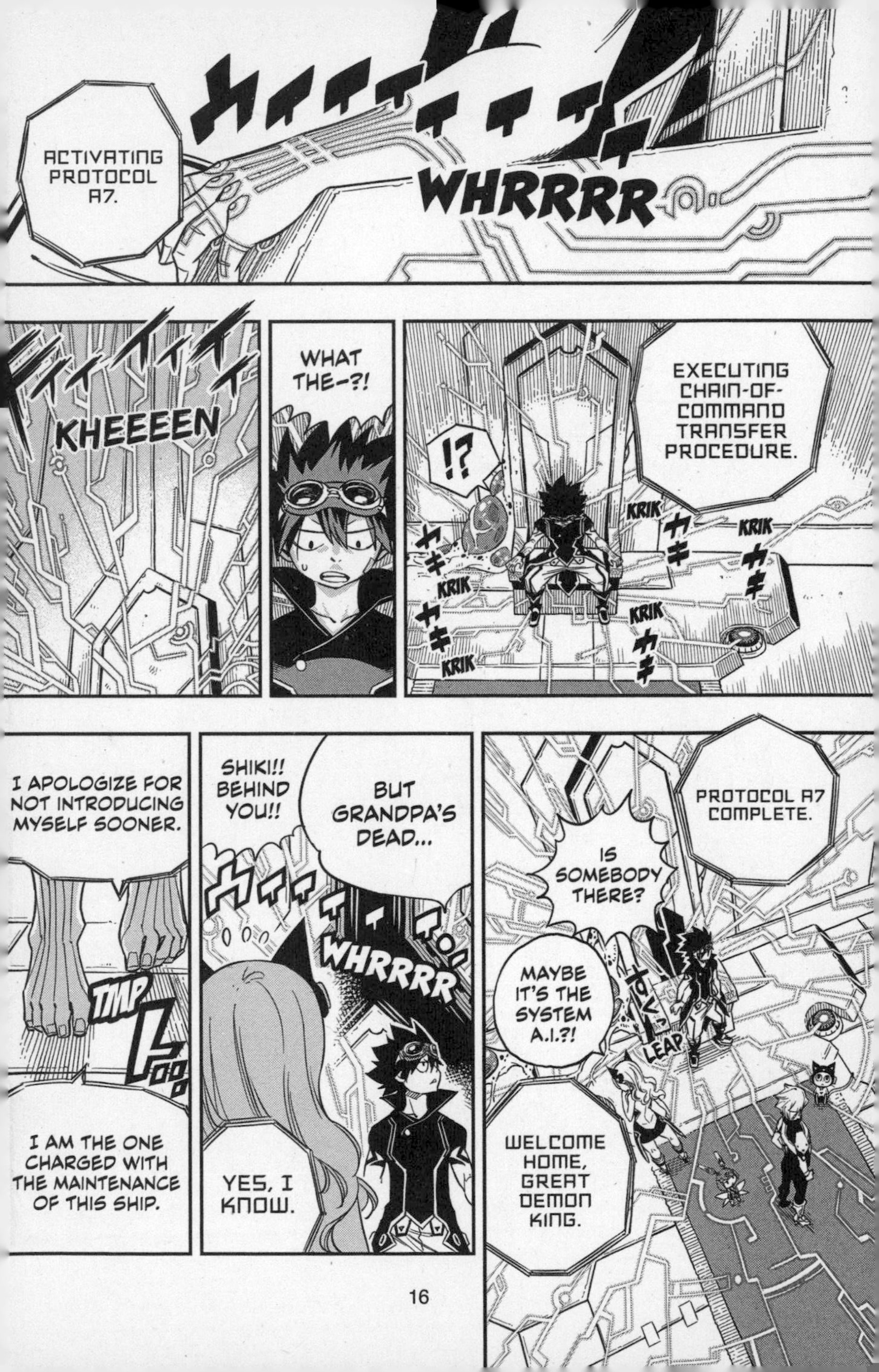
ACTIVATING PROTOCOL A7.
WHRRRR
EXECUTING CHAIN-OF-COMMAND TRANSFER PROCEDURE.
!?
KRIK
KRIK
KRIK
KRIK
KRIK
WHAT THE-?!
KHEEEEN
PROTOCOL A7 COMPLETE.
IS SOMEBODY THERE?
MAYBE IT'S THE SYSTEM A.I.?!
LEAP
WELCOME HOME, GREAT DEMON KING.
BUT GRANDPA'S DEAD...
SHIKI!! BEHIND YOU!!
WHRRRR
YES, I KNOW.
I APOLOGIZE FOR NOT INTRODUCING MYSELF SOONER.
TMP
I AM THE ONE CHARGED WITH THE MAINTENANCE OF THIS SHIP.

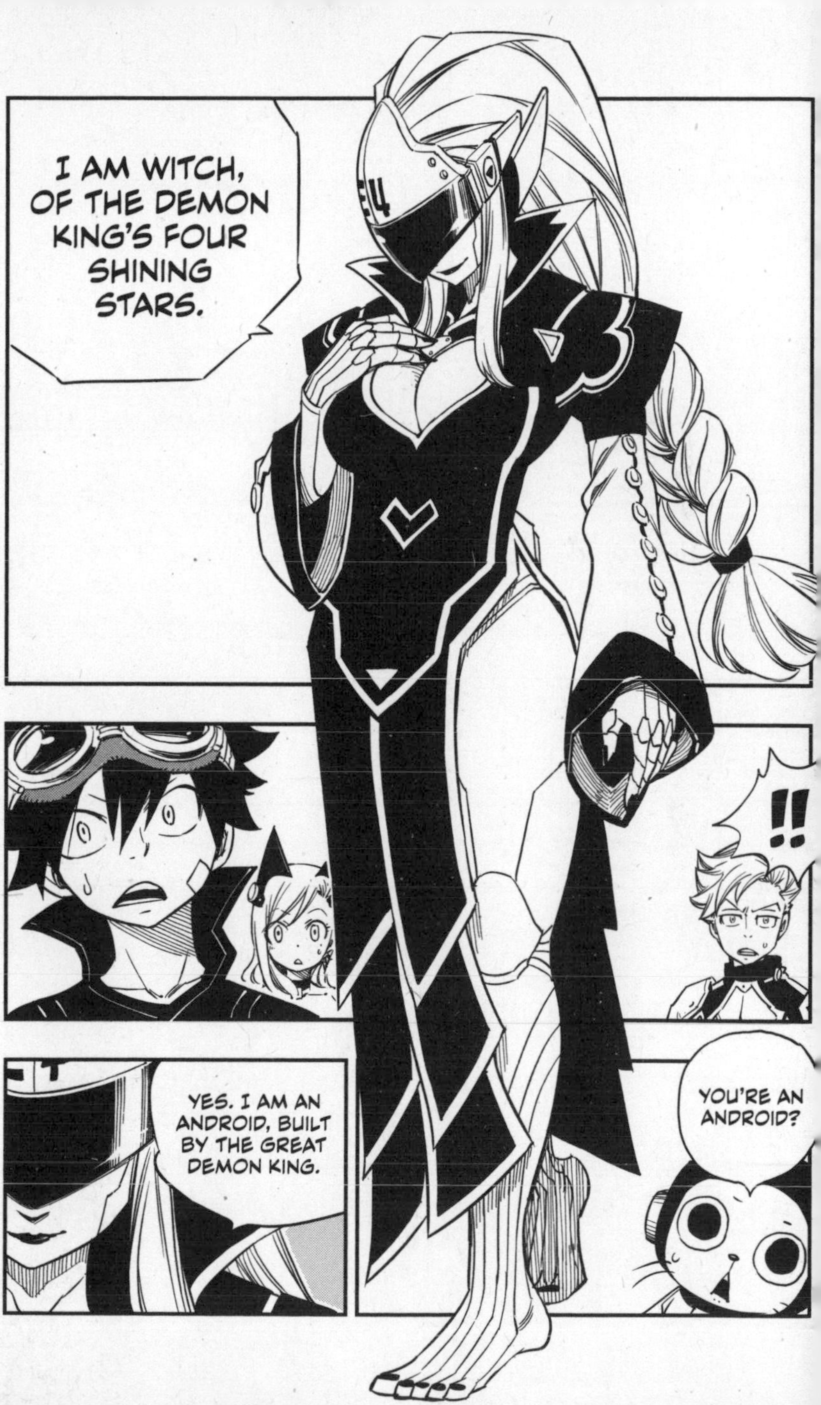
I AM WITCH, OF THE DEMON KING'S FOUR SHINING STARS.
!!
YOU'RE AN ANDROID?
YES. I AM AN ANDROID, BUILT BY THE GREAT DEMON KING.

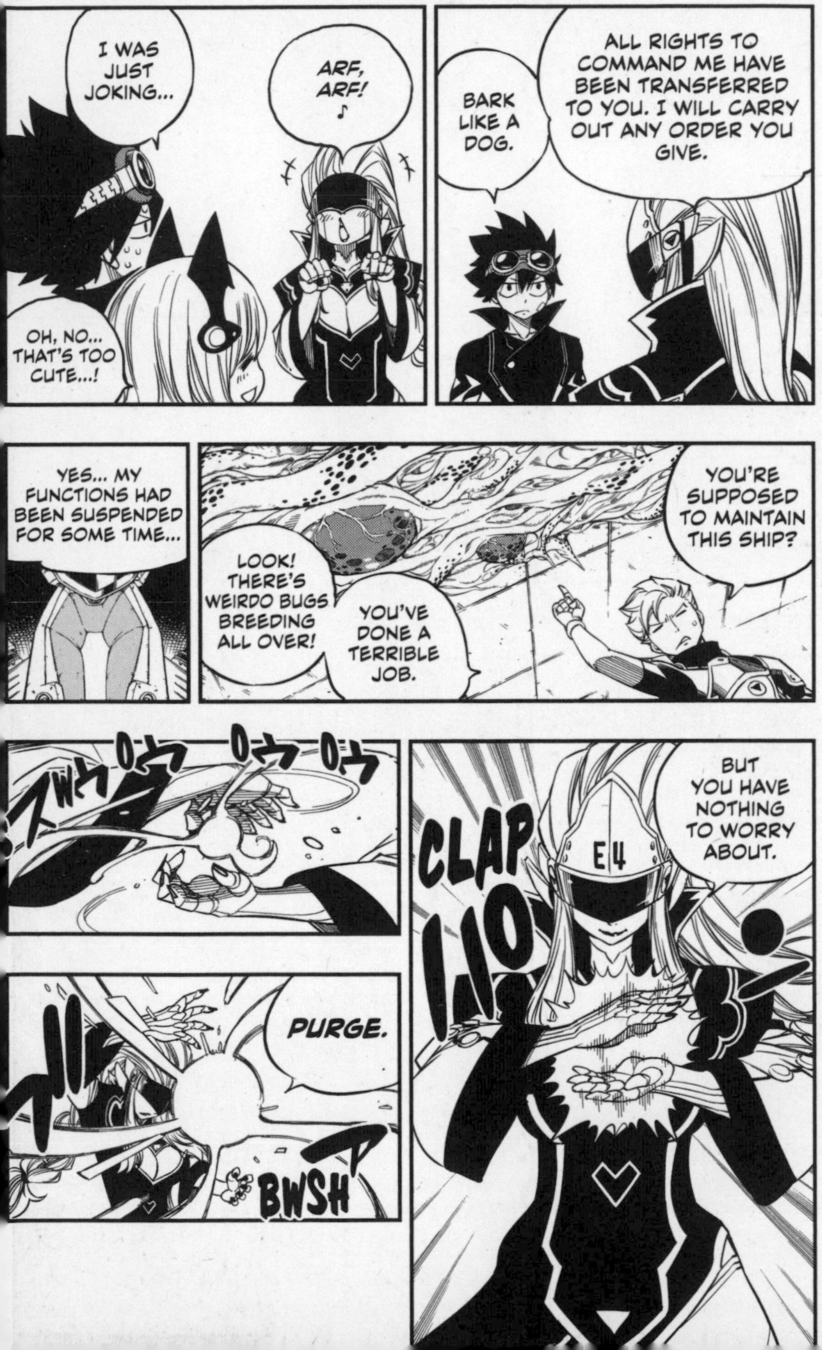
ALL RIGHTS TO COMMAND ME HAVE BEEN TRANSFERRED TO YOU. I WILL CARRY OUT ANY ORDER YOU GIVE.
BARK LIKE A DOG.
ARF, ARF! ♪
I WAS JUST JOKING...
OH, NO... THAT'S TOO CUTE...!
YOU'RE SUPPOSED TO MAINTAIN THIS SHIP?
LOOK! THERE'S WEIRDO BUGS BREEDING ALL OVER!
YOU'VE DONE A TERRIBLE JOB.
YES... MY FUNCTIONS HAD BEEN SUSPENDED FOR SOME TIME...
BUT YOU HAVE NOTHING TO WORRY ABOUT.
CLAP
E4
PURGE.
BWSH

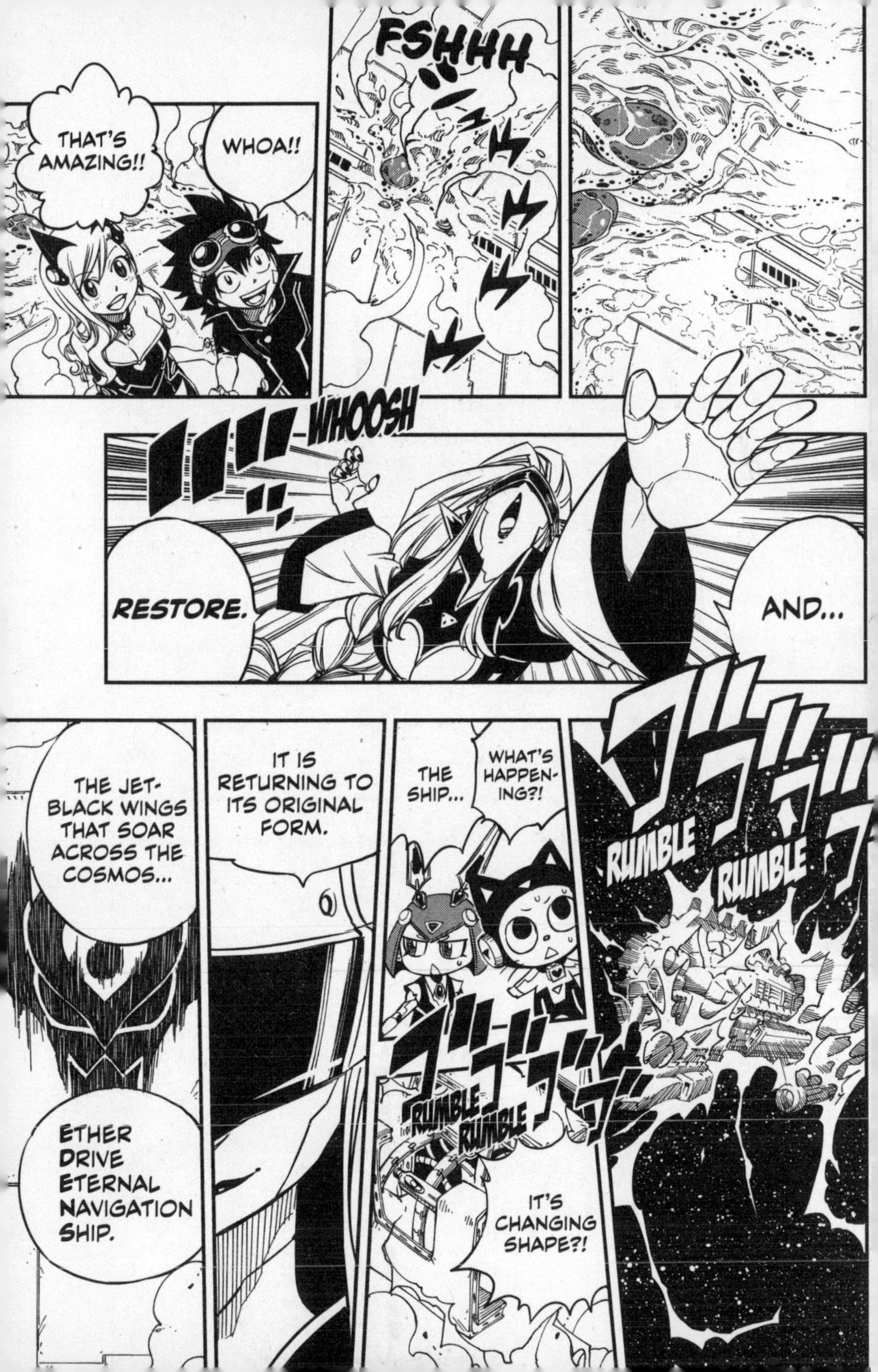
FSHHH
WHOA!!
THAT'S AMAZING!!
WHOOSH
AND...
RESTORE.
RUMBLE
RUMBLE
WHAT'S HAPPENING?!
THE SHIP...
RUMBLE
RUMBLE
IT'S CHANGING SHAPE?!
IT IS RETURNING TO ITS ORIGINAL FORM.
THE JET-BLACK WINGS THAT SOAR ACROSS THE COSMOS...
ETHER DRIVE ETERNAL NAVIGATION SHIP.

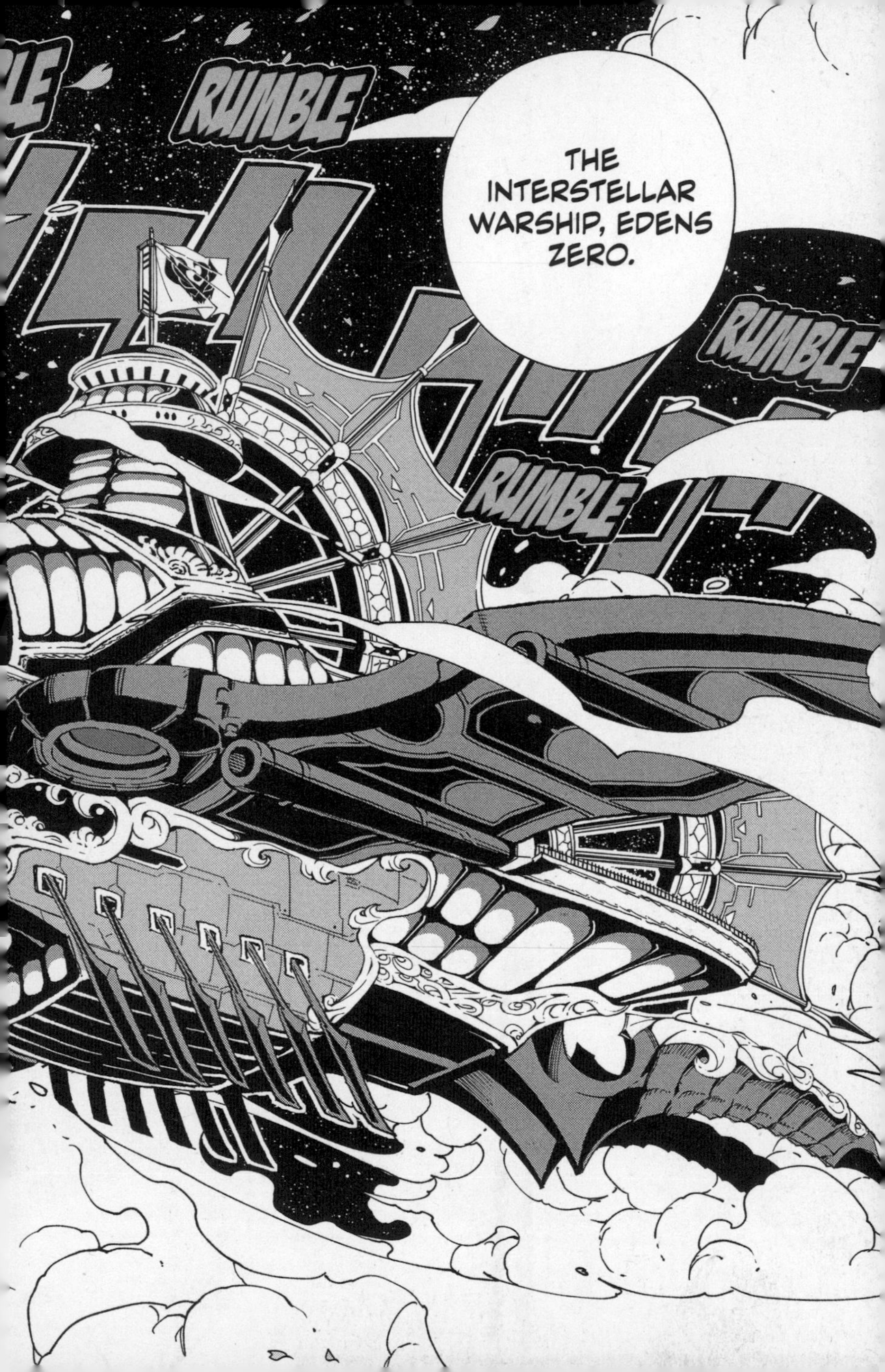
THE INTERSTELLAR WARSHIP, EDENS ZERO.
RUMBLE
RUMBLE
RUMBLE

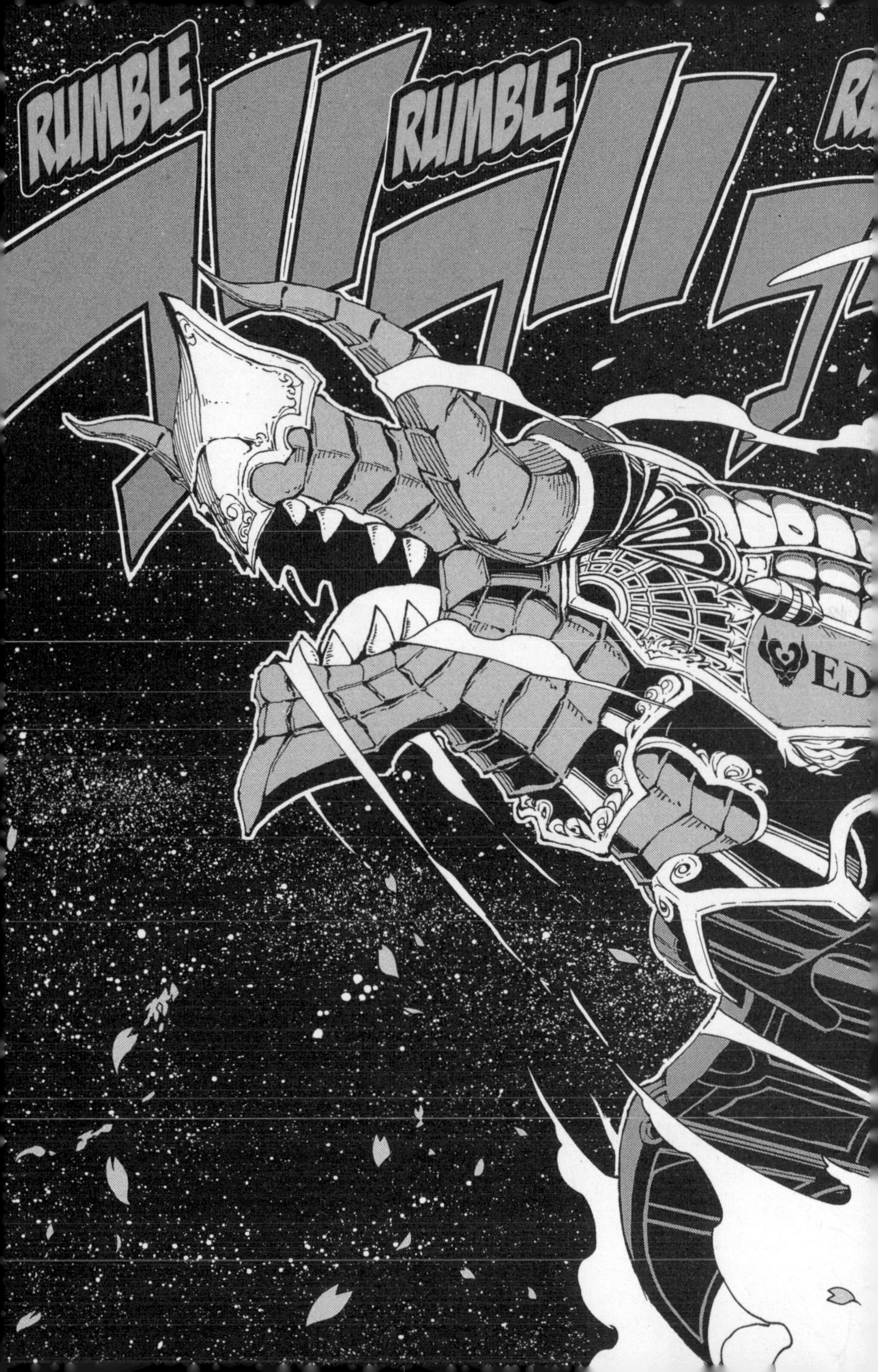
RUMBLE
RUMBLE

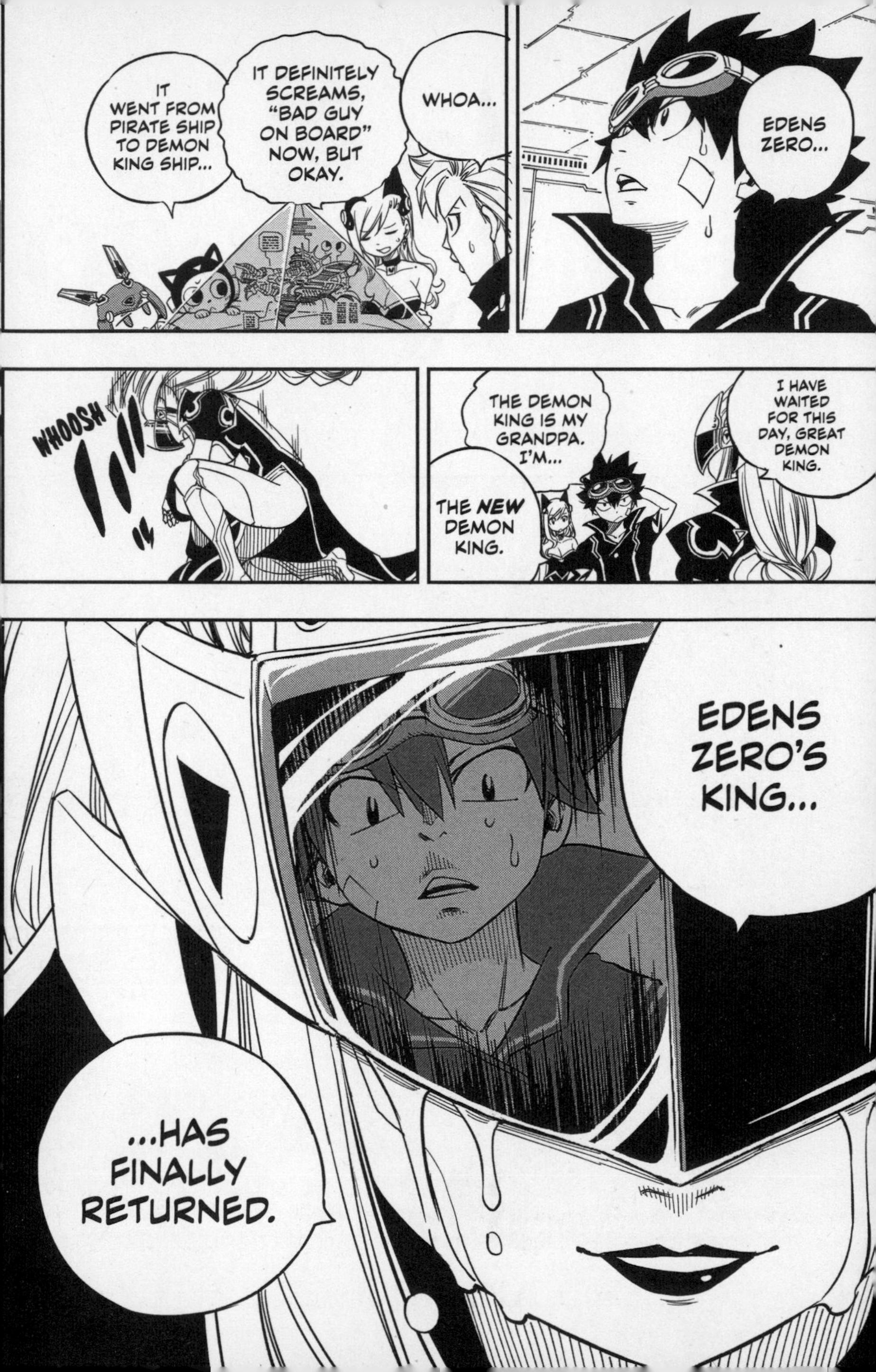
EDENS ZERO...
WHOA...
IT DEFINITELY SCREAMS, "BAD GUY ON BOARD" NOW, BUT OKAY.
IT WENT FROM PIRATE SHIP TO DEMON KING SHIP...
I HAVE WAITED FOR THIS DAY, GREAT DEMON KING.
THE DEMON KING IS MY GRANDPA. I'M...
THE *NEW* DEMON KING.
WHOOSH
EDENS ZERO'S KING...
...HAS FINALLY RETURNED.

EDENS ZERO

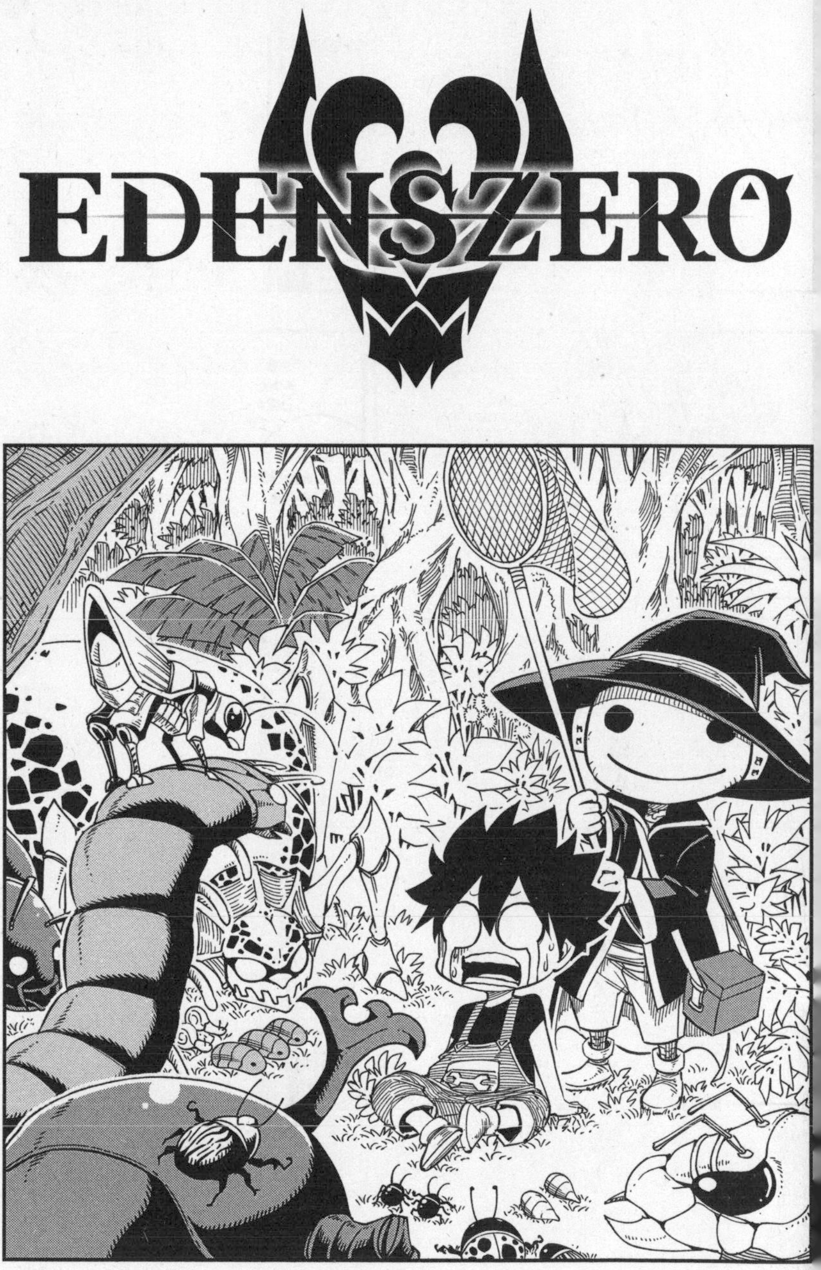

CHAPTER 16: SISTER

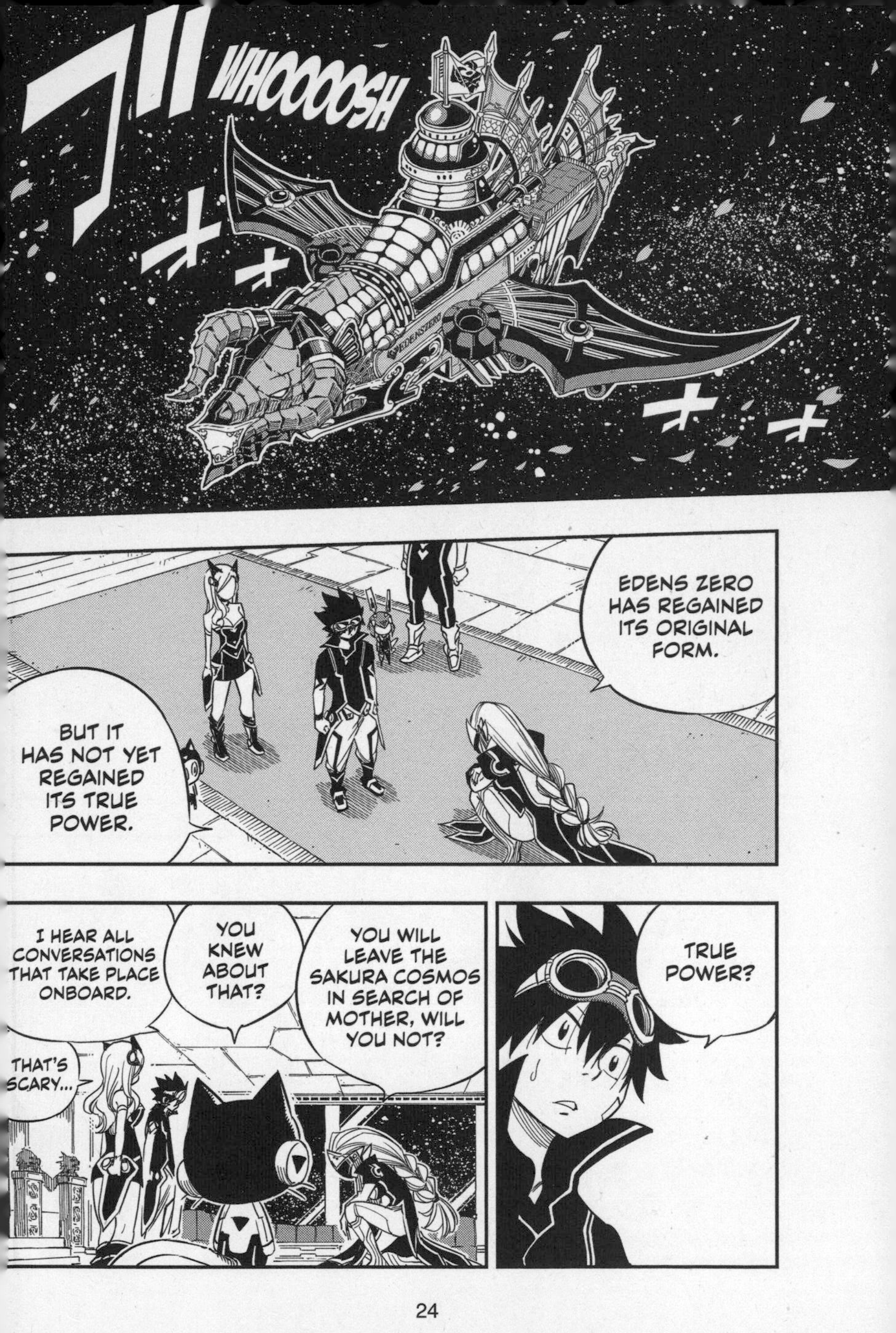
WHOOOOOSH
EDENS ZERO HAS REGAINED ITS ORIGINAL FORM.
BUT IT HAS NOT YET REGAINED ITS TRUE POWER.
TRUE POWER?
YOU WILL LEAVE THE SAKURA COSMOS IN SEARCH OF MOTHER, WILL YOU NOT?
YOU KNEW ABOUT THAT?
I HEAR ALL CONVERSATIONS THAT TAKE PLACE ONBOARD.
THAT'S SCARY...

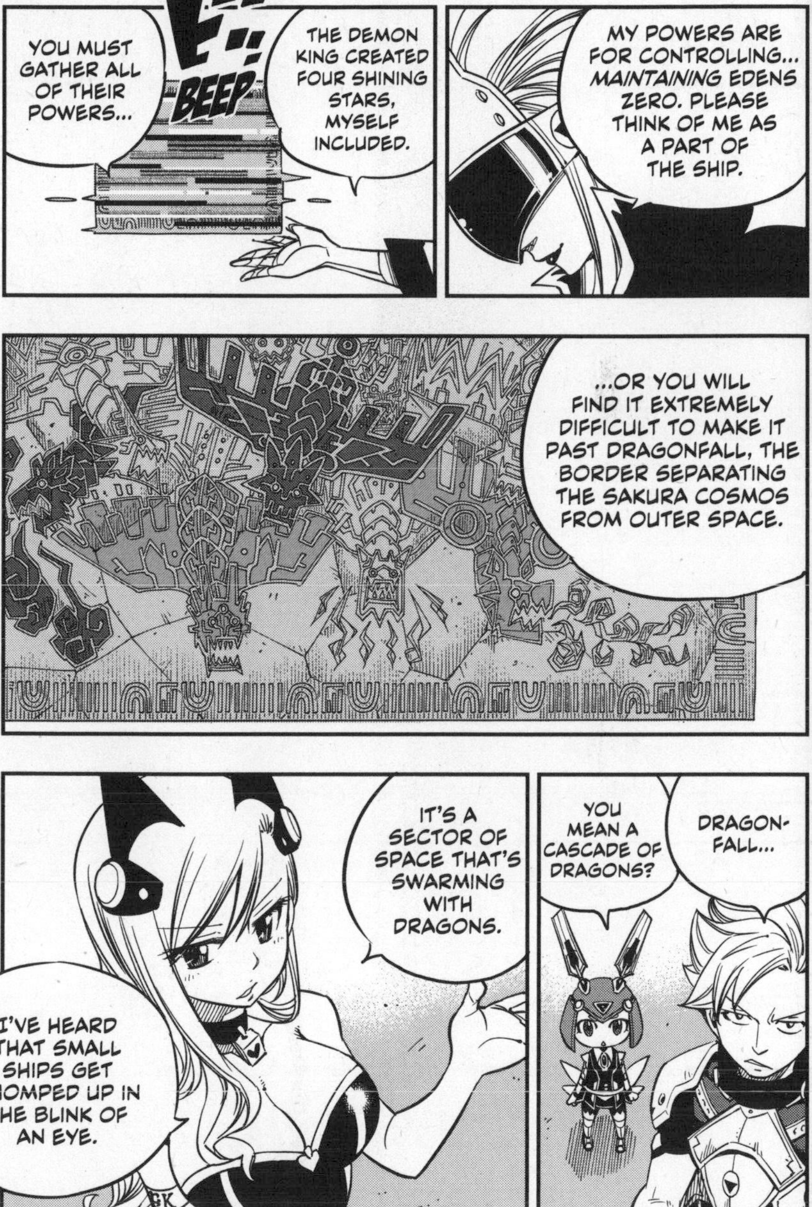
MY POWERS ARE FOR CONTROLLING... *MAINTAINING* EDENS ZERO. PLEASE THINK OF ME AS A PART OF THE SHIP.
THE DEMON KING CREATED FOUR SHINING STARS, MYSELF INCLUDED.
BEEP
YOU MUST GATHER ALL OF THEIR POWERS...
...OR YOU WILL FIND IT EXTREMELY DIFFICULT TO MAKE IT PAST DRAGONFALL, THE BORDER SEPARATING THE SAKURA COSMOS FROM OUTER SPACE.
DRAGON-FALL...
YOU MEAN A CASCADE OF DRAGONS?
IT'S A SECTOR OF SPACE THAT'S SWARMING WITH DRAGONS.
I'VE HEARD THAT SMALL SHIPS GET CHOMPED UP IN THE BLINK OF AN EYE.

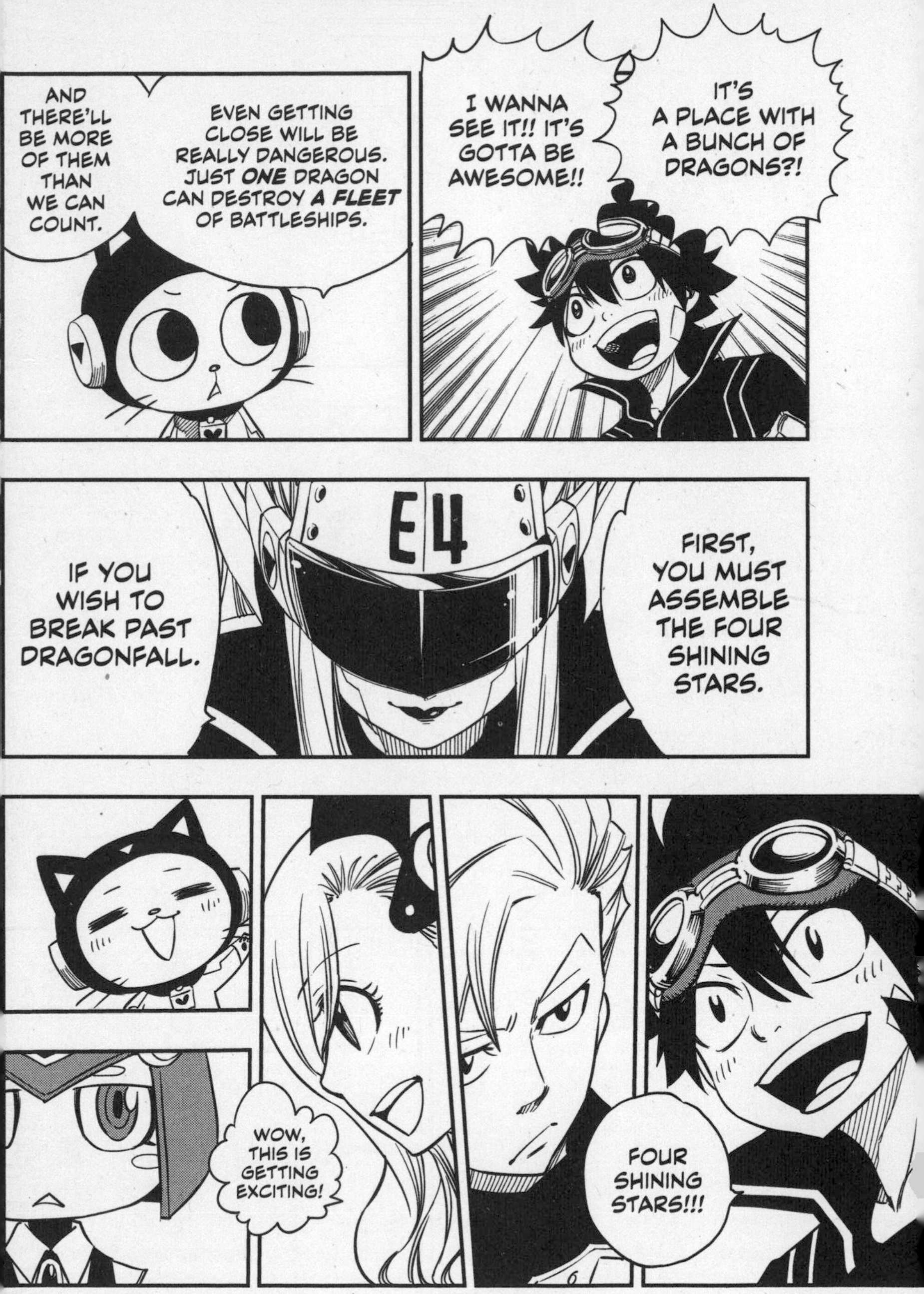
IT'S A PLACE WITH A BUNCH OF DRAGONS?!
I WANNA SEE IT!! IT'S GOTTA BE AWESOME!!
EVEN GETTING CLOSE WILL BE REALLY DANGEROUS. JUST ONE DRAGON CAN DESTROY A FLEET OF BATTLESHIPS.
AND THERE'LL BE MORE OF THEM THAN WE CAN COUNT.
E4
FIRST, YOU MUST ASSEMBLE THE FOUR SHINING STARS.
IF YOU WISH TO BREAK PAST DRAGONFALL.
FOUR SHINING STARS!!!
WOW, THIS IS GETTING EXCITING!

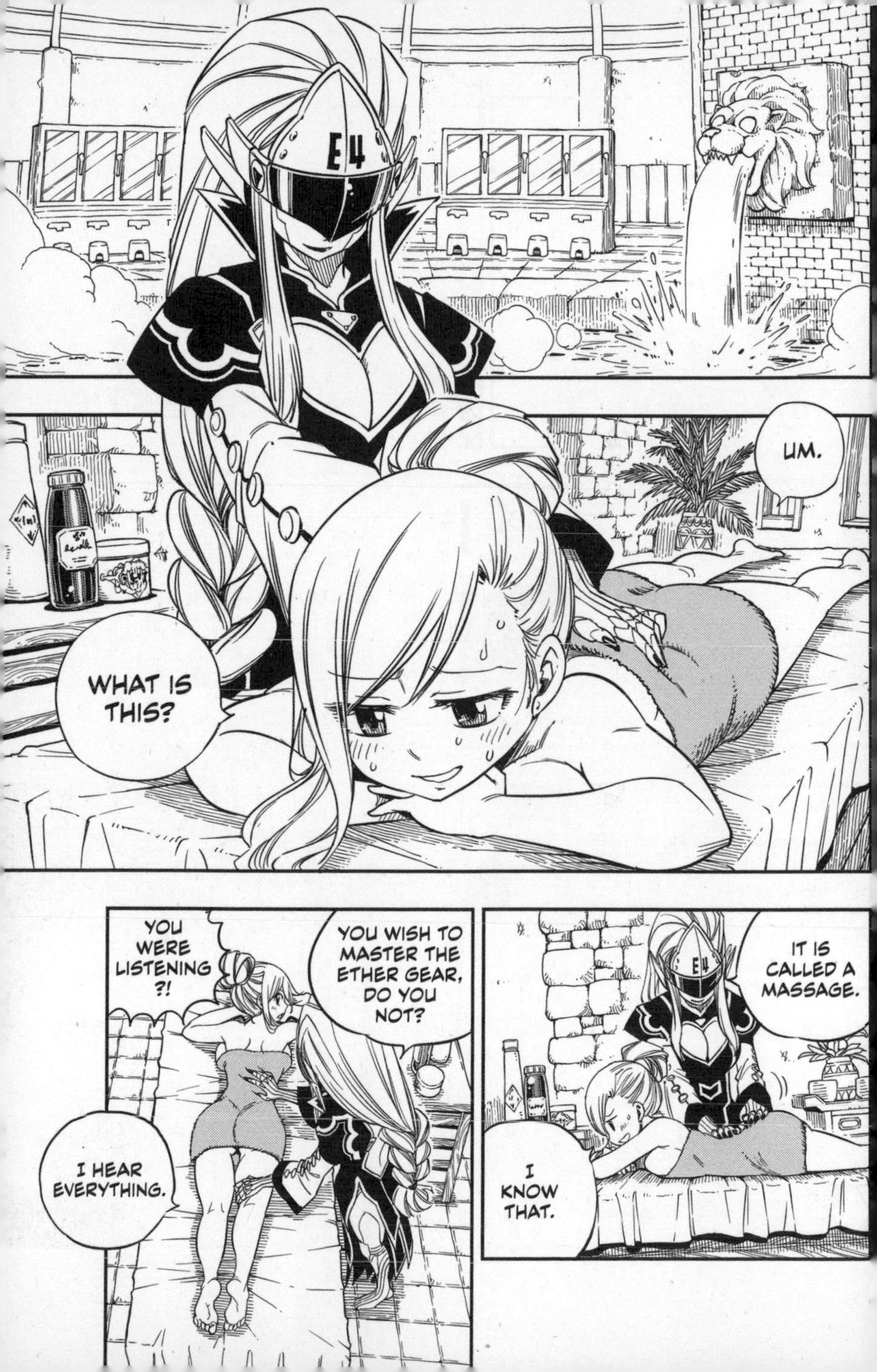
UM.
WHAT IS THIS?
IT IS CALLED A MASSAGE.
I KNOW THAT.
YOU WISH TO MASTER THE ETHER GEAR, DO YOU NOT?
YOU WERE LISTENING?!
I HEAR EVERYTHING.

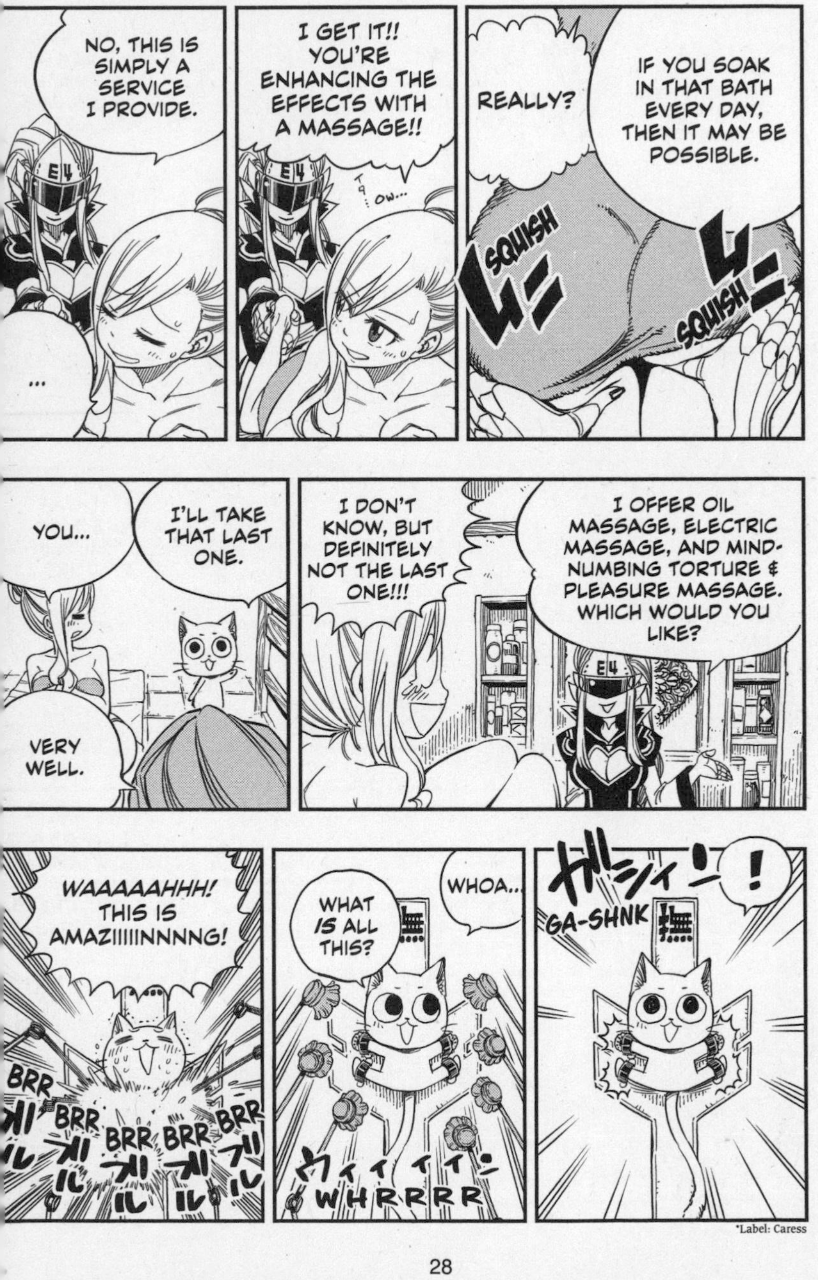
IF YOU SOAK IN THAT BATH EVERY DAY, THEN IT MAY BE POSSIBLE.
REALLY?
SQUISH
SQUISH
I GET IT!! YOU'RE ENHANCING THE EFFECTS WITH A MASSAGE!!
OW...
NO, THIS IS SIMPLY A SERVICE I PROVIDE.
...
I OFFER OIL MASSAGE, ELECTRIC MASSAGE, AND MIND-NUMBING TORTURE & PLEASURE MASSAGE. WHICH WOULD YOU LIKE?
I DON'T KNOW, BUT DEFINITELY NOT THE LAST ONE!!!
I'LL TAKE THAT LAST ONE.
YOU...
VERY WELL.
!
GA-SHNK
WHOA...
WHAT IS ALL THIS?
WHRRRRR
WAAAAAHHH! THIS IS AMAZIIIIINNNNG!
BRR
BRR
BRR
BRR
BRR

*Label: Caress

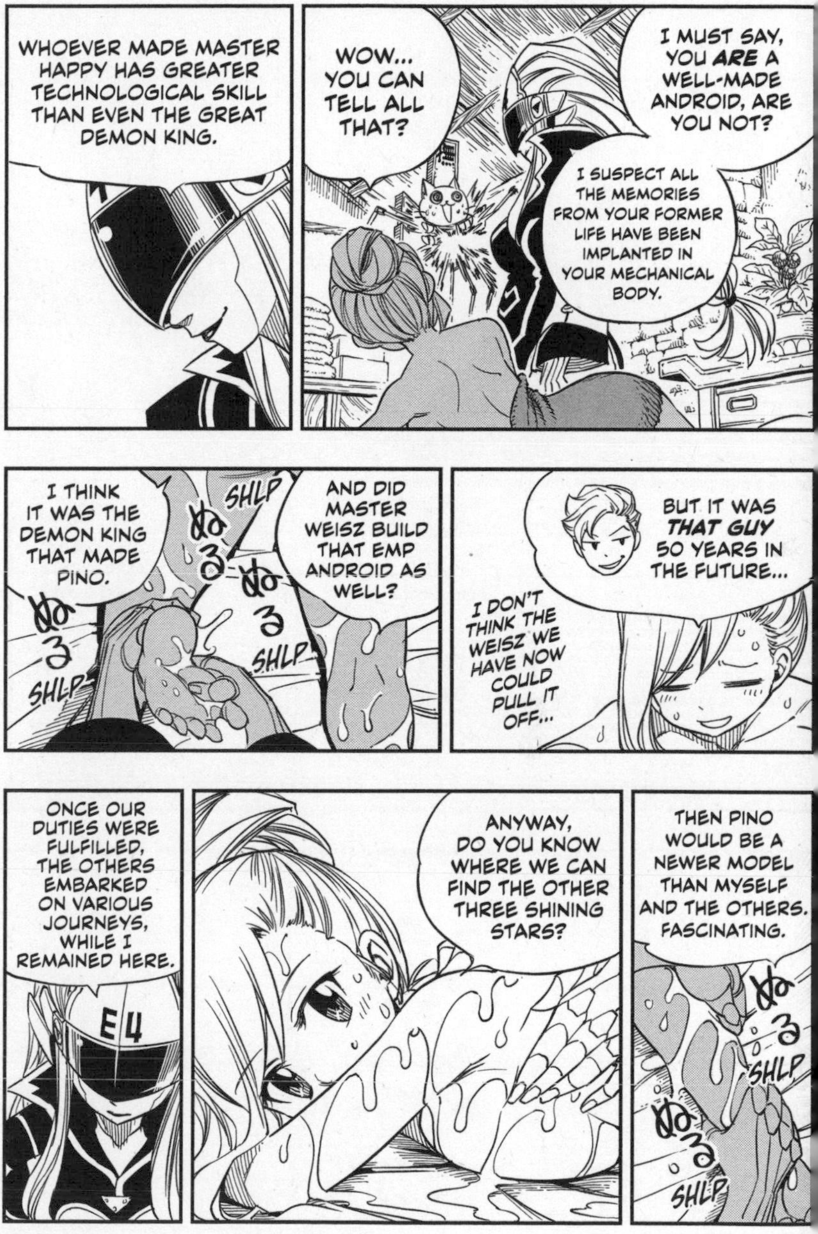

I MUST SAY, YOU **ARE** A WELL-MADE ANDROID, ARE YOU NOT?
I SUSPECT ALL THE MEMORIES FROM YOUR FORMER LIFE HAVE BEEN IMPLANTED IN YOUR MECHANICAL BODY.
WOW... YOU CAN TELL ALL THAT?
WHOEVER MADE MASTER HAPPY HAS GREATER TECHNOLOGICAL SKILL THAN EVEN THE GREAT DEMON KING.
BUT IT WAS **THAT GUY** 50 YEARS IN THE FUTURE...
I DON'T THINK THE WEISZ WE HAVE NOW COULD PULL IT OFF...
AND DID MASTER WEISZ BUILD THAT EMP ANDROID AS WELL?
SHLP
ぬる
ぬる
SHLP
I THINK IT WAS THE DEMON KING THAT MADE PINO.
ぬる
SHLP
THEN PINO WOULD BE A NEWER MODEL THAN MYSELF AND THE OTHERS. FASCINATING.
ぬる
SHLP
ぬる
SHLP
ANYWAY, DO YOU KNOW WHERE WE CAN FIND THE OTHER THREE SHINING STARS?
ONCE OUR DUTIES WERE FULFILLED, THE OTHERS EMBARKED ON VARIOUS JOURNEYS, WHILE I REMAINED HERE.
E4

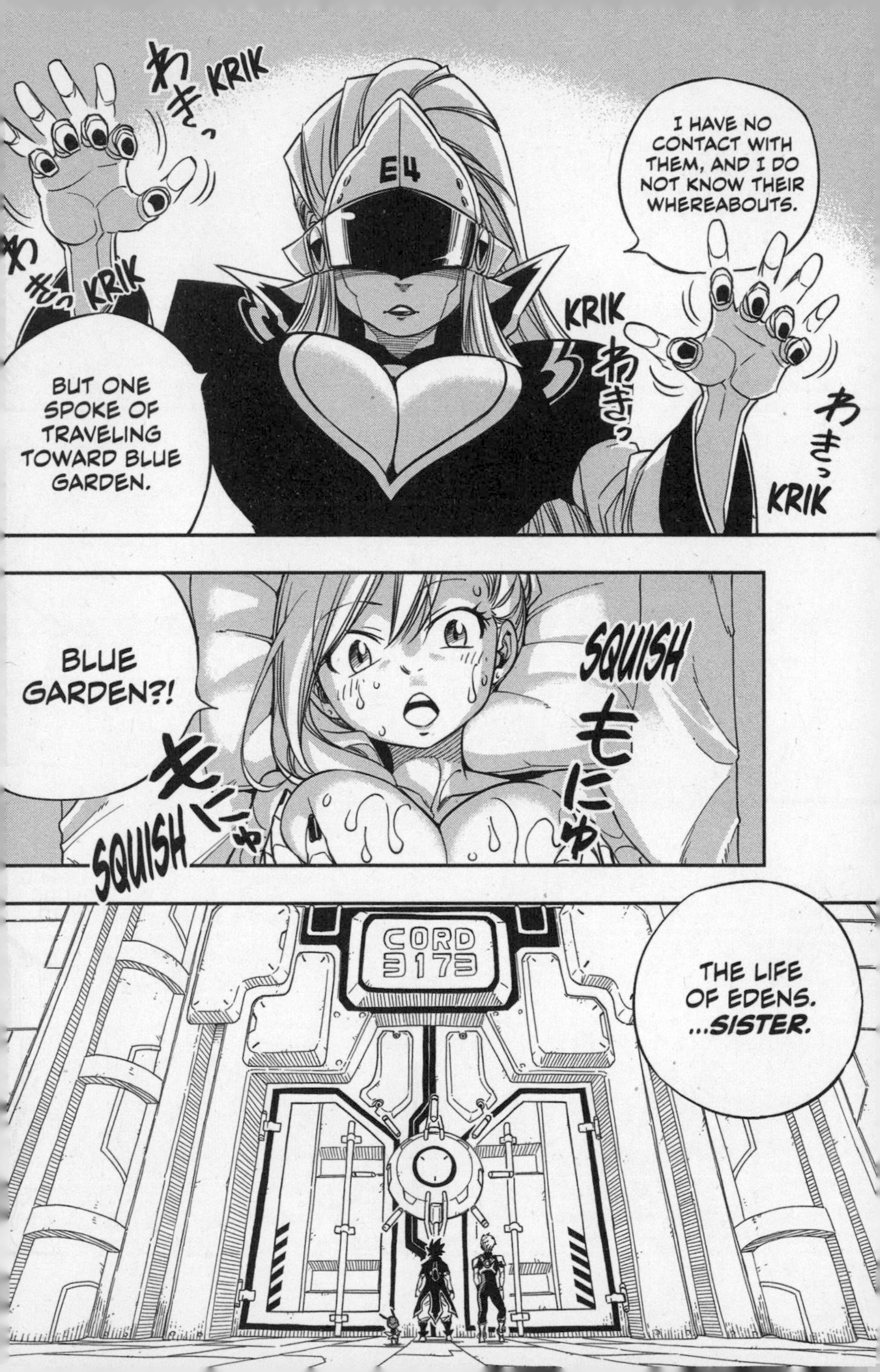

I HAVE NO CONTACT WITH THEM, AND I DO NOT KNOW THEIR WHEREABOUTS.
わきっ KRIK
KRIK わきっ
わきっ KRIK
わきっ KRIK
わきっ KRIK
BUT ONE SPOKE OF TRAVELING TOWARD BLUE GARDEN.
SQUISH もにゅ
BLUE GARDEN?!
もにゅ SQUISH
THE LIFE OF EDENS. ...*SISTER.*
CORD 3173

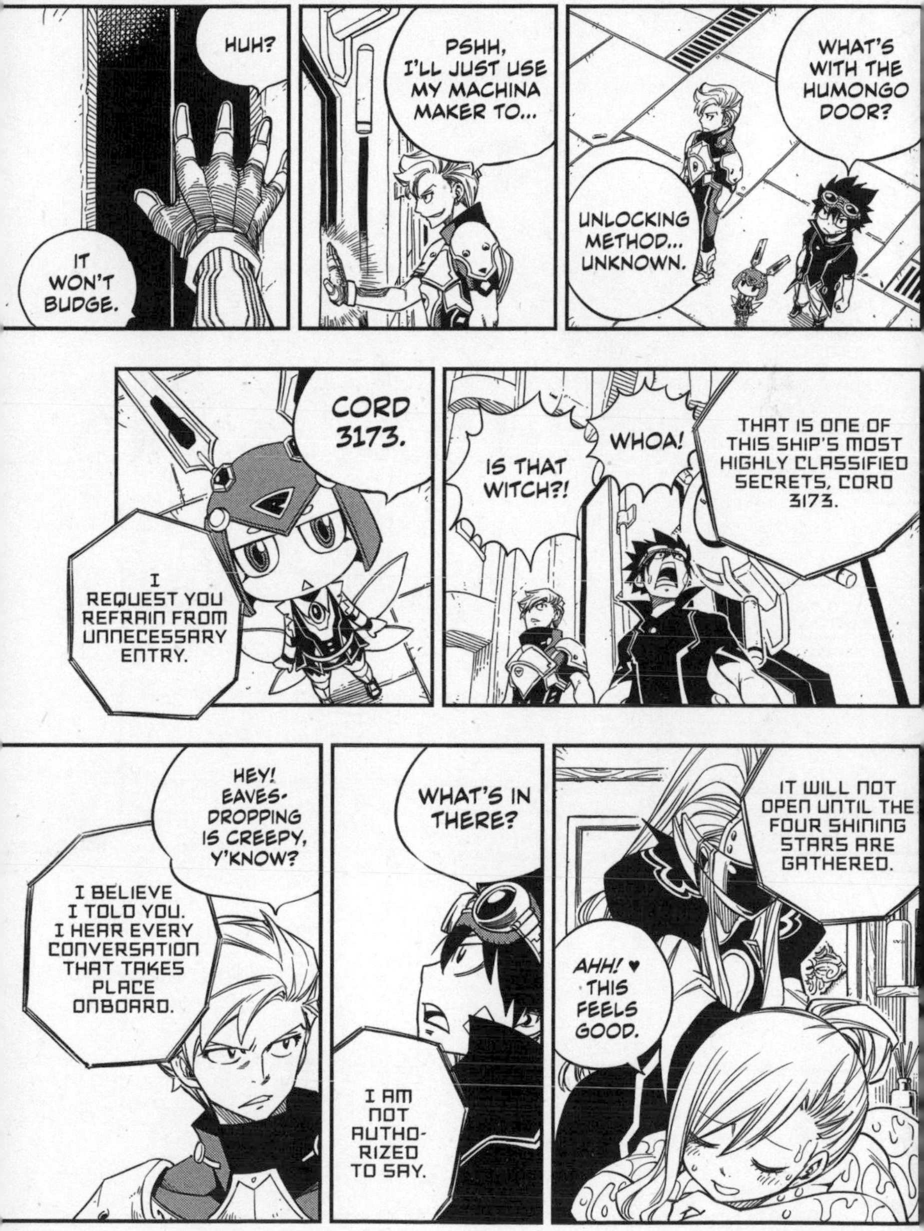
WHAT'S WITH THE HUMONGO DOOR?
UNLOCKING METHOD... UNKNOWN.
PSHH, I'LL JUST USE MY MACHINA MAKER TO...
HUH?
IT WON'T BUDGE.
THAT IS ONE OF THIS SHIP'S MOST HIGHLY CLASSIFIED SECRETS, CORD 3173.
WHOA!
IS THAT WITCH?!
CORD 3173.
I REQUEST YOU REFRAIN FROM UNNECESSARY ENTRY.
IT WILL NOT OPEN UNTIL THE FOUR SHINING STARS ARE GATHERED.
AHH! ♥ THIS FEELS GOOD.
WHAT'S IN THERE?
I AM NOT AUTHO-RIZED TO SAY.
HEY! EAVES-DROPPING IS CREEPY, Y'KNOW?
I BELIEVE I TOLD YOU. I HEAR EVERY CONVERSATION THAT TAKES PLACE ONBOARD.

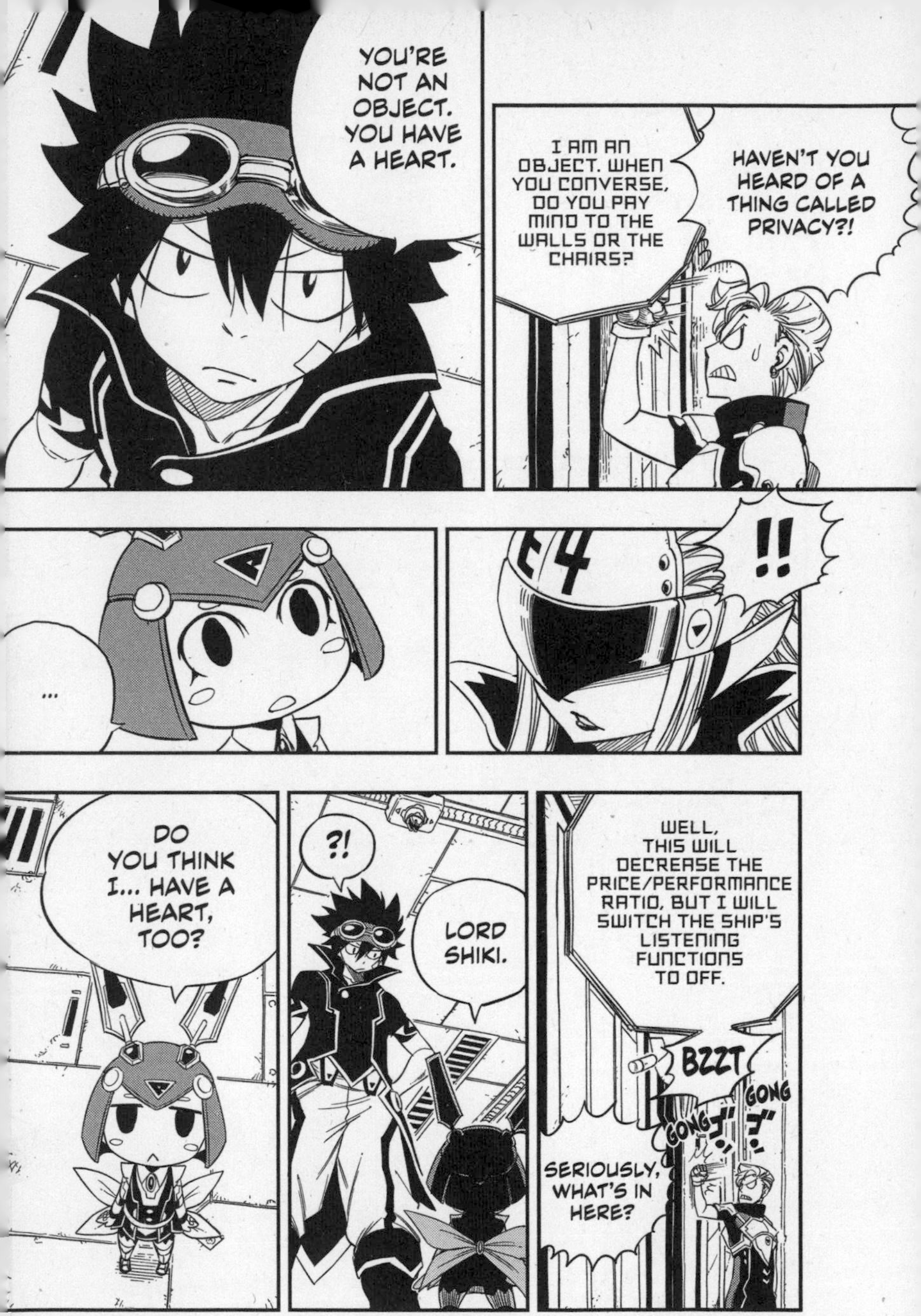
HAVEN'T YOU HEARD OF A THING CALLED PRIVACY?!
I AM AN OBJECT. WHEN YOU CONVERSE, DO YOU PAY MIND TO THE WALLS OR THE CHAIRS?
YOU'RE NOT AN OBJECT. YOU HAVE A HEART.
!!
...
WELL, THIS WILL DECREASE THE PRICE/PERFORMANCE RATIO, BUT I WILL SWITCH THE SHIP'S LISTENING FUNCTIONS TO OFF.
BZZT
GONG
GONG
SERIOUSLY, WHAT'S IN HERE?
?!
LORD SHIKI.
DO YOU THINK I... HAVE A HEART, TOO?

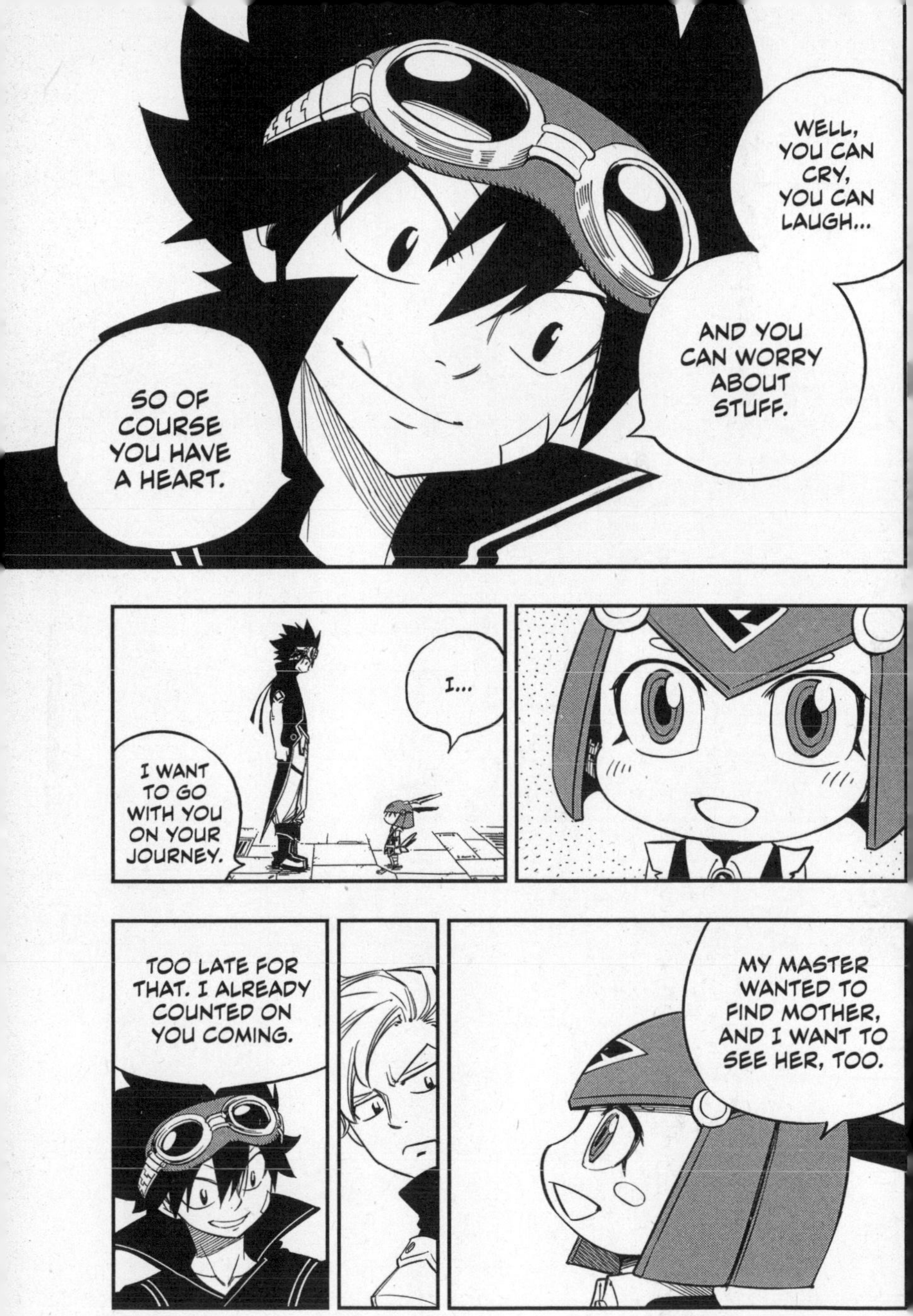
WELL, YOU CAN CRY, YOU CAN LAUGH...
AND YOU CAN WORRY ABOUT STUFF.
SO OF COURSE YOU HAVE A HEART.
I...
I WANT TO GO WITH YOU ON YOUR JOURNEY.
MY MASTER WANTED TO FIND MOTHER, AND I WANT TO SEE HER, TOO.
TOO LATE FOR THAT. I ALREADY COUNTED ON YOU COMING.

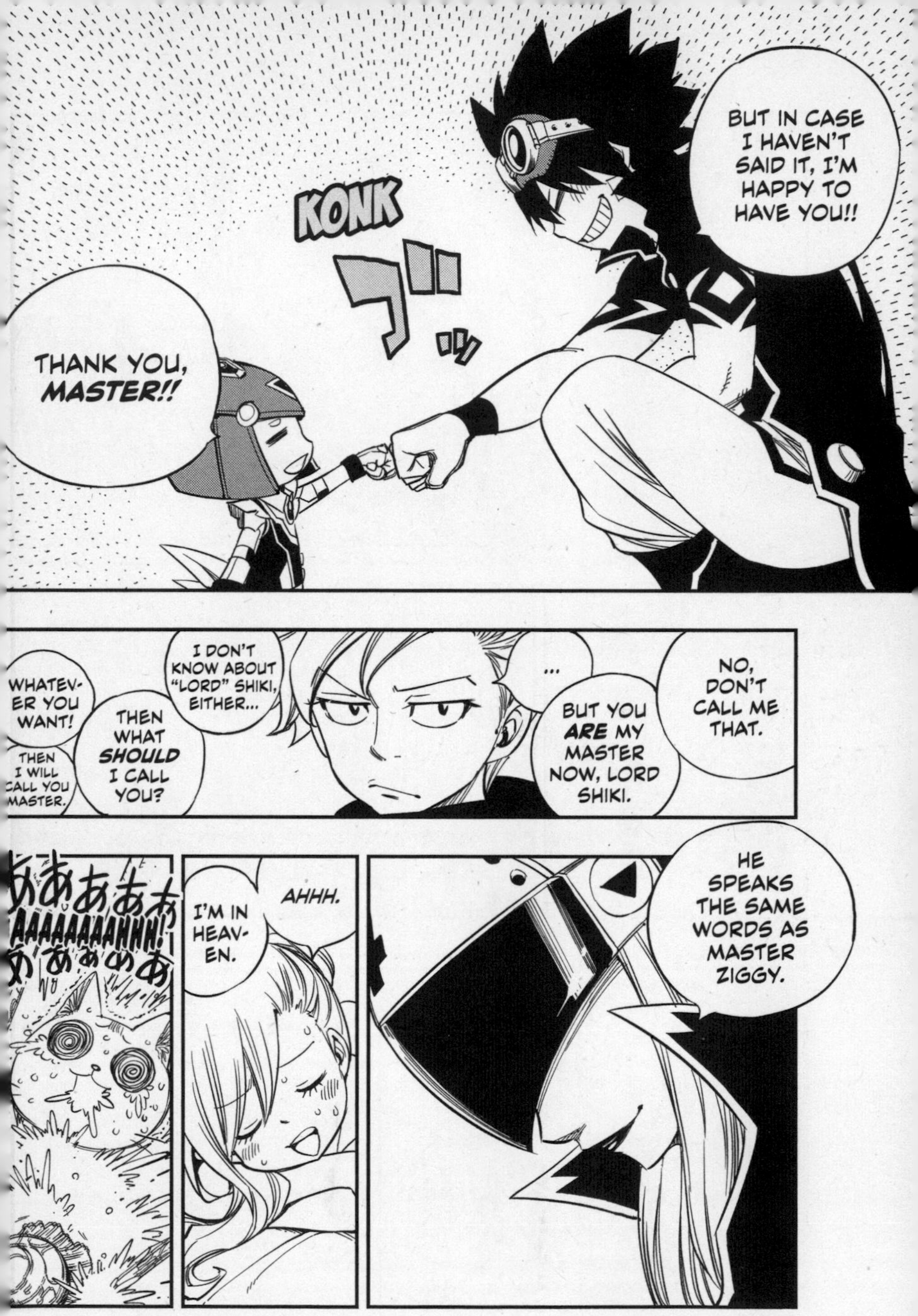
BUT IN CASE I HAVEN'T SAID IT, I'M HAPPY TO HAVE YOU!!
KONK
ゴッ
THANK YOU, *MASTER!!*
NO, DON'T CALL ME THAT.
BUT YOU *ARE* MY MASTER NOW, LORD SHIKI.
...
I DON'T KNOW ABOUT "LORD" SHIKI, EITHER...
THEN WHAT *SHOULD* I CALL YOU?
WHATEVER YOU WANT!
THEN I WILL CALL YOU MASTER.
HE SPEAKS THE SAME WORDS AS MASTER ZIGGY.
AHHH.
I'M IN HEAVEN.
AAAAAAAAAHHH!

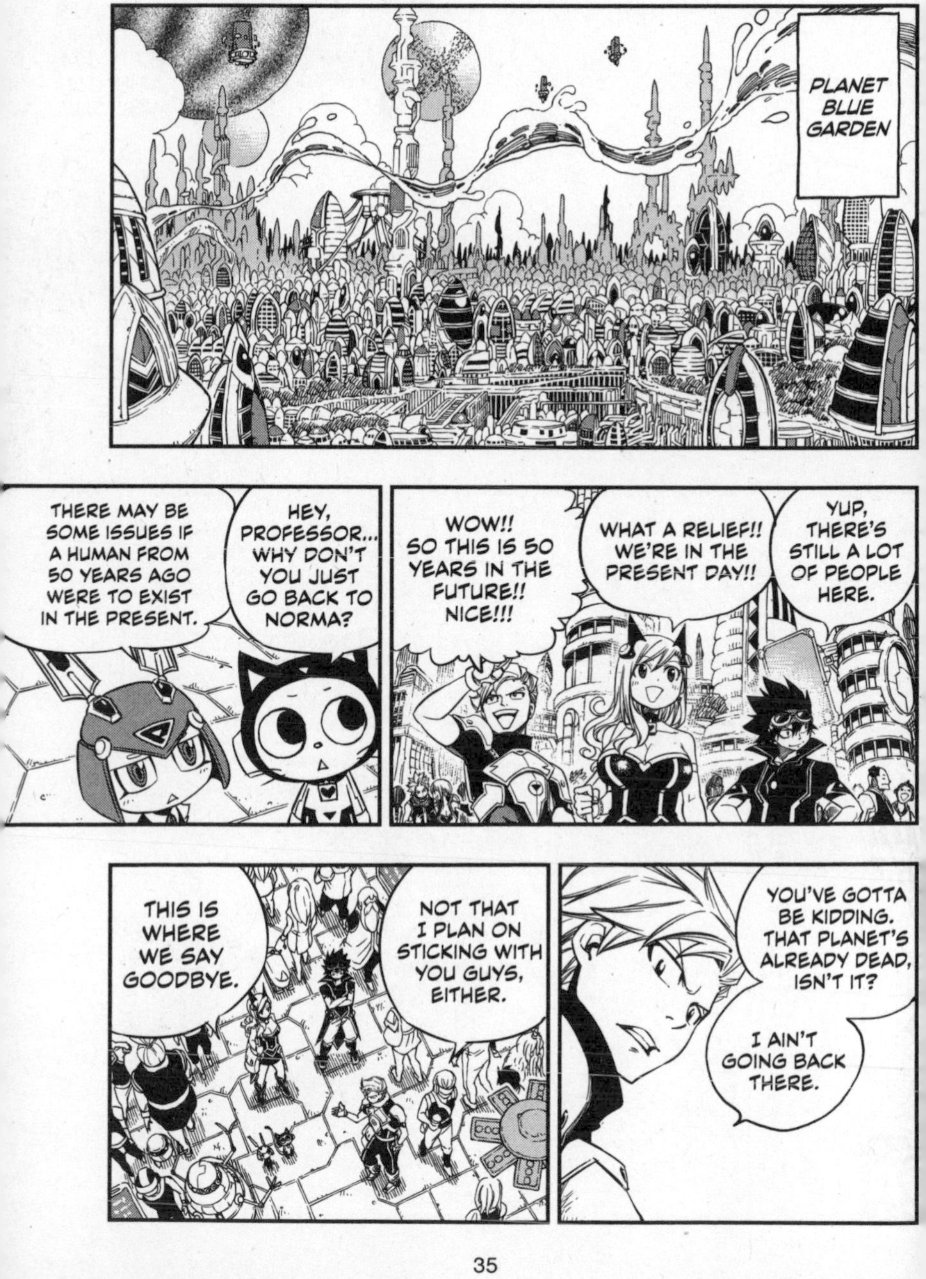
PLANET BLUE GARDEN
YUP, THERE'S STILL A LOT OF PEOPLE HERE.
WHAT A RELIEF!! WE'RE IN THE PRESENT DAY!!
WOW!! SO THIS IS 50 YEARS IN THE FUTURE!! NICE!!!
HEY, PROFESSOR... WHY DON'T YOU JUST GO BACK TO NORMA?
THERE MAY BE SOME ISSUES IF A HUMAN FROM 50 YEARS AGO WERE TO EXIST IN THE PRESENT.
YOU'VE GOTTA BE KIDDING. THAT PLANET'S ALREADY DEAD, ISN'T IT?
I AIN'T GOING BACK THERE.
NOT THAT I PLAN ON STICKING WITH YOU GUYS, EITHER.
THIS IS WHERE WE SAY GOODBYE.

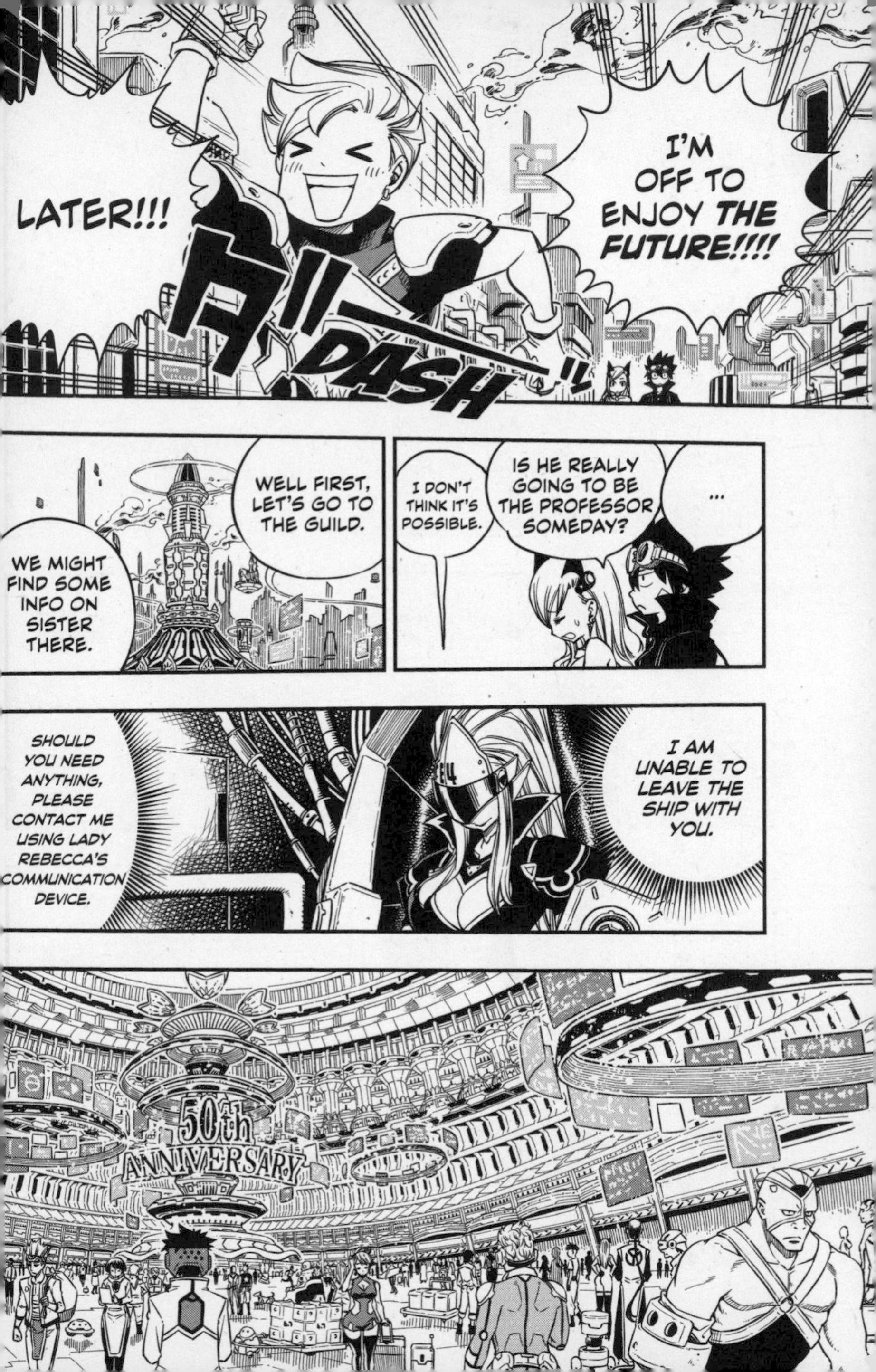
I'M OFF TO ENJOY THE FUTURE!!!!
LATER!!!
DASH
...
IS HE REALLY GOING TO BE THE PROFESSOR SOMEDAY?
I DON'T THINK IT'S POSSIBLE.
WELL FIRST, LET'S GO TO THE GUILD.
WE MIGHT FIND SOME INFO ON SISTER THERE.
I AM UNABLE TO LEAVE THE SHIP WITH YOU.
SHOULD YOU NEED ANYTHING, PLEASE CONTACT ME USING LADY REBECCA'S COMMUNICATION DEVICE.
50th ANNIVERSARY

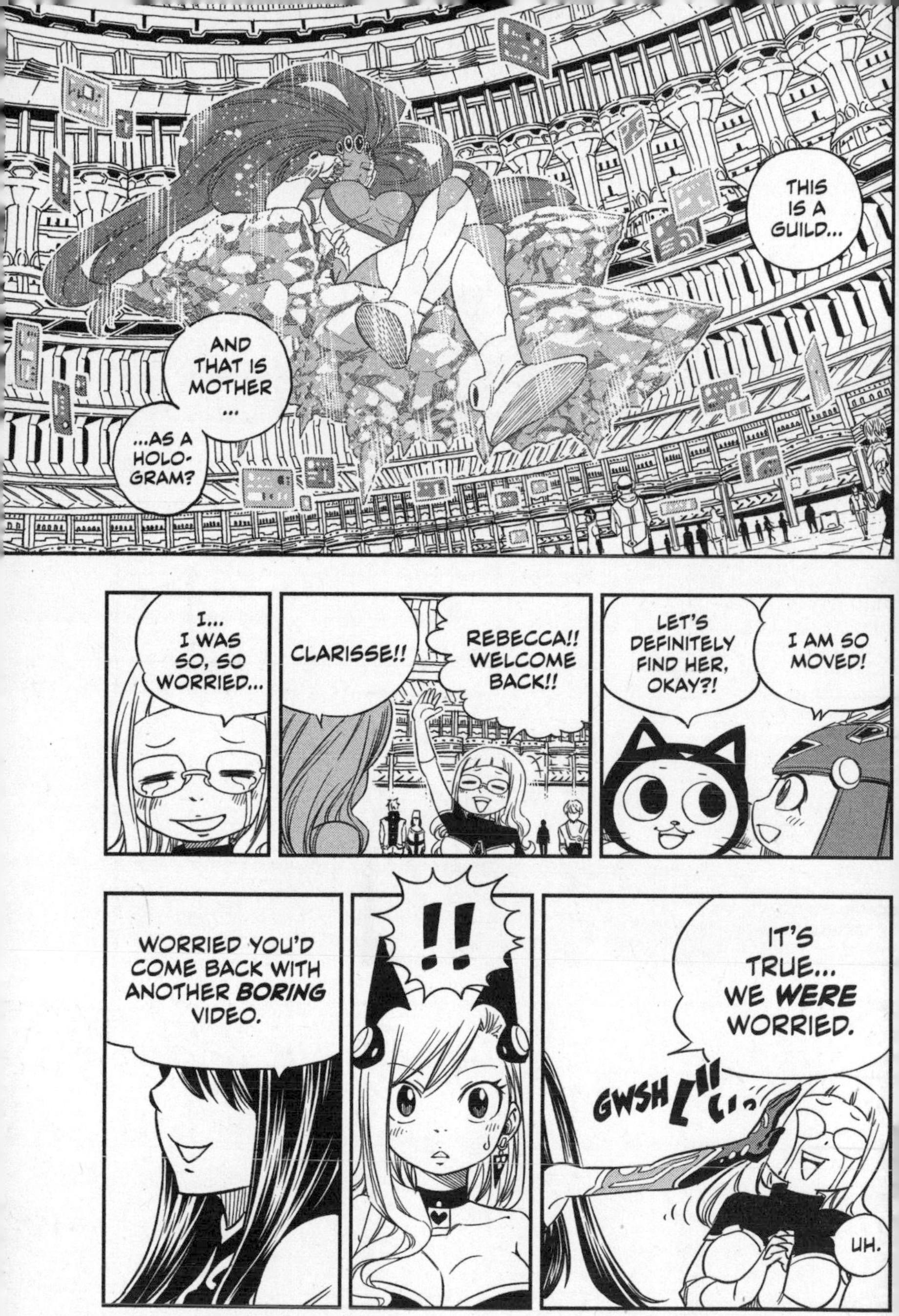
THIS IS A GUILD...
AND THAT IS MOTHER ...
...AS A HOLOGRAM?
I AM SO MOVED!
LET'S DEFINITELY FIND HER, OKAY?!
REBECCA!! WELCOME BACK!!
CLARISSE!!
I... I WAS SO, SO WORRIED...
IT'S TRUE... WE WERE WORRIED.
GWSH
UH.
!!
WORRIED YOU'D COME BACK WITH ANOTHER BORING VIDEO.

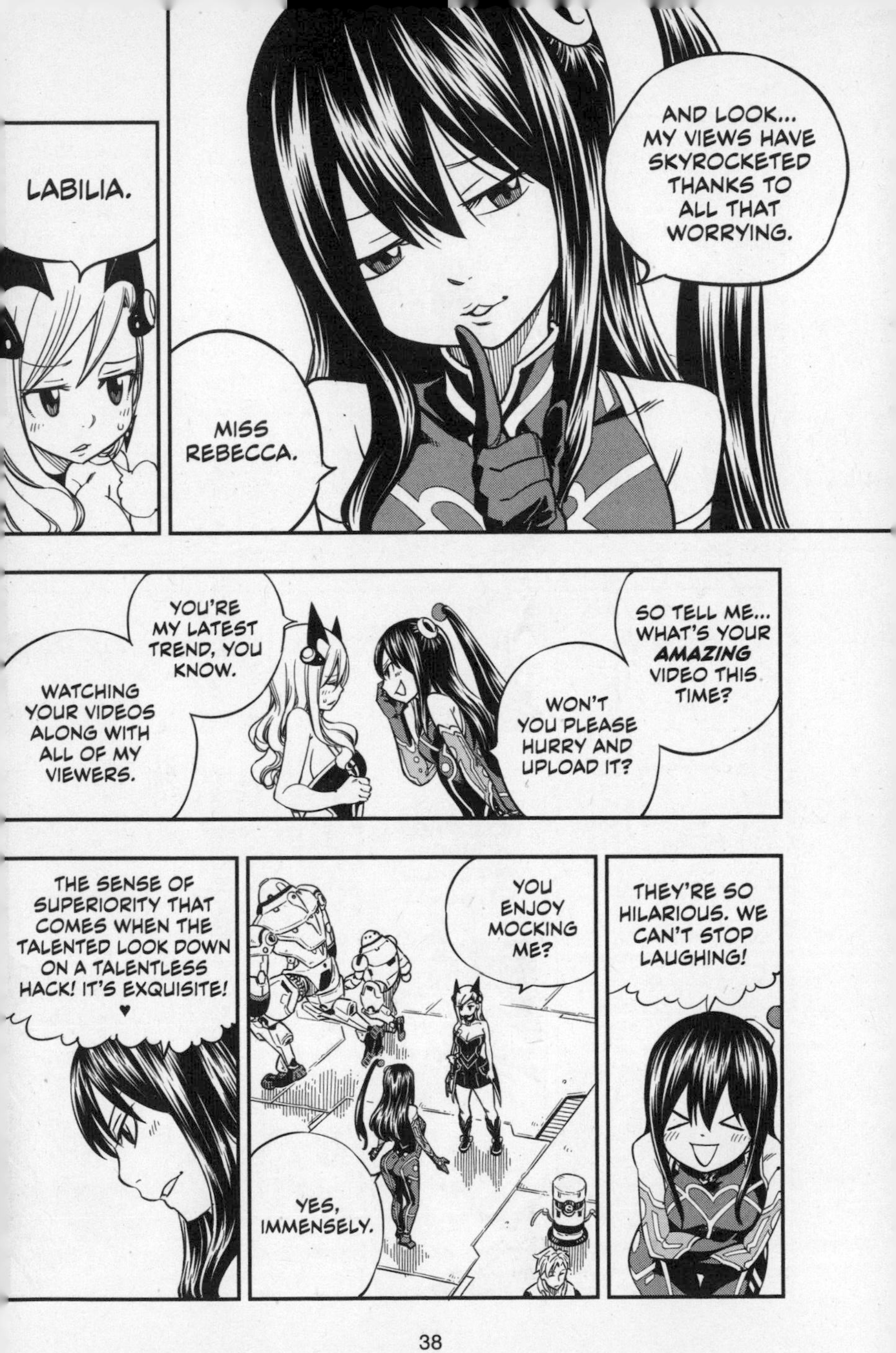
AND LOOK... MY VIEWS HAVE SKYROCKETED THANKS TO ALL THAT WORRYING.
MISS REBECCA.
LABILIA.
SO TELL ME... WHAT'S YOUR *AMAZING* VIDEO THIS TIME?
WON'T YOU PLEASE HURRY AND UPLOAD IT?
YOU'RE MY LATEST TREND, YOU KNOW.
WATCHING YOUR VIDEOS ALONG WITH ALL OF MY VIEWERS.
THEY'RE SO HILARIOUS. WE CAN'T STOP LAUGHING!
YOU ENJOY MOCKING ME?
YES, IMMENSELY.
THE SENSE OF SUPERIORITY THAT COMES WHEN THE TALENTED LOOK DOWN ON A TALENTLESS HACK! IT'S EXQUISITE! ♥

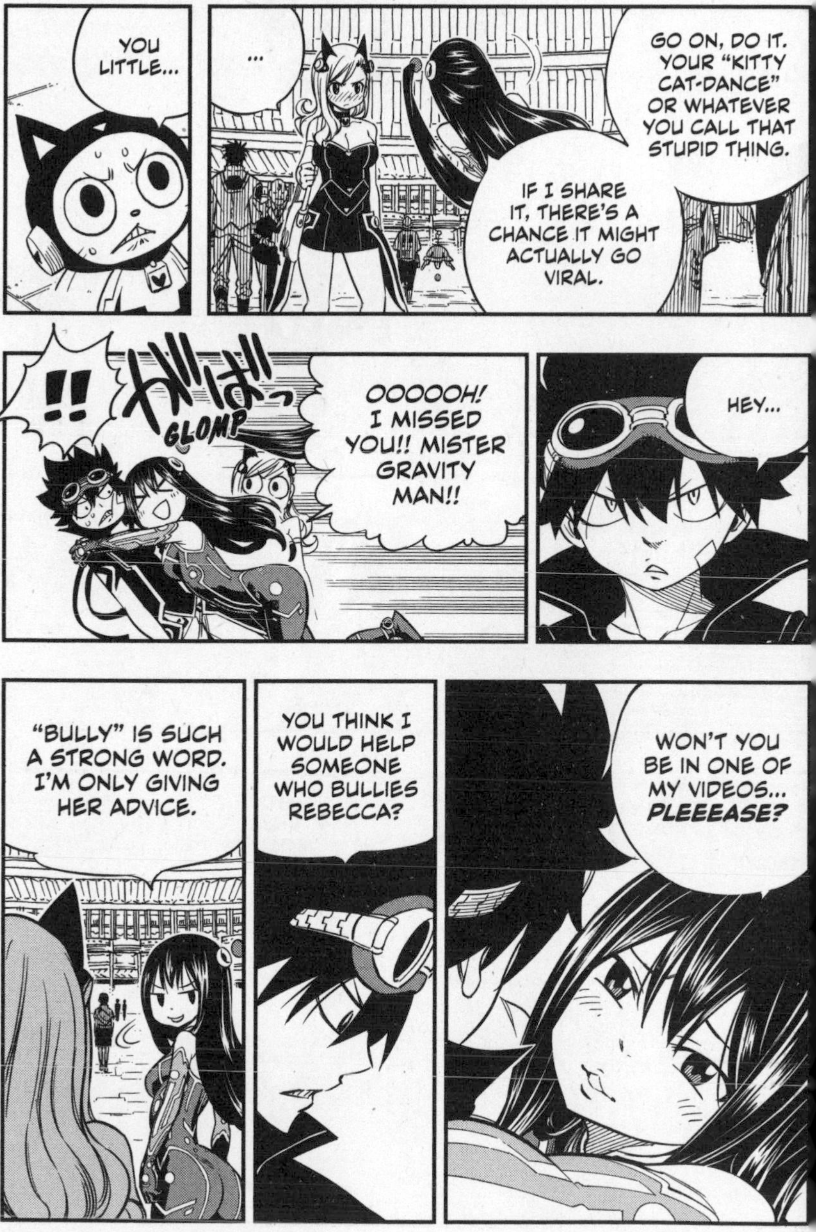
GO ON, DO IT. YOUR “KITTY CAT-DANCE” OR WHATEVER YOU CALL THAT STUPID THING.
...
IF I SHARE IT, THERE'S A CHANCE IT MIGHT ACTUALLY GO VIRAL.
YOU LITTLE...
HEY...
OOOOOH! I MISSED YOU!! MISTER GRAVITY MAN!!
GLOMP
!!
WON'T YOU BE IN ONE OF MY VIDEOS... *PLEEEASE?*
YOU THINK I WOULD HELP SOMEONE WHO BULLIES REBECCA?
“BULLY” IS SUCH A STRONG WORD. I'M ONLY GIVING HER ADVICE.

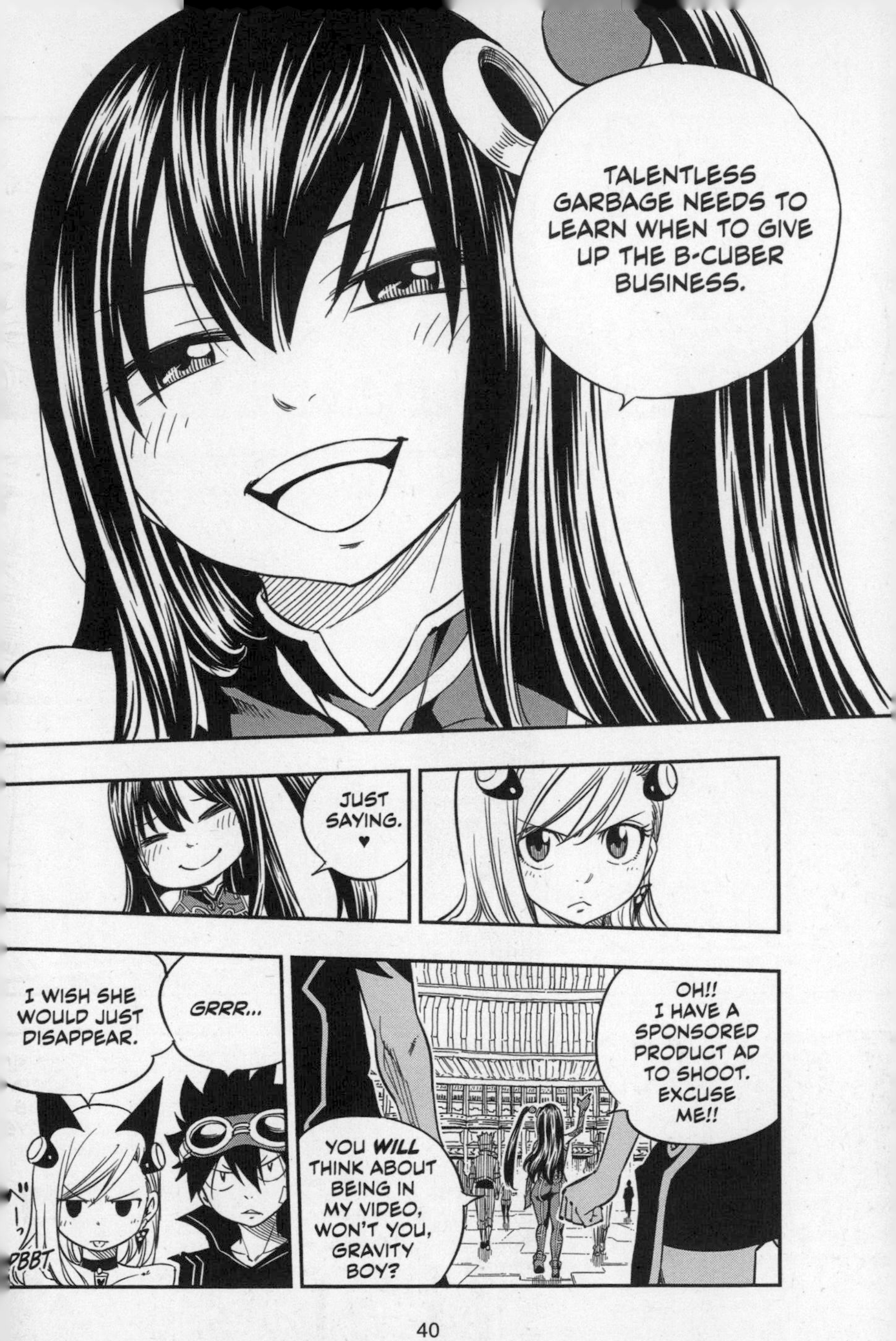
TALENTLESS GARBAGE NEEDS TO LEARN WHEN TO GIVE UP THE B-CUBER BUSINESS.
JUST SAYING. ♥
OH!! I HAVE A SPONSORED PRODUCT AD TO SHOOT. EXCUSE ME!!
YOU *WILL* THINK ABOUT BEING IN MY VIDEO, WON'T YOU, GRAVITY BOY?
GRRR...
I WISH SHE WOULD JUST DISAPPEAR.
PBBT

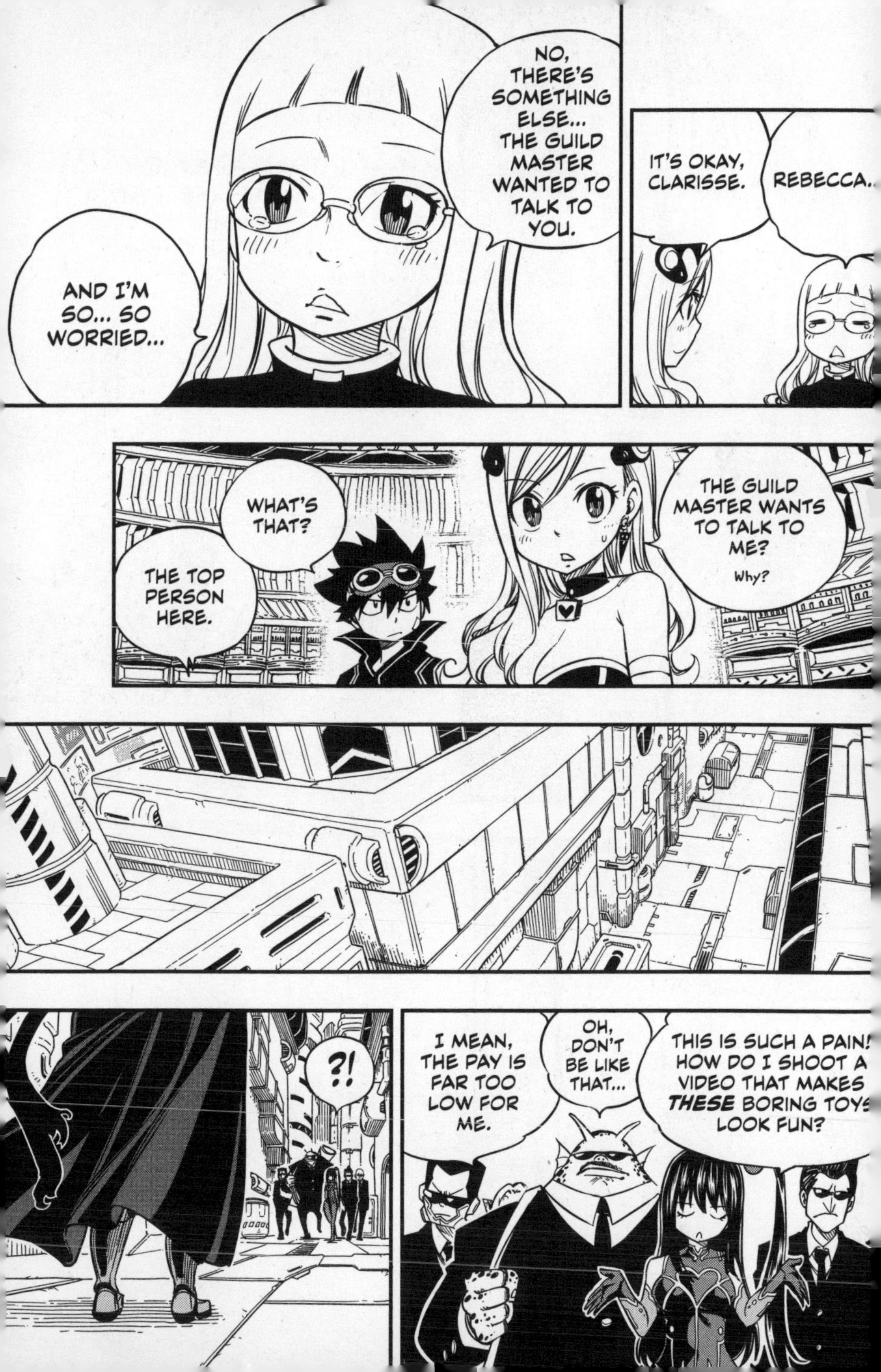
REBECCA...
IT'S OKAY, CLARISSE.
NO, THERE'S SOMETHING ELSE... THE GUILD MASTER WANTED TO TALK TO YOU.
AND I'M SO... SO WORRIED...
THE GUILD MASTER WANTS TO TALK TO ME? Why?
WHAT'S THAT?
THE TOP PERSON HERE.
THIS IS SUCH A PAIN! HOW DO I SHOOT A VIDEO THAT MAKES *THESE* BORING TOYS LOOK FUN?
OH, DON'T BE LIKE THAT...
I MEAN, THE PAY IS FAR TOO LOW FOR ME.
?!

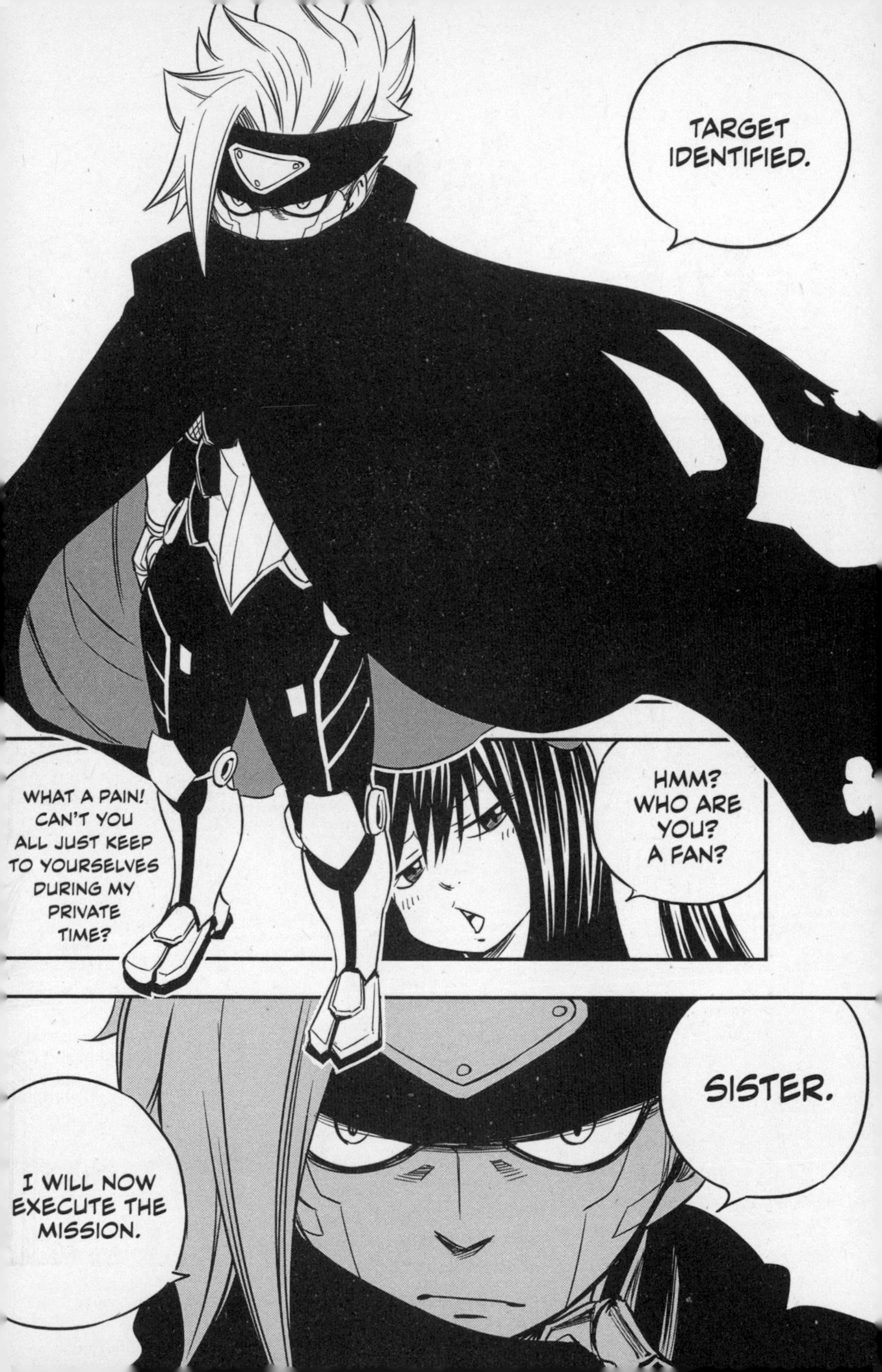
TARGET IDENTIFIED.
HMM? WHO ARE YOU? A FAN?
WHAT A PAIN! CAN'T YOU ALL JUST KEEP TO YOURSELVES DURING MY PRIVATE TIME?
SISTER.
I WILL NOW EXECUTE THE MISSION.

EDENS ZERO

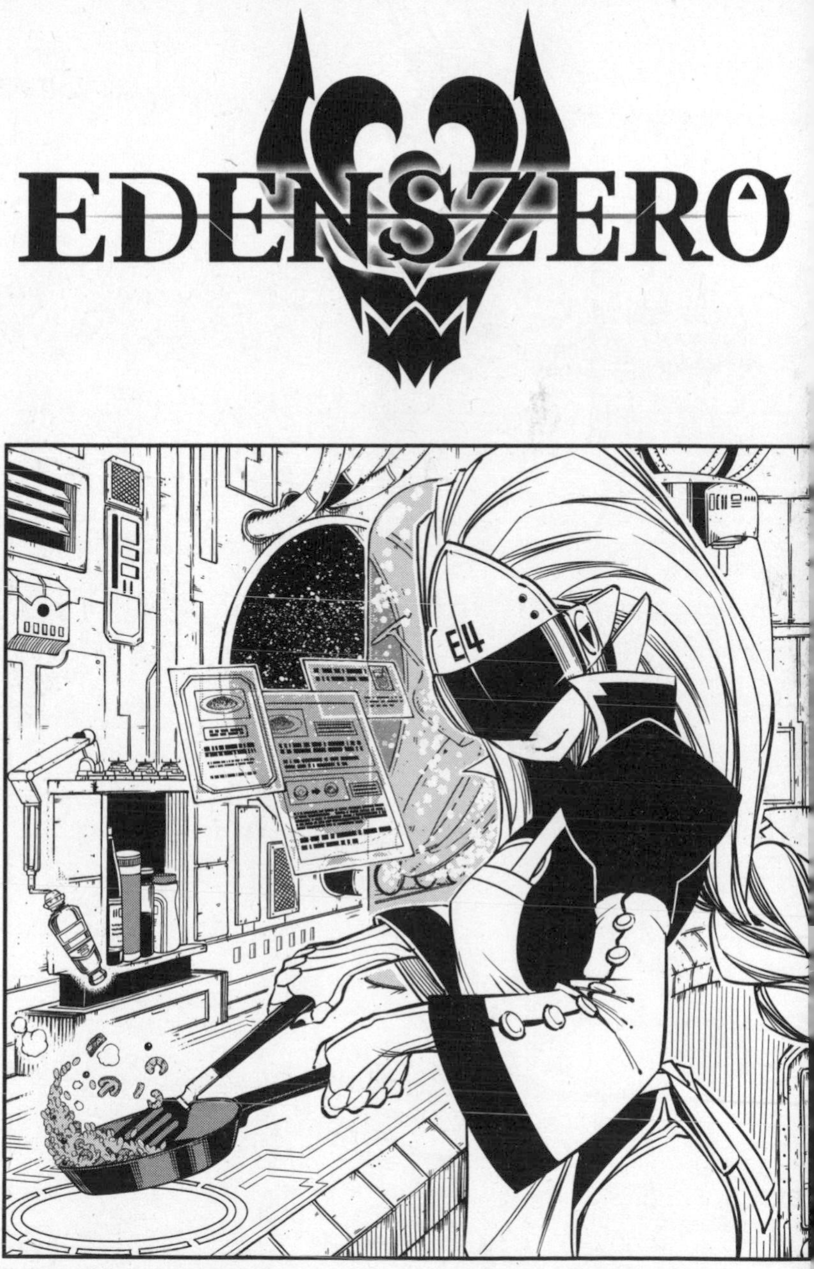
E4

CHAPTER 17: THE COLLECTION

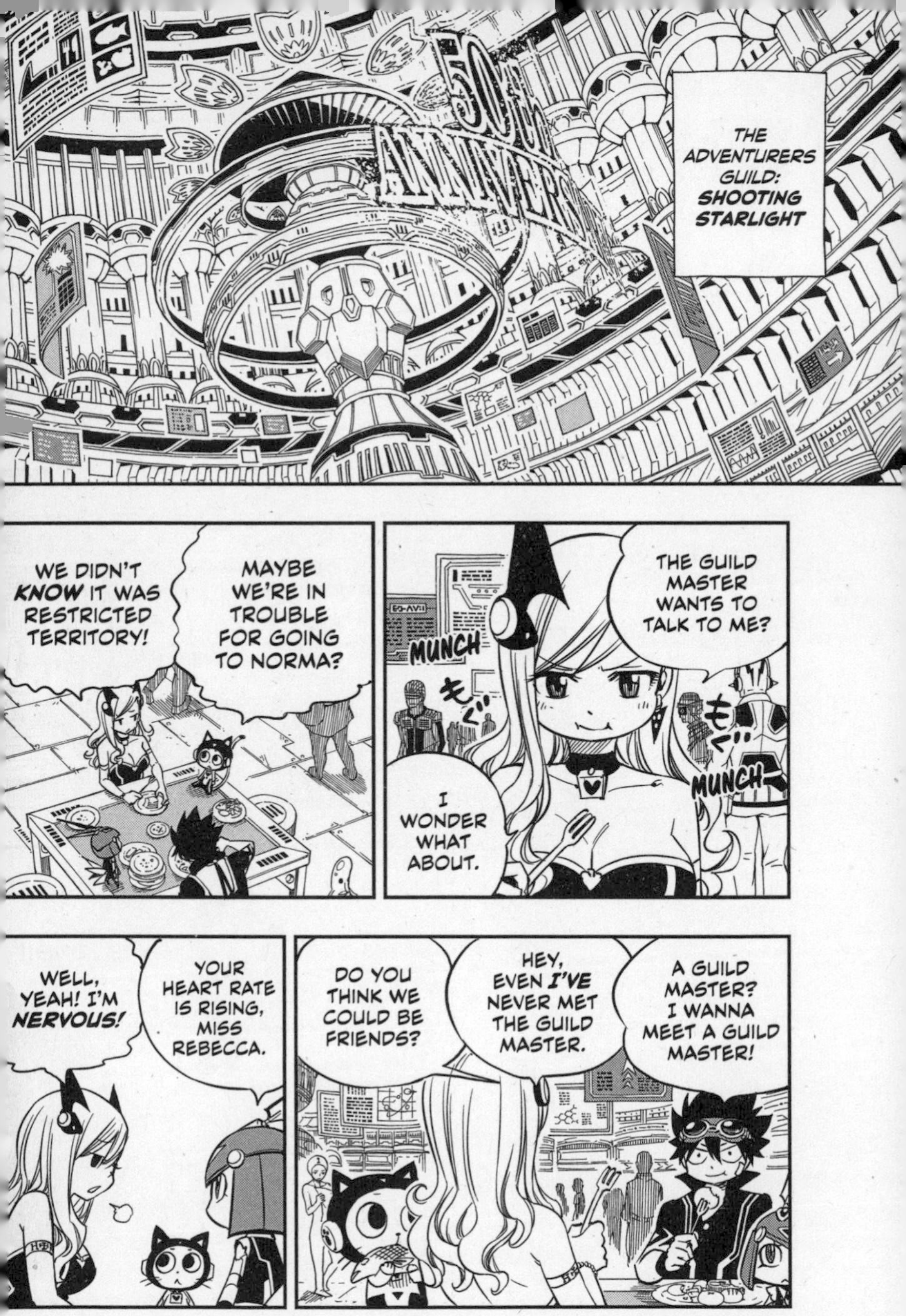

THE ADVENTURERS GUILD: SHOOTING STARLIGHT
THE GUILD MASTER WANTS TO TALK TO ME?
MUNCH
もぐ
もぐ
MUNCH
I WONDER WHAT ABOUT.
MAYBE WE'RE IN TROUBLE FOR GOING TO NORMA?
WE DIDN'T KNOW IT WAS RESTRICTED TERRITORY!
A GUILD MASTER? I WANNA MEET A GUILD MASTER!
HEY, EVEN I'VE NEVER MET THE GUILD MASTER.
DO YOU THINK WE COULD BE FRIENDS?
YOUR HEART RATE IS RISING, MISS REBECCA.
WELL, YEAH! I'M NERVOUS!

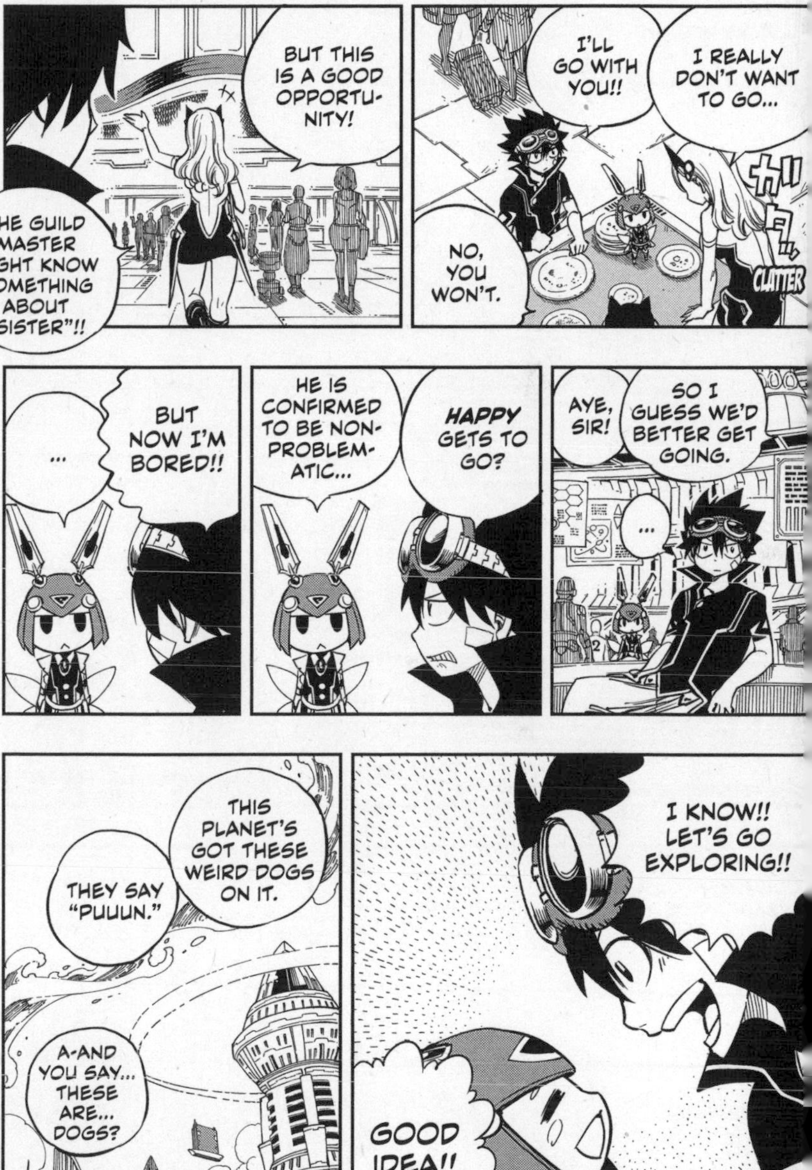
I REALLY DON'T WANT TO GO...
I'LL GO WITH YOU!!
NO, YOU WON'T.
CLATTER
BUT THIS IS A GOOD OPPORTU-NITY!
THE GUILD MASTER MIGHT KNOW SOMETHING ABOUT "SISTER"!!
SO I GUESS WE'D BETTER GET GOING.
AYE, SIR!
...
HAPPY GETS TO GO?
HE IS CONFIRMED TO BE NON-PROBLEM-ATIC...
BUT NOW I'M BORED!!
...
I KNOW!! LET'S GO EXPLORING!!
GOOD IDEA!!
THIS PLANET'S GOT THESE WEIRD DOGS ON IT.
THEY SAY "PUUUN."
A-AND YOU SAY... THESE ARE... DOGS?

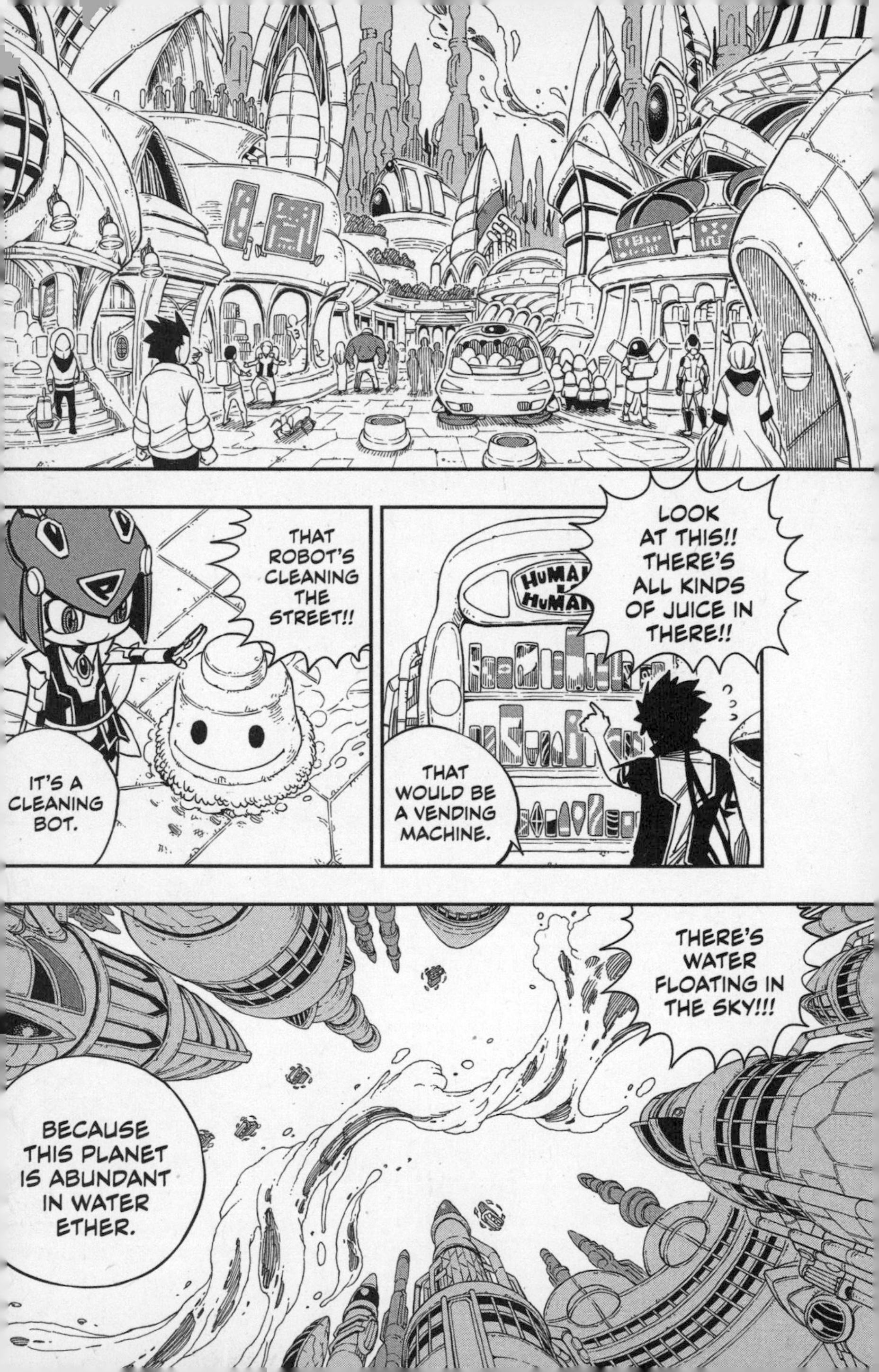
LOOK AT THIS!! THERE'S ALL KINDS OF JUICE IN THERE!!
THAT WOULD BE A VENDING MACHINE.
THAT ROBOT'S CLEANING THE STREET!!
IT'S A CLEANING BOT.
THERE'S WATER FLOATING IN THE SKY!!!
BECAUSE THIS PLANET IS ABUNDANT IN WATER ETHER.

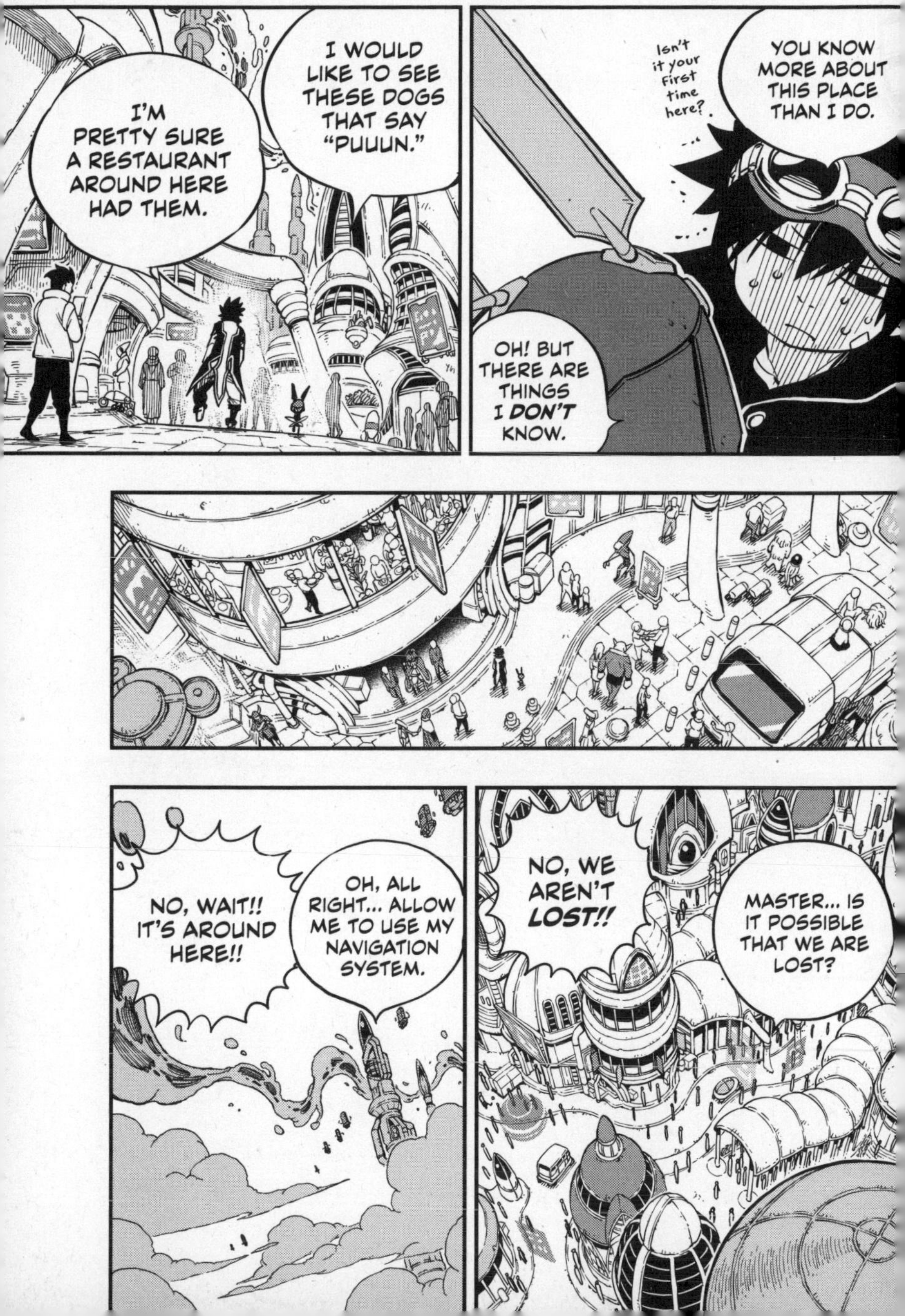
YOU KNOW MORE ABOUT THIS PLACE THAN I DO.
Isn't it your first time here?
...
OH! BUT THERE ARE THINGS I *DON'T* KNOW.
I WOULD LIKE TO SEE THESE DOGS THAT SAY "PUUUN."
I'M PRETTY SURE A RESTAURANT AROUND HERE HAD THEM.
MASTER... IS IT POSSIBLE THAT WE ARE LOST?
NO, WE AREN'T *LOST!!*
OH, ALL RIGHT... ALLOW ME TO USE MY NAVIGATION SYSTEM.
NO, WAIT!! IT'S AROUND HERE!!

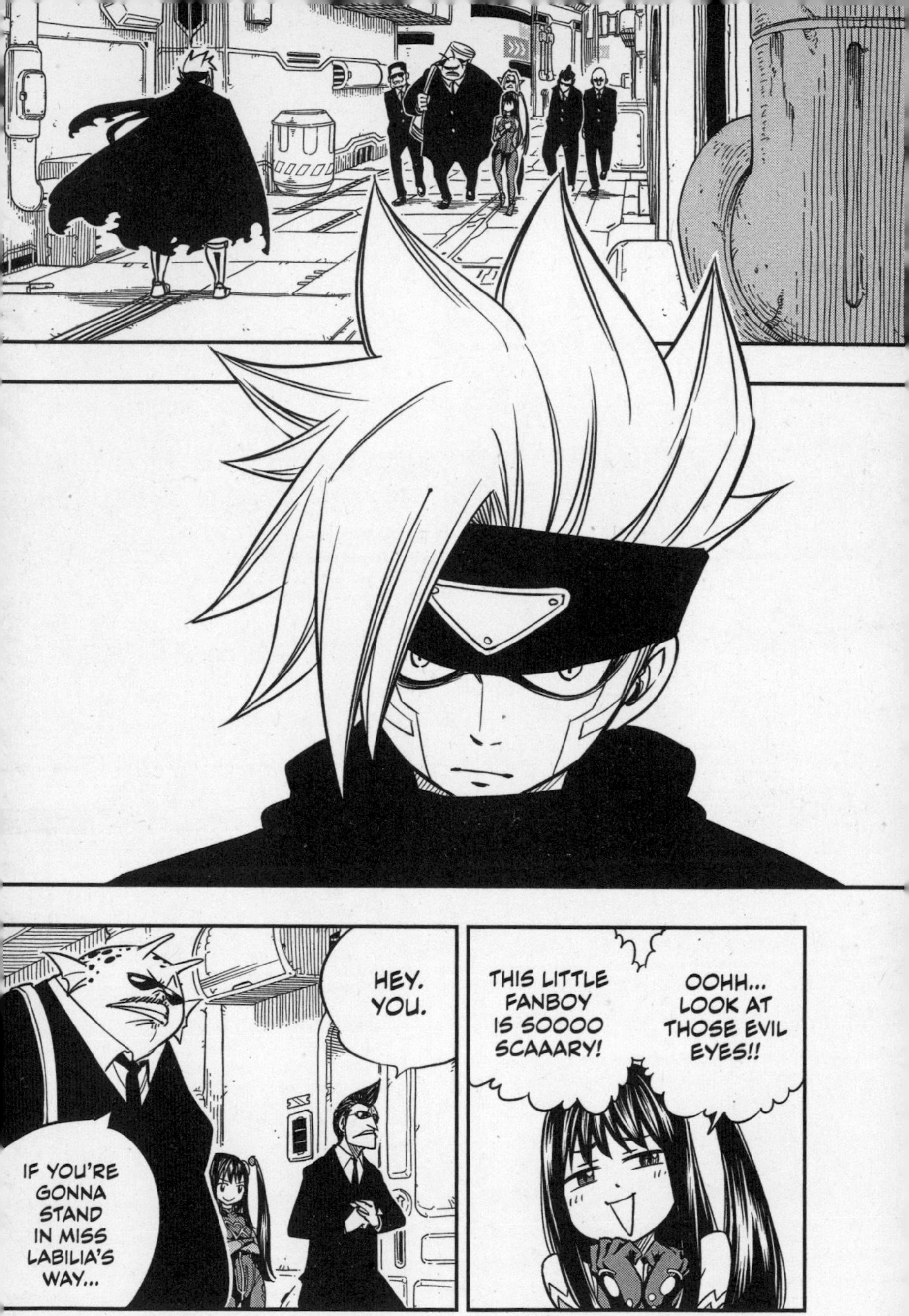
OOHH... LOOK AT THOSE EVIL EYES!!
THIS LITTLE FANBOY IS SOOOO SCAAARY!
HEY. YOU.
IF YOU'RE GONNA STAND IN MISS LABILIA'S WAY...

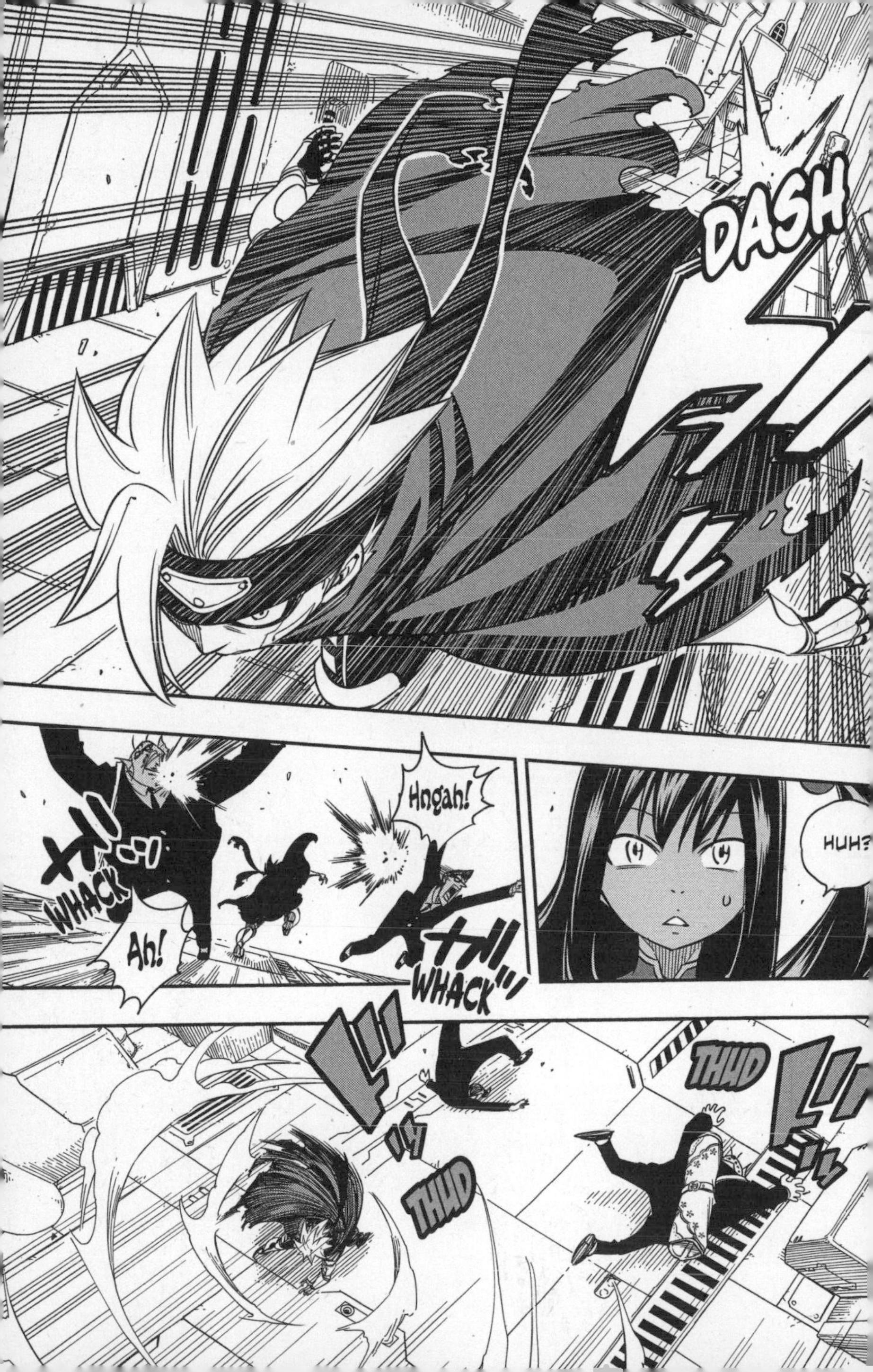
DASH
HUH?
Hngah!
WHACK
WHACK
Ah!
THUD
THUD

YOU GOT IT!!

YOU LITTLE...!

WHAT THE—!! THIS GUY'S TROUBLE!!!

NUMBER 3!! NUMBER 4!!

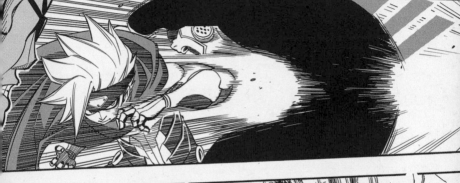

NUMBER 5!!!

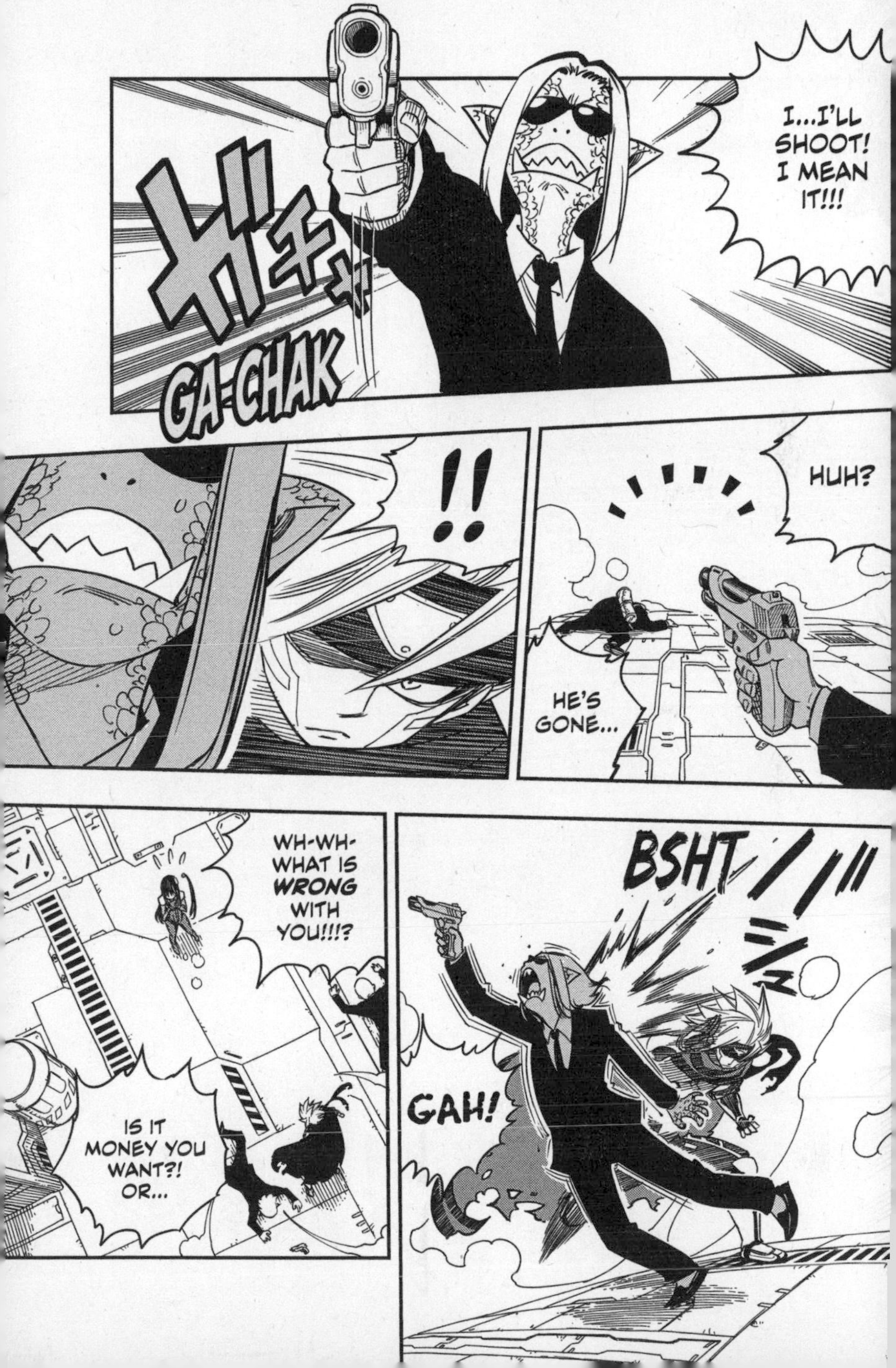
I...I'LL SHOOT! I MEAN IT!!!
ガチャ
GA-CHAK
HUH?
HE'S GONE...
!!
BSHT
GAH!
WH-WH-WHAT IS **WRONG** WITH YOU!!!?
IS IT MONEY YOU WANT?! OR...

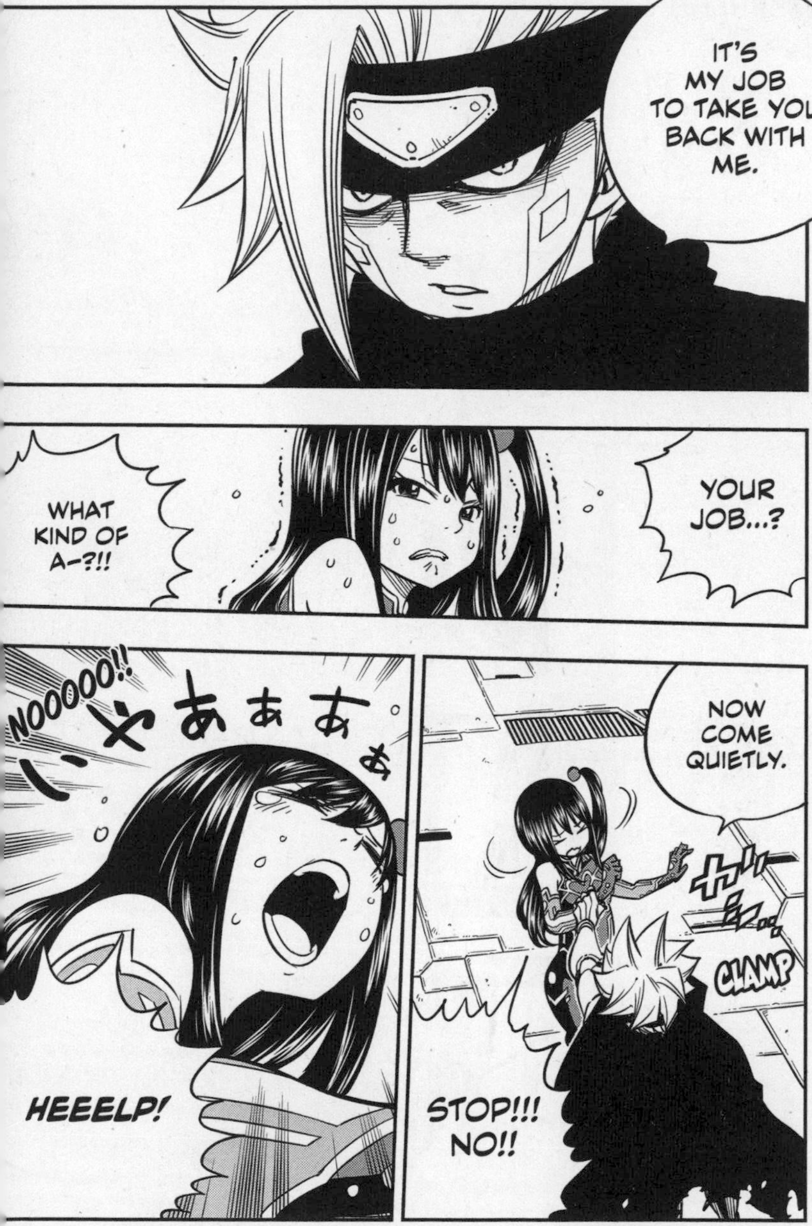
IT'S MY JOB TO TAKE YOU BACK WITH ME.
YOUR JOB...?
WHAT KIND OF A–?!!
NOW COME QUIETLY.
CLAMP
STOP!!! NO!!
NOOOOO!!
いやああああ
HEEELP!

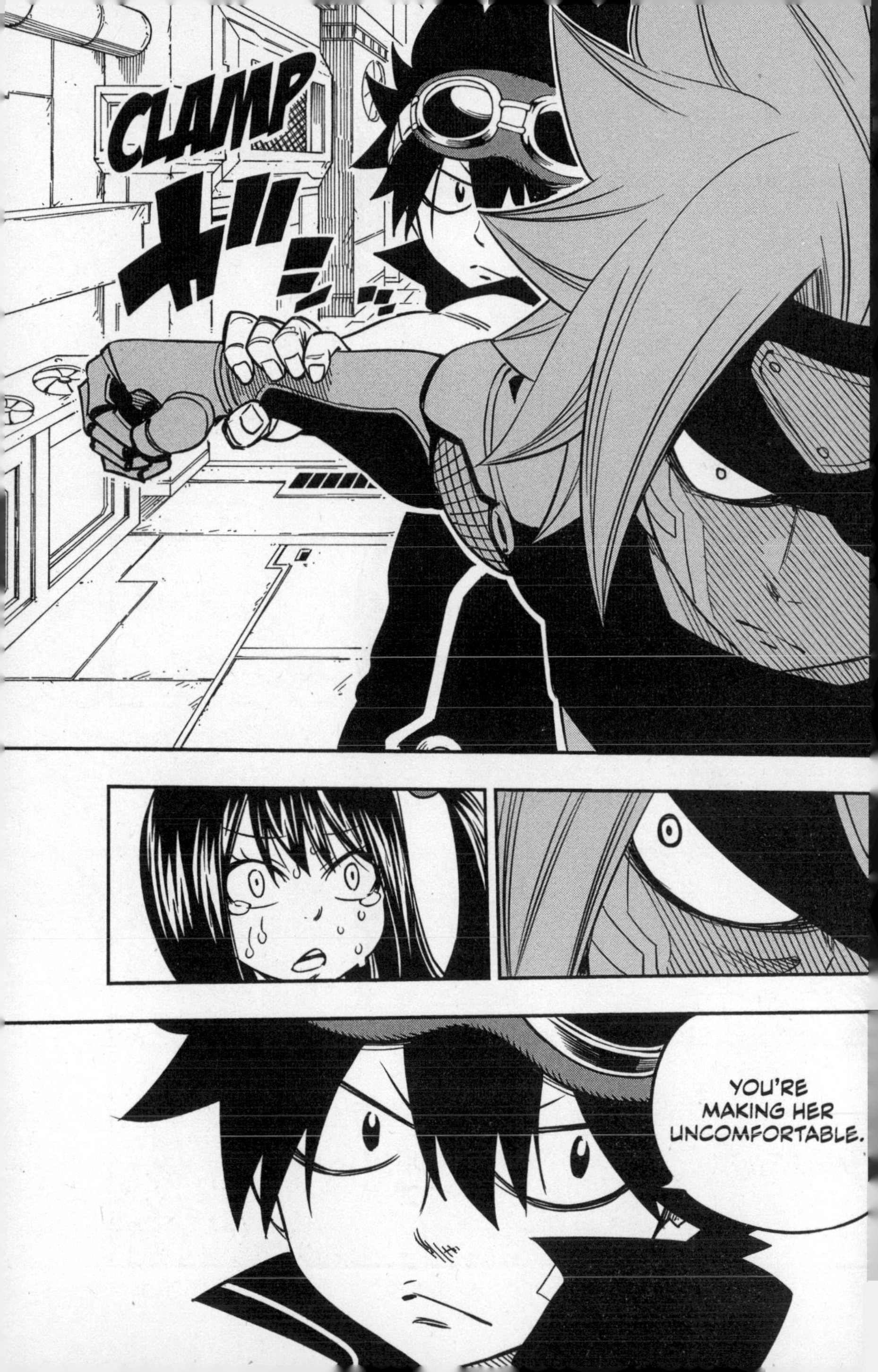
CLAMP
YOU'RE MAKING HER UNCOMFORTABLE.

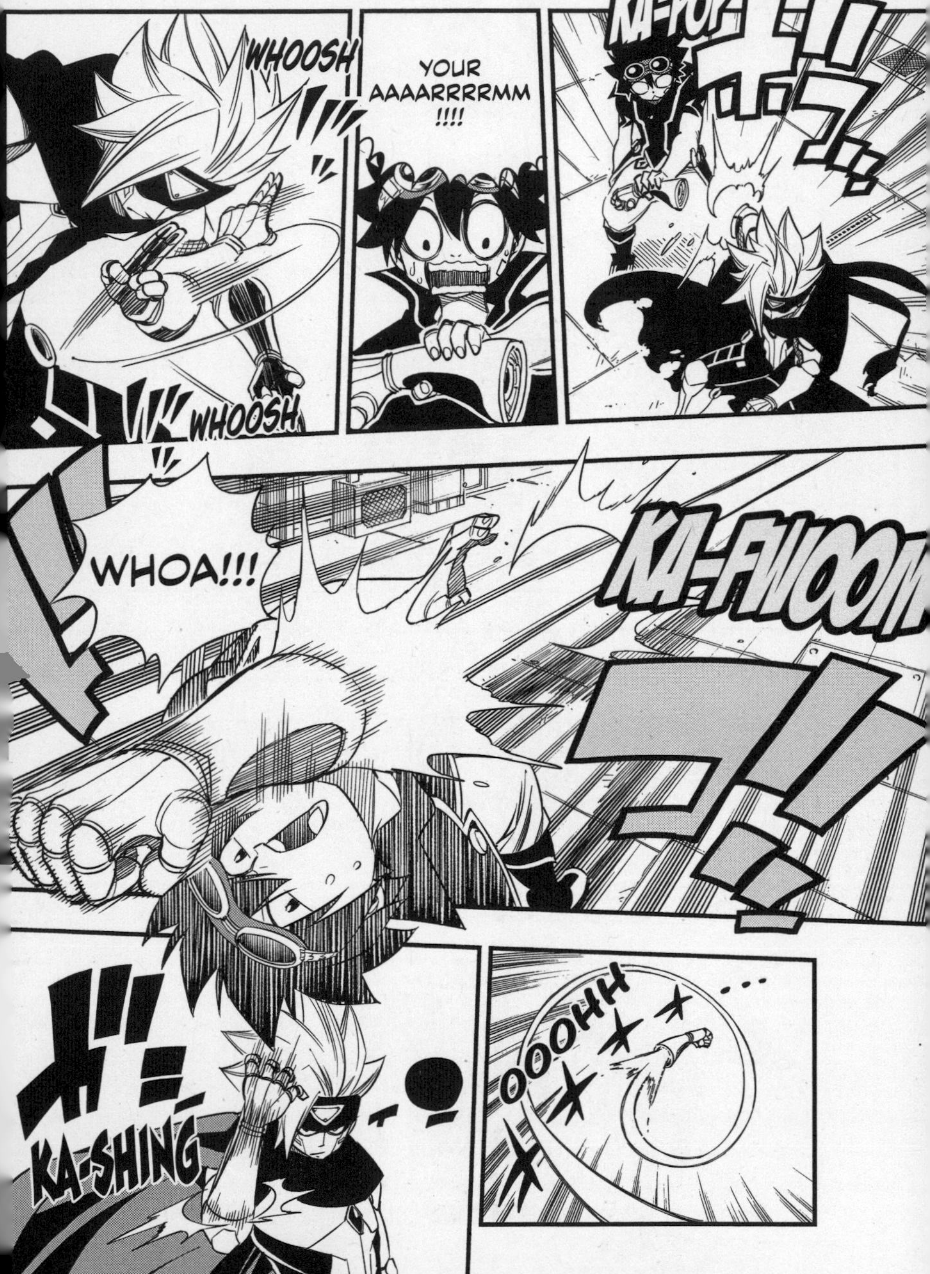
KA-POP
YOUR AAAARRRRMM !!!!
WHOOSH
WHOOSH
KA-FWOOM
WHOA!!!
OOOHH ...
KA-SHING

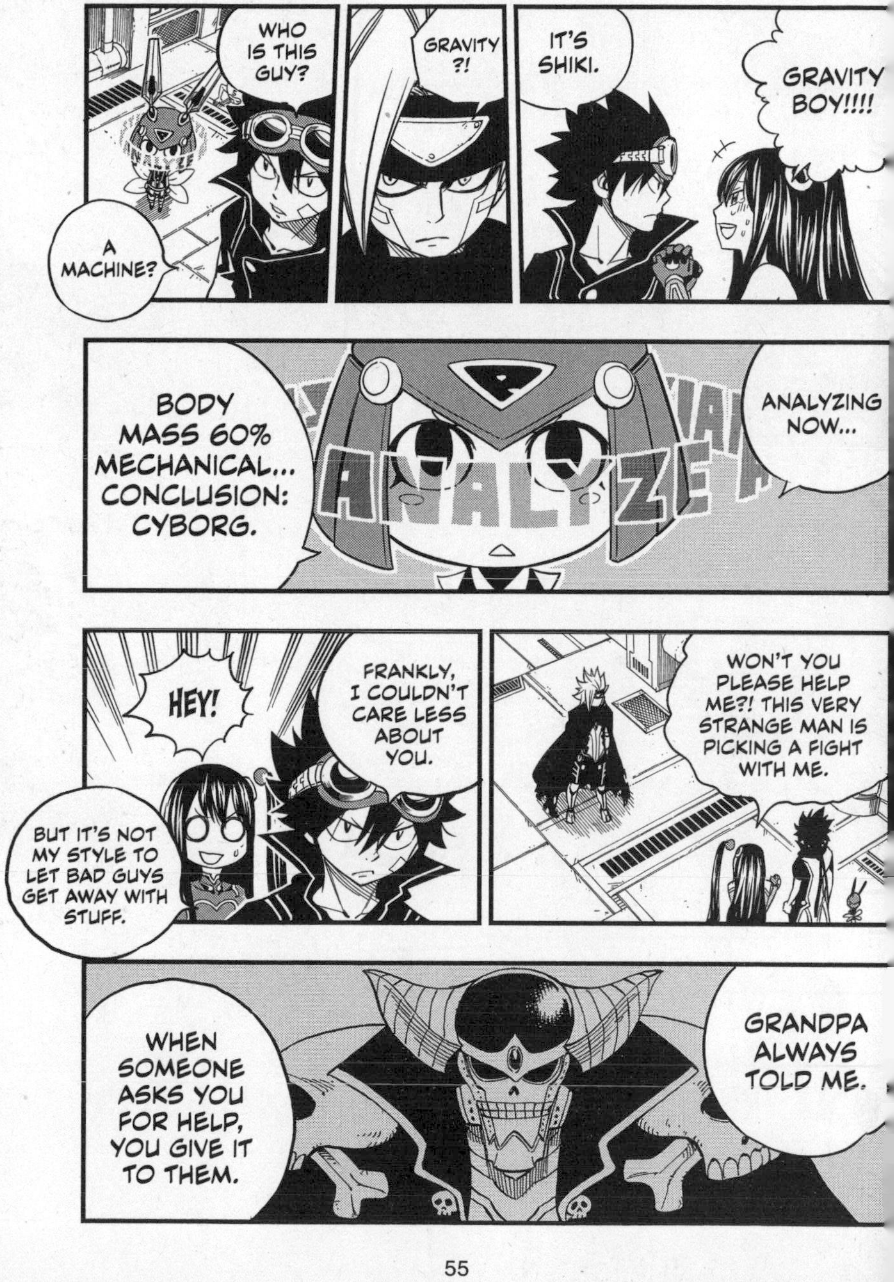
GRAVITY BOY!!!!
IT'S SHIKI.
GRAVITY ?!
WHO IS THIS GUY?
ANALYZE
A MACHINE?
ANALYZING NOW...
ANALYZE
BODY MASS 60% MECHANICAL... CONCLUSION: CYBORG.
WON'T YOU PLEASE HELP ME?! THIS VERY STRANGE MAN IS PICKING A FIGHT WITH ME.
FRANKLY, I COULDN'T CARE LESS ABOUT YOU.
HEY!
BUT IT'S NOT MY STYLE TO LET BAD GUYS GET AWAY WITH STUFF.
GRANDPA ALWAYS TOLD ME.
WHEN SOMEONE ASKS YOU FOR HELP, YOU GIVE IT TO THEM.

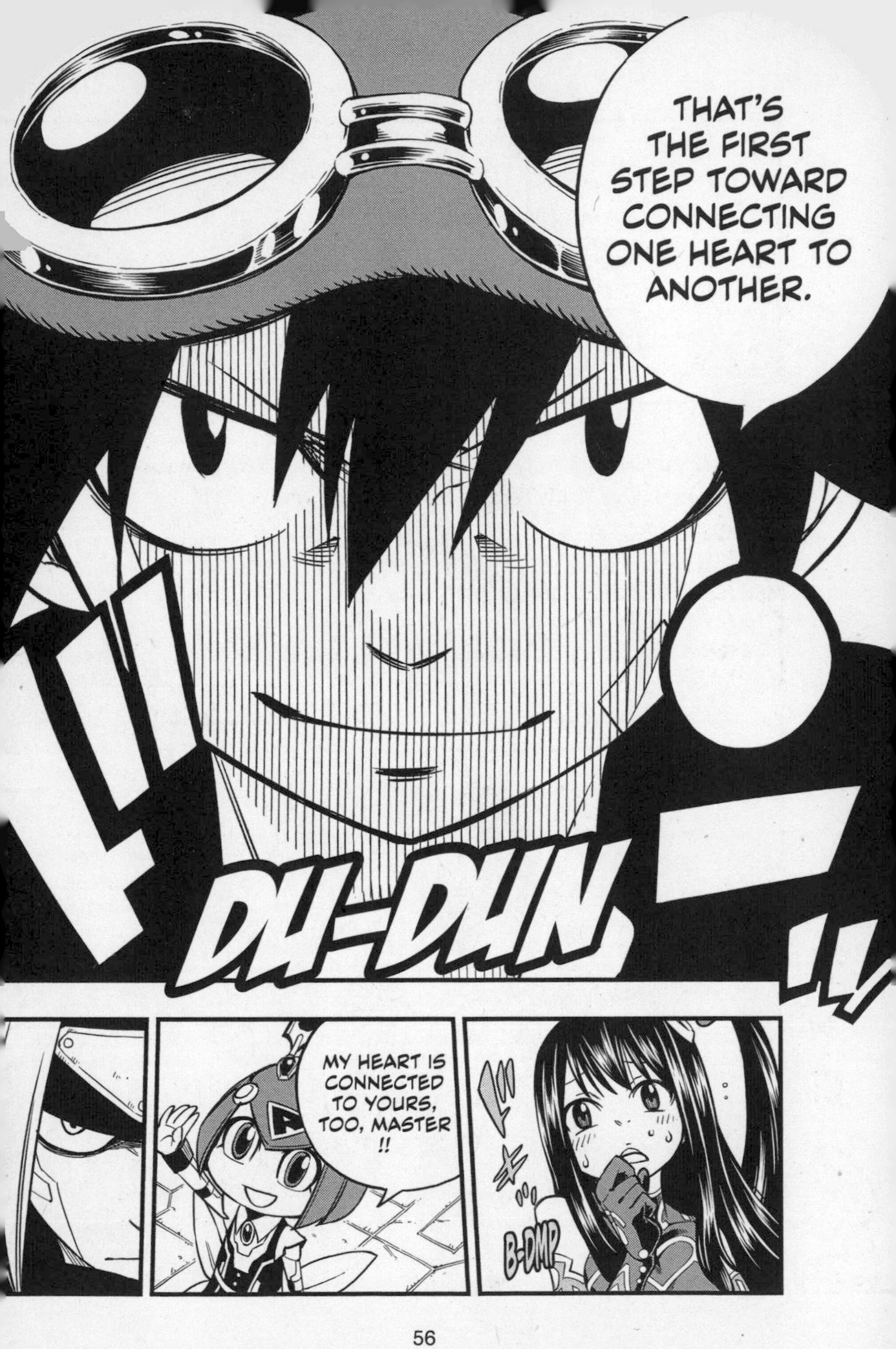
THAT'S THE FIRST STEP TOWARD CONNECTING ONE HEART TO ANOTHER.
DU-DUN
B-DMP
MY HEART IS CONNECTED TO YOURS, TOO, MASTER !!

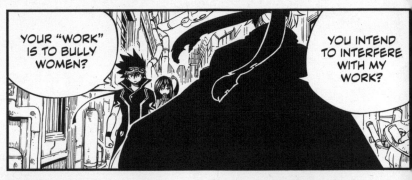

YOU INTEND TO INTERFERE WITH MY WORK?
YOUR "WORK" IS TO BULLY WOMEN?
MY WORK IS TO TAKE PEOPLE WITH ME.
EVEN IF THEY DON'T WANT TO GO?
THE TARGET'S FEELINGS ARE IRRELEVANT.
YOU'LL NEVER CONNECT ANY HEARTS LIKE THAT.
I HAVE NO NEED FOR HEARTS.
カキ
KRIK
カキ
KRIK

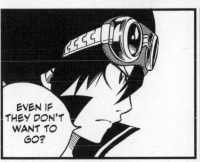

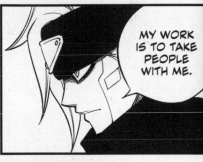

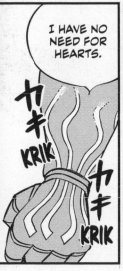

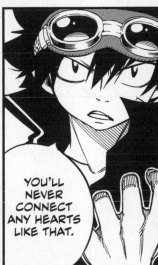

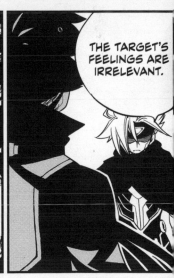

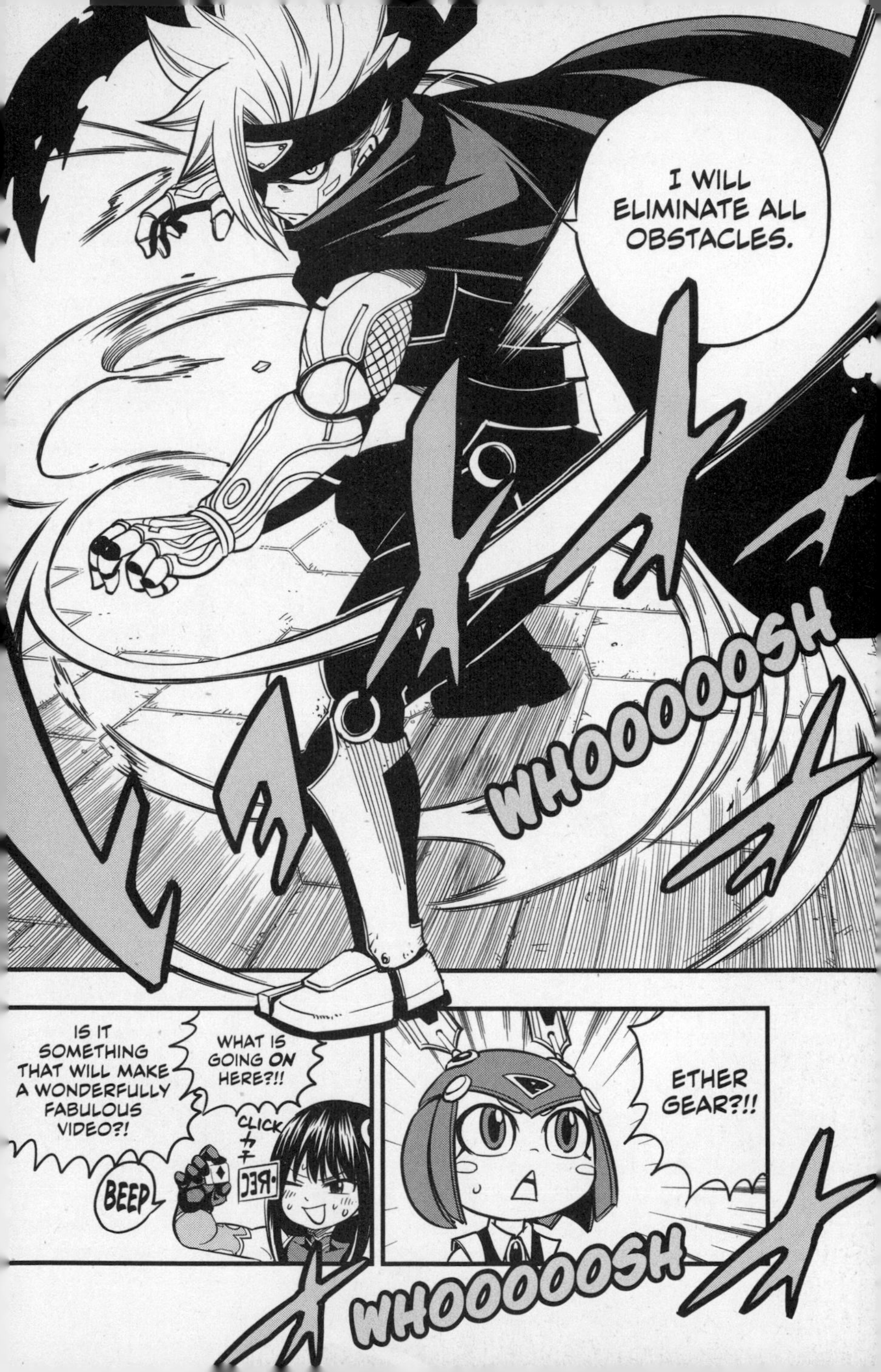
I WILL ELIMINATE ALL OBSTACLES.
WHOOOOOOSH
ETHER GEAR?!!
WHAT IS GOING ON HERE?!!
IS IT SOMETHING THAT WILL MAKE A WONDERFULLY FABULOUS VIDEO?!
CLICK
カチ
BEEP
WHOOOOOOSH

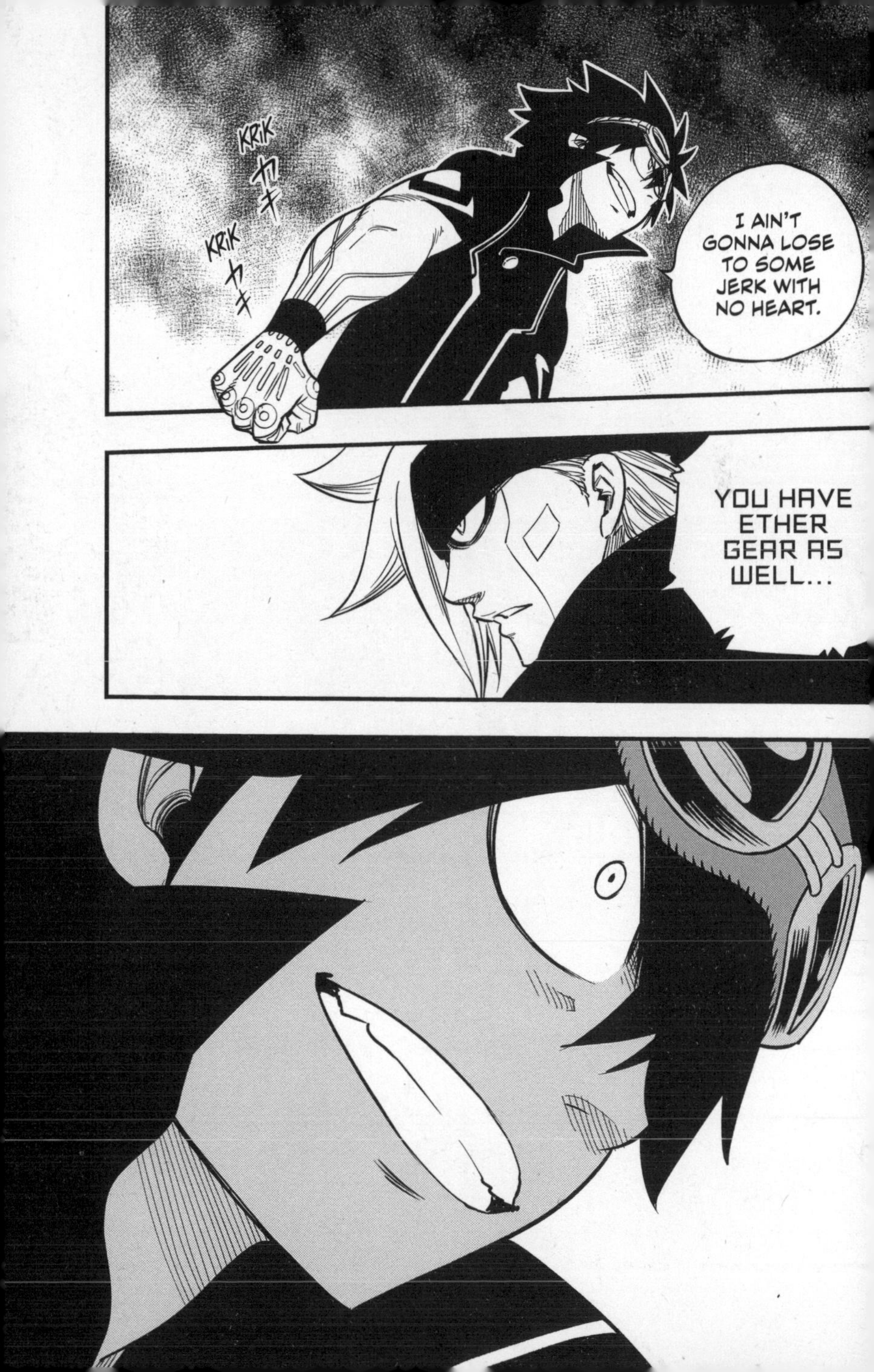
I AIN'T GONNA LOSE TO SOME JERK WITH NO HEART.
KRIK
カキ
KRIK
カキ
YOU HAVE ETHER GEAR AS WELL...

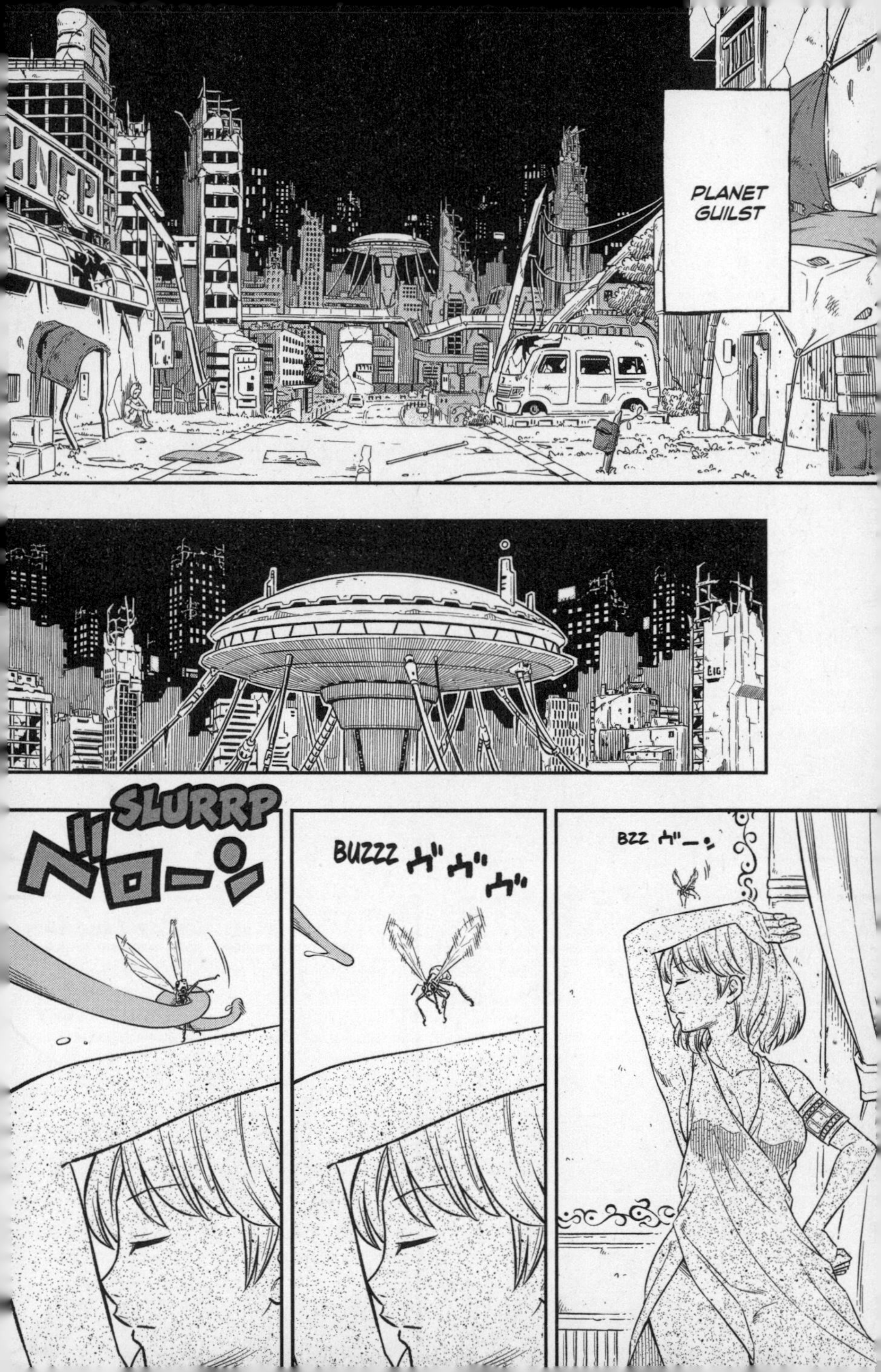
PLANET GUILST
BZZ ヴー
BUZZZ ヴヴヴ
SLURRP ベローン

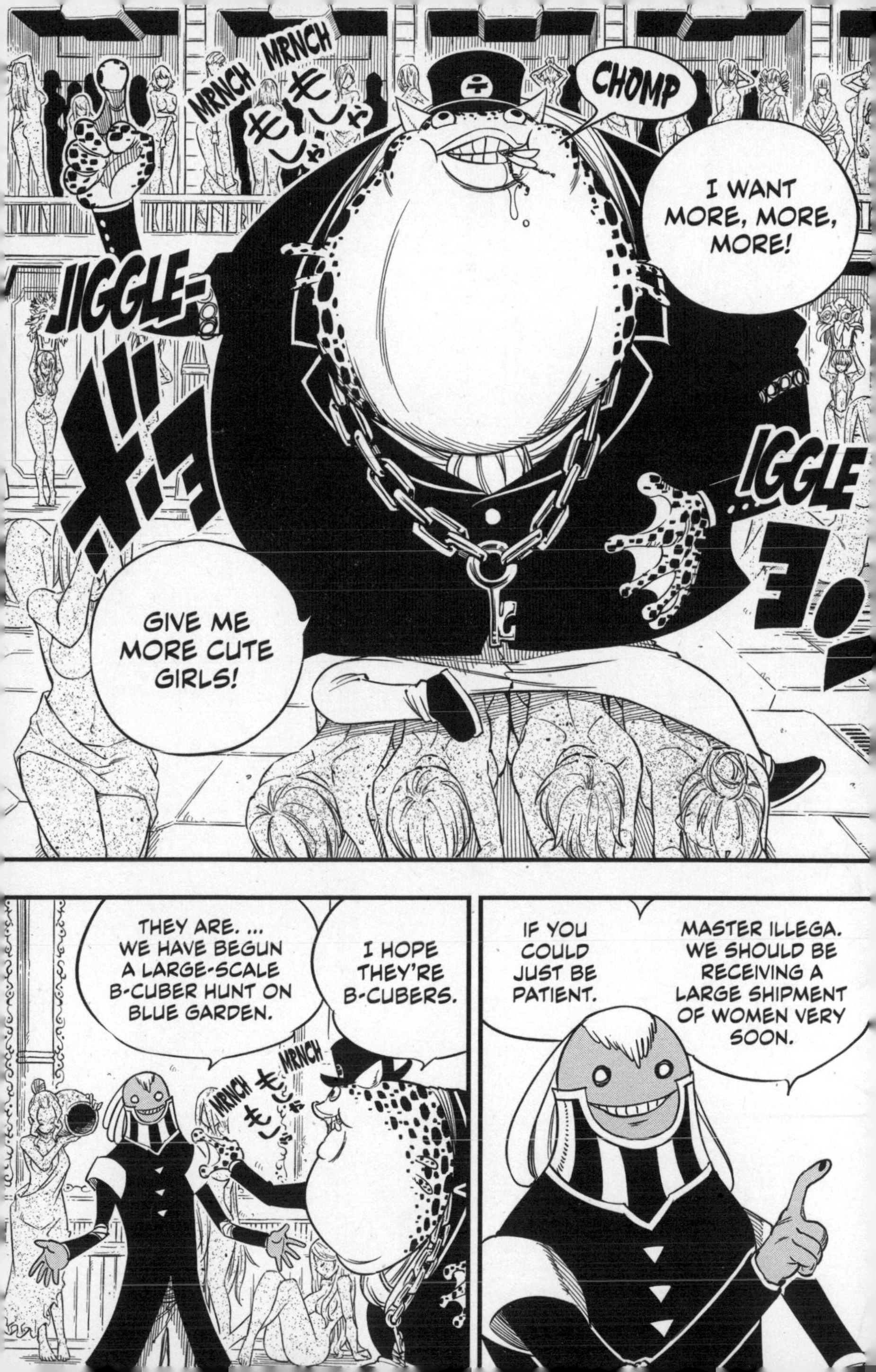
CHOMP
I WANT MORE, MORE, MORE!
MRNCH MRNCH
もしゃもしゃ
IGGLE
JIGGLE
GIVE ME MORE CUTE GIRLS!
MASTER ILLEGA. WE SHOULD BE RECEIVING A LARGE SHIPMENT OF WOMEN VERY SOON.
IF YOU COULD JUST BE PATIENT.
I HOPE THEY'RE B-CUBERS.
THEY ARE. ... WE HAVE BEGUN A LARGE-SCALE B-CUBER HUNT ON BLUE GARDEN.
MRNCH MRNCH
もしゃもしゃ

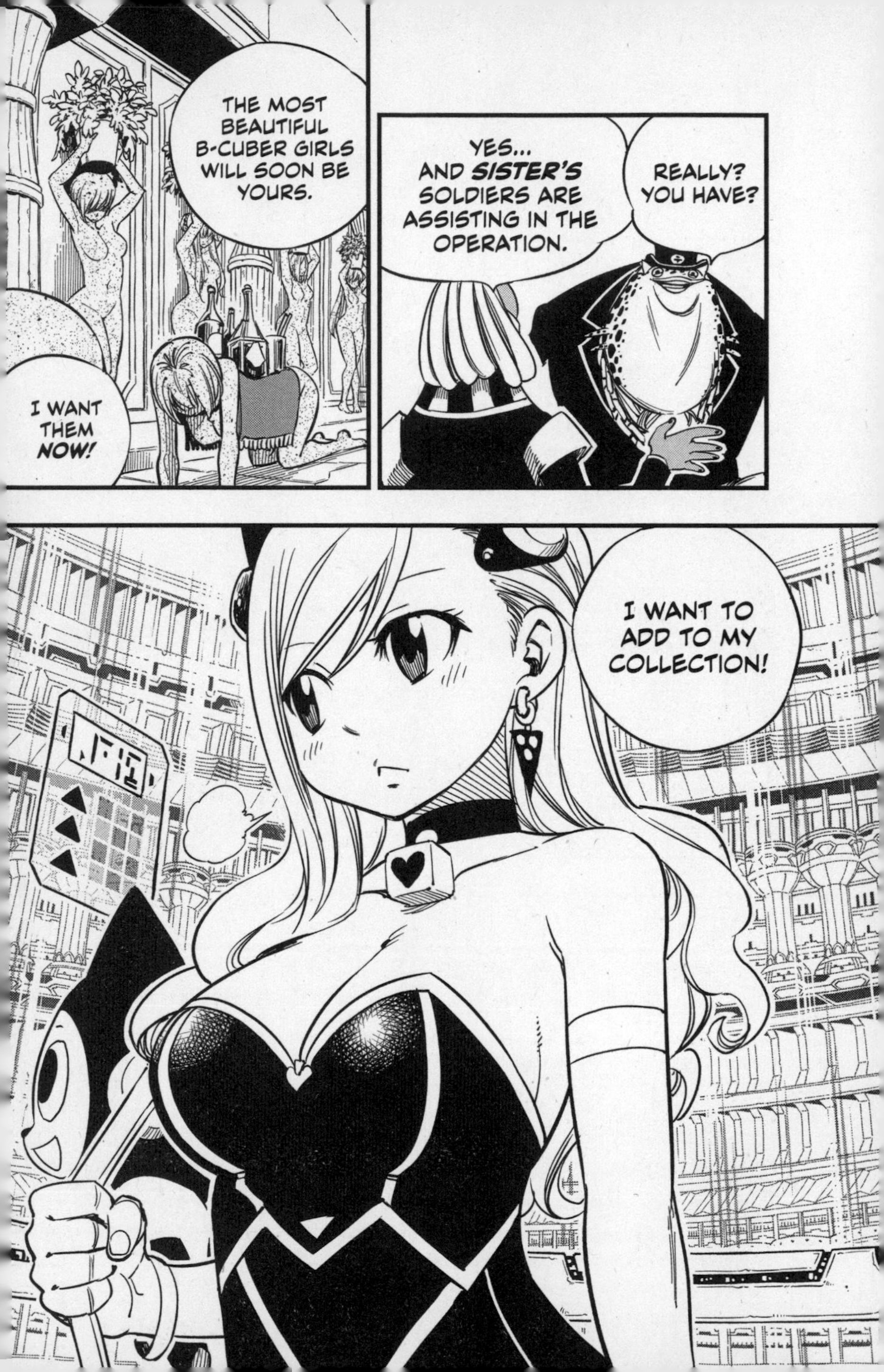
REALLY? YOU HAVE?
YES... AND SISTER'S SOLDIERS ARE ASSISTING IN THE OPERATION.
THE MOST BEAUTIFUL B-CUBER GIRLS WILL SOON BE YOURS.
I WANT THEM NOW!
I WANT TO ADD TO MY COLLECTION!

EDENS ZERO

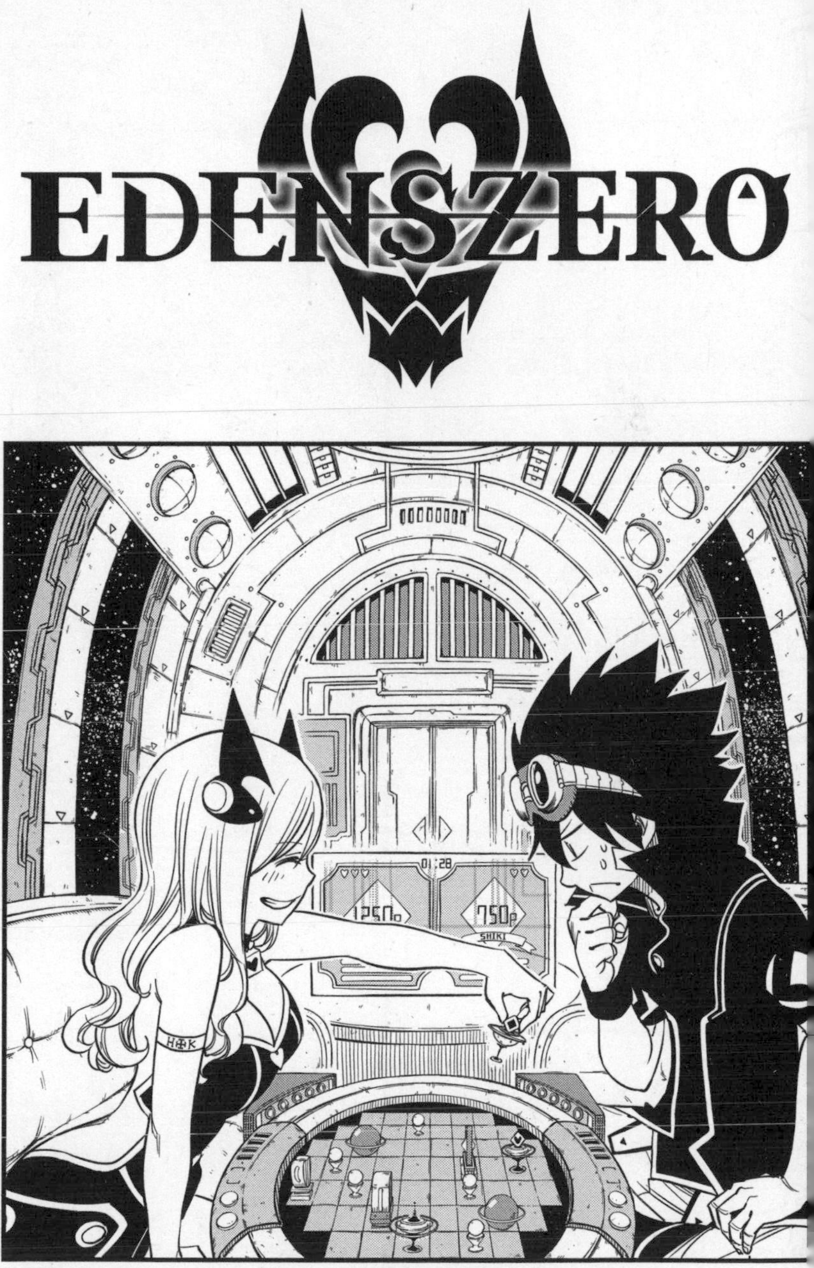
01:28
1250p
750p
SHIKI

CHAPTER 18: WIND HOWLS ON THE HIGHWAY

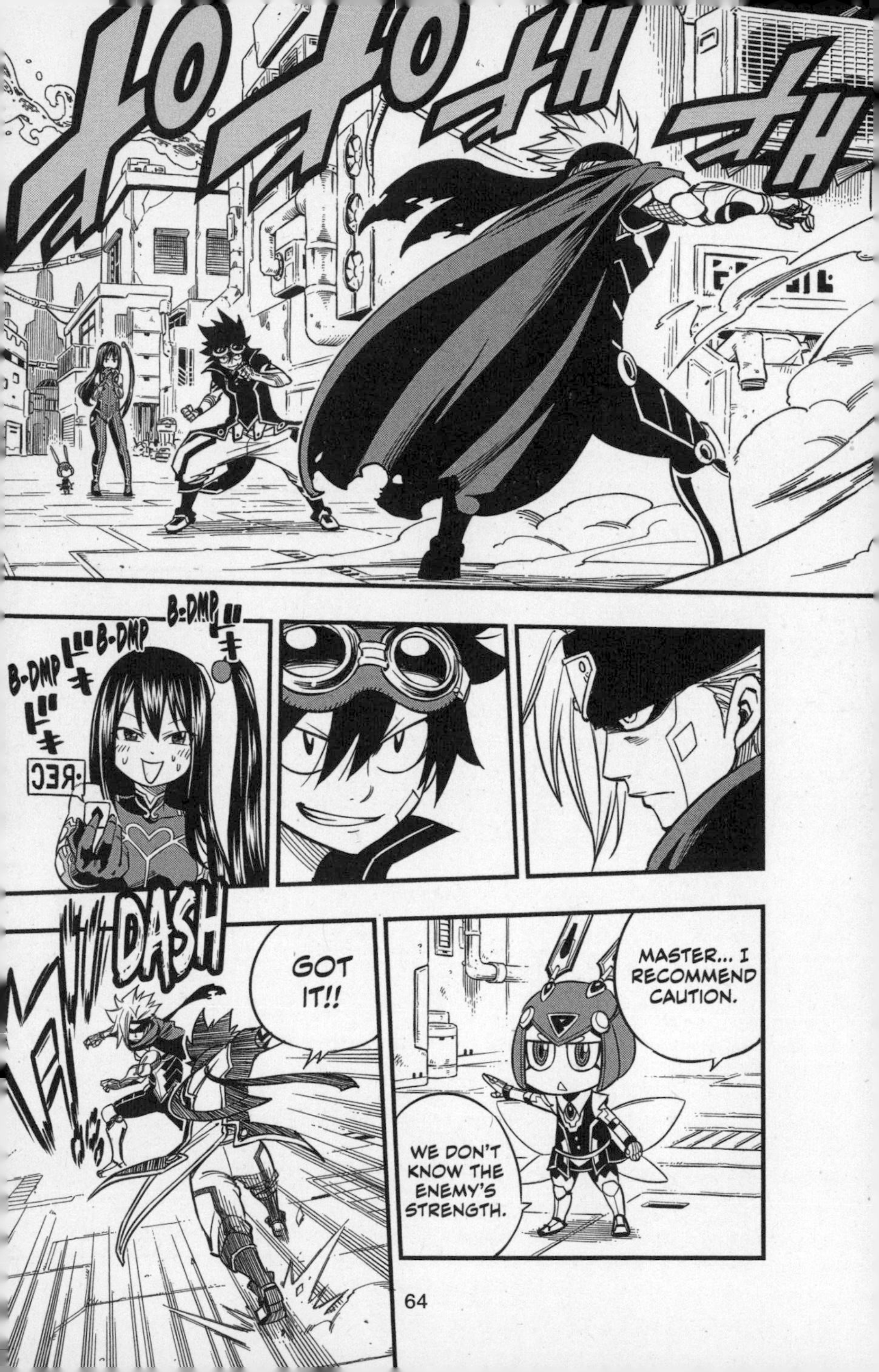
B-DMP
B-DMP
B-DMP
REC
MASTER... I RECOMMEND CAUTION.
WE DON'T KNOW THE ENEMY'S STRENGTH.
DASH
GOT IT!!

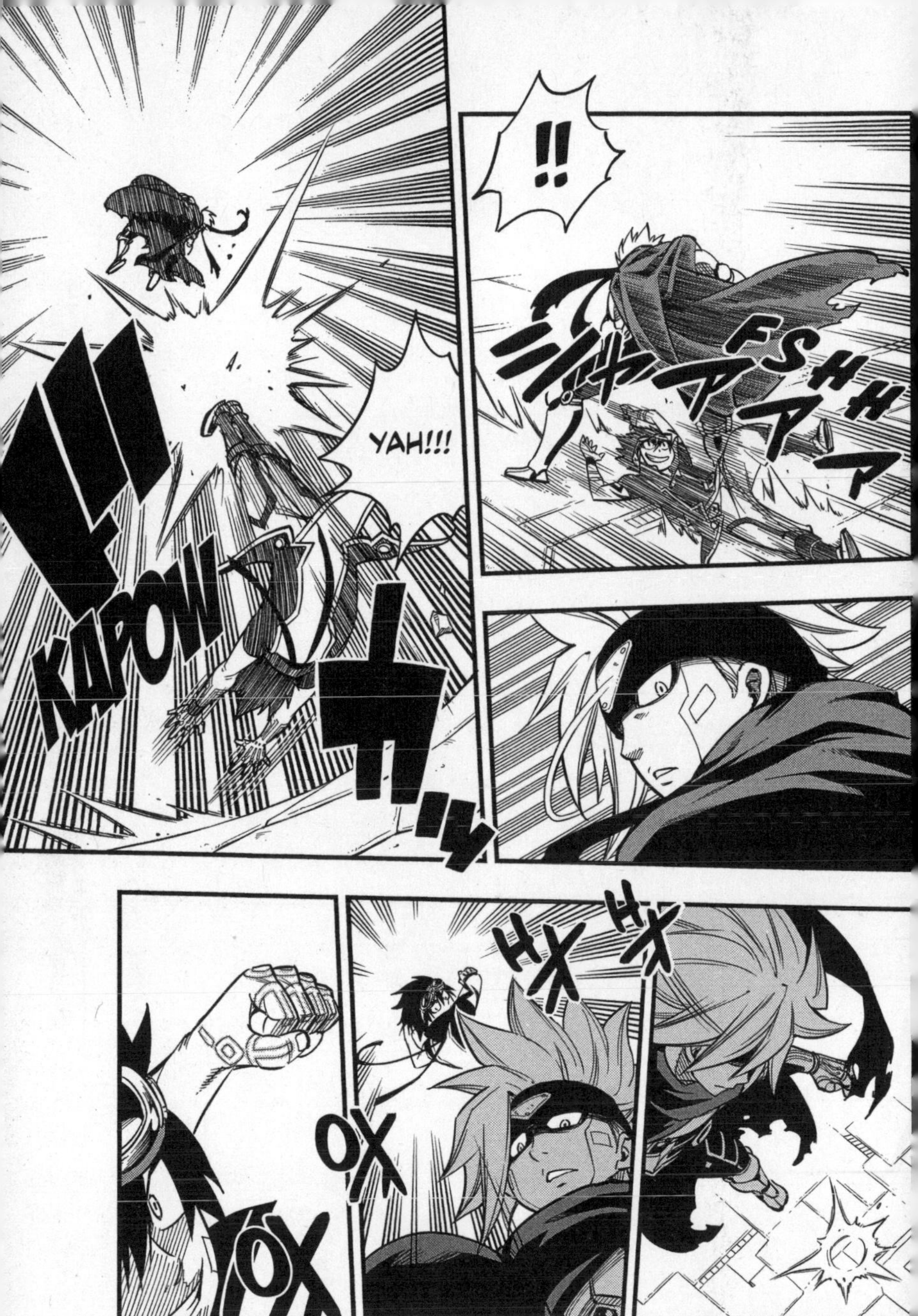
!!
FSHH
YAH!!!
KAPOW
HX
HX
OX
OX

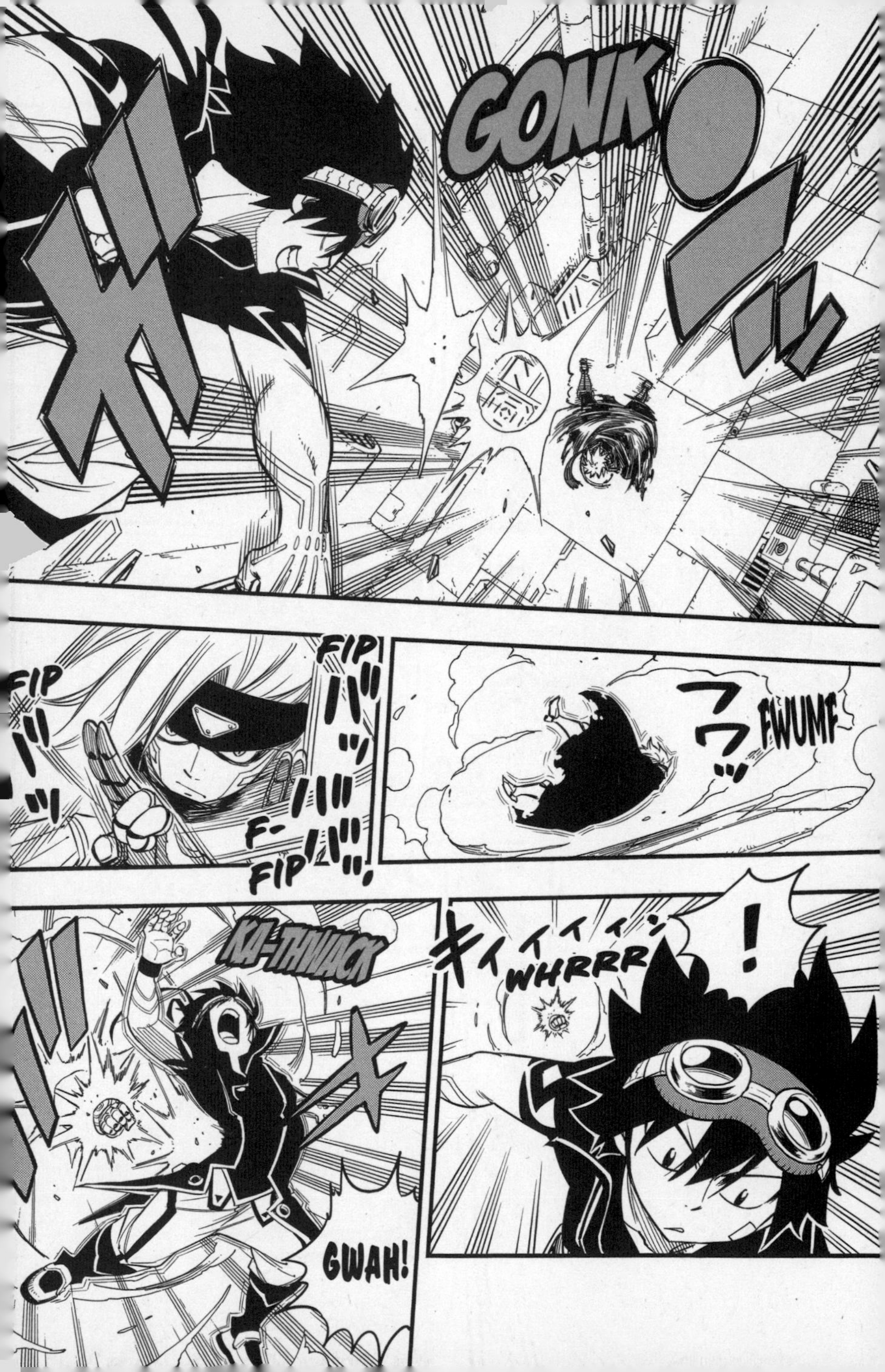

GONK
FWUMF
フワッ
FIP
FIP
F-
FIP
キイイイン
WHRRR
!
KA-THWACK
GWAH!

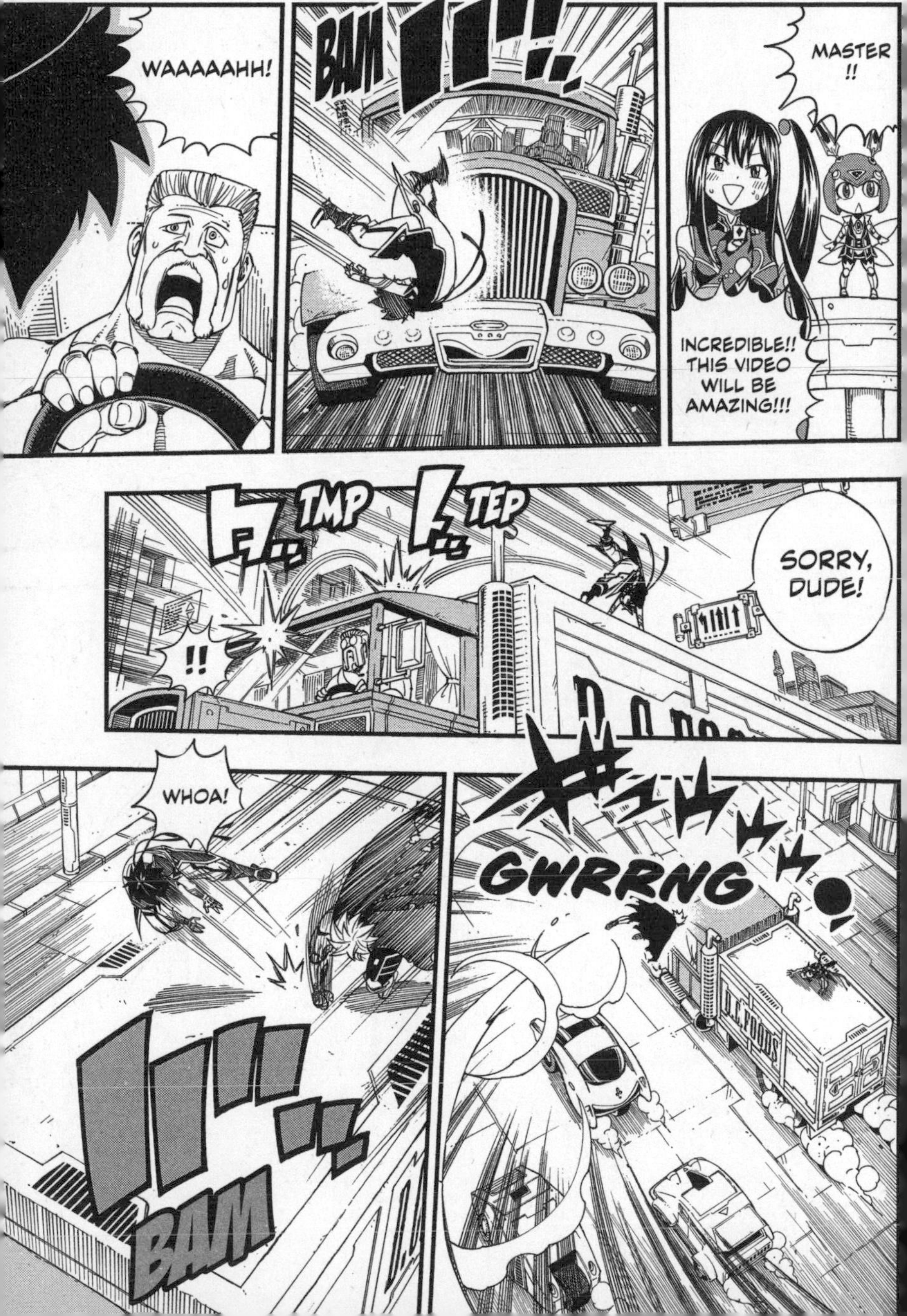
MASTER !!
INCREDIBLE!! THIS VIDEO WILL BE AMAZING!!!
BAM
WAAAAAHH!
SORRY, DUDE!
TEP
TMP
!!
GWRRNG
WHOA!
BAM

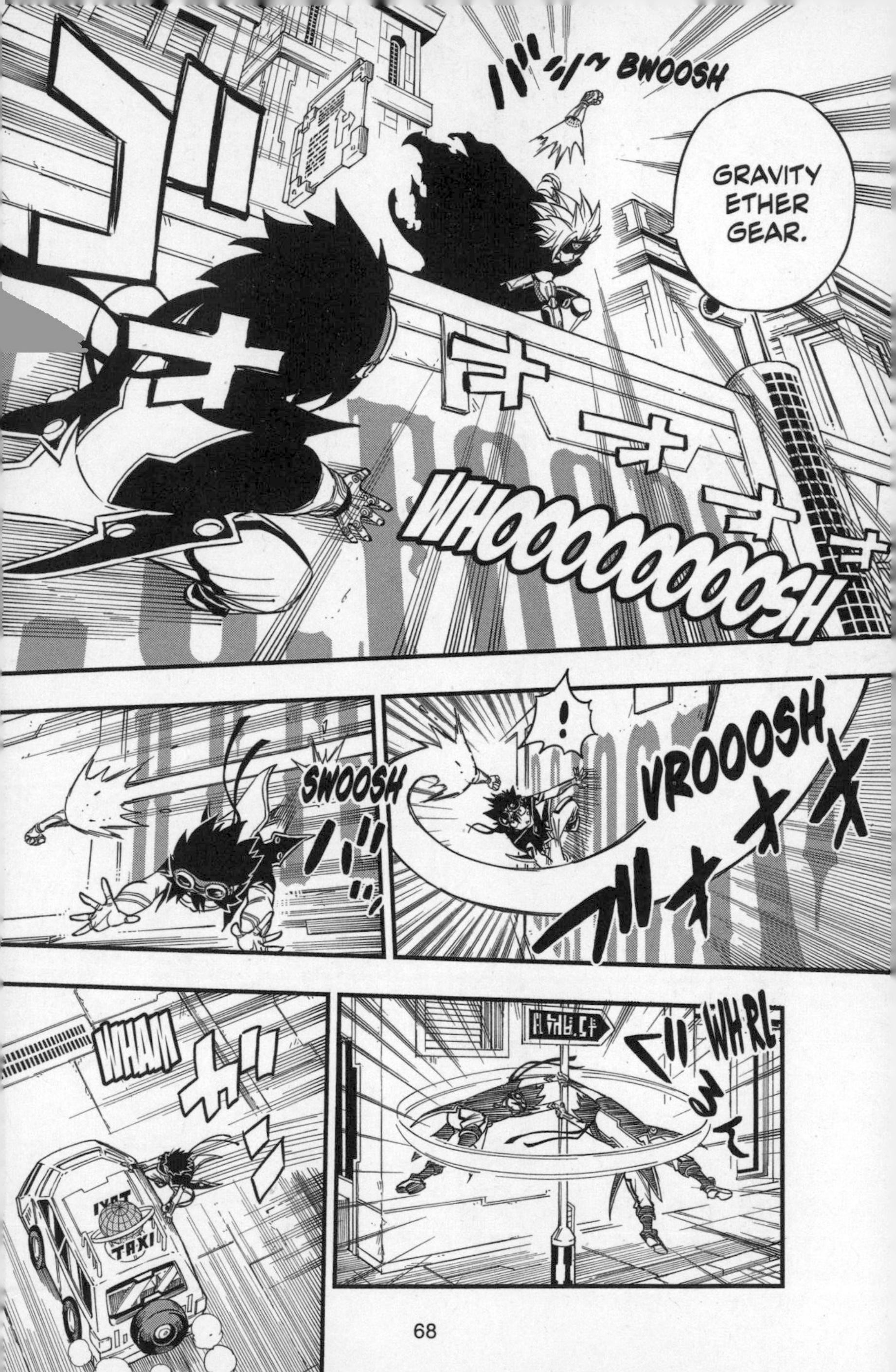
BWOOSH
GRAVITY ETHER GEAR.
WHOOOOOOOOOSH
!
VROOOSH
SWOOSH
WHIRL
WHAM
TAXI

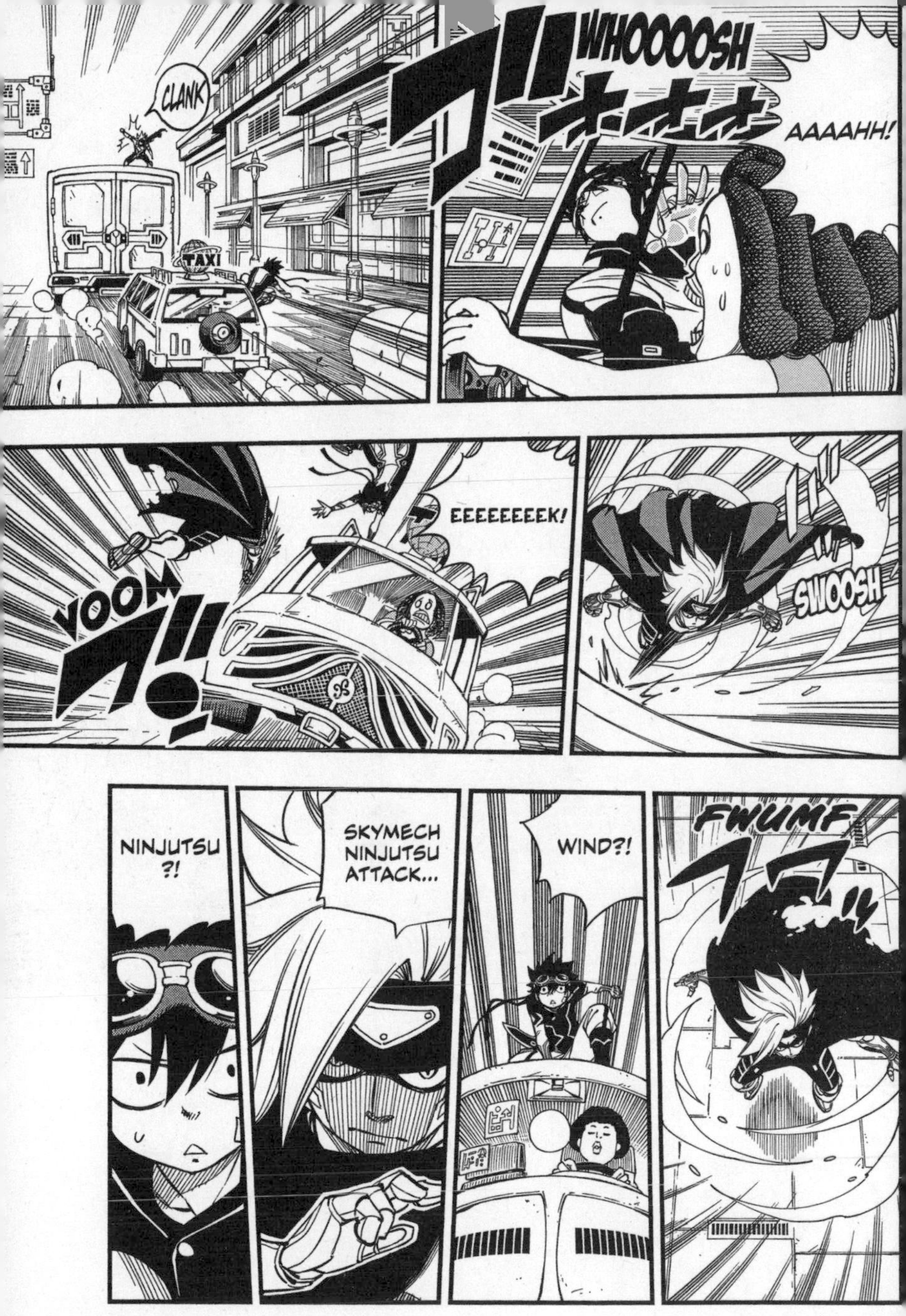
WHOOOOSH
AAAAHH!
CLANK
TAXI
SWOOSH
EEEEEEEEK!
VOOM
FWUMF
WIND?!
SKYMECH NINJUTSU ATTACK...
NINJUTSU ?!

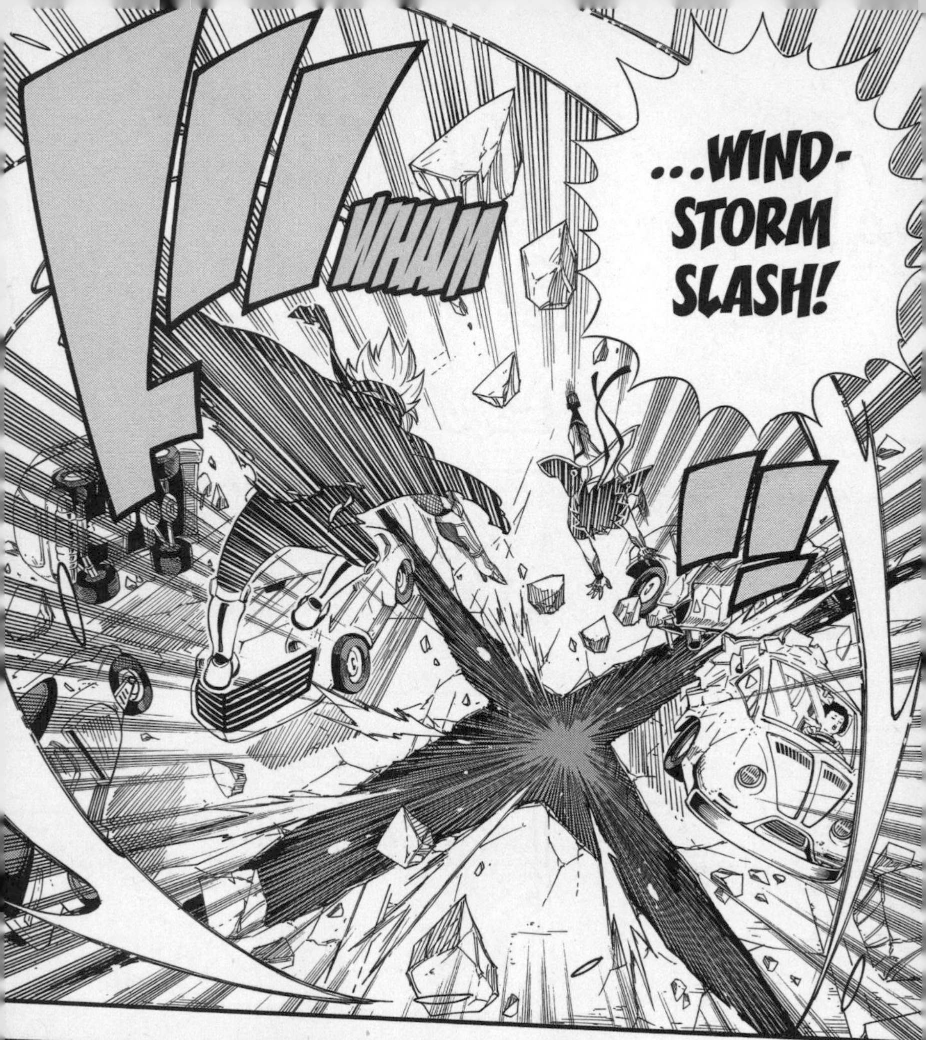
...WIND-
STORM
SLASH!
WHAM

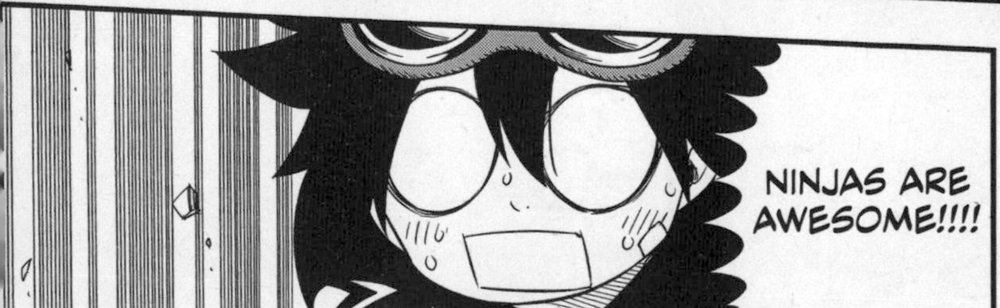
NINJAS ARE
AWESOME!!!!

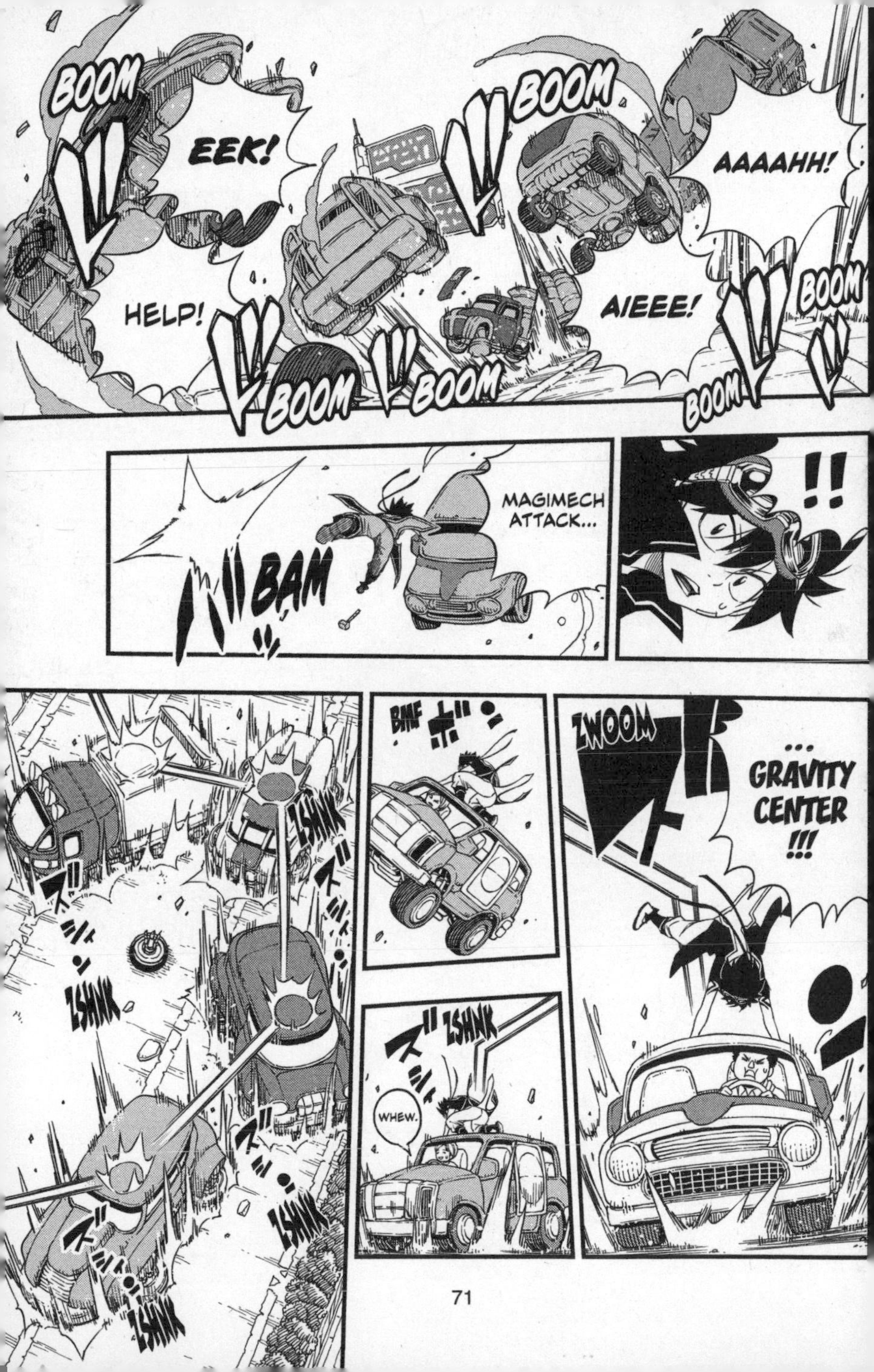
BOOM
AAAAHH!
BOOM
AIEEE!
BOOM
EEK!
BOOM
HELP!
BOOM
BOOM
!!
MAGIMECH ATTACK...
BAM
... GRAVITY CENTER !!!
ZWOOM
BMF
ZSHNK
WHEW.
ZSHNK
ZSHNK
ZSHNK
ZSHNK

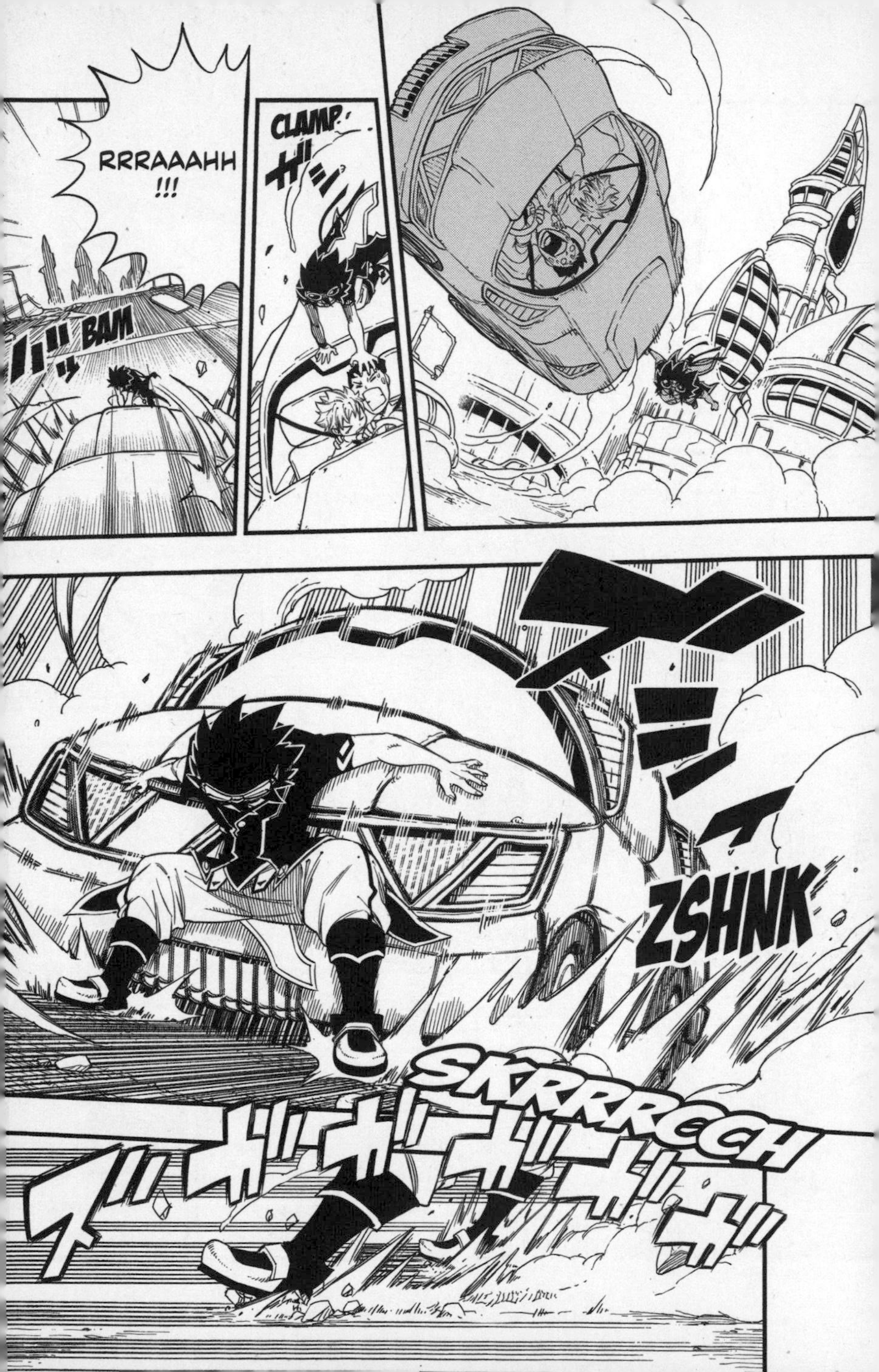
CLAMP
RRRAAAHH!!!
BAM
ZSHNK
SKRRRCCH

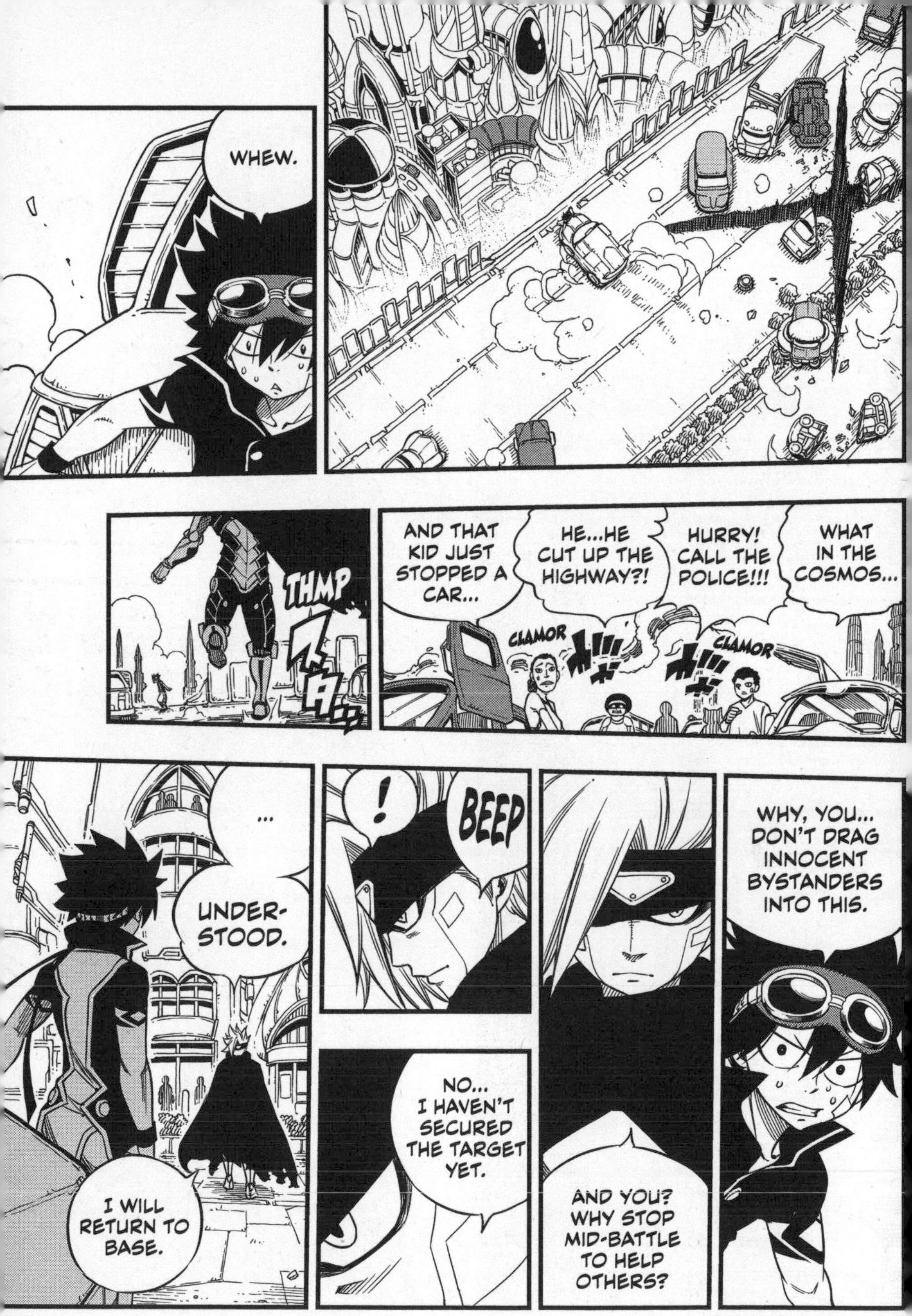
WHEW.
WHAT IN THE COSMOS...
HURRY! CALL THE POLICE!!!
HE...HE CUT UP THE HIGHWAY?!
AND THAT KID JUST STOPPED A CAR...
CLAMOR
CLAMOR
THMP
WHY, YOU... DON'T DRAG INNOCENT BYSTANDERS INTO THIS.
AND YOU? WHY STOP MID-BATTLE TO HELP OTHERS?
BEEP
!
NO... I HAVEN'T SECURED THE TARGET YET.
...
UNDER-STOOD.
I WILL RETURN TO BASE.

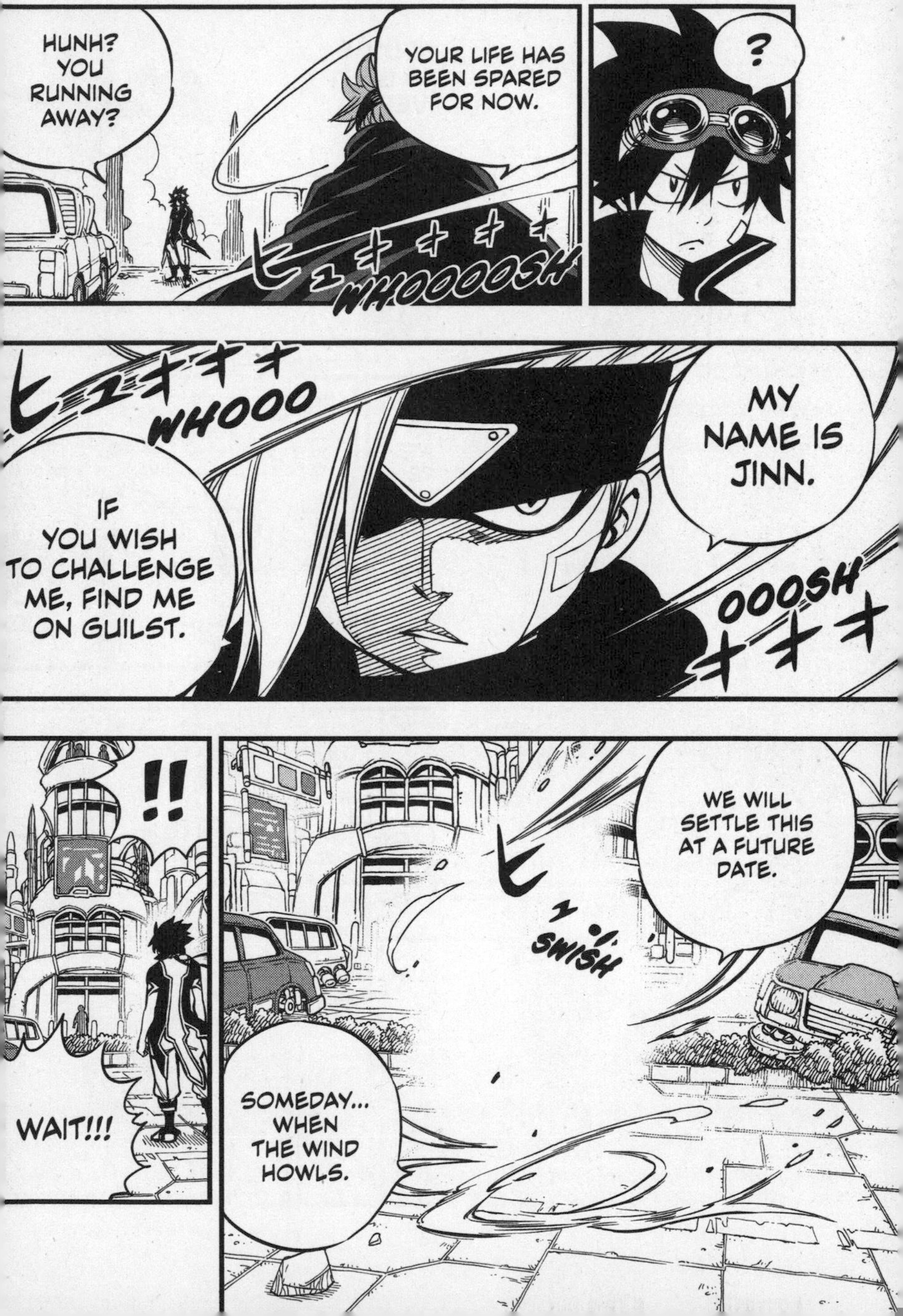
?
YOUR LIFE HAS BEEN SPARED FOR NOW.
HUNH? YOU RUNNING AWAY?
ヒュオオオオ
WHOOOOOSH
MY NAME IS JINN.
ヒュオオオ
WHOOO
OOOSH
オオオ
IF YOU WISH TO CHALLENGE ME, FIND ME ON GUILST.
WE WILL SETTLE THIS AT A FUTURE DATE.
ヒュッ
SWISH
SOMEDAY... WHEN THE WIND HOWLS.
!!
WAIT!!!

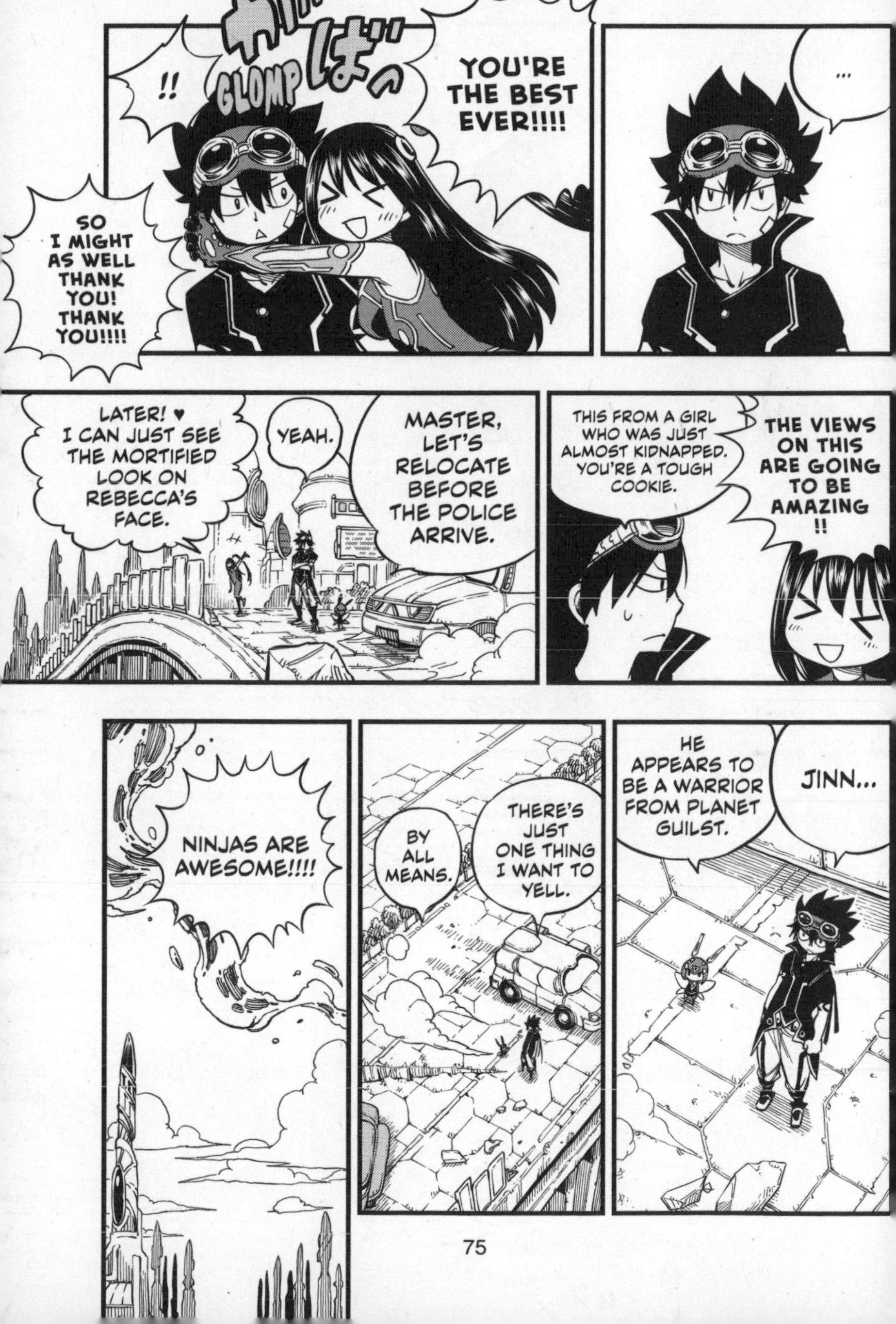
...
YOU'RE THE BEST EVER!!!!
GLOMP
!!
SO I MIGHT AS WELL THANK YOU! THANK YOU!!!!
THE VIEWS ON THIS ARE GOING TO BE AMAZING !!
THIS FROM A GIRL WHO WAS JUST ALMOST KIDNAPPED. YOU'RE A TOUGH COOKIE.
MASTER, LET'S RELOCATE BEFORE THE POLICE ARRIVE.
YEAH.
LATER! ♥ I CAN JUST SEE THE MORTIFIED LOOK ON REBECCA'S FACE.
JINN...
HE APPEARS TO BE A WARRIOR FROM PLANET GUILST.
THERE'S JUST ONE THING I WANT TO YELL.
BY ALL MEANS.
NINJAS ARE AWESOME!!!!

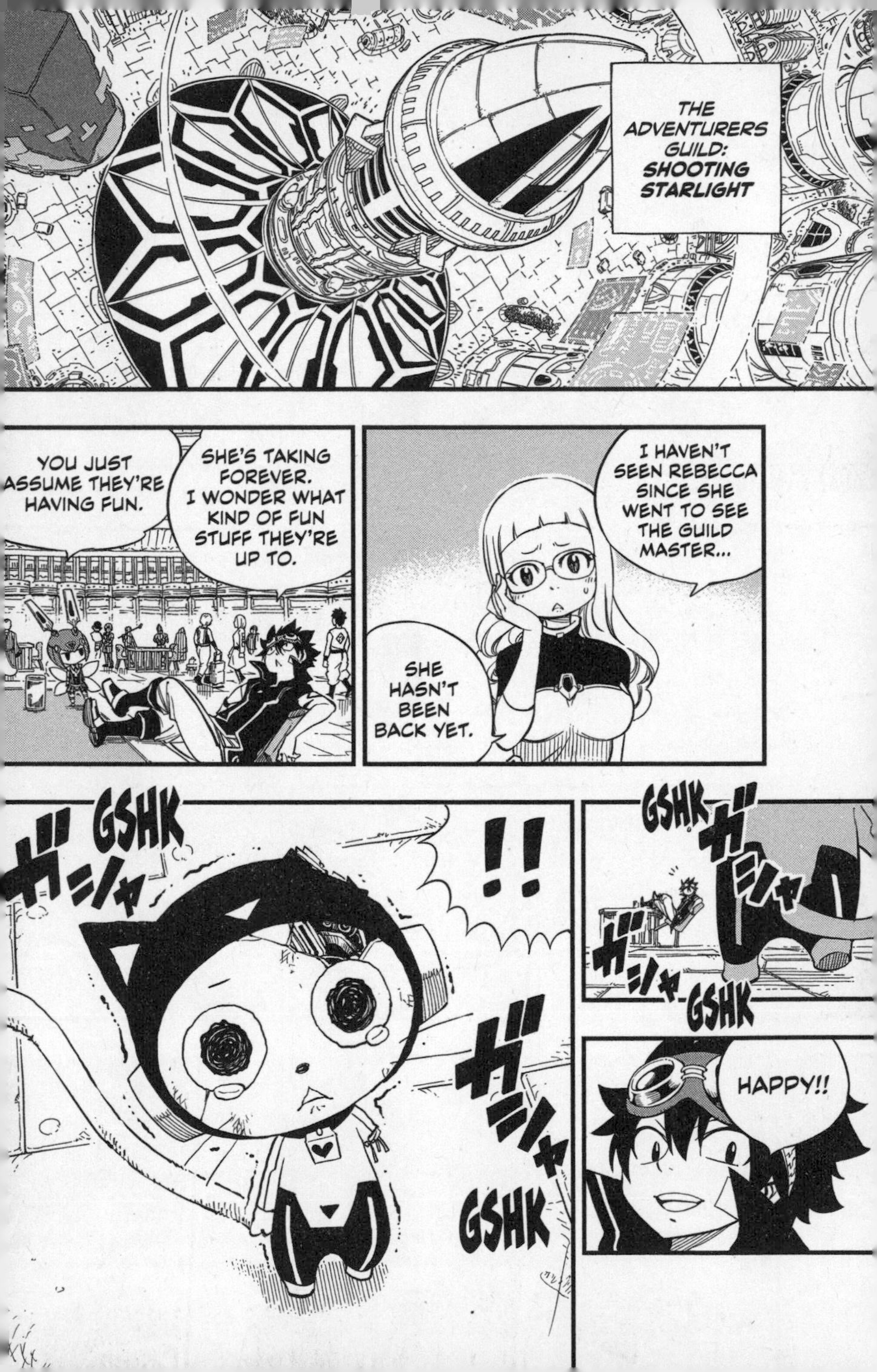

THE ADVENTURERS GUILD: SHOOTING STARLIGHT
I HAVEN'T SEEN REBECCA SINCE SHE WENT TO SEE THE GUILD MASTER...
SHE HASN'T BEEN BACK YET.
SHE'S TAKING FOREVER. I WONDER WHAT KIND OF FUN STUFF THEY'RE UP TO.
YOU JUST ASSUME THEY'RE HAVING FUN.
GSHK
GSHK
HAPPY!!
GSHK
!!
GSHK

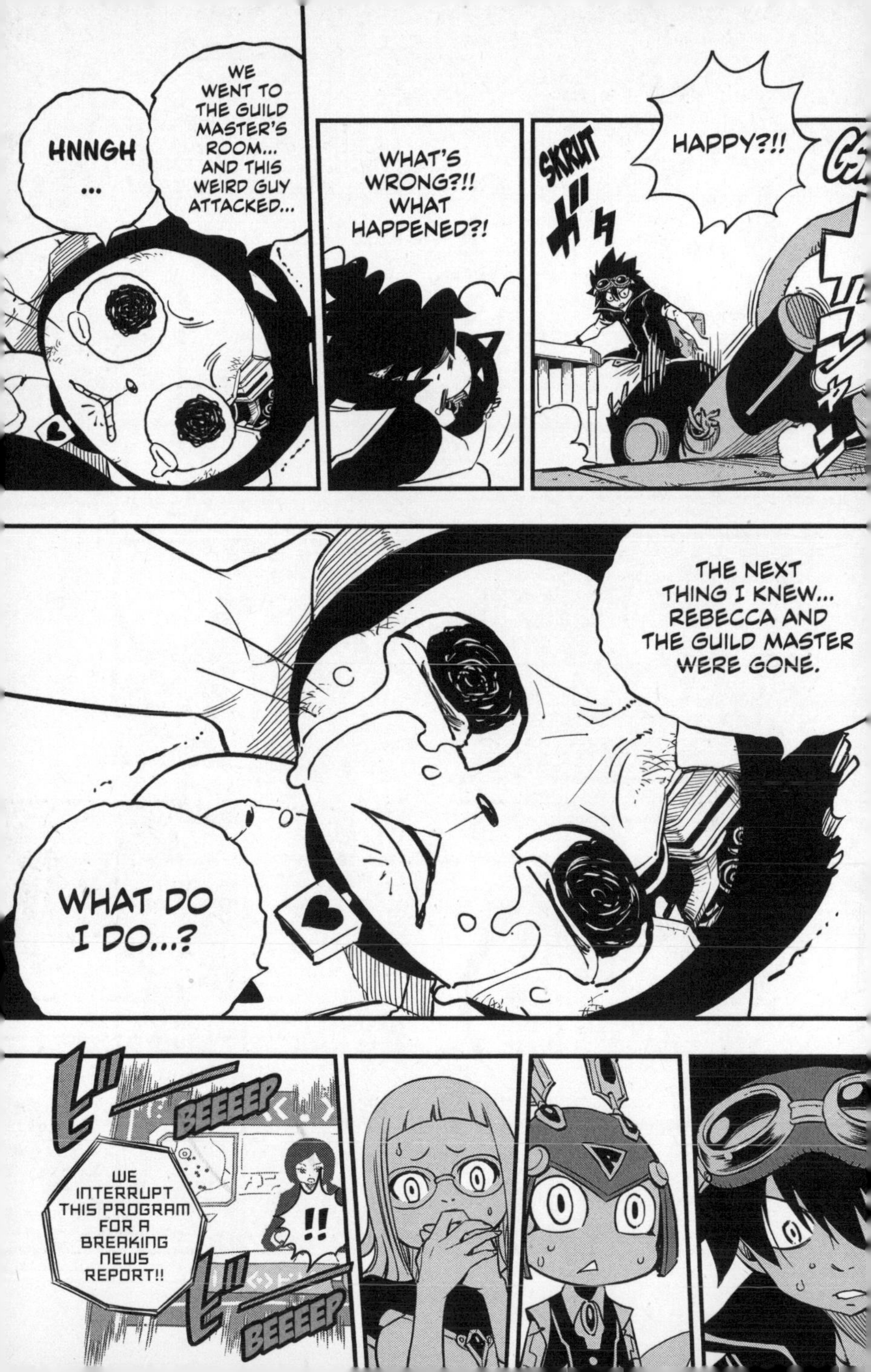

HAPPY?!!
SKRUT
WHAT'S WRONG?!! WHAT HAPPENED?!
WE WENT TO THE GUILD MASTER'S ROOM... AND THIS WEIRD GUY ATTACKED...
HNNGH ...
THE NEXT THING I KNEW... REBECCA AND THE GUILD MASTER WERE GONE.
WHAT DO I DO...?
BEEEEP
WE INTERRUPT THIS PROGRAM FOR A BREAKING NEWS REPORT!!
!!
BEEEEP

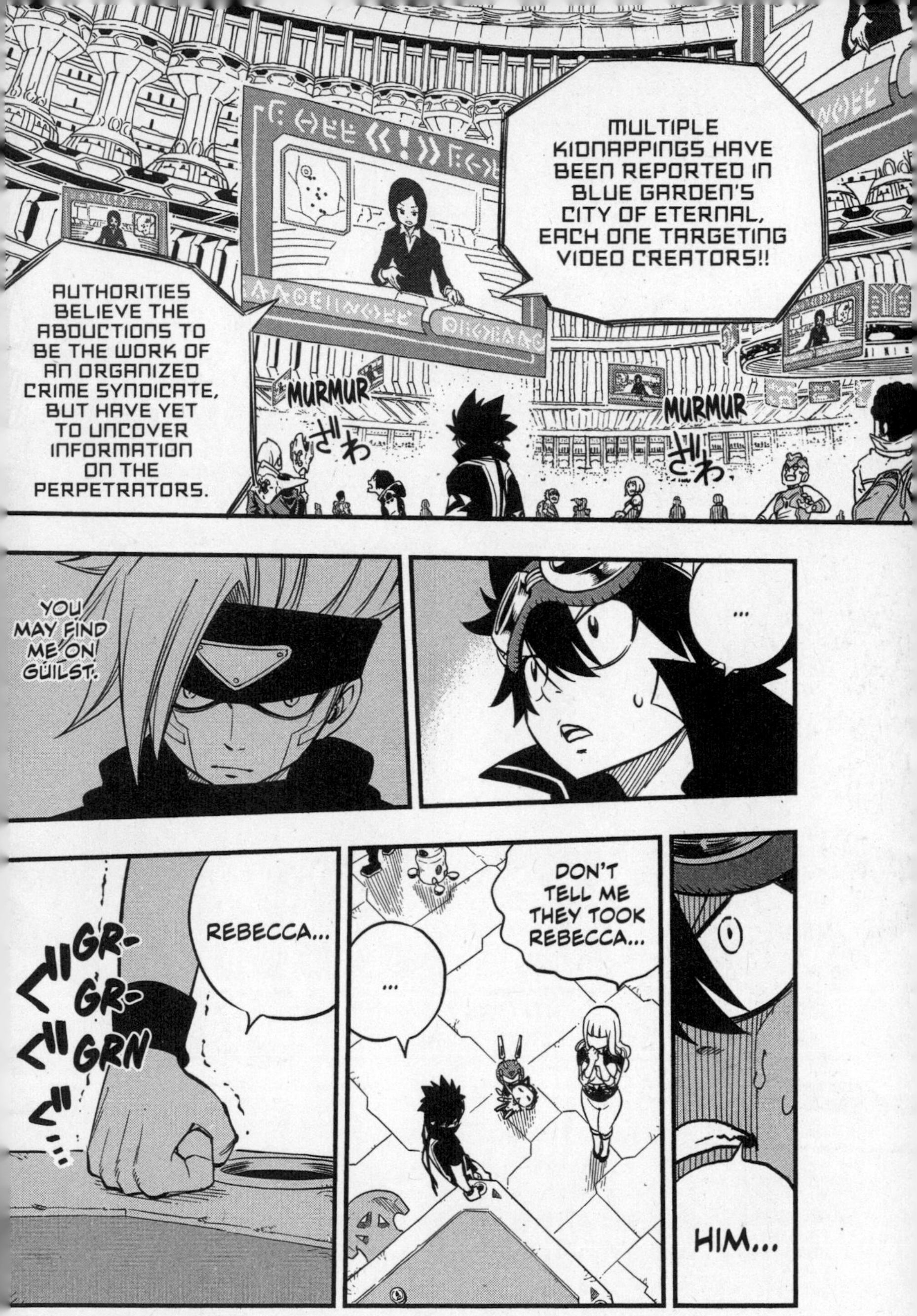
MULTIPLE KIDNAPPINGS HAVE BEEN REPORTED IN BLUE GARDEN'S CITY OF ETERNAL, EACH ONE TARGETING VIDEO CREATORS!!
AUTHORITIES BELIEVE THE ABDUCTIONS TO BE THE WORK OF AN ORGANIZED CRIME SYNDICATE, BUT HAVE YET TO UNCOVER INFORMATION ON THE PERPETRATORS.
MURMUR
ざわ
MURMUR
ざわ
...
YOU MAY FIND ME ON GUILST.
HIM...
DON'T TELL ME THEY TOOK REBECCA...
...
REBECCA...
GR-
GR-
GRN

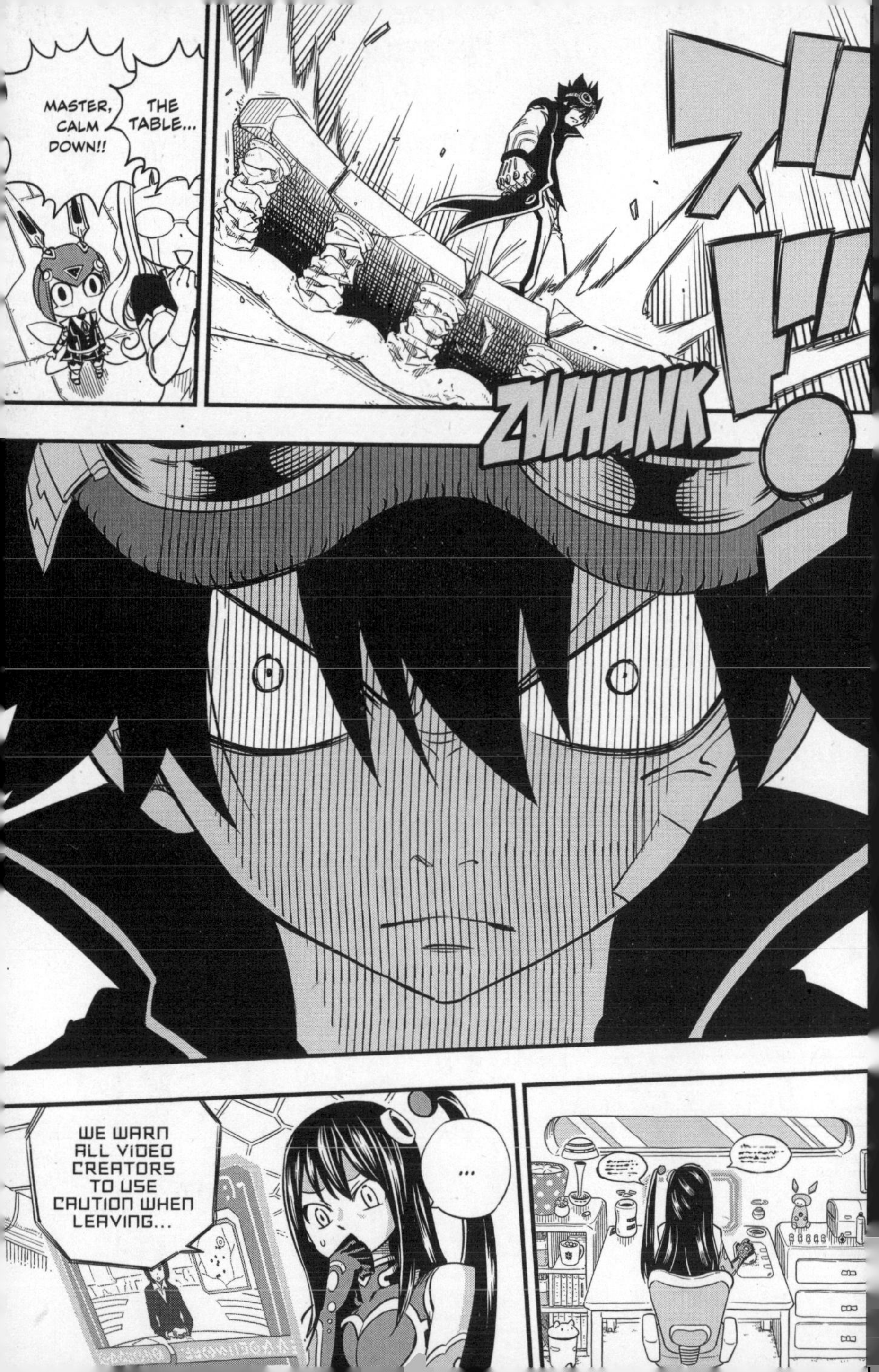
ズド!!
ZWHUNK
THE TABLE...
MASTER, CALM DOWN!!
WE WARN ALL VIDEO CREATORS TO USE CAUTION WHEN LEAVING...
...

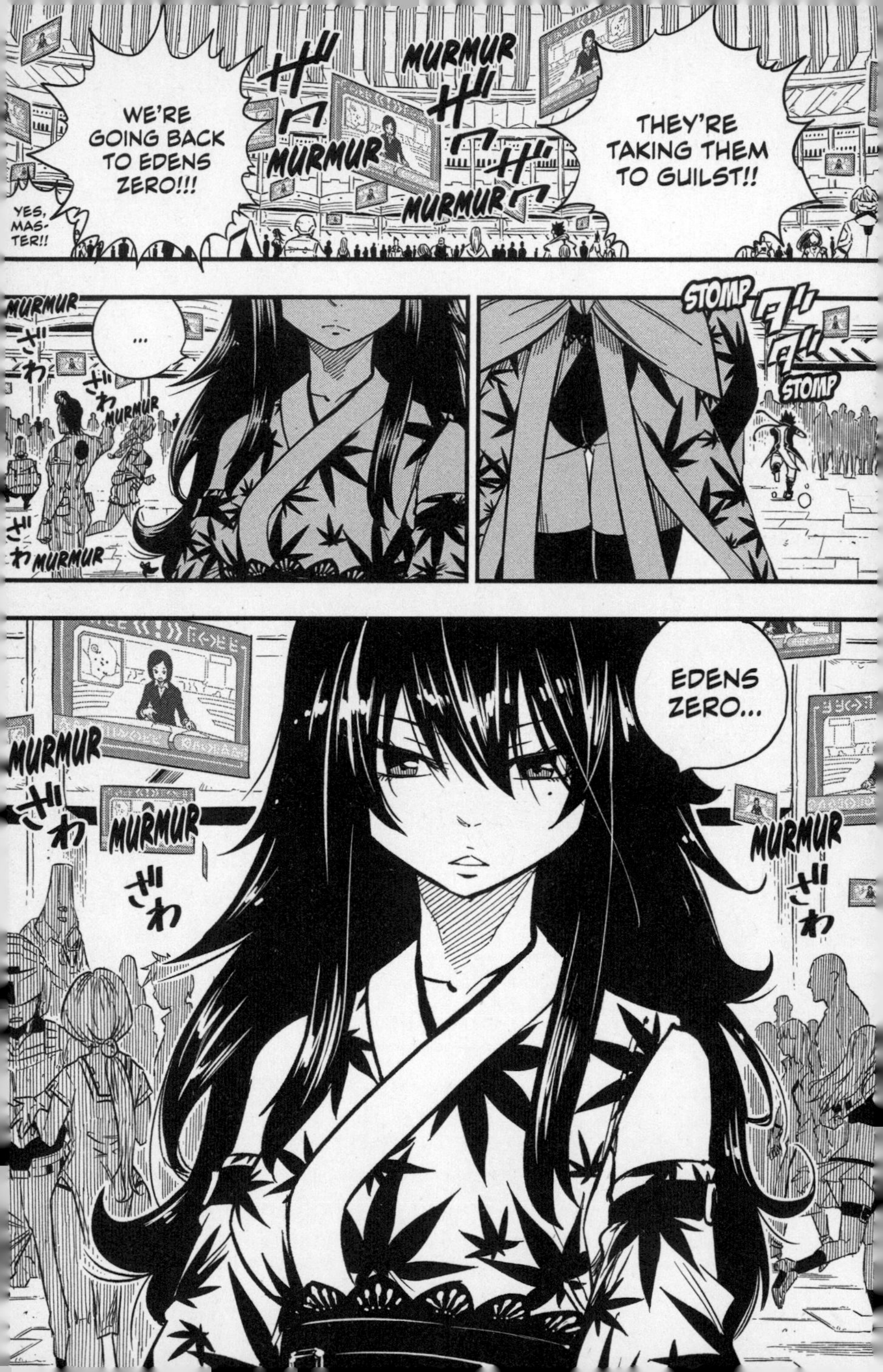
THEY'RE TAKING THEM TO GUILST!!
MURMUR
ザワ
MURMUR
ザワ
MURMUR
ザワ
WE'RE GOING BACK TO EDENS ZERO!!!
YES, MAS-TER!!
STOMP
タッ
タッ
STOMP
MURMUR
ざわ
...
ざわ
MURMUR
ざわ
MURMUR
EDENS ZERO...
MURMUR
ざわ
MURMUR
ざわ
MURMUR
ざわ
ざわ

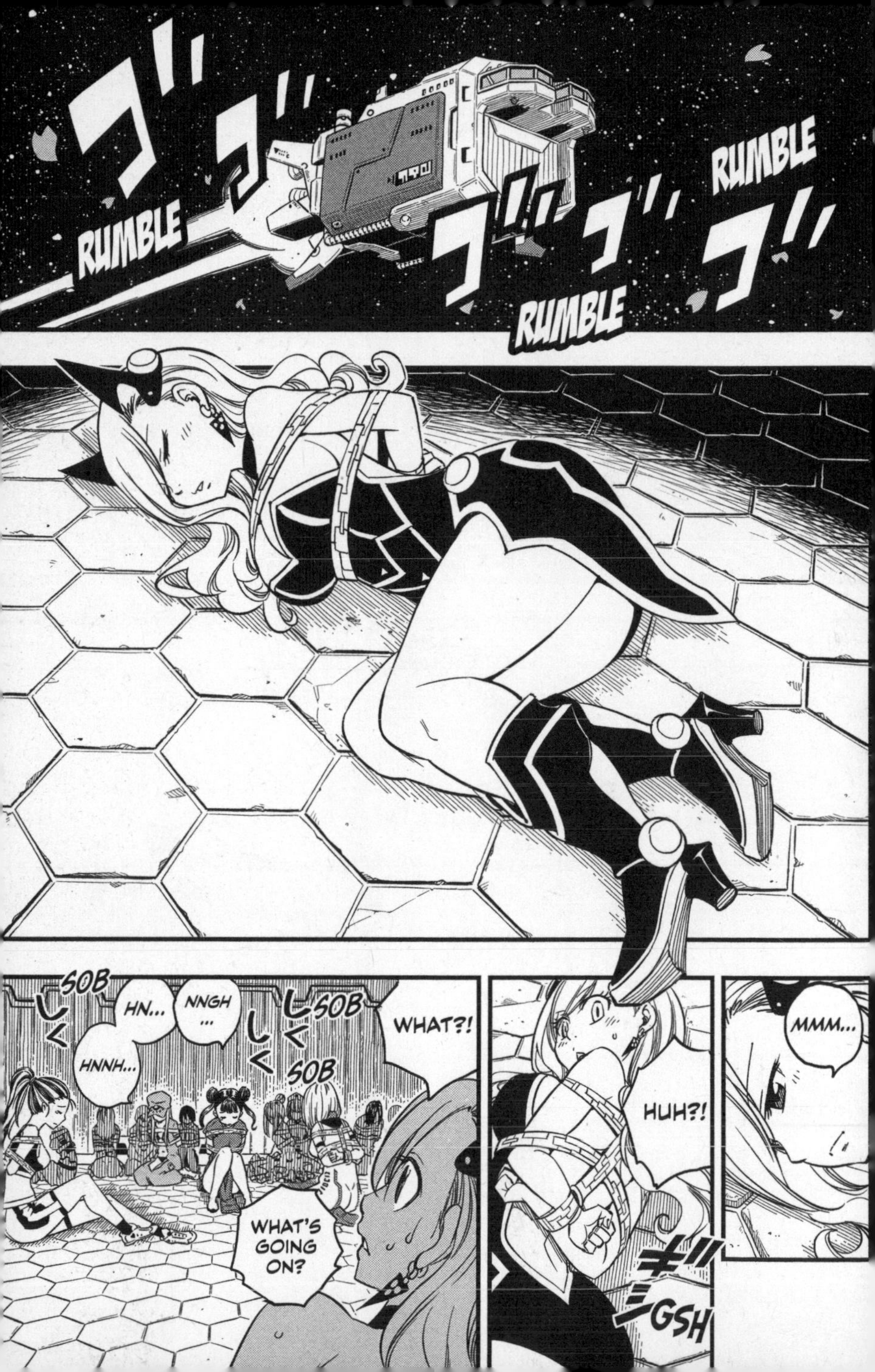
RUMBLE
RUMBLE
RUMBLE
MMM...
HUH?!
GSH
WHAT?!
SOB
NNGH ...
HN...
SOB
HNNH...
SOB
WHAT'S GOING ON?

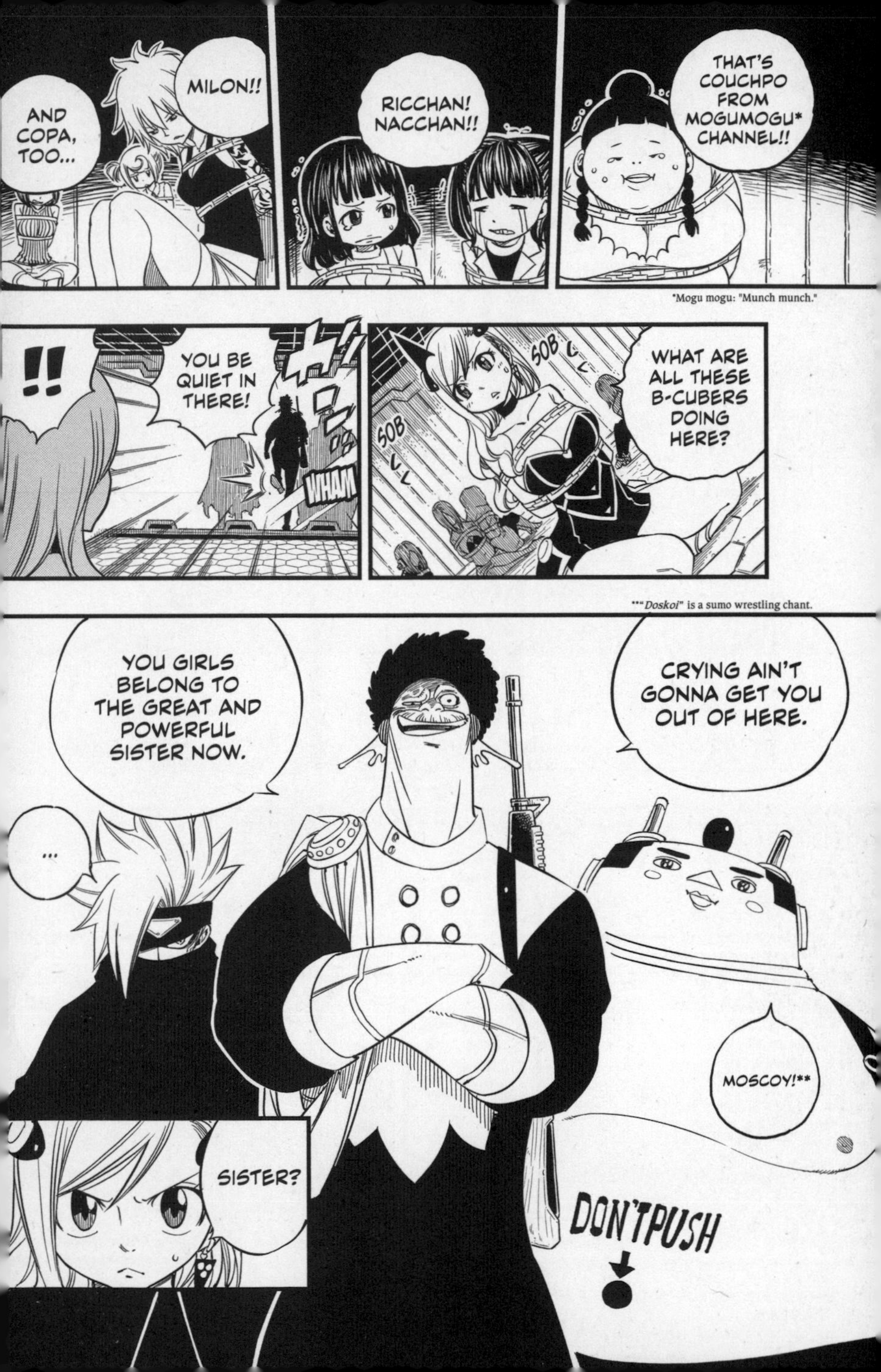
THAT'S COUCHPO FROM MOGUMOGU* CHANNEL!!
RICCHAN! NACCHAN!!
MILON!!
AND COPA, TOO...
SOB
WHAT ARE ALL THESE B-CUBERS DOING HERE?
SOB
YOU BE QUIET IN THERE!
WHAM
!!
CRYING AIN'T GONNA GET YOU OUT OF HERE.
YOU GIRLS BELONG TO THE GREAT AND POWERFUL SISTER NOW.
MOSCOY!**
...
SISTER?
DON'T PUSH

*Mogu mogu: "Munch munch."

**"*Doskoi*" is a sumo wrestling chant.

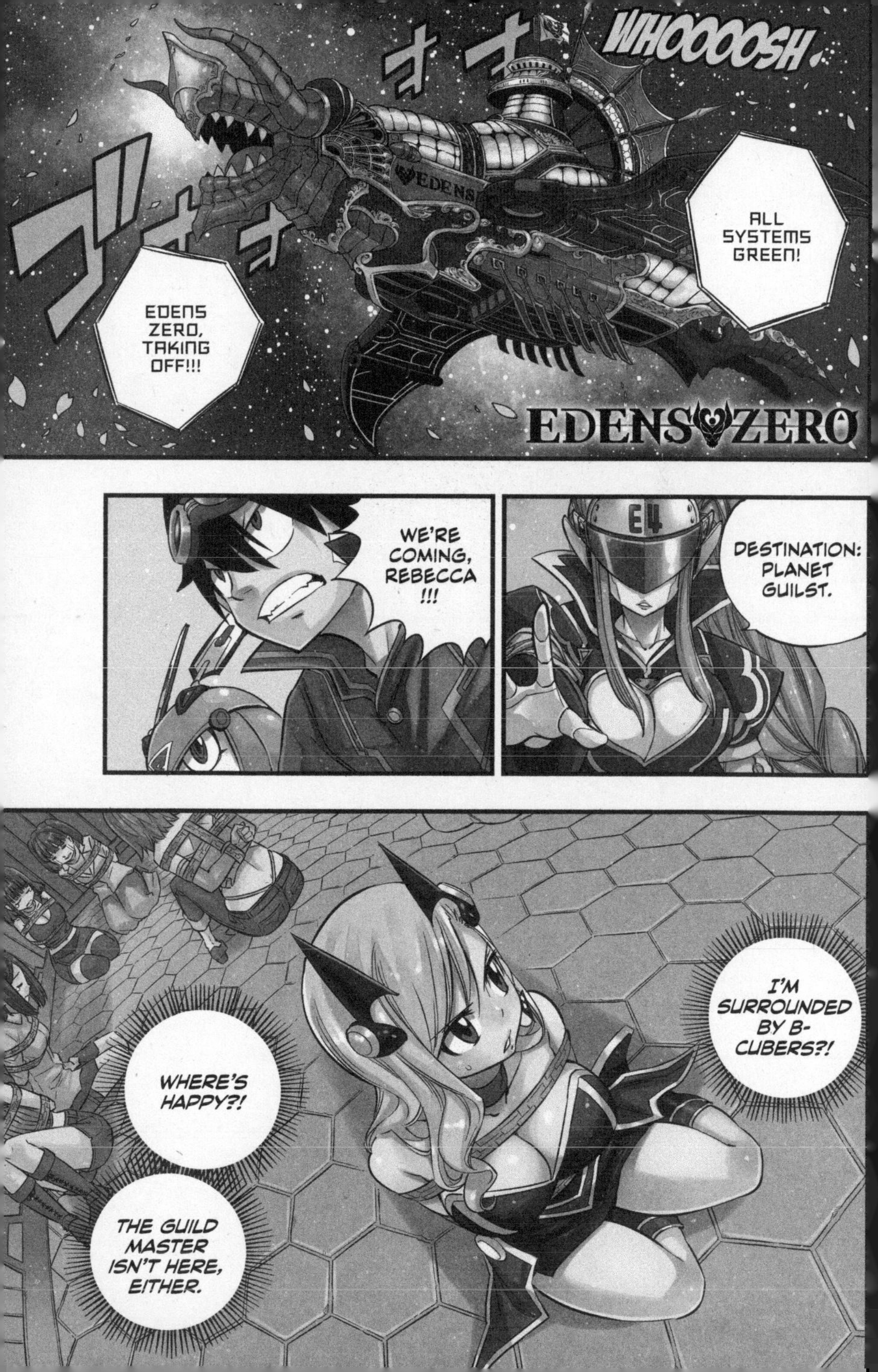
WHOOOOSH
ALL SYSTEMS GREEN!
EDENS ZERO, TAKING OFF!!!
EDENS ZERO
DESTINATION: PLANET GUILST.
WE'RE COMING, REBECCA!!!
I'M SURROUNDED BY B-CUBERS?!
WHERE'S HAPPY?!
THE GUILD MASTER ISN'T HERE, EITHER.

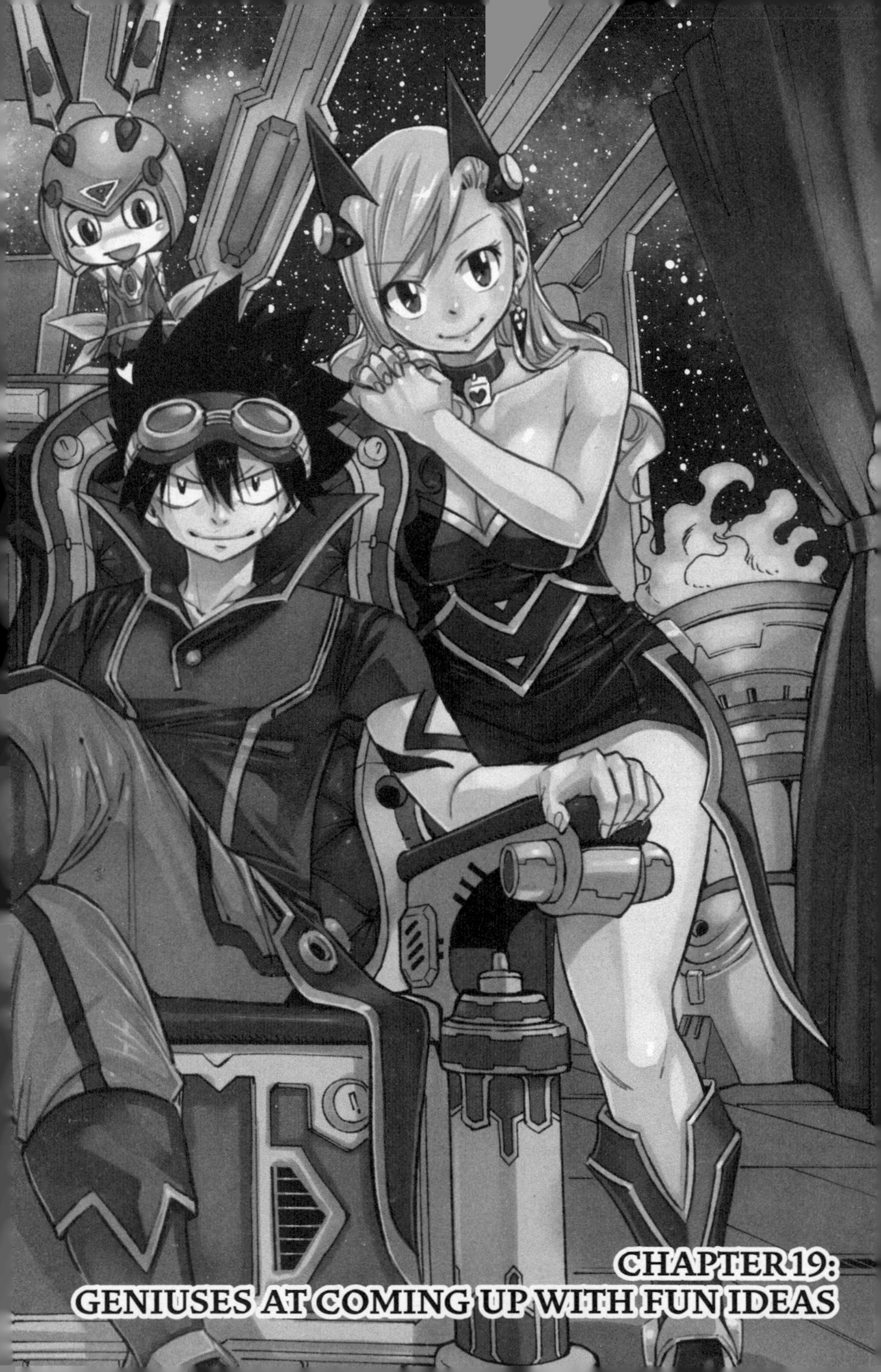
CHAPTER 19:
GENIUSES AT COMING UP WITH FUN IDEAS

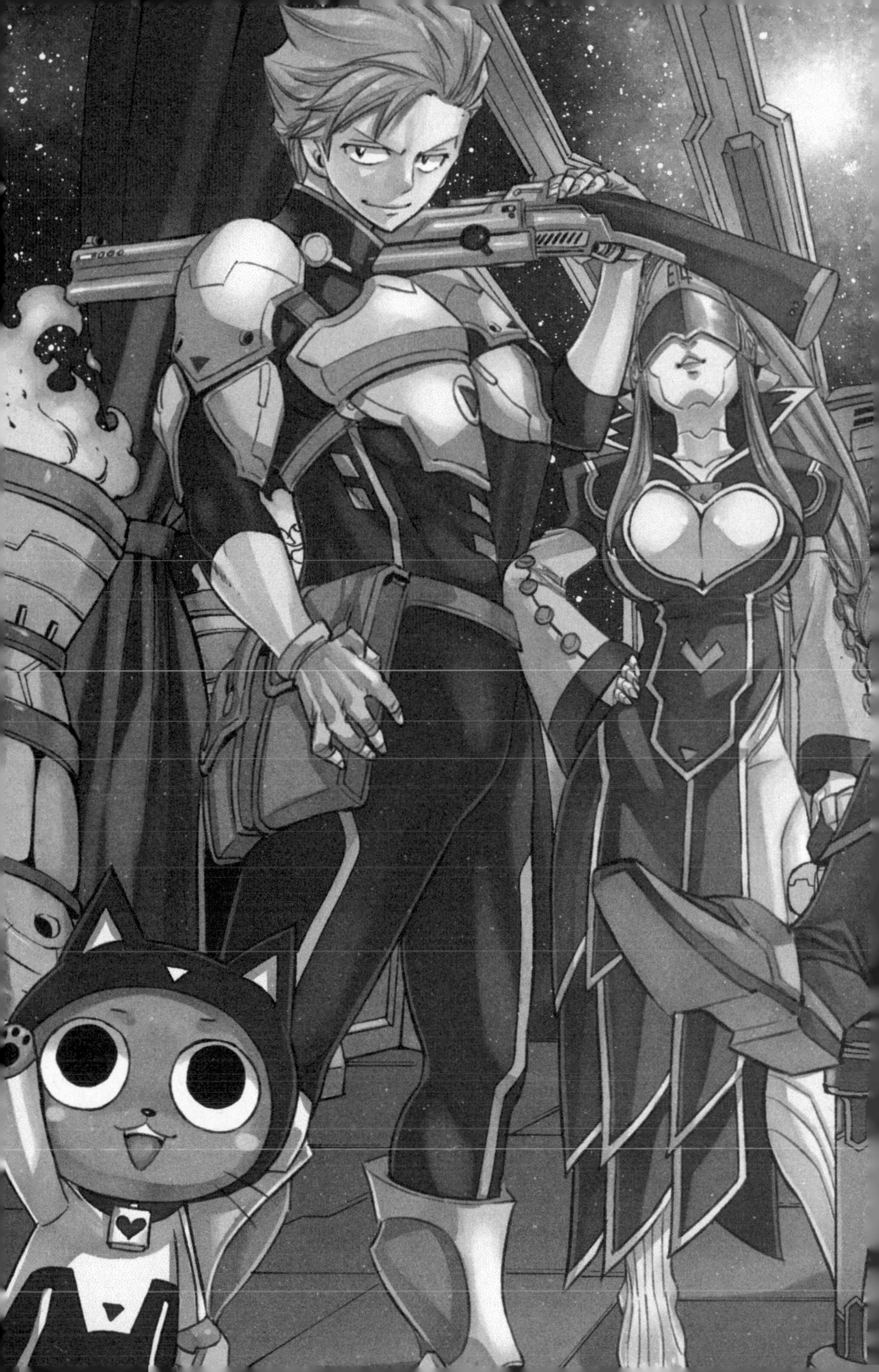

EZ DRAWING

IT'S TIME TO PRESENT OUR FIRST BATCH OF FAN DRAWINGS!

(DAISUKE NAKAYAMA, KANAGAWA)

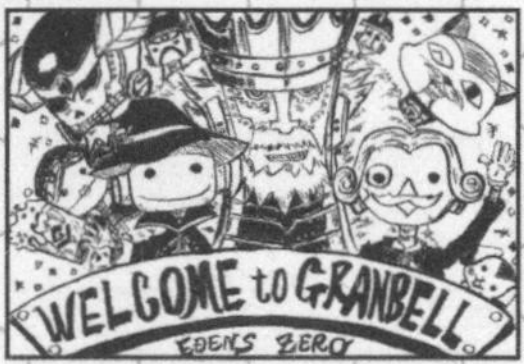
WELCOME to GRANBELL
EDEN'S ZERO

◀ THEY WERE SHIKI'S FIRST FRIENDS, AND THEY WERE ALL FABULOUS ACTORS.

(SHUNPEI HIGASHIYAMA, GUNMA)

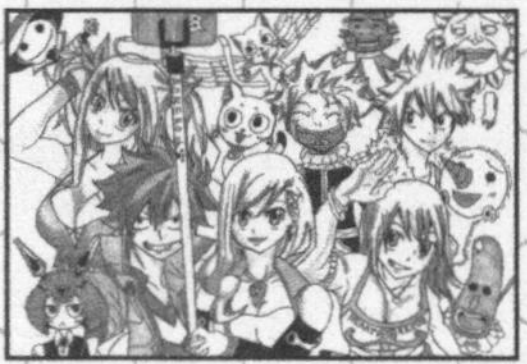

◀ IF THEY ALL TEAMED UP, A VIDEO WITH MORE THAN A MILLION VIEWS MIGHT JUST BE POSSIBLE!

(YŌSEI, OSAKA)

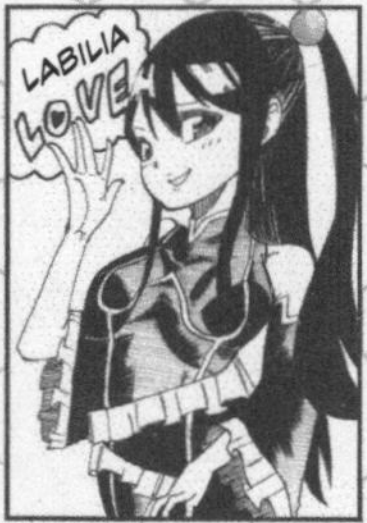
LABILIA
LOVE

▲ I BET LABILIA FANS ARE SUPER LOYAL!

(REN, HOKKAIDO)

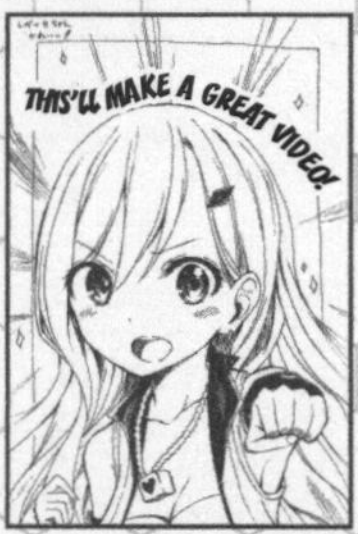
THIS'LL MAKE A GREAT VIDEO!

▲ THE FIRST STEP IN MAKING A GOOD VIDEO IS KNOWING HOW TO LOOK AT THE CAMERA!

(MOMOKA KODAMA, EHIME)

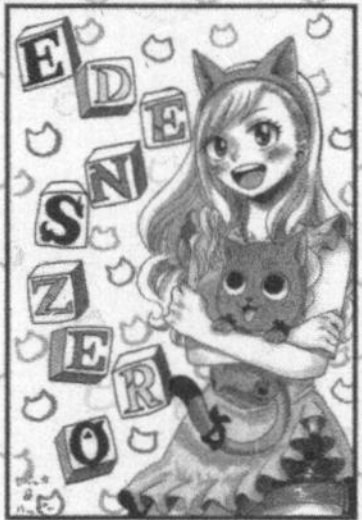
EDENS ZERO

▲ EVEN THE PATTERN BEHIND HER HAS CAT EARS IS CUTE. SUCH ATTENTION TO DETAIL!

(SS, AICHI)

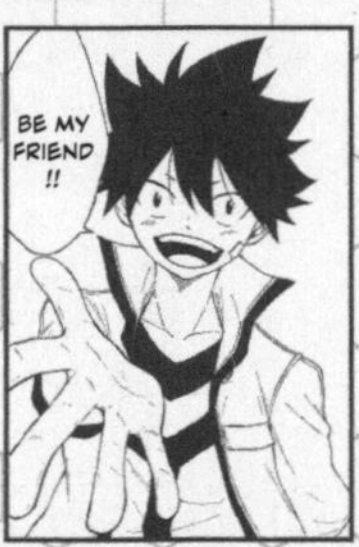
BE MY FRIEND !!

▲ IF HE'S THIS DIRECT, HOW CAN ANYONE SAY NO?

(RYŪTARŌ YAMAMOTO, NAGASAKI)

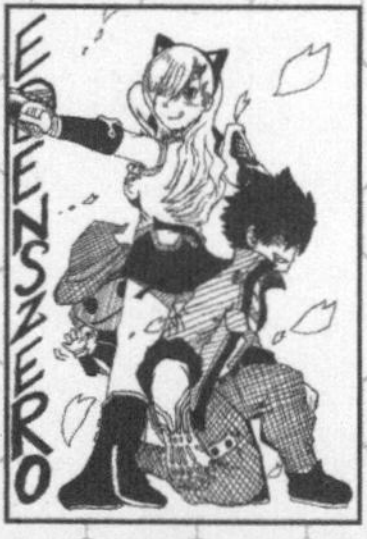
EDENSZERO

▲ STRIKING A POSE IN A STORM OF SAKURA PETALS!

(BANWOLF, KANAGAWA)

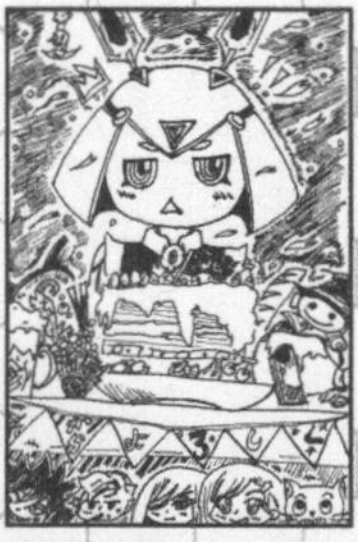

▲ WHO IS PINO CARRYING SNACKS TO?

(NAOYA AOKI, CHIBA)

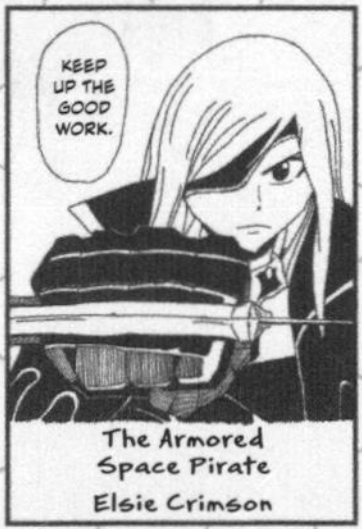
KEEP UP THE GOOD WORK.
The Armored Space Pirate Elsie Crimson

▲ A SPACE PIRATE'S GOTTA HAVE AN EYEPATCH!

(ENTARŌ, NIIGATA)

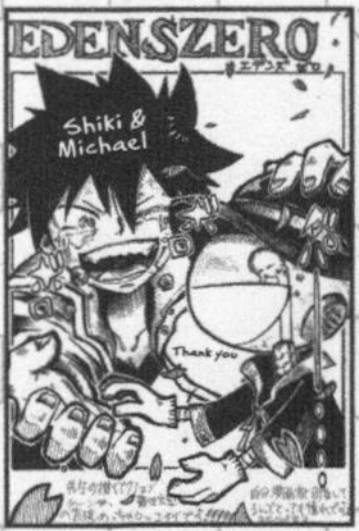
EDENSZERO
Shiki & Michael
Thank you

▲ GOOD LUCK ON YOUR DREAM OF BEING A MANGA ARTIST!

EDITOR'S NOTE: DRAWING SUBMISSIONS LIMITED TO JAPAN.

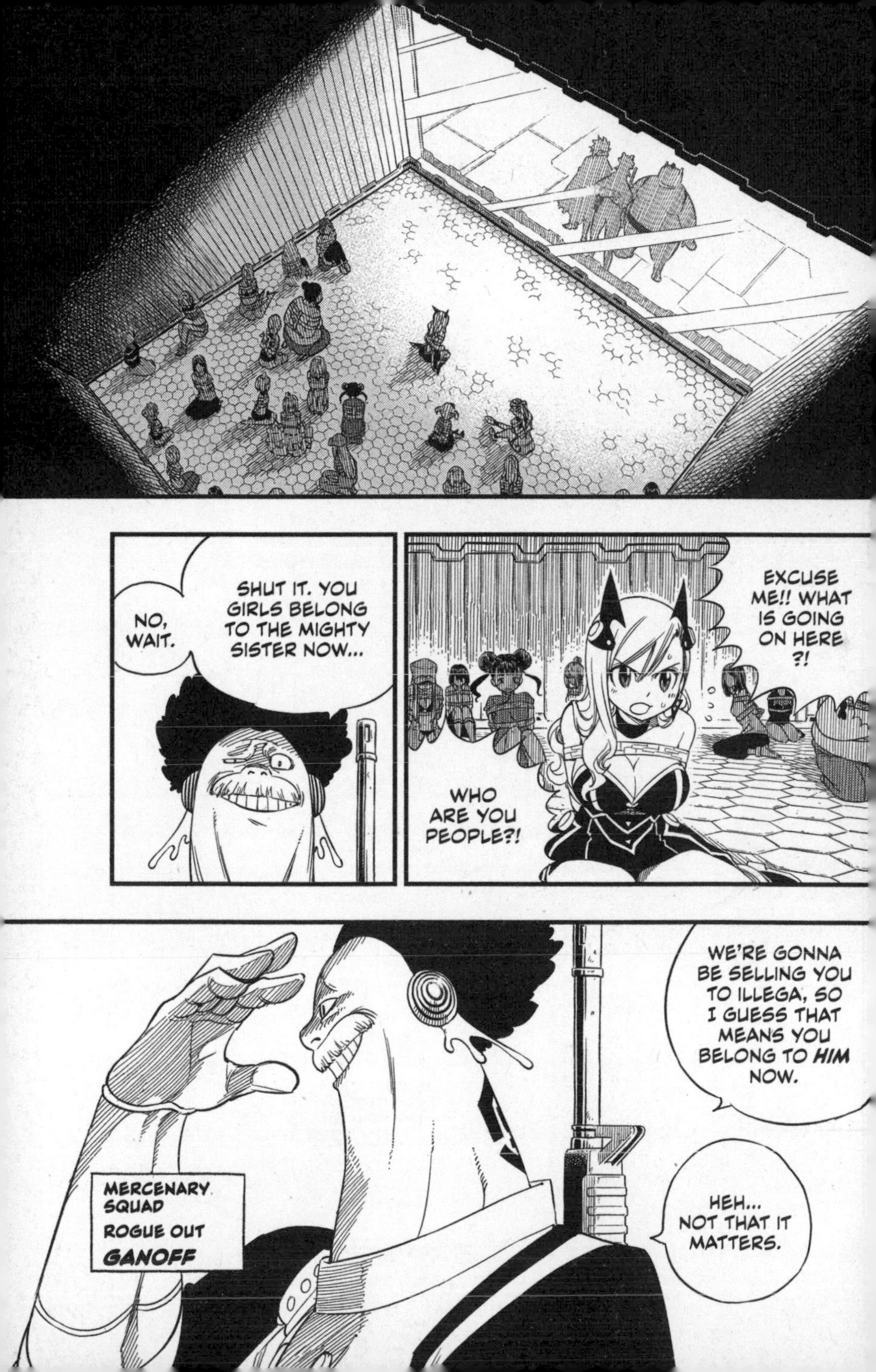
EXCUSE ME!! WHAT IS GOING ON HERE?!
WHO ARE YOU PEOPLE?!
SHUT IT. YOU GIRLS BELONG TO THE MIGHTY SISTER NOW...
NO, WAIT.
WE'RE GONNA BE SELLING YOU TO ILLEGA, SO I GUESS THAT MEANS YOU BELONG TO *HIM* NOW.
HEH... NOT THAT IT MATTERS.
MERCENARY SQUAD
ROGUE OUT
GANOFF

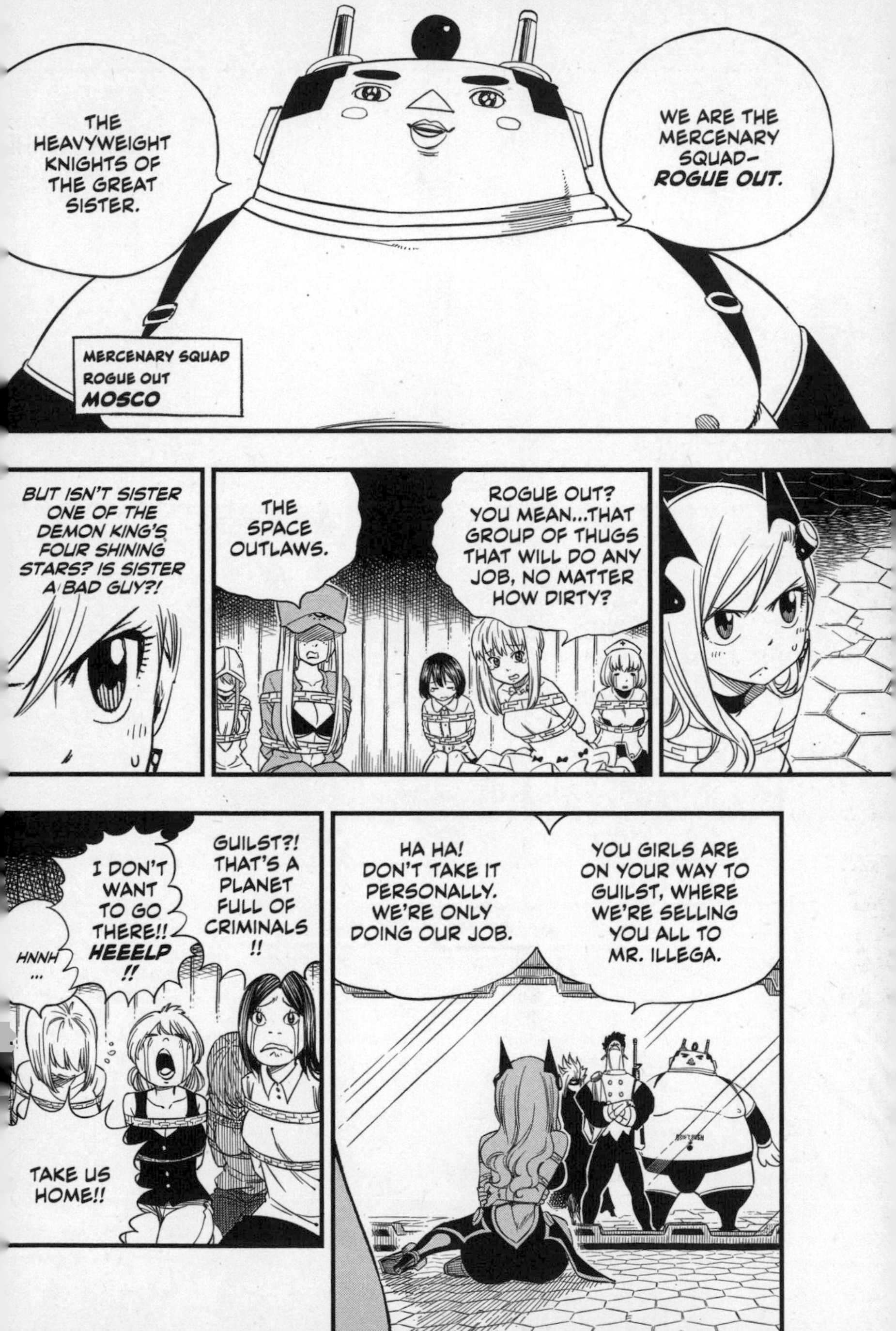
WE ARE THE MERCENARY SQUAD— ROGUE OUT.
THE HEAVYWEIGHT KNIGHTS OF THE GREAT SISTER.
MERCENARY SQUAD ROGUE OUT MOSCO
ROGUE OUT? YOU MEAN...THAT GROUP OF THUGS THAT WILL DO ANY JOB, NO MATTER HOW DIRTY?
THE SPACE OUTLAWS.
BUT ISN'T SISTER ONE OF THE DEMON KING'S FOUR SHINING STARS? IS SISTER A BAD GUY?!
YOU GIRLS ARE ON YOUR WAY TO GUILST, WHERE WE'RE SELLING YOU ALL TO MR. ILLEGA.
HA HA! DON'T TAKE IT PERSONALLY. WE'RE ONLY DOING OUR JOB.
GUILST?! THAT'S A PLANET FULL OF CRIMINALS !!
I DON'T WANT TO GO THERE!! HEEELP !!
HNNH ...
TAKE US HOME!!

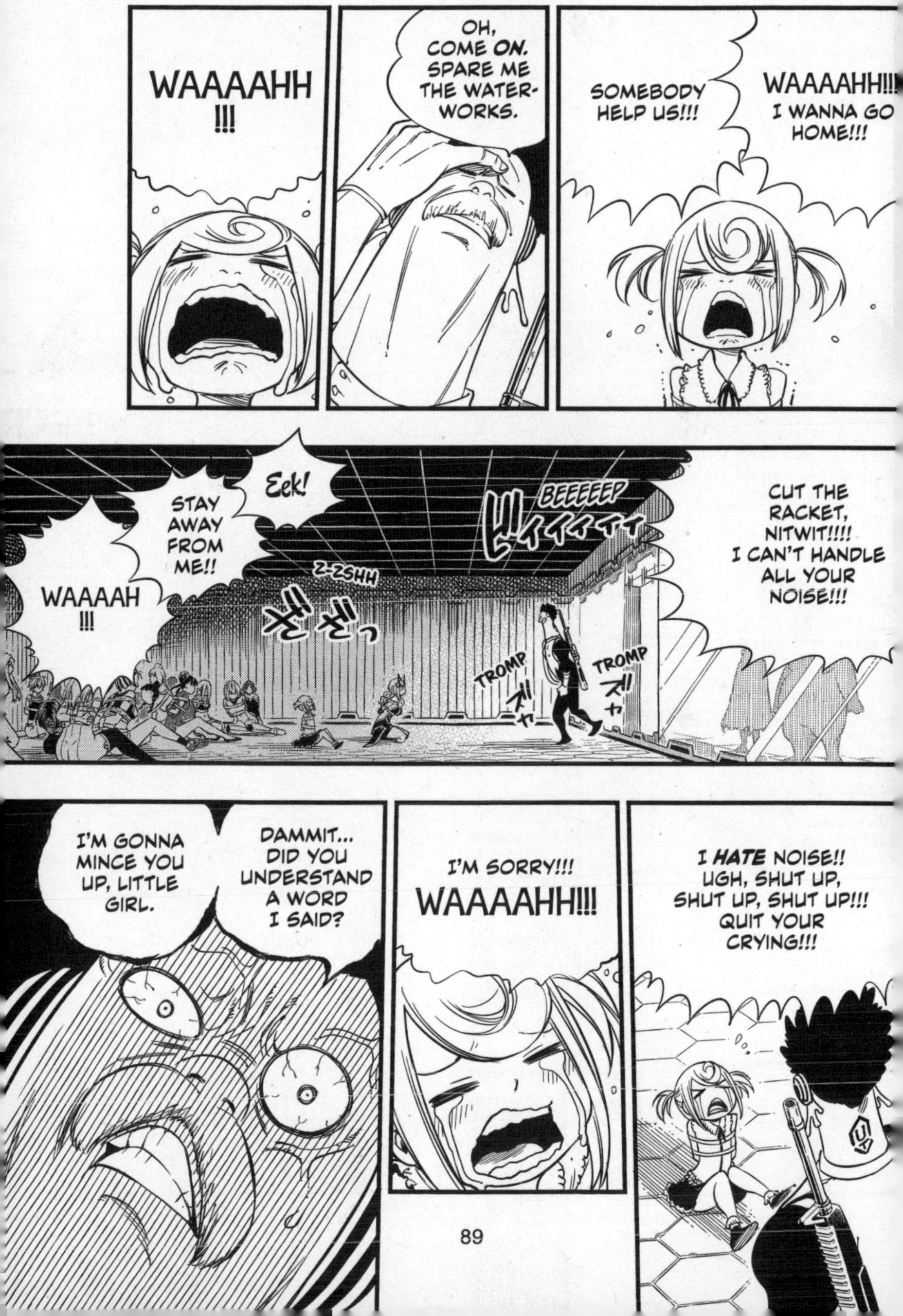
WAAAAHH!!! I WANNA GO HOME!!!
SOMEBODY HELP US!!!
OH, COME ON. SPARE ME THE WATER-WORKS.
WAAAAHH !!!
CUT THE RACKET, NITWIT!!!! I CAN'T HANDLE ALL YOUR NOISE!!!
BEEEEEP
TROMP
TROMP
Z-ZSHH
Eek!
STAY AWAY FROM ME!!
WAAAAH !!!
I HATE NOISE!! UGH, SHUT UP, SHUT UP, SHUT UP!!! QUIT YOUR CRYING!!!
I'M SORRY!!!
WAAAAHH!!!
DAMMIT... DID YOU UNDERSTAND A WORD I SAID?
I'M GONNA MINCE YOU UP, LITTLE GIRL.

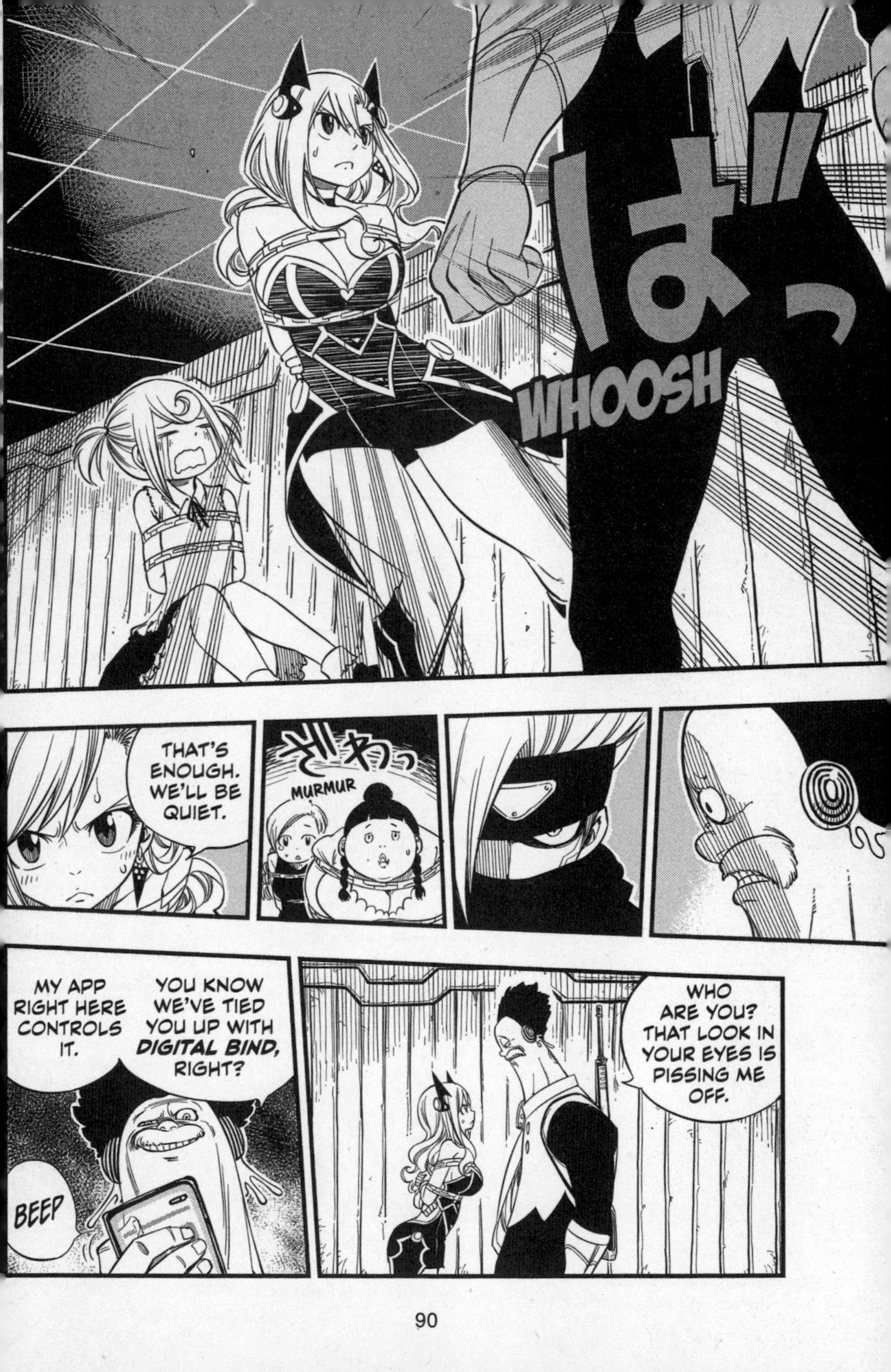
ばっ
WHOOSH
ざわっ
MURMUR
THAT'S ENOUGH. WE'LL BE QUIET.
WHO ARE YOU? THAT LOOK IN YOUR EYES IS PISSING ME OFF.
YOU KNOW WE'VE TIED YOU UP WITH *DIGITAL BIND*, RIGHT?
MY APP RIGHT HERE CONTROLS IT.
BEEP

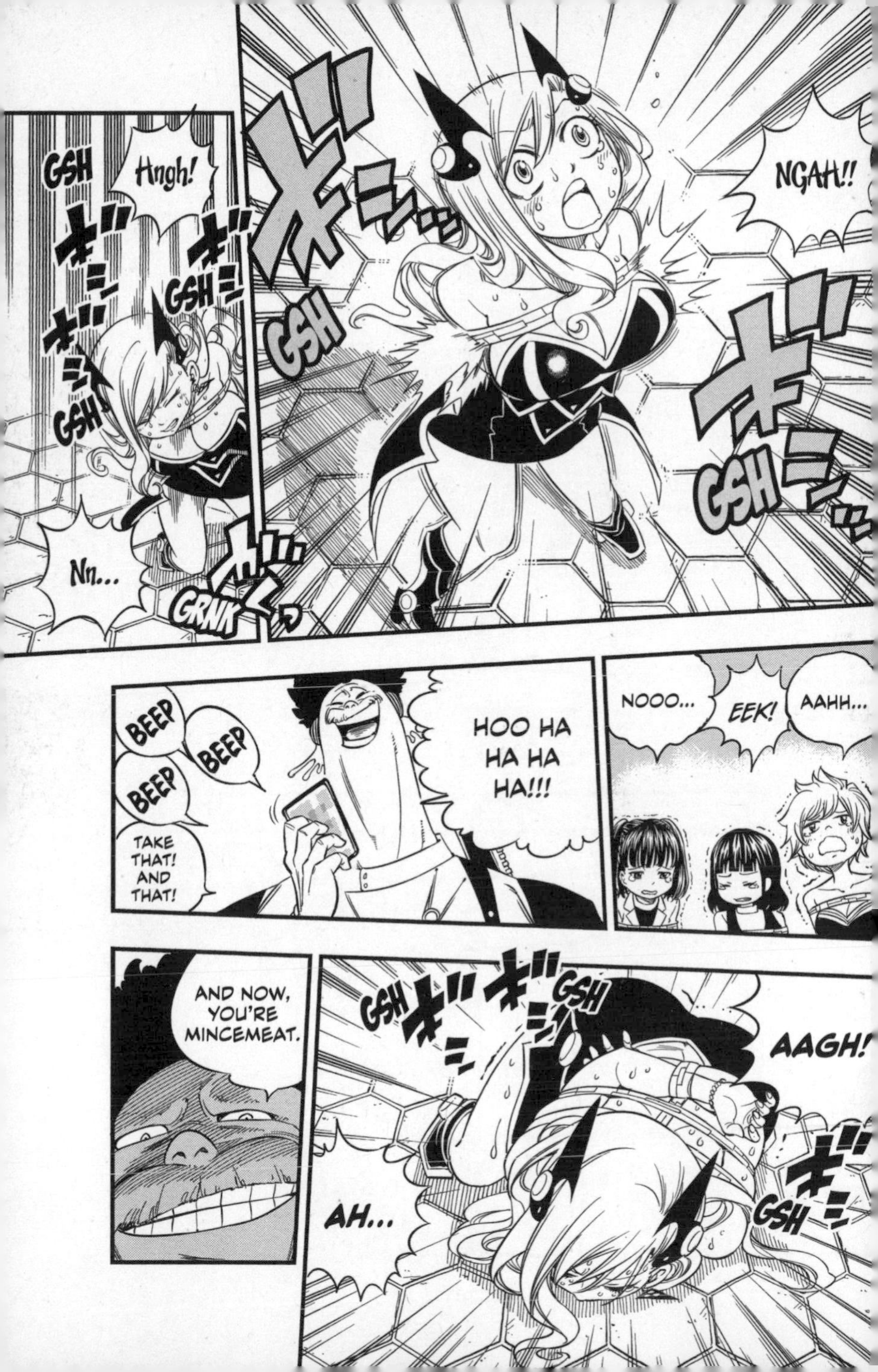
NGAH!!
GSH
GSH
GSH
Hngh!
GSH
GSH
GSH
Nn...
GRNK
AAHH...
EEK!
NOOO...
HOO HA HA HA HA!!!
BEEP
BEEP
BEEP
TAKE THAT! AND THAT!
AAGH!
GSH
GSH
GSH
AH...
AND NOW, YOU'RE MINCEMEAT.

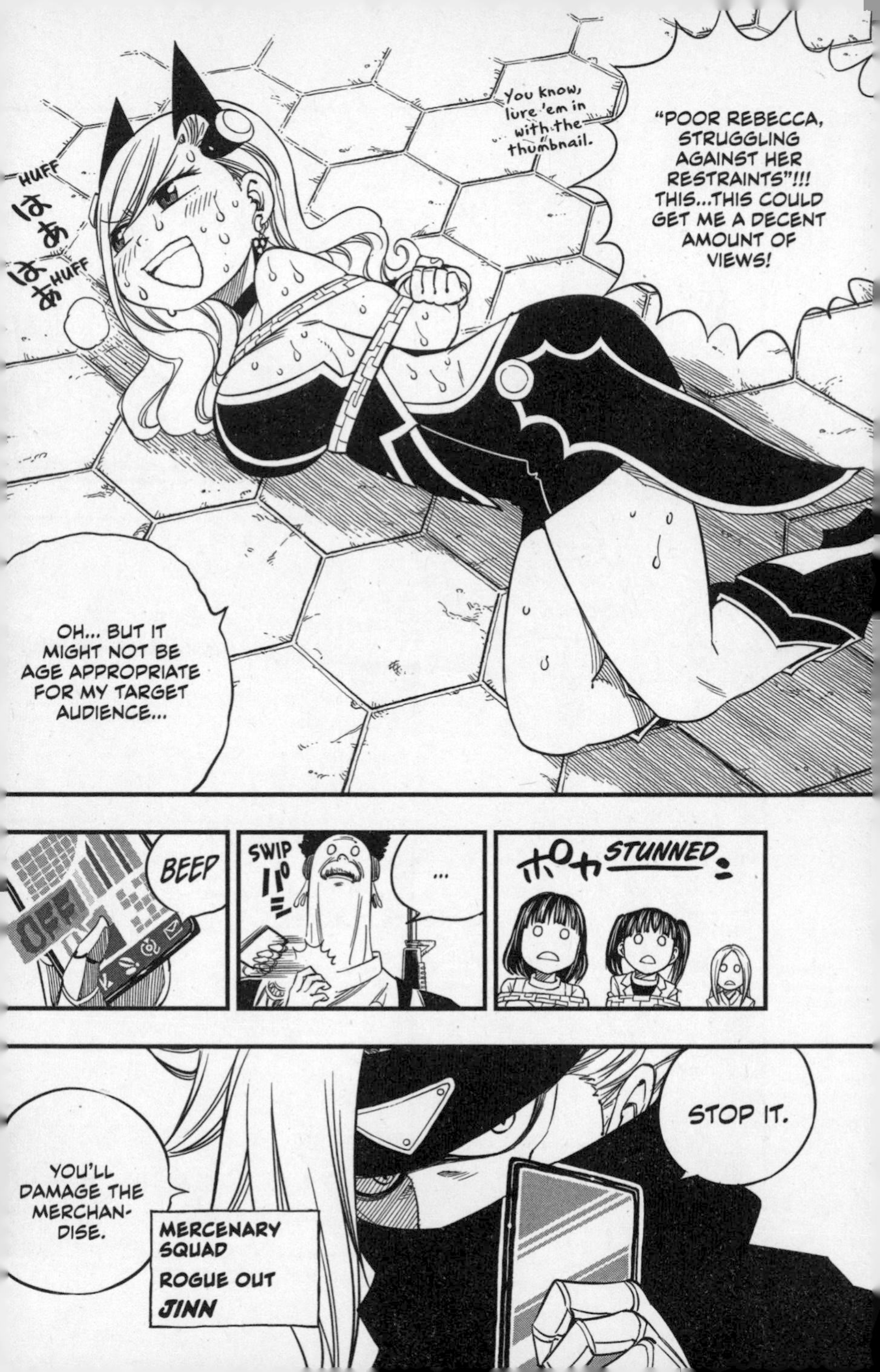
"POOR REBECCA, STRUGGLING AGAINST HER RESTRAINTS"!!! THIS...THIS COULD GET ME A DECENT AMOUNT OF VIEWS!
You know, lure 'em in with the thumbnail.
HUFF はあ
はあ HUFF
OH... BUT IT MIGHT NOT BE AGE APPROPRIATE FOR MY TARGET AUDIENCE...
ポカ STUNNED
SWIP パ
...
BEEP
OFF
STOP IT.
YOU'LL DAMAGE THE MERCHAN-DISE.
MERCENARY SQUAD
ROGUE OUT
JINN

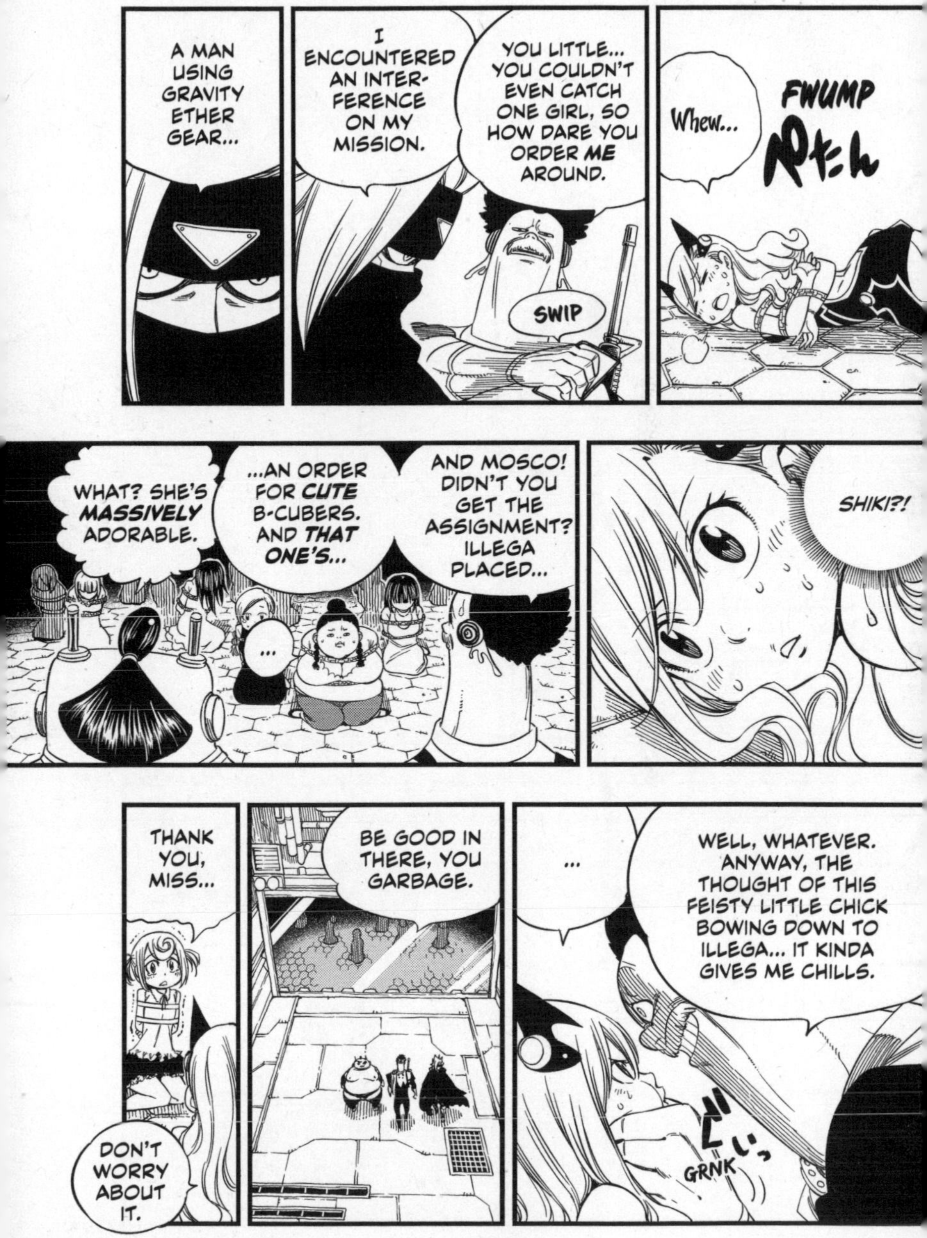

Whew...
FWUMP
ぺたん
YOU LITTLE... YOU COULDN'T EVEN CATCH ONE GIRL, SO HOW DARE YOU ORDER *ME* AROUND.
I ENCOUNTERED AN INTERFERENCE ON MY MISSION.
SWIP
A MAN USING GRAVITY ETHER GEAR...
SHIKI?!
AND MOSCO! DIDN'T YOU GET THE ASSIGNMENT? ILLEGA PLACED...
...AN ORDER FOR *CUTE* B-CUBERS. AND *THAT ONE'S...*
WHAT? SHE'S *MASSIVELY* ADORABLE.
...
WELL, WHATEVER. ANYWAY, THE THOUGHT OF THIS FEISTY LITTLE CHICK BOWING DOWN TO ILLEGA... IT KINDA GIVES ME CHILLS.
...
GRNK
BE GOOD IN THERE, YOU GARBAGE.
THANK YOU, MISS...
DON'T WORRY ABOUT IT.

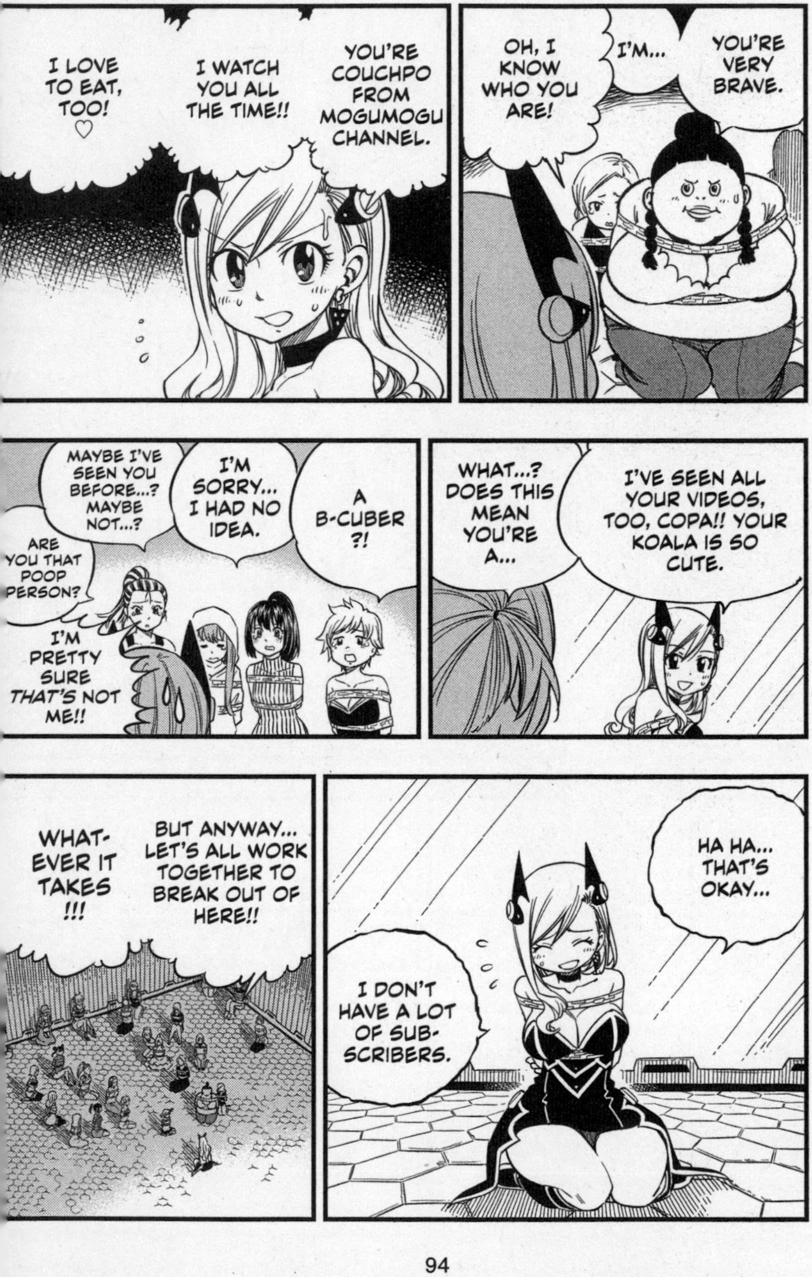
YOU'RE VERY BRAVE.
I'M...
OH, I KNOW WHO YOU ARE!
YOU'RE COUCHPO FROM MOGUMOGU CHANNEL.
I WATCH YOU ALL THE TIME!!
I LOVE TO EAT, TOO! ♡
I'VE SEEN ALL YOUR VIDEOS, TOO, COPA!! YOUR KOALA IS SO CUTE.
WHAT...? DOES THIS MEAN YOU'RE A...
A B-CUBER?!
I'M SORRY... I HAD NO IDEA.
MAYBE I'VE SEEN YOU BEFORE...? MAYBE NOT...?
ARE YOU THAT POOP PERSON?
I'M PRETTY SURE *THAT'S* NOT ME!!
HA HA... THAT'S OKAY...
I DON'T HAVE A LOT OF SUB-SCRIBERS.
BUT ANYWAY... LET'S ALL WORK TOGETHER TO BREAK OUT OF HERE!!
WHAT-EVER IT TAKES!!!

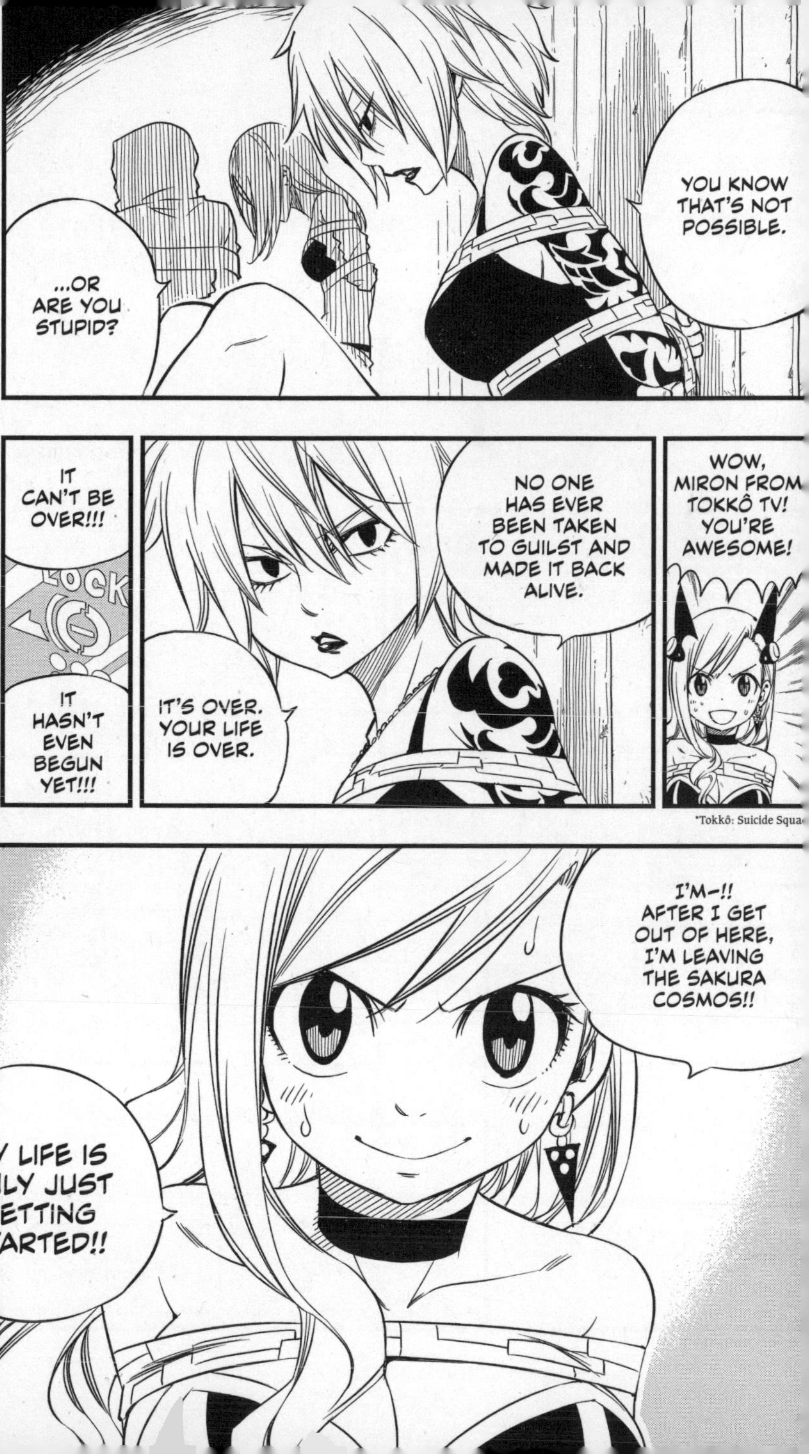
YOU KNOW THAT'S NOT POSSIBLE.
...OR ARE YOU STUPID?
WOW, MIRON FROM TOKKÔ TV! YOU'RE AWESOME!
NO ONE HAS EVER BEEN TAKEN TO GUILST AND MADE IT BACK ALIVE.
IT'S OVER. YOUR LIFE IS OVER.
IT CAN'T BE OVER!!!
LOCK
IT HASN'T EVEN BEGUN YET!!!
I'M-!! AFTER I GET OUT OF HERE, I'M LEAVING THE SAKURA COSMOS!!
MY LIFE IS ONLY JUST GETTING STARTED!!

*Tokkô: Suicide Squa

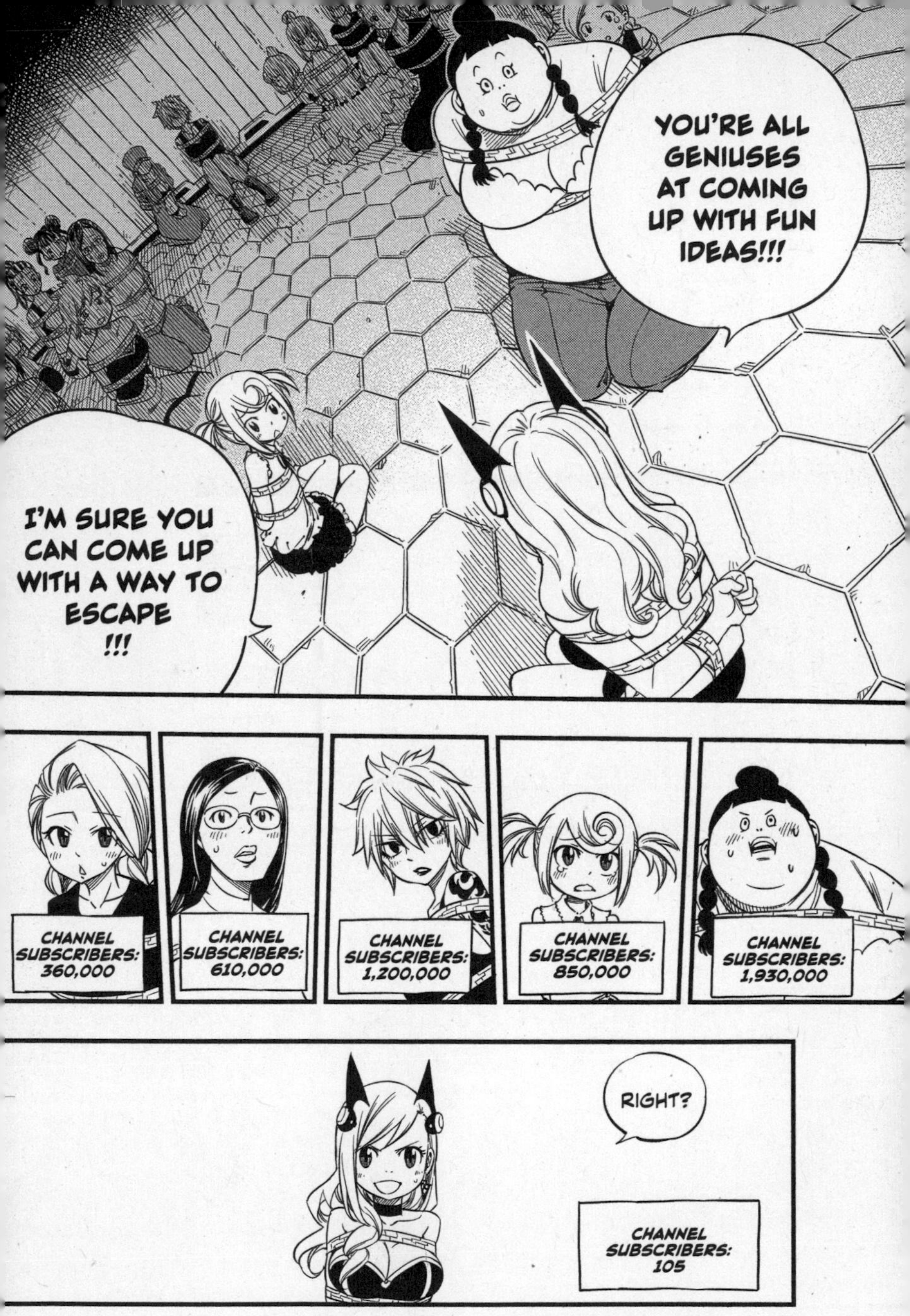
YOU'RE ALL GENIUSES AT COMING UP WITH FUN IDEAS!!!
I'M SURE YOU CAN COME UP WITH A WAY TO ESCAPE !!!
CHANNEL SUBSCRIBERS: 1,930,000
CHANNEL SUBSCRIBERS: 850,000
CHANNEL SUBSCRIBERS: 1,200,000
CHANNEL SUBSCRIBERS: 610,000
CHANNEL SUBSCRIBERS: 360,000
RIGHT?
CHANNEL SUBSCRIBERS: 105

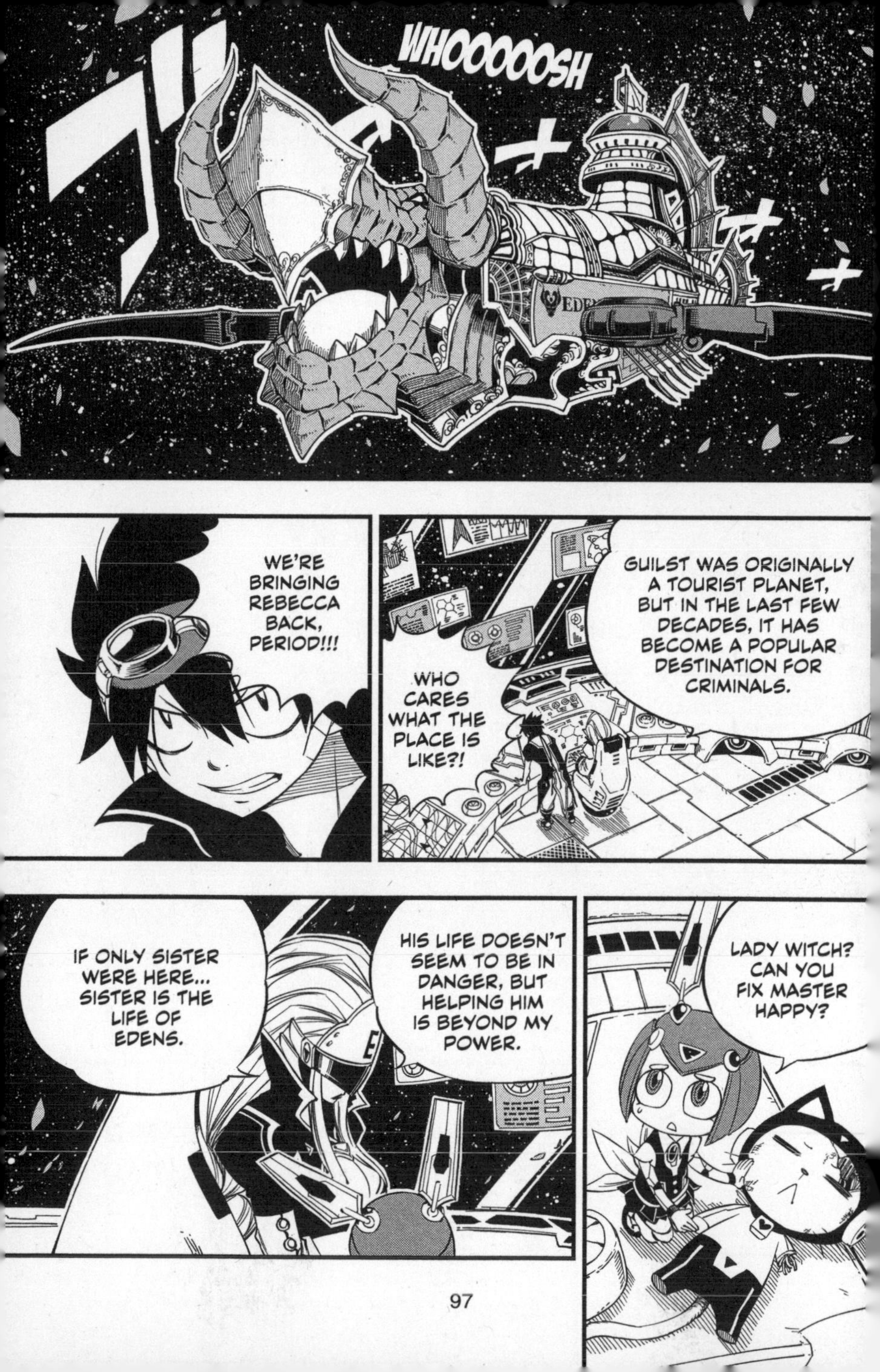
WHOOOOOSH
GUILST WAS ORIGINALLY A TOURIST PLANET, BUT IN THE LAST FEW DECADES, IT HAS BECOME A POPULAR DESTINATION FOR CRIMINALS.
WHO CARES WHAT THE PLACE IS LIKE?!
WE'RE BRINGING REBECCA BACK, PERIOD!!!
LADY WITCH? CAN YOU FIX MASTER HAPPY?
HIS LIFE DOESN'T SEEM TO BE IN DANGER, BUT HELPING HIM IS BEYOND MY POWER.
IF ONLY SISTER WERE HERE... SISTER IS THE LIFE OF EDENS.

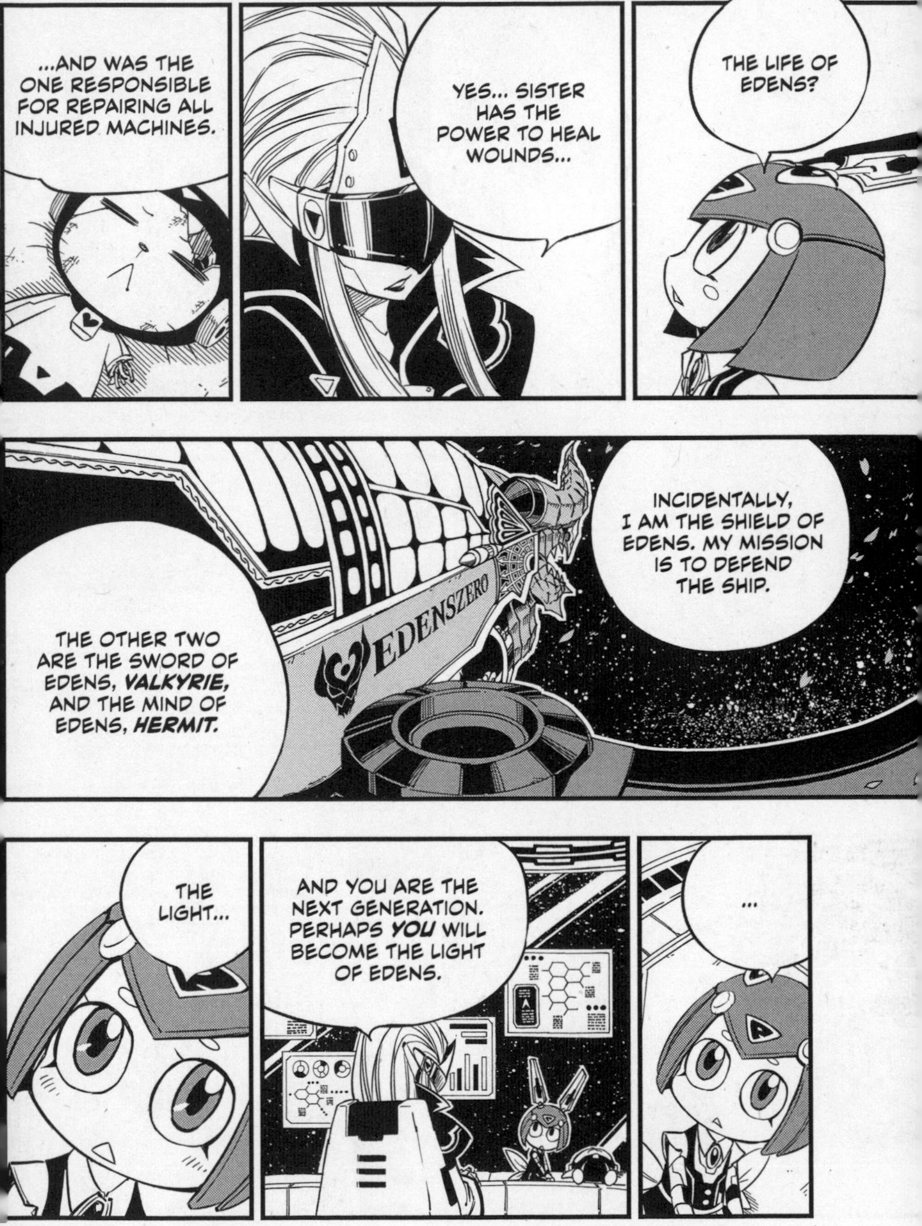
THE LIFE OF EDENS?
YES... SISTER HAS THE POWER TO HEAL WOUNDS...
...AND WAS THE ONE RESPONSIBLE FOR REPAIRING ALL INJURED MACHINES.
INCIDENTALLY, I AM THE SHIELD OF EDENS. MY MISSION IS TO DEFEND THE SHIP.
EDENSZERO
THE OTHER TWO ARE THE SWORD OF EDENS, *VALKYRIE,* AND THE MIND OF EDENS, *HERMIT.*
...
AND YOU ARE THE NEXT GENERATION. PERHAPS *YOU* WILL BECOME THE LIGHT OF EDENS.
THE LIGHT...

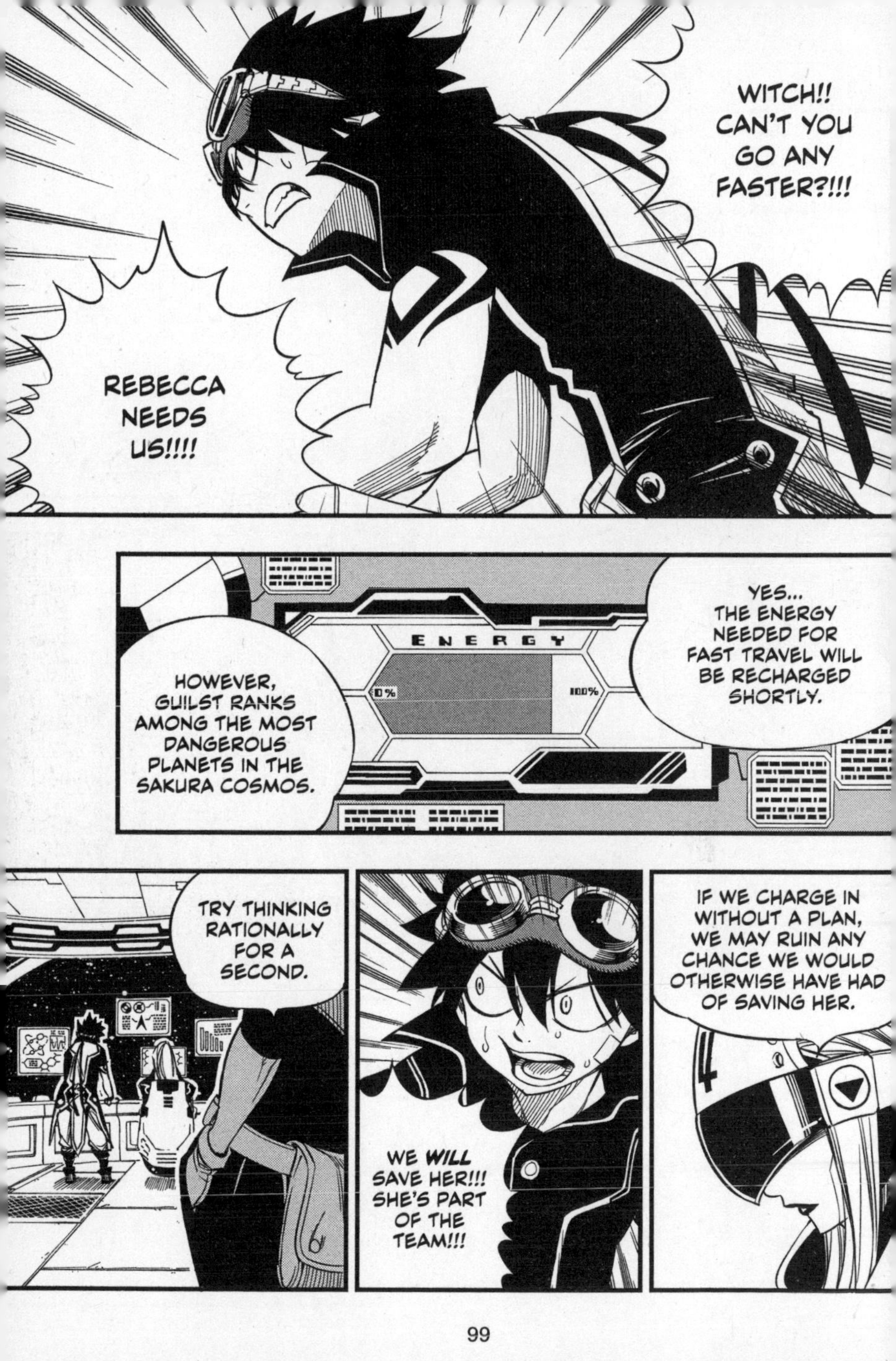
WITCH!! CAN'T YOU GO ANY FASTER?!!!
REBECCA NEEDS US!!!!
YES... THE ENERGY NEEDED FOR FAST TRAVEL WILL BE RECHARGED SHORTLY.
ENERGY
0%
100%
HOWEVER, GUILST RANKS AMONG THE MOST DANGEROUS PLANETS IN THE SAKURA COSMOS.
IF WE CHARGE IN WITHOUT A PLAN, WE MAY RUIN ANY CHANCE WE WOULD OTHERWISE HAVE HAD OF SAVING HER.
WE *WILL* SAVE HER!!! SHE'S PART OF THE TEAM!!!
TRY THINKING RATIONALLY FOR A SECOND.

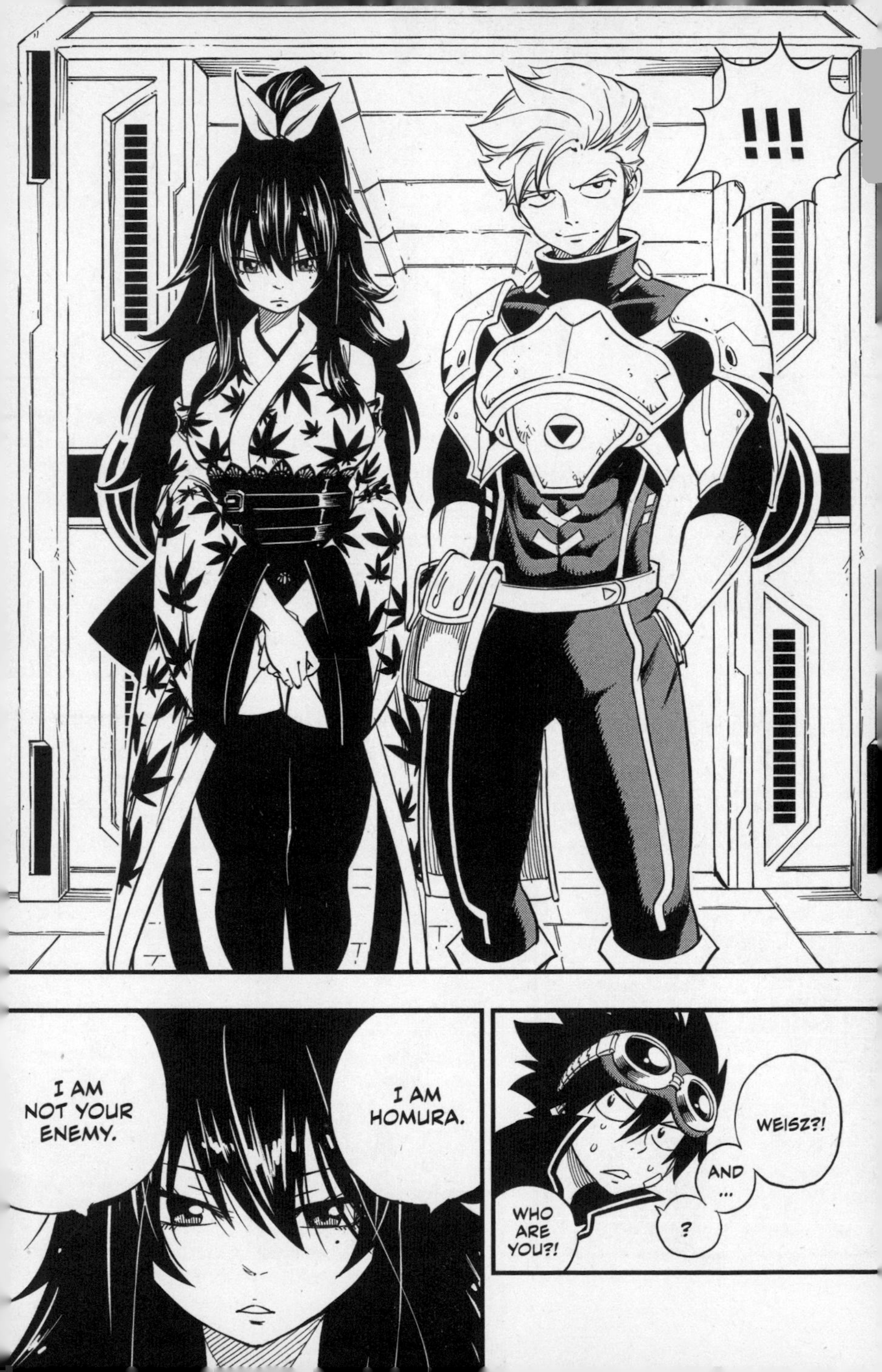
!!!
WEISZ?!
AND ...
?
WHO ARE YOU?!
I AM HOMURA.
I AM NOT YOUR ENEMY.

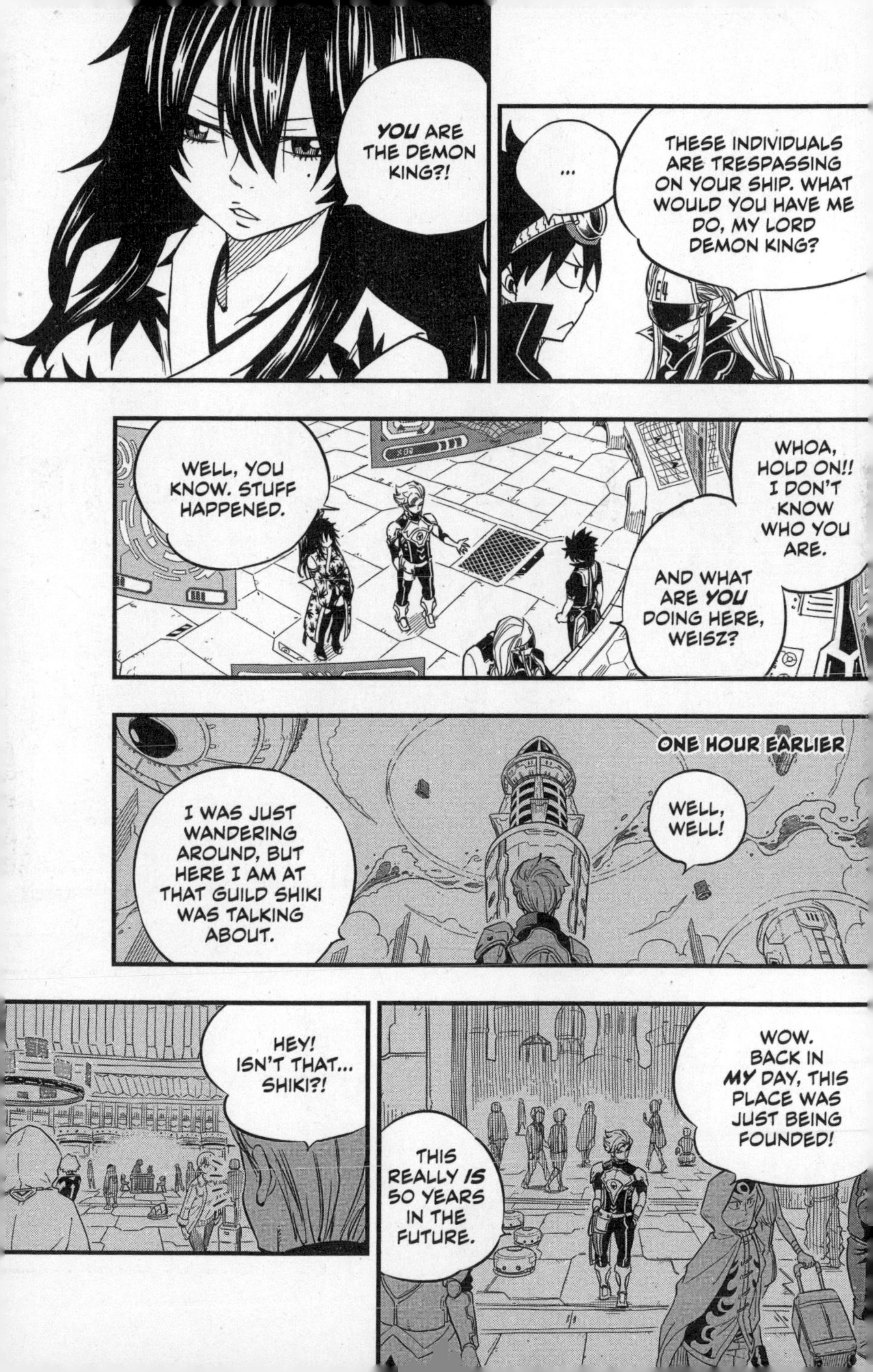
THESE INDIVIDUALS ARE TRESPASSING ON YOUR SHIP. WHAT WOULD YOU HAVE ME DO, MY LORD DEMON KING?
...
YOU ARE THE DEMON KING?!
WHOA, HOLD ON!! I DON'T KNOW WHO YOU ARE.
AND WHAT ARE *YOU* DOING HERE, WEISZ?
WELL, YOU KNOW. STUFF HAPPENED.
ONE HOUR EARLIER
WELL, WELL!
I WAS JUST WANDERING AROUND, BUT HERE I AM AT THAT GUILD SHIKI WAS TALKING ABOUT.
WOW. BACK IN *MY* DAY, THIS PLACE WAS JUST BEING FOUNDED!
THIS REALLY *IS* 50 YEARS IN THE FUTURE.
HEY! ISN'T THAT... SHIKI?!

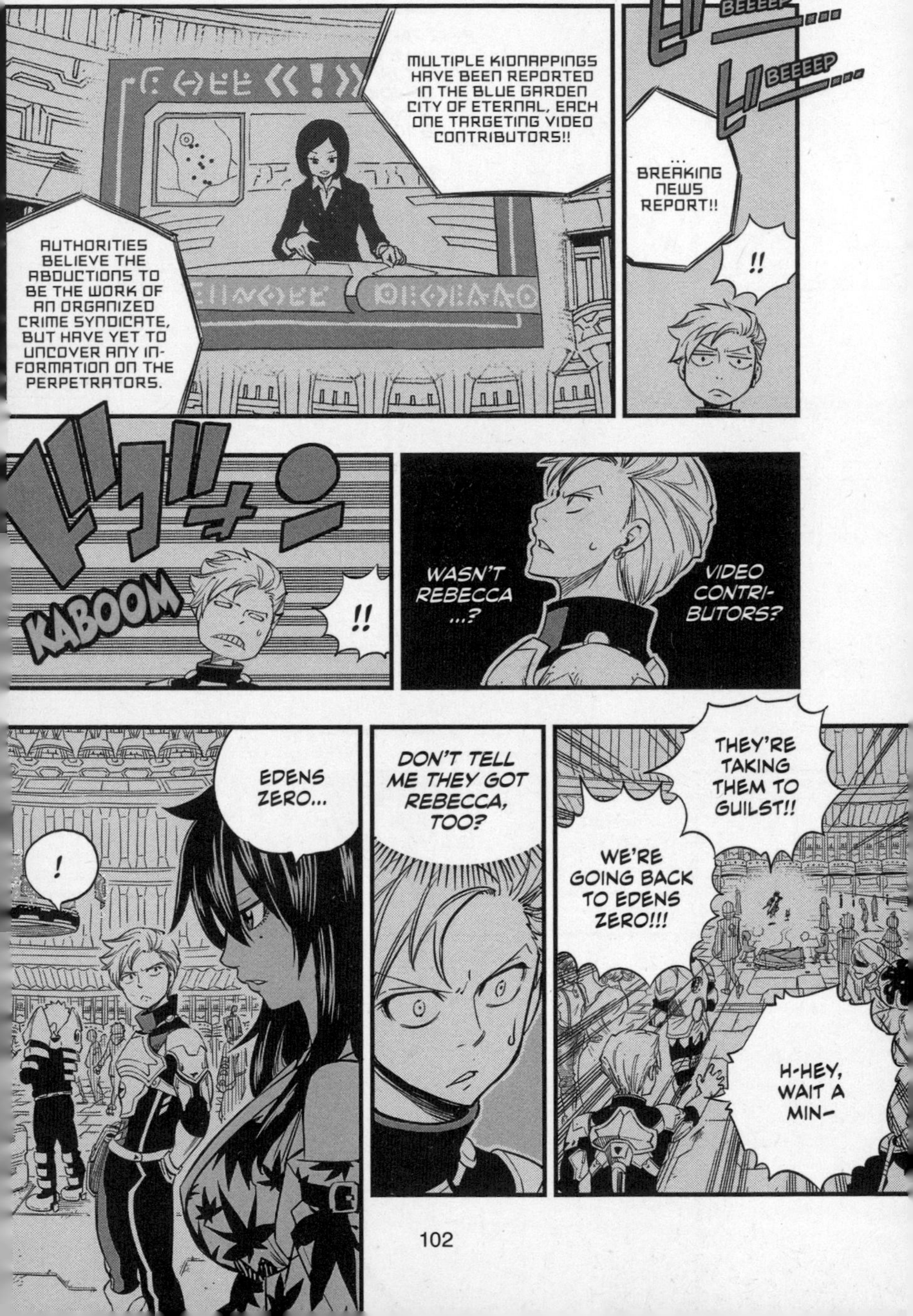
BEEEEP.....
BEEEEP.....
... BREAKING NEWS REPORT!!
!!
MULTIPLE KIDNAPPINGS HAVE BEEN REPORTED IN THE BLUE GARDEN CITY OF ETERNAL, EACH ONE TARGETING VIDEO CONTRIBUTORS!!
AUTHORITIES BELIEVE THE ABDUCTIONS TO BE THE WORK OF AN ORGANIZED CRIME SYNDICATE, BUT HAVE YET TO UNCOVER ANY INFORMATION ON THE PERPETRATORS.
VIDEO CONTRIBUTORS?
WASN'T REBECCA ...?
KABOOM
!!
THEY'RE TAKING THEM TO GUILST!!
WE'RE GOING BACK TO EDENS ZERO!!!
H-HEY, WAIT A MIN-
DON'T TELL ME THEY GOT REBECCA, TOO?
EDENS ZERO...
!

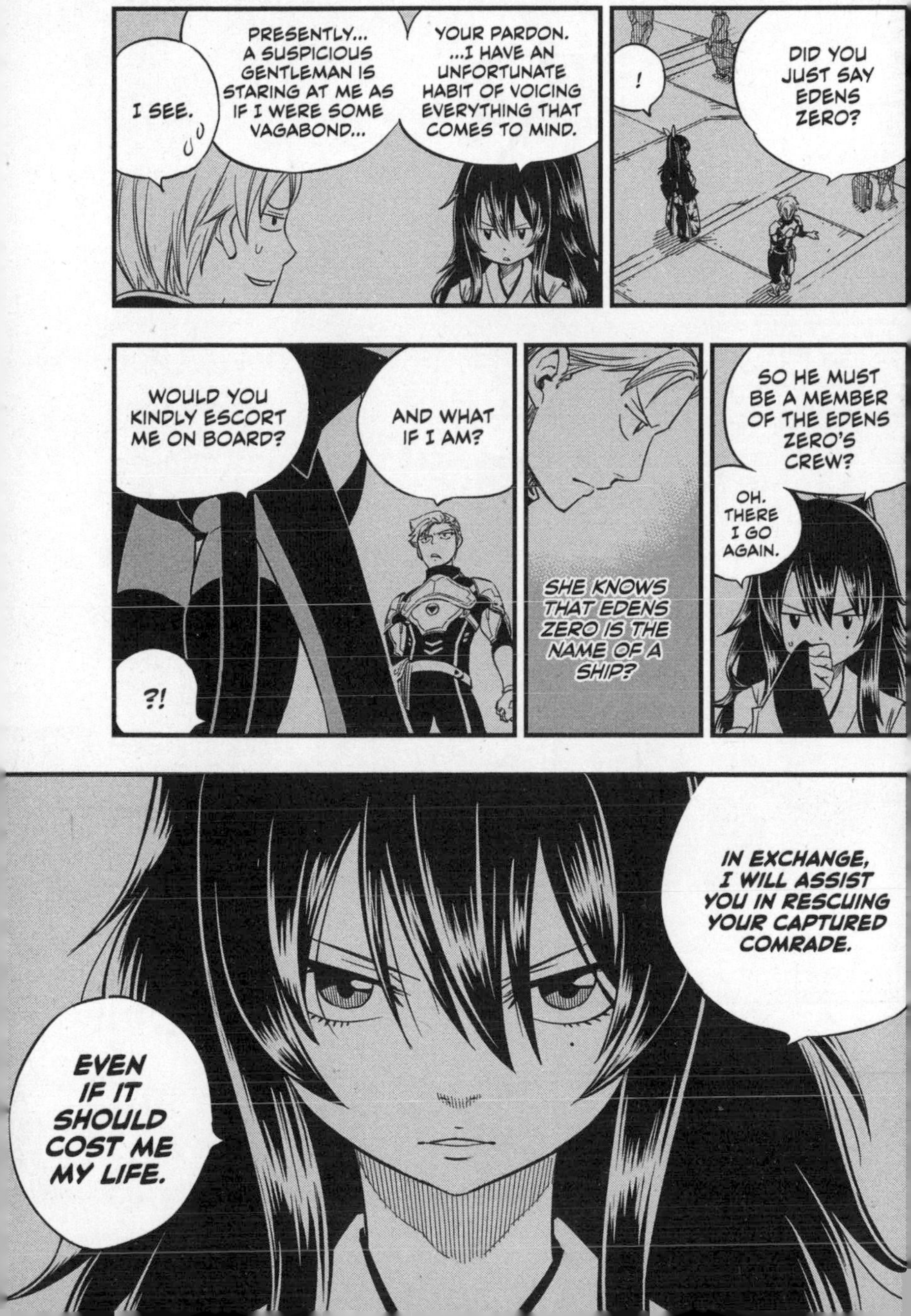
DID YOU JUST SAY EDENS ZERO?
!
YOUR PARDON. ...I HAVE AN UNFORTUNATE HABIT OF VOICING EVERYTHING THAT COMES TO MIND.
PRESENTLY... A SUSPICIOUS GENTLEMAN IS STARING AT ME AS IF I WERE SOME VAGABOND...
I SEE.
SO HE MUST BE A MEMBER OF THE EDENS ZERO'S CREW?
OH. THERE I GO AGAIN.
SHE KNOWS THAT EDENS ZERO IS THE NAME OF A SHIP?
AND WHAT IF I AM?
WOULD YOU KINDLY ESCORT ME ON BOARD?
?!
IN EXCHANGE, I WILL ASSIST YOU IN RESCUING YOUR CAPTURED COMRADE.
EVEN IF IT SHOULD COST ME MY LIFE.

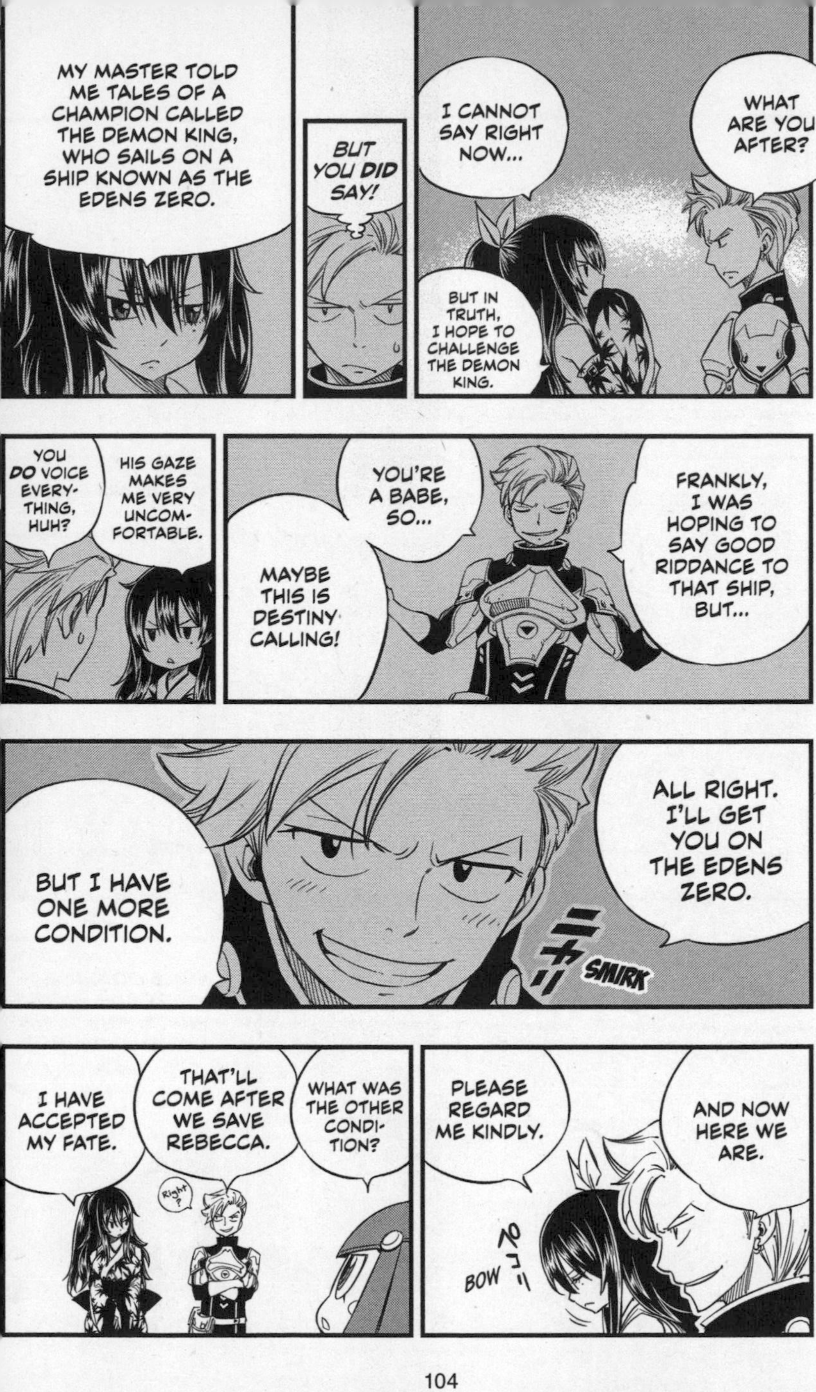
WHAT ARE YOU AFTER?
I CANNOT SAY RIGHT NOW...
BUT IN TRUTH, I HOPE TO CHALLENGE THE DEMON KING.
BUT YOU **DID** SAY!
MY MASTER TOLD ME TALES OF A CHAMPION CALLED THE DEMON KING, WHO SAILS ON A SHIP KNOWN AS THE EDENS ZERO.
FRANKLY, I WAS HOPING TO SAY GOOD RIDDANCE TO THAT SHIP, BUT...
YOU'RE A BABE, SO...
MAYBE THIS IS DESTINY CALLING!
HIS GAZE MAKES ME VERY UNCOMFORTABLE.
YOU **DO** VOICE EVERYTHING, HUH?
ALL RIGHT. I'LL GET YOU ON THE EDENS ZERO.
ニヤッ
SMIRK
BUT I HAVE ONE MORE CONDITION.
AND NOW HERE WE ARE.
PLEASE REGARD ME KINDLY.
ペコッ
BOW
WHAT WAS THE OTHER CONDITION?
THAT'LL COME AFTER WE SAVE REBECCA.
Right?
I HAVE ACCEPTED MY FATE.

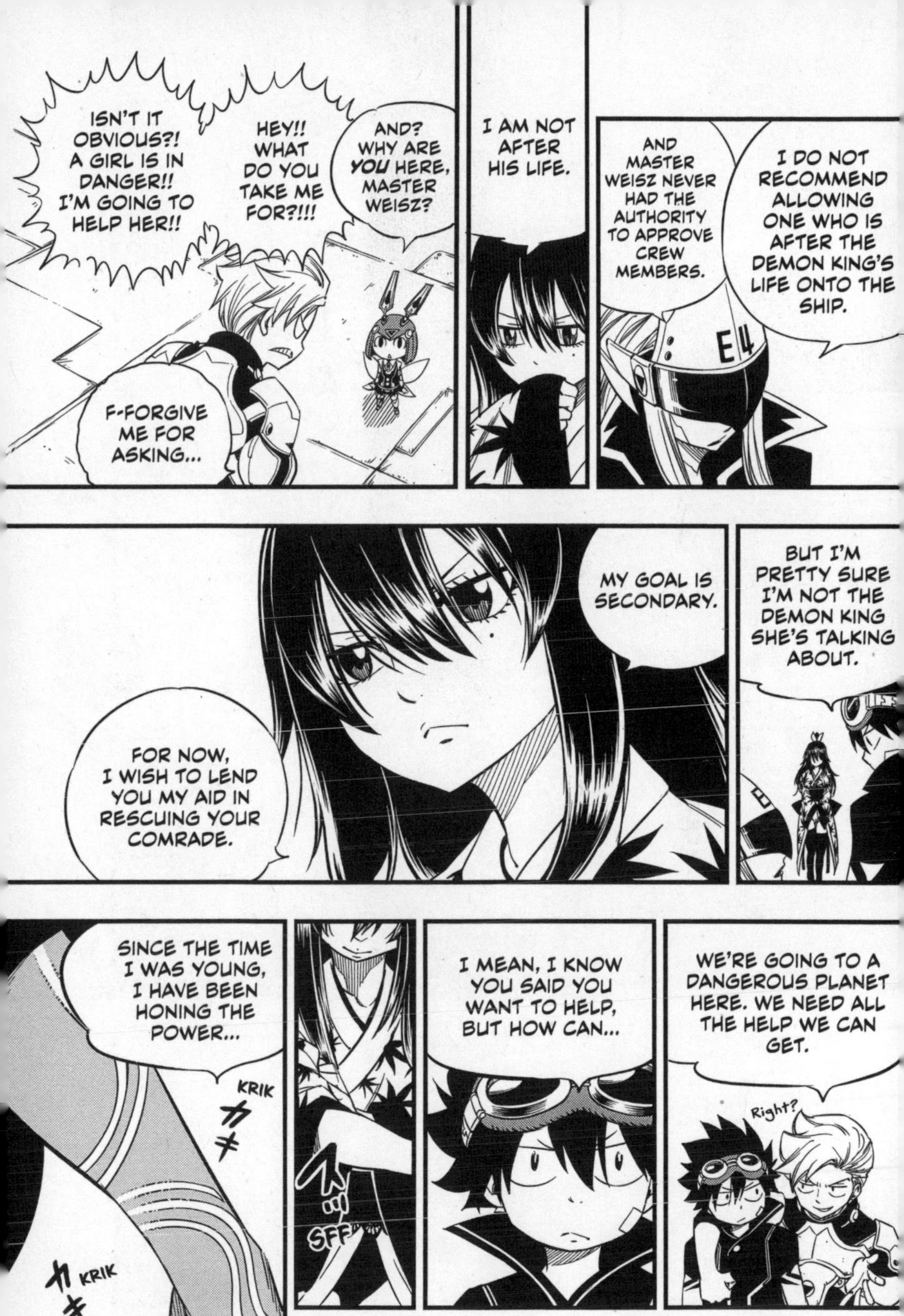
I DO NOT RECOMMEND ALLOWING ONE WHO IS AFTER THE DEMON KING'S LIFE ONTO THE SHIP.
AND MASTER WEISZ NEVER HAD THE AUTHORITY TO APPROVE CREW MEMBERS.
E4
I AM NOT AFTER HIS LIFE.
AND? WHY ARE *YOU* HERE, MASTER WEISZ?
HEY!! WHAT DO YOU TAKE ME FOR?!!!
ISN'T IT OBVIOUS?! A GIRL IS IN DANGER!! I'M GOING TO HELP HER!!
F-FORGIVE ME FOR ASKING...
BUT I'M PRETTY SURE I'M NOT THE DEMON KING SHE'S TALKING ABOUT.
MY GOAL IS SECONDARY.
FOR NOW, I WISH TO LEND YOU MY AID IN RESCUING YOUR COMRADE.
WE'RE GOING TO A DANGEROUS PLANET HERE. WE NEED ALL THE HELP WE CAN GET.
Right?
I MEAN, I KNOW YOU SAID YOU WANT TO HELP, BUT HOW CAN...
SFF
SINCE THE TIME I WAS YOUNG, I HAVE BEEN HONING THE POWER...
KRIK
KRIK

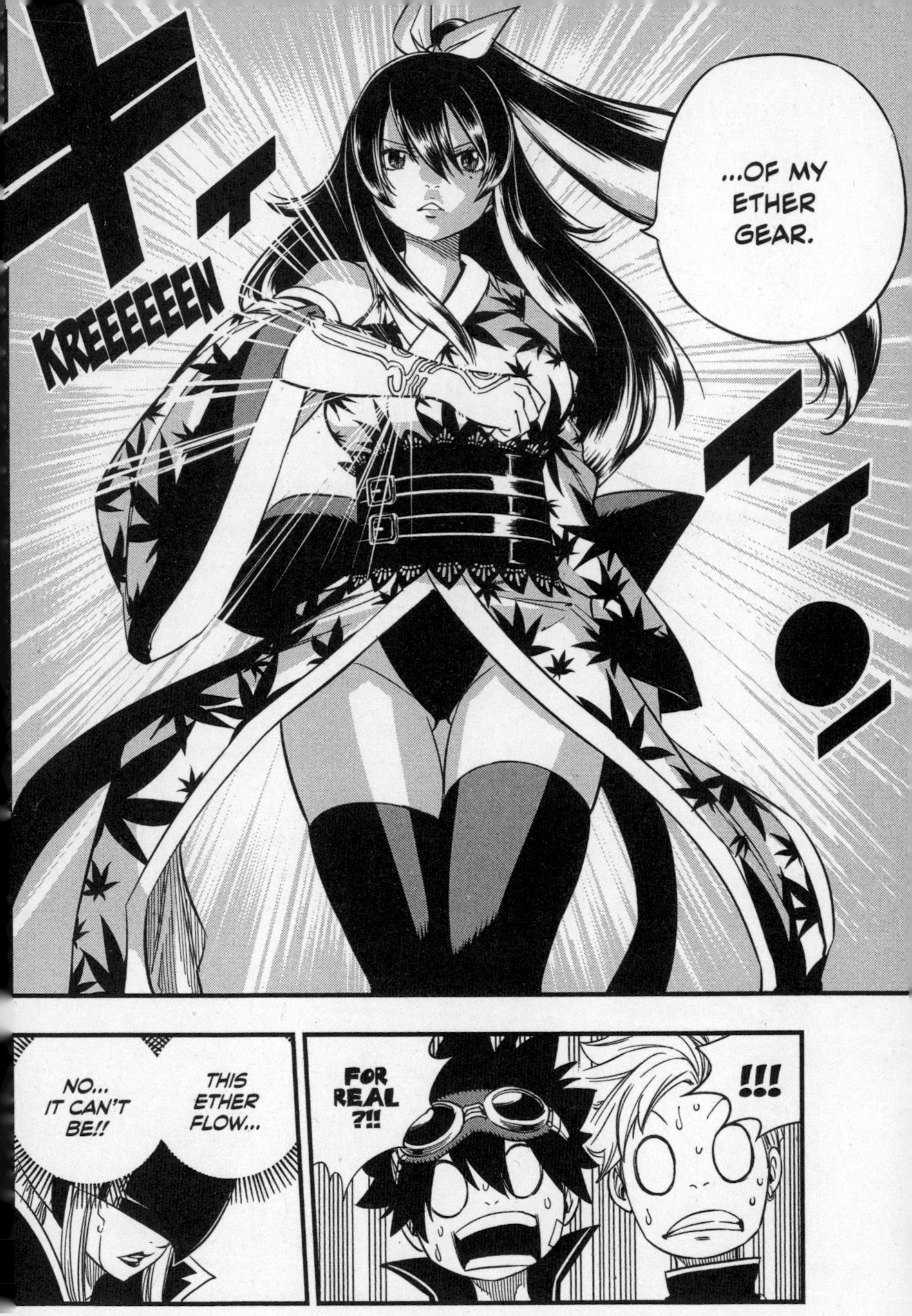
...OF MY ETHER GEAR.
KREEEEEEN
!!!
FOR REAL ?!!
THIS ETHER FLOW...
NO... IT CAN'T BE!!

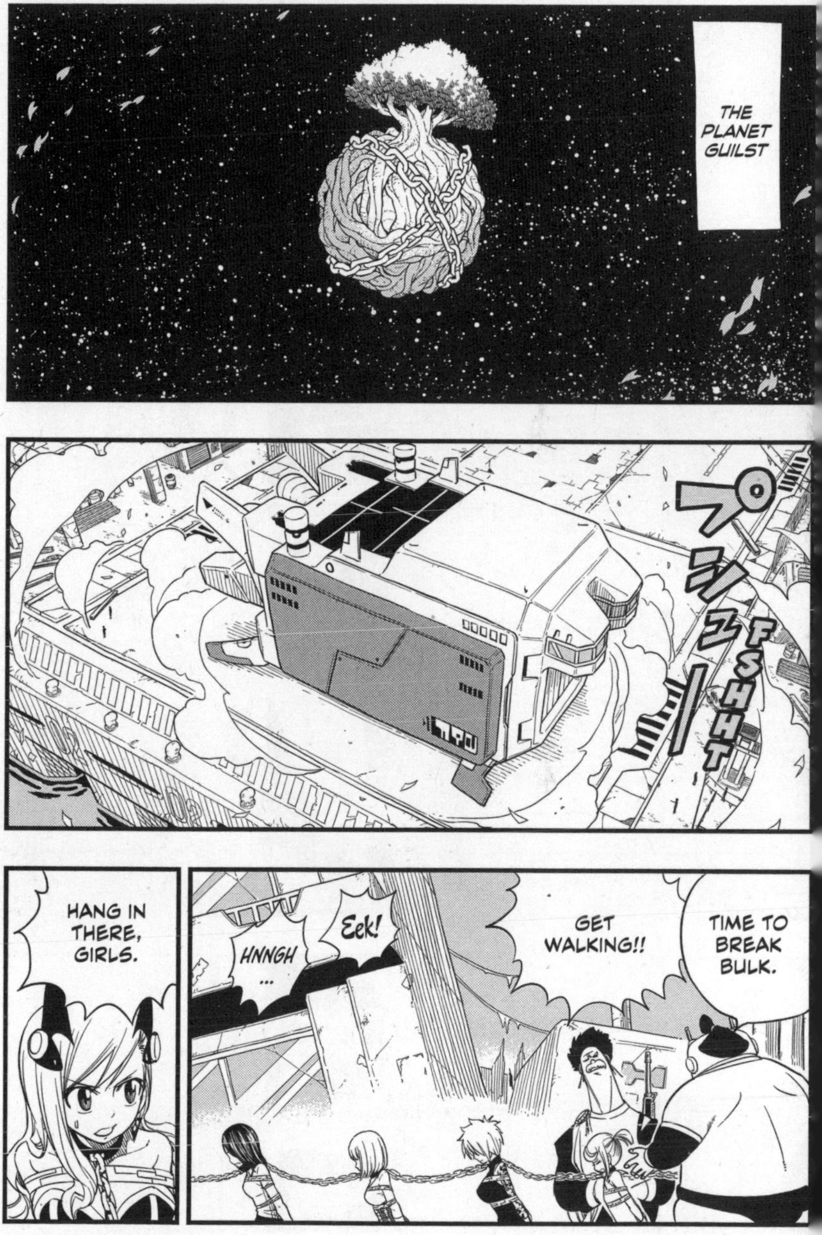
THE PLANET GUILST
プシュー
FSHHT
TIME TO BREAK BULK.
GET WALKING!!
Eek!
HNNGH ...
HANG IN THERE, GIRLS.

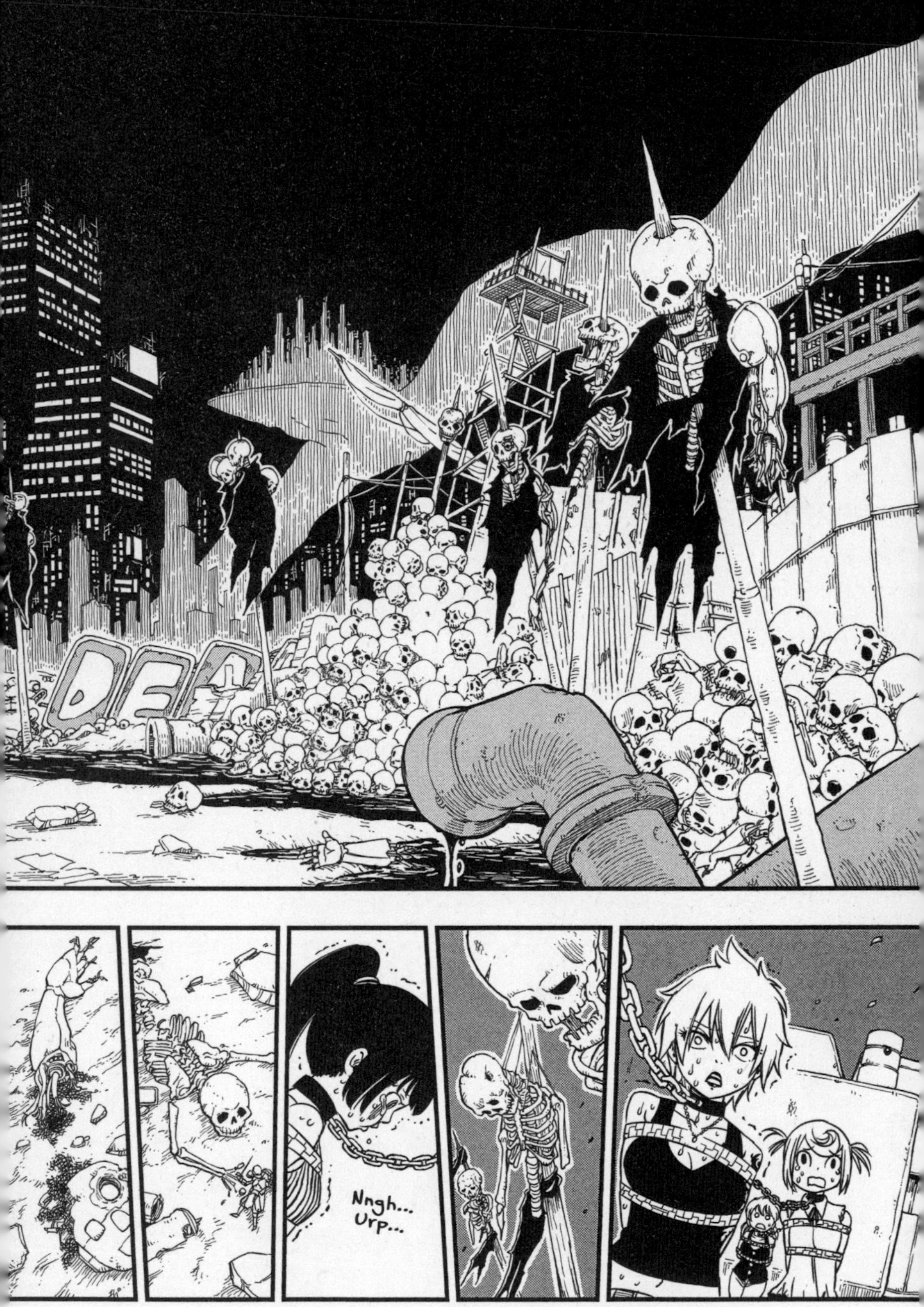
Nngh... Urp...

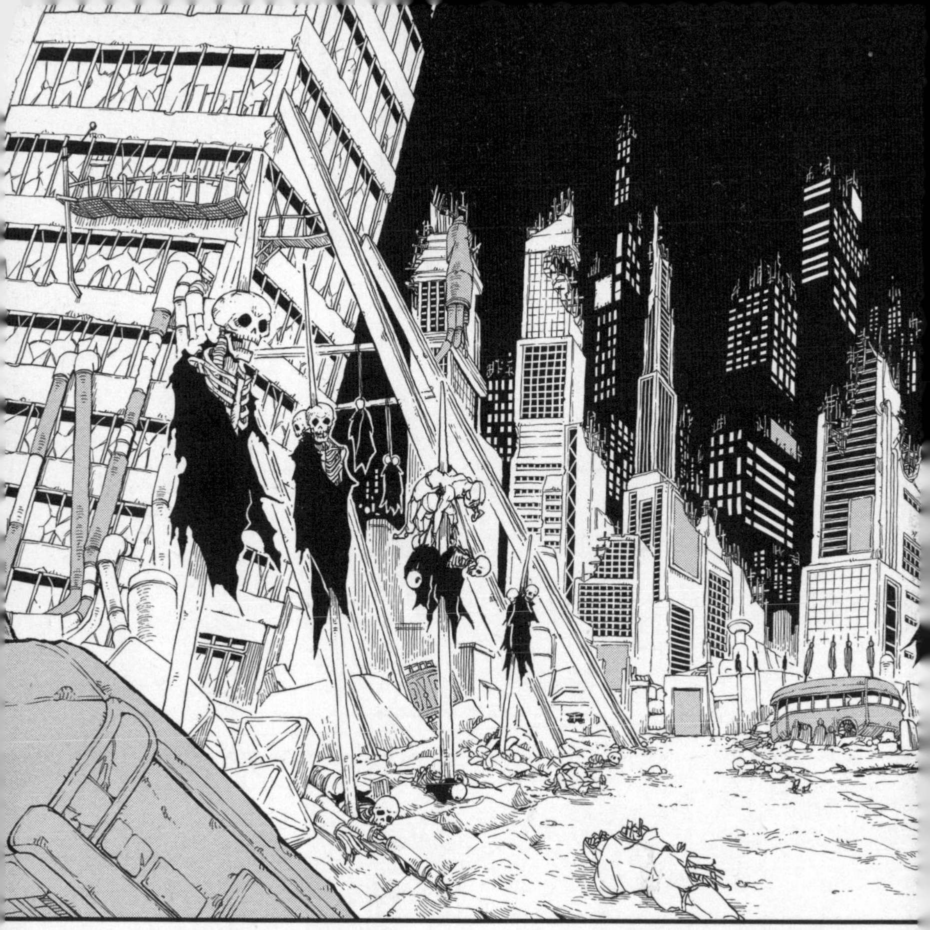

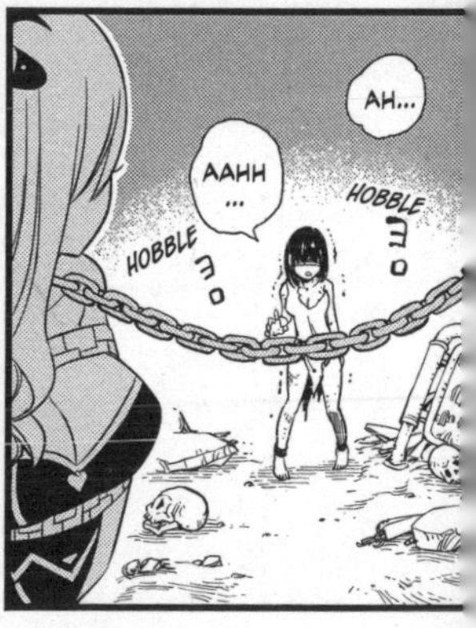
AH...
AAHH ...
HOBBLE ヨロ
HOBBLE ヨロ

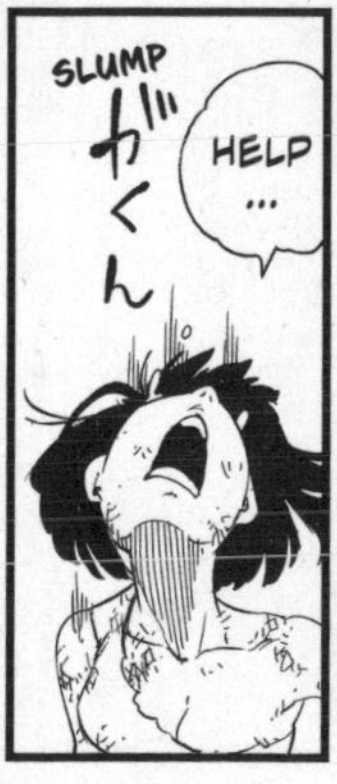
SLUMP がくん。
HELP ...

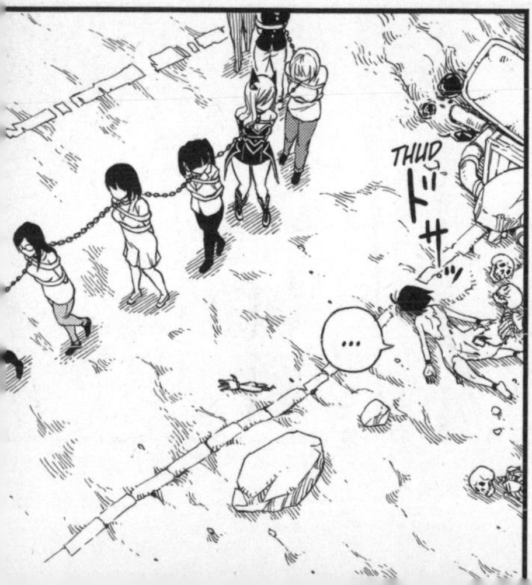
THUD ドサッ
...

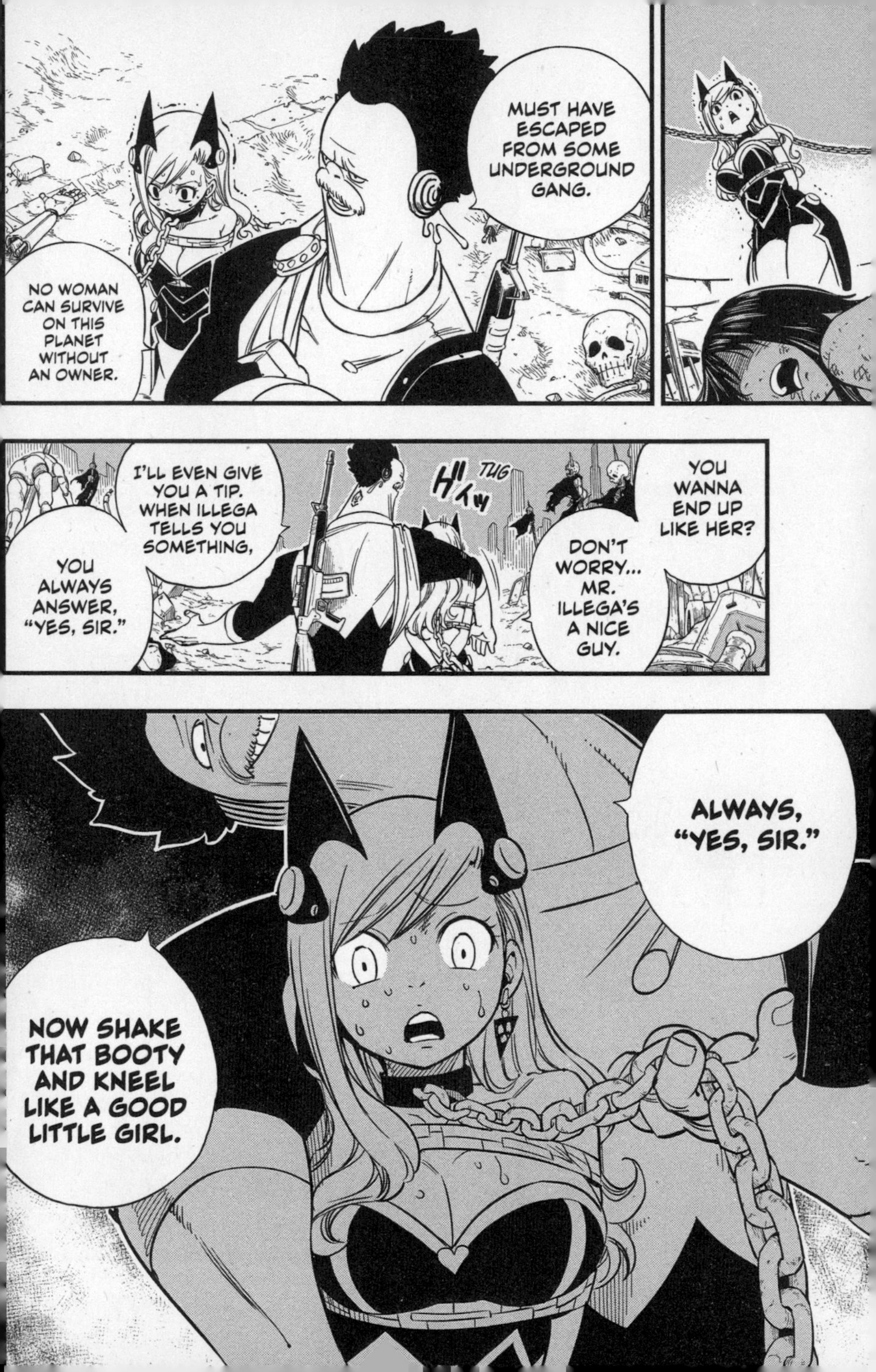
MUST HAVE ESCAPED FROM SOME UNDERGROUND GANG.
NO WOMAN CAN SURVIVE ON THIS PLANET WITHOUT AN OWNER.
YOU WANNA END UP LIKE HER?
DON'T WORRY... MR. ILLEGA'S A NICE GUY.
グイッ TUG
I'LL EVEN GIVE YOU A TIP. WHEN ILLEGA TELLS YOU SOMETHING,
YOU ALWAYS ANSWER, "YES, SIR."
ALWAYS, "YES, SIR."
NOW SHAKE THAT BOOTY AND KNEEL LIKE A GOOD LITTLE GIRL.

EDENS ZERO

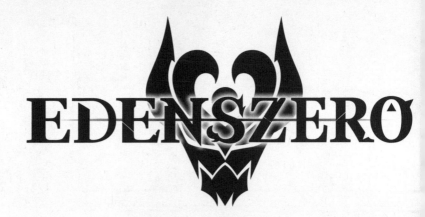

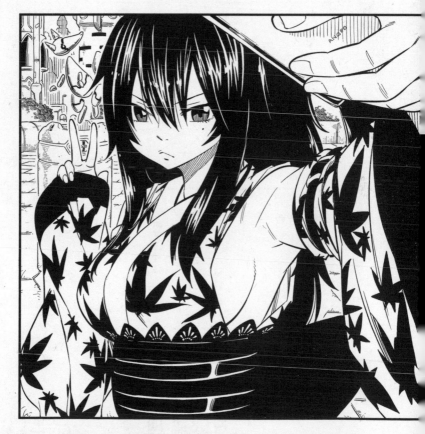

CHAPTER 20: PLANET GUILST

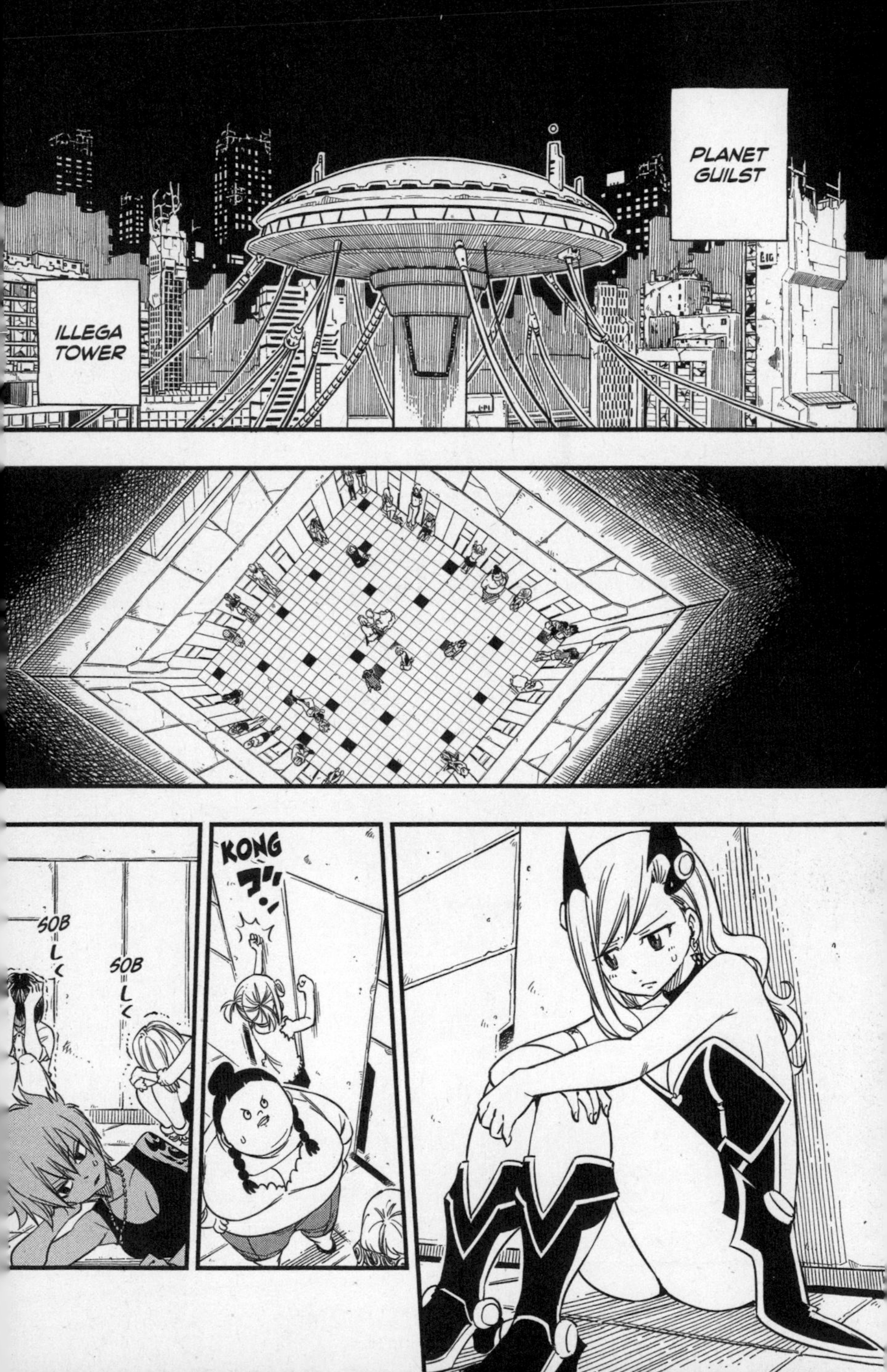

PLANET GUILST
ILLEGA TOWER
KONG
ゴッ
SOB
しく
SOB
しく

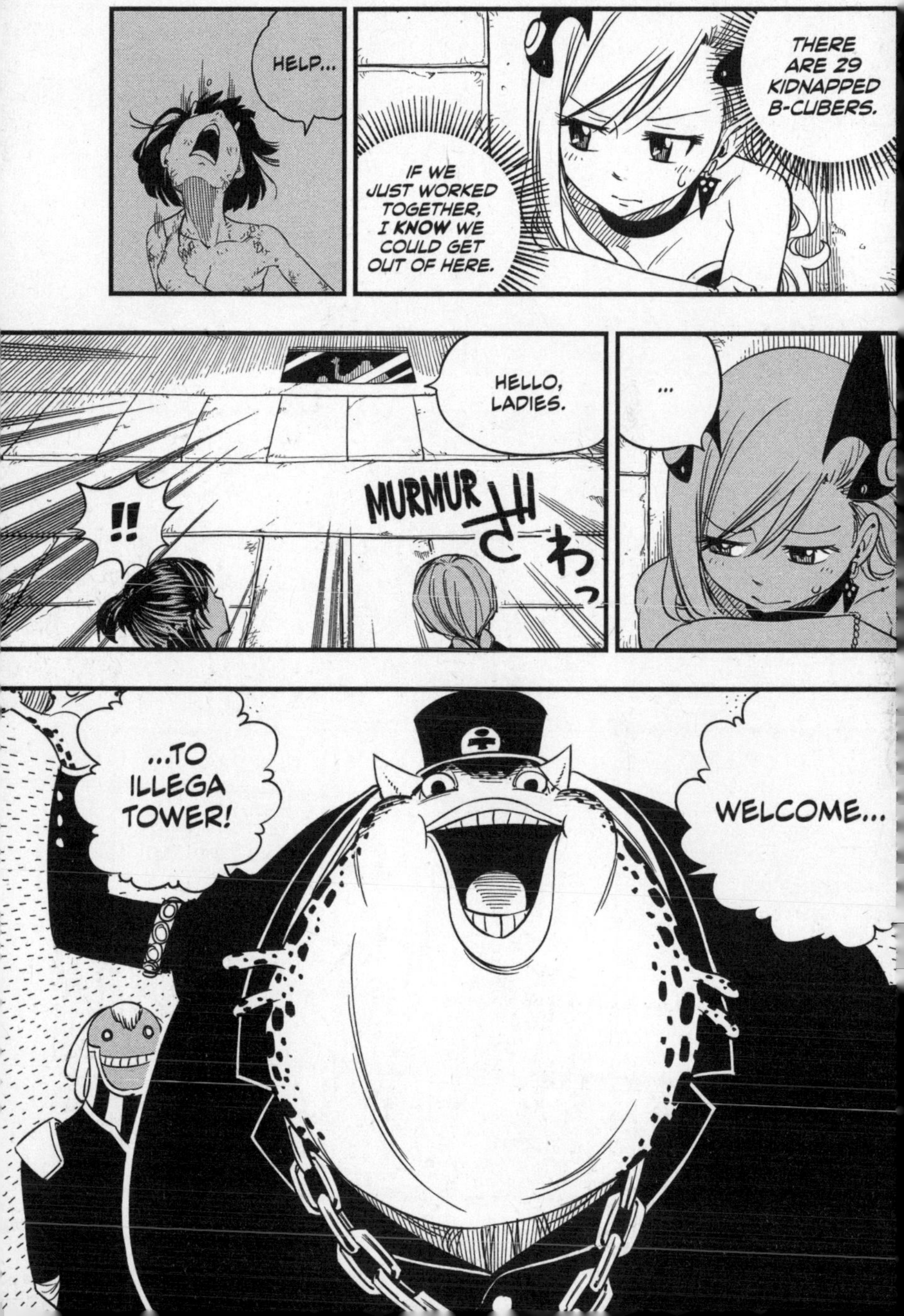
THERE ARE 29 KIDNAPPED B-CUBERS.
IF WE JUST WORKED TOGETHER, I KNOW WE COULD GET OUT OF HERE.
HELP...
...
HELLO, LADIES.
MURMUR
ざわっ
!!
WELCOME...
...TO ILLEGA TOWER!

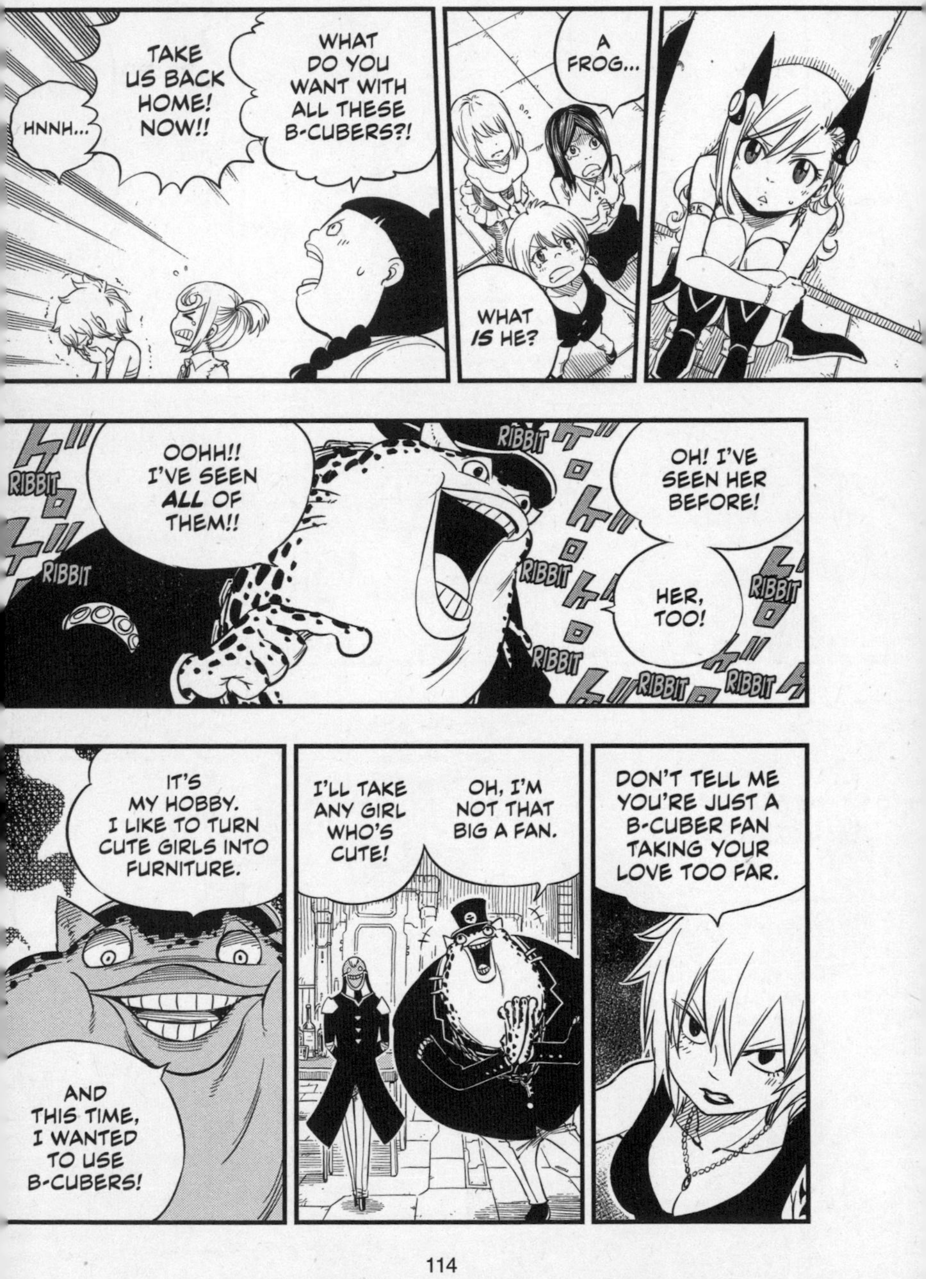
A FROG...
WHAT IS HE?
WHAT DO YOU WANT WITH ALL THESE B-CUBERS?!
TAKE US BACK HOME! NOW!!
HNNH...
RIBBIT
OH! I'VE SEEN HER BEFORE!
HER, TOO!
RIBBIT
RIBBIT
RIBBIT
RIBBIT
RIBBIT
OOHH!! I'VE SEEN ALL OF THEM!!
RIBBIT
RIBBIT
DON'T TELL ME YOU'RE JUST A B-CUBER FAN TAKING YOUR LOVE TOO FAR.
OH, I'M NOT THAT BIG A FAN.
I'LL TAKE ANY GIRL WHO'S CUTE!
IT'S MY HOBBY. I LIKE TO TURN CUTE GIRLS INTO FURNITURE.
AND THIS TIME, I WANTED TO USE B-CUBERS!

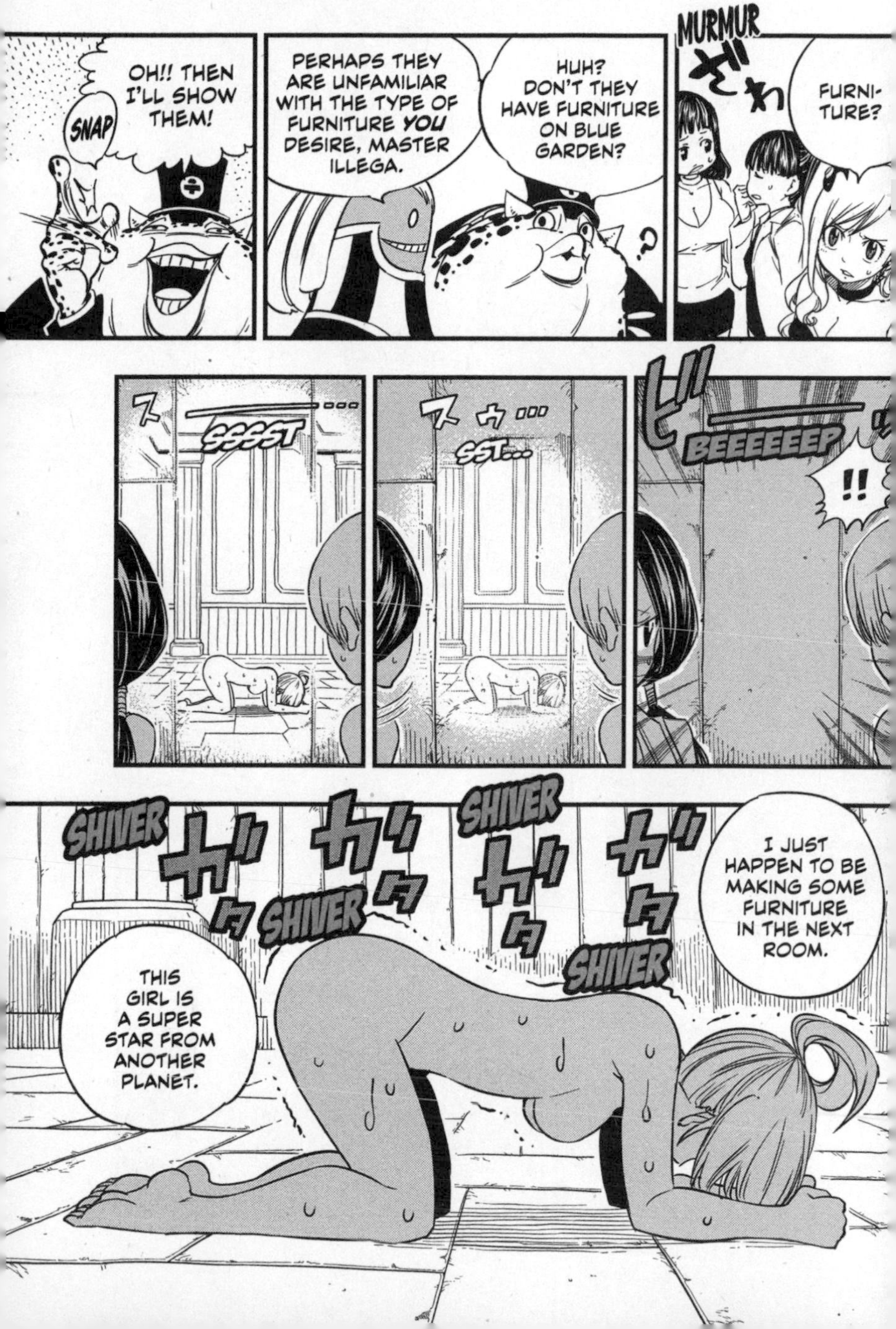
MURMUR
ざわ
FURNI-TURE?
HUH? DON'T THEY HAVE FURNITURE ON BLUE GARDEN?
PERHAPS THEY ARE UNFAMILIAR WITH THE TYPE OF FURNITURE *YOU* DESIRE, MASTER ILLEGA.
OH!! THEN I'LL SHOW THEM!
SNAP
ビー
BEEEEEEP
!!
スゥ…
SST...
ス—…
SSSST
I JUST HAPPEN TO BE MAKING SOME FURNITURE IN THE NEXT ROOM.
ガタ
SHIVER
ガタ
SHIVER
ガタ
SHIVER
ガタ
SHIVER
THIS GIRL IS A SUPER STAR FROM ANOTHER PLANET.

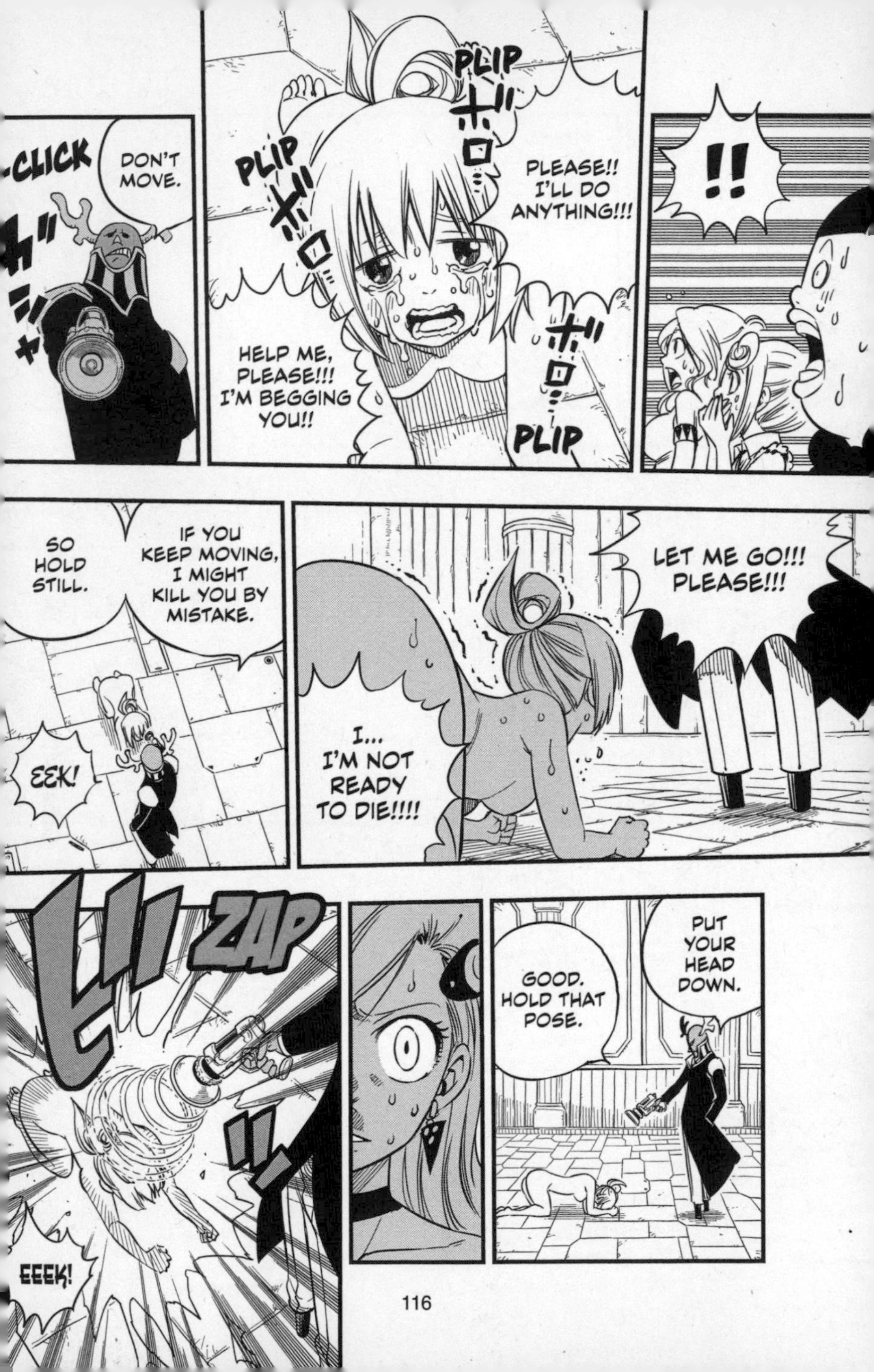
!!
PLIP
PLEASE!! I'LL DO ANYTHING!!!
PLIP
HELP ME, PLEASE!!! I'M BEGGING YOU!!
PLIP
DON'T MOVE.
-CLICK
LET ME GO!!! PLEASE!!!
I... I'M NOT READY TO DIE!!!!
IF YOU KEEP MOVING, I MIGHT KILL YOU BY MISTAKE.
SO HOLD STILL.
EEK!
PUT YOUR HEAD DOWN.
GOOD. HOLD THAT POSE.
ZAP
EEEK!

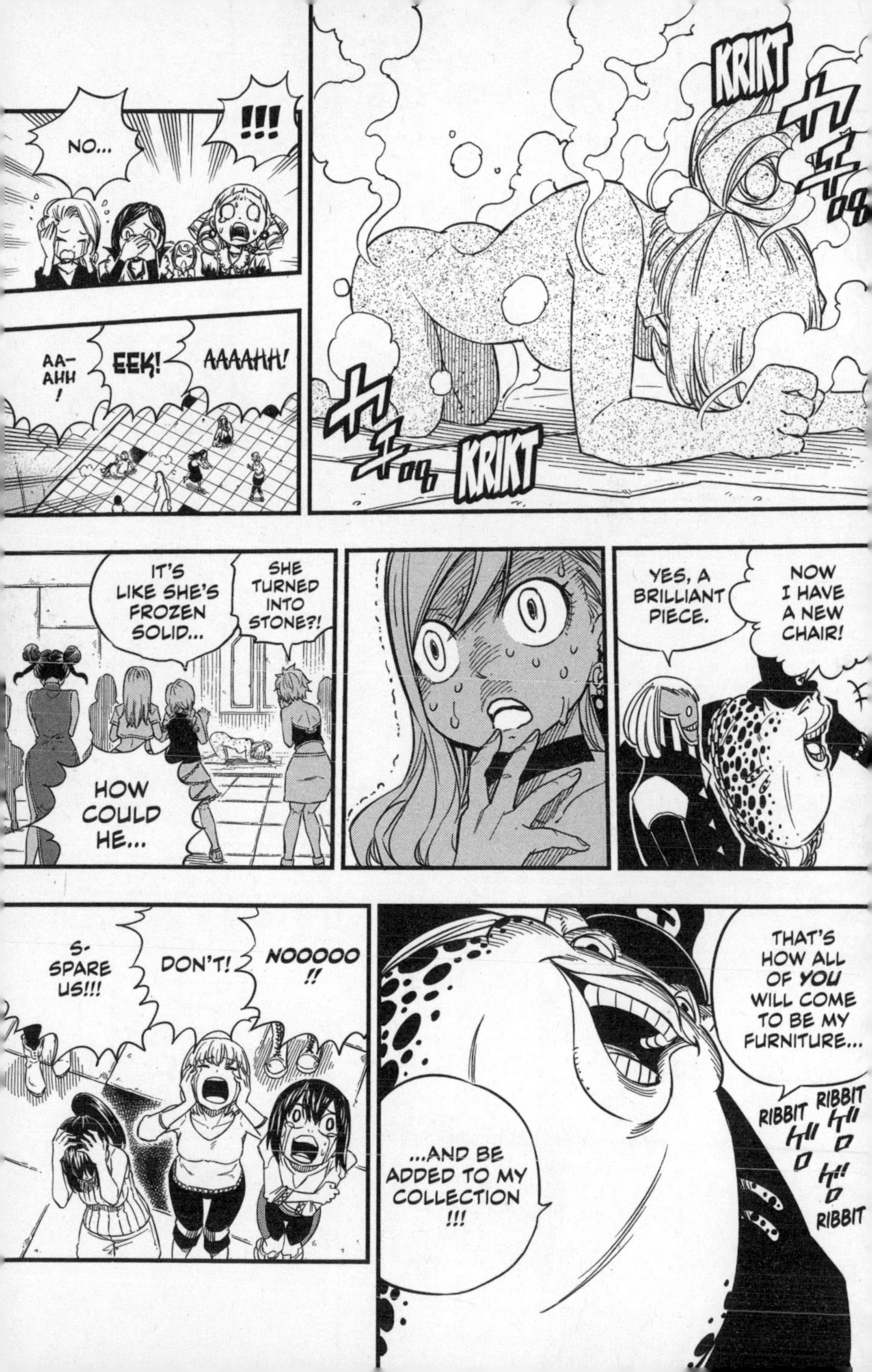

KRIKT
KRIKT
!!!
NO...
AAAAHH!
EEK!
AA-AHH!
NOW I HAVE A NEW CHAIR!
YES, A BRILLIANT PIECE.
SHE TURNED INTO STONE?!
IT'S LIKE SHE'S FROZEN SOLID...
HOW COULD HE...
THAT'S HOW ALL OF *YOU* WILL COME TO BE MY FURNITURE...
RIBBIT ゲロ
RIBBIT ゲロ
RIBBIT ゲロ
...AND BE ADDED TO MY COLLECTION!!!
NOOOOO!!
DON'T!
S-SPARE US!!!

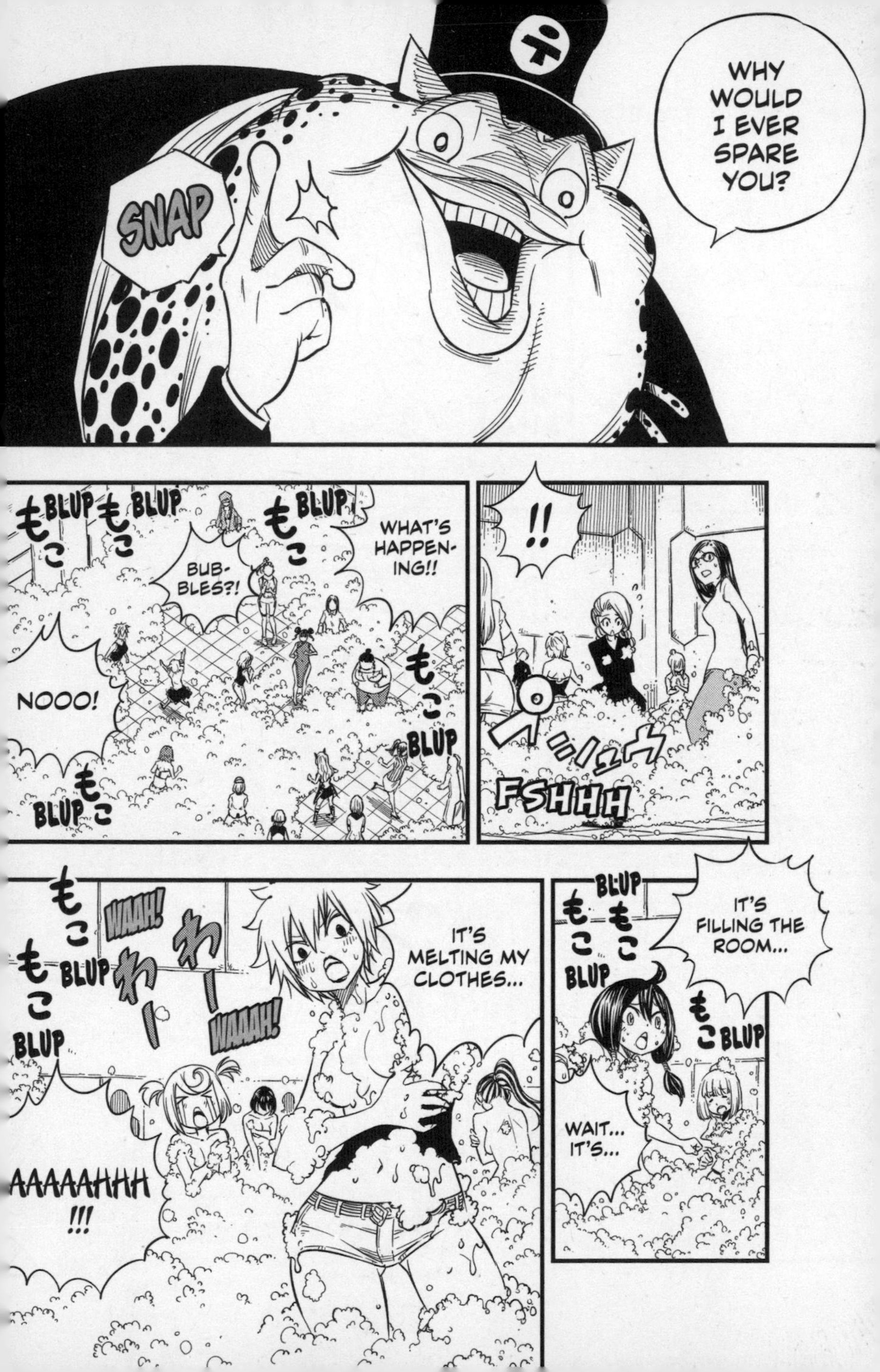
WHY WOULD I EVER SPARE YOU?
SNAP
!!
プシュウ
FSHHH
もこ BLUP
WHAT'S HAPPEN-ING!!
もこ BLUP
BUB-BLES?!
もこ BLUP
もこ BLUP
NOOO!
もこ BLUP
もこ BLUP
IT'S FILLING THE ROOM...
BLUP もこ
もこ BLUP
もこ BLUP
WAIT... IT'S...
IT'S MELTING MY CLOTHES...
わー
WAAAH!
わー
WAAH!
もこ
もこ BLUP
BLUP
AAAAAHHH!!!

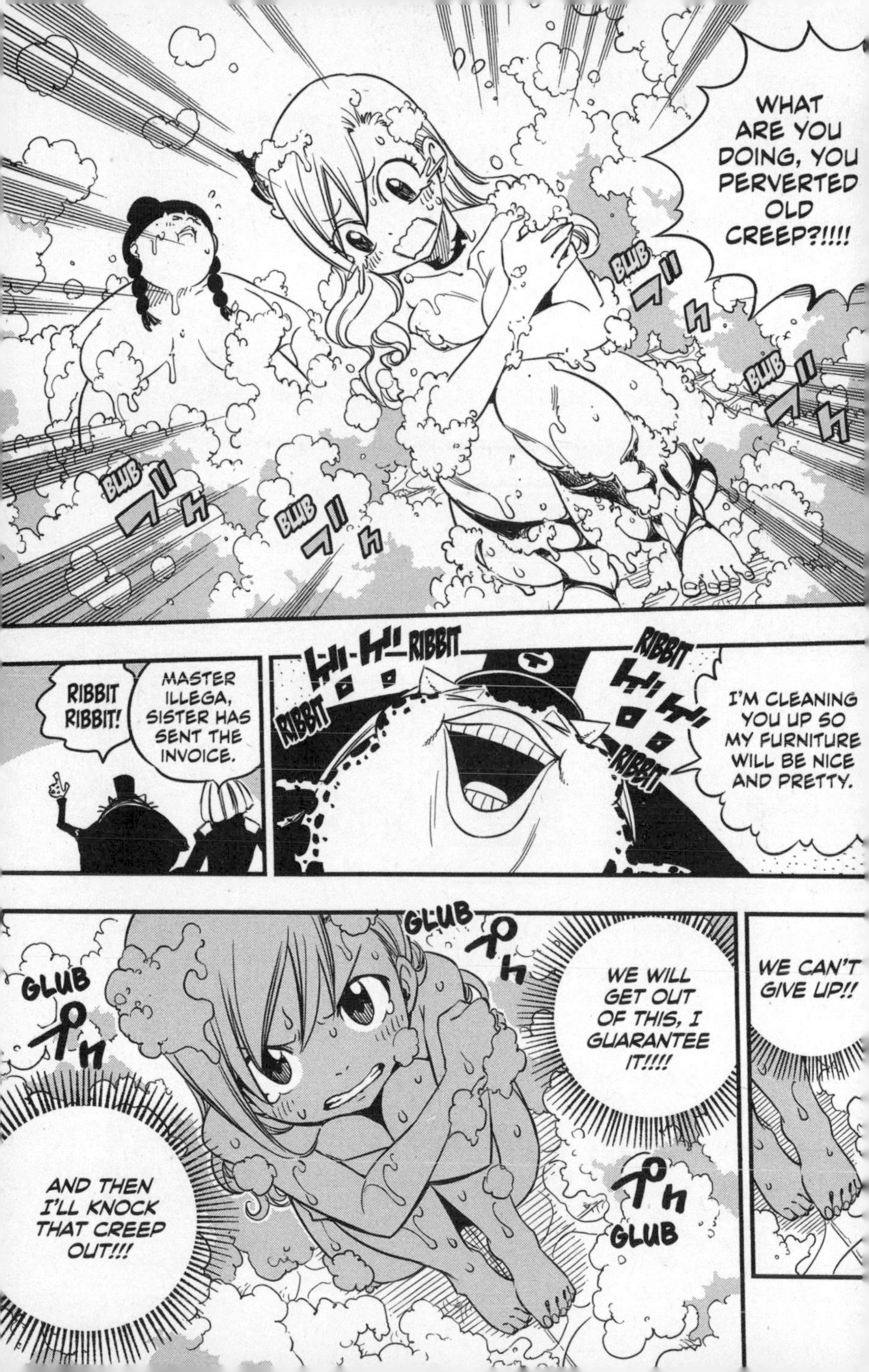
WHAT ARE YOU DOING, YOU PERVERTED OLD CREEP?!!!!
BLUB
BLUB
BLUB
BLUB
RIBBIT
RIBBIT
I'M CLEANING YOU UP SO MY FURNITURE WILL BE NICE AND PRETTY.
RIBBIT
RIBBIT
MASTER ILLEGA, SISTER HAS SENT THE INVOICE.
RIBBIT RIBBIT!
WE CAN'T GIVE UP!!
GLUB
WE WILL GET OUT OF THIS, I GUARANTEE IT!!!!
GLUB
AND THEN I'LL KNOCK THAT CREEP OUT!!!
GLUB

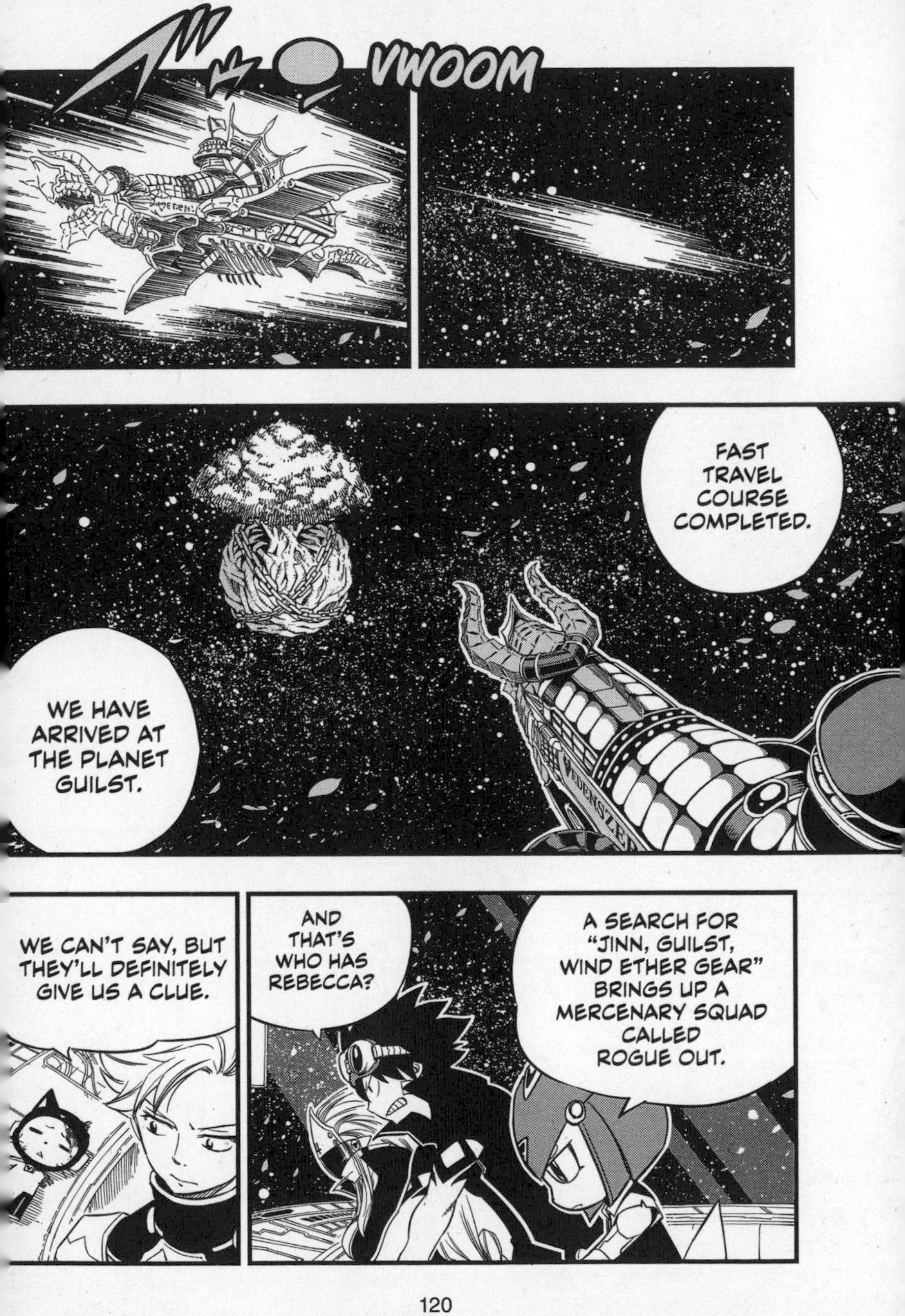
VWOOM
FAST TRAVEL COURSE COMPLETED.
WE HAVE ARRIVED AT THE PLANET GUILST.
A SEARCH FOR "JINN, GUILST, WIND ETHER GEAR" BRINGS UP A MERCENARY SQUAD CALLED ROGUE OUT.
AND THAT'S WHO HAS REBECCA?
WE CAN'T SAY, BUT THEY'LL DEFINITELY GIVE US A CLUE.

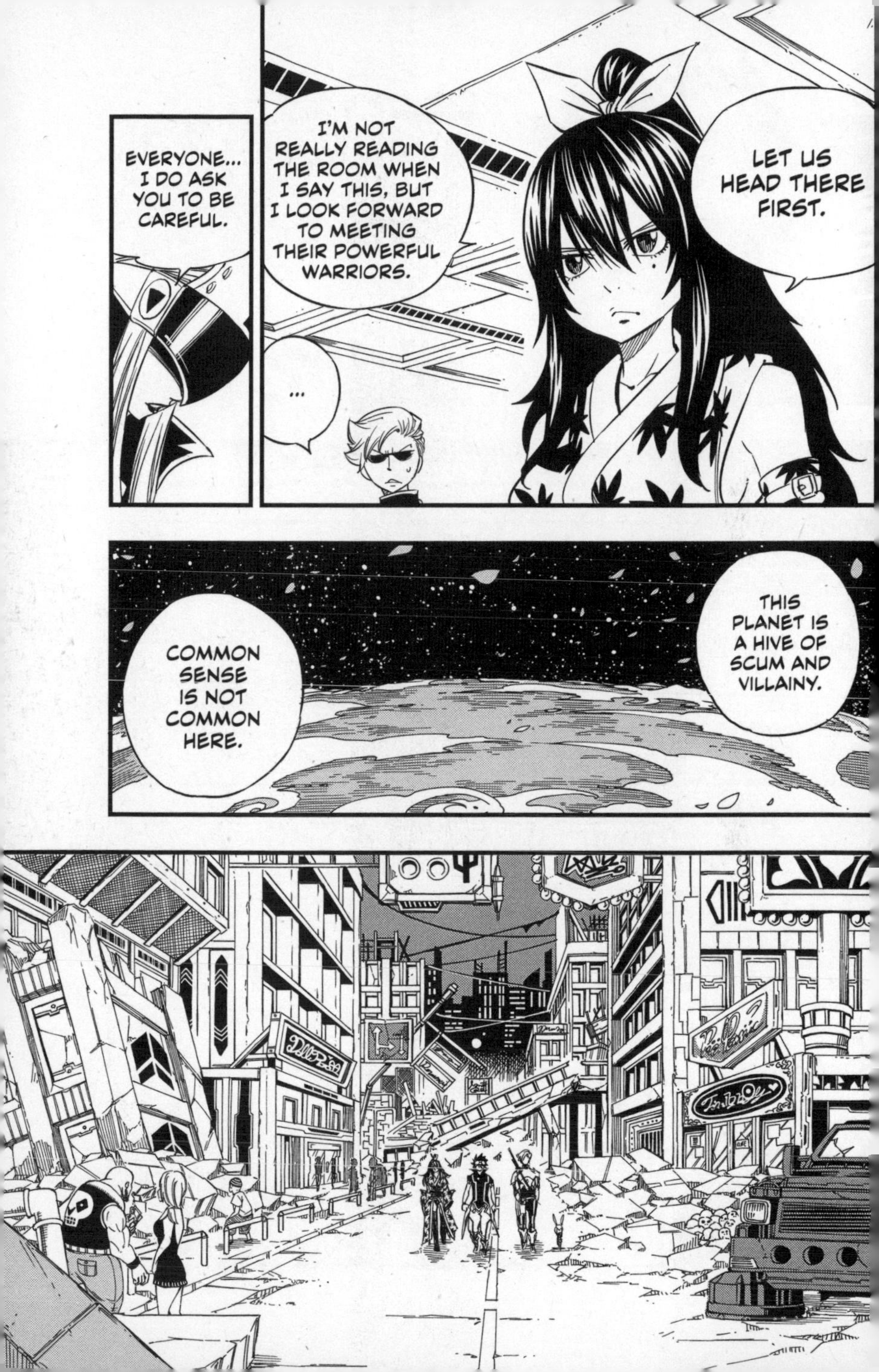
LET US HEAD THERE FIRST.
I'M NOT REALLY READING THE ROOM WHEN I SAY THIS, BUT I LOOK FORWARD TO MEETING THEIR POWERFUL WARRIORS.
...
EVERYONE... I DO ASK YOU TO BE CAREFUL.
THIS PLANET IS A HIVE OF SCUM AND VILLAINY.
COMMON SENSE IS NOT COMMON HERE.

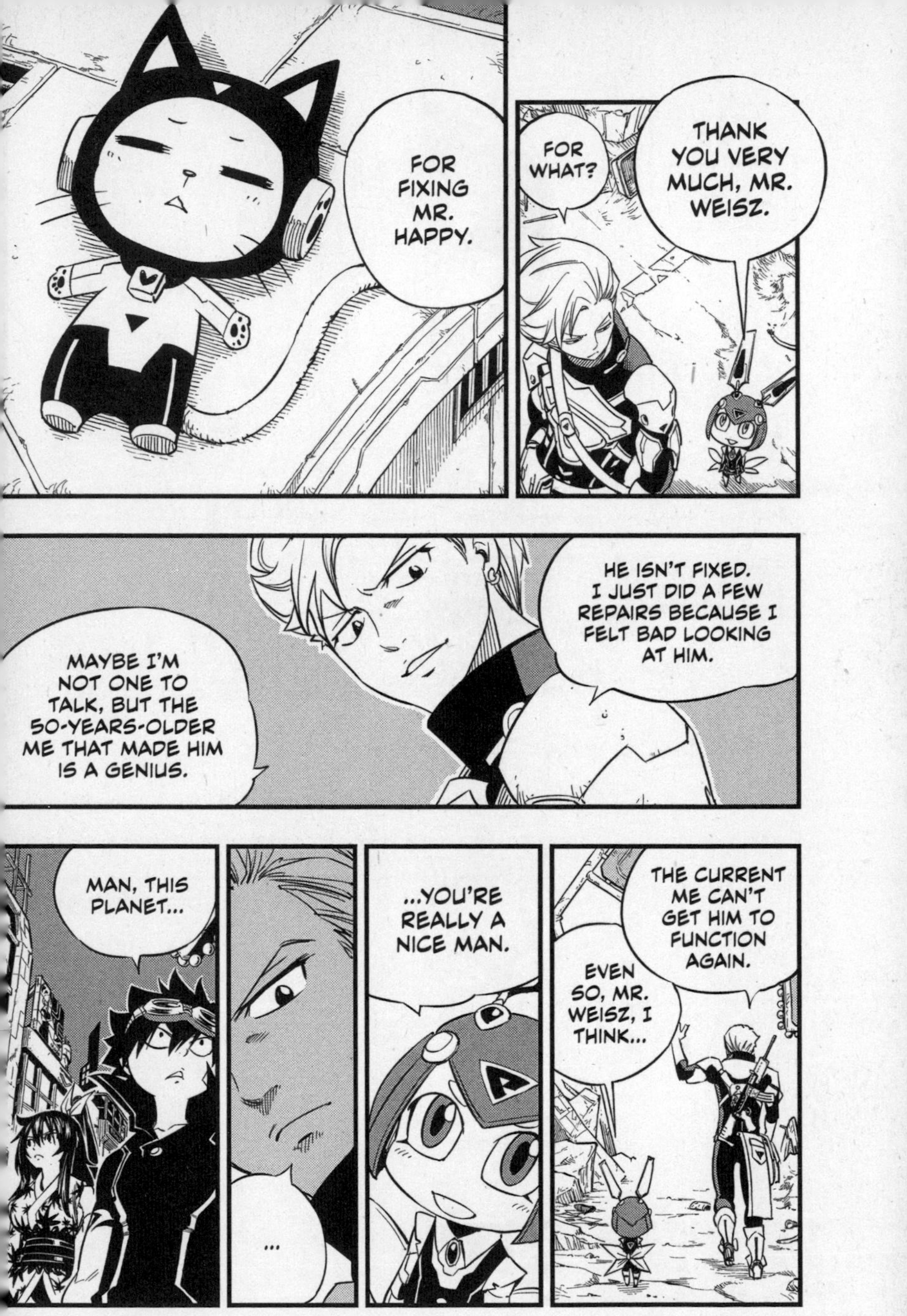
THANK YOU VERY MUCH, MR. WEISZ.
FOR WHAT?
FOR FIXING MR. HAPPY.
HE ISN'T FIXED. I JUST DID A FEW REPAIRS BECAUSE I FELT BAD LOOKING AT HIM.
MAYBE I'M NOT ONE TO TALK, BUT THE 50-YEARS-OLDER ME THAT MADE HIM IS A GENIUS.
THE CURRENT ME CAN'T GET HIM TO FUNCTION AGAIN.
EVEN SO, MR. WEISZ, I THINK...
...YOU'RE REALLY A NICE MAN.
...
MAN, THIS PLANET...

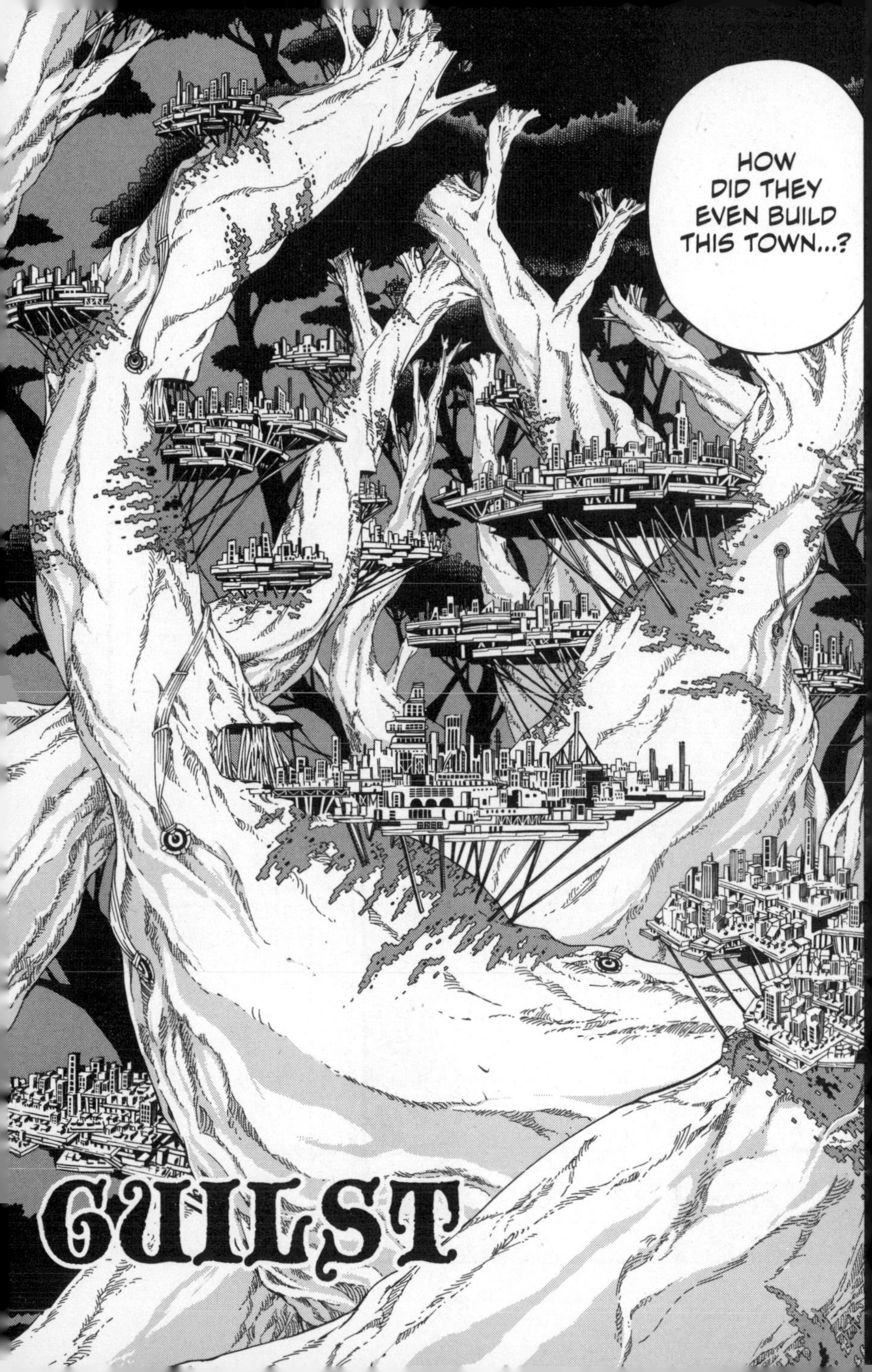
HOW DID THEY EVEN BUILD THIS TOWN...?
GUILST

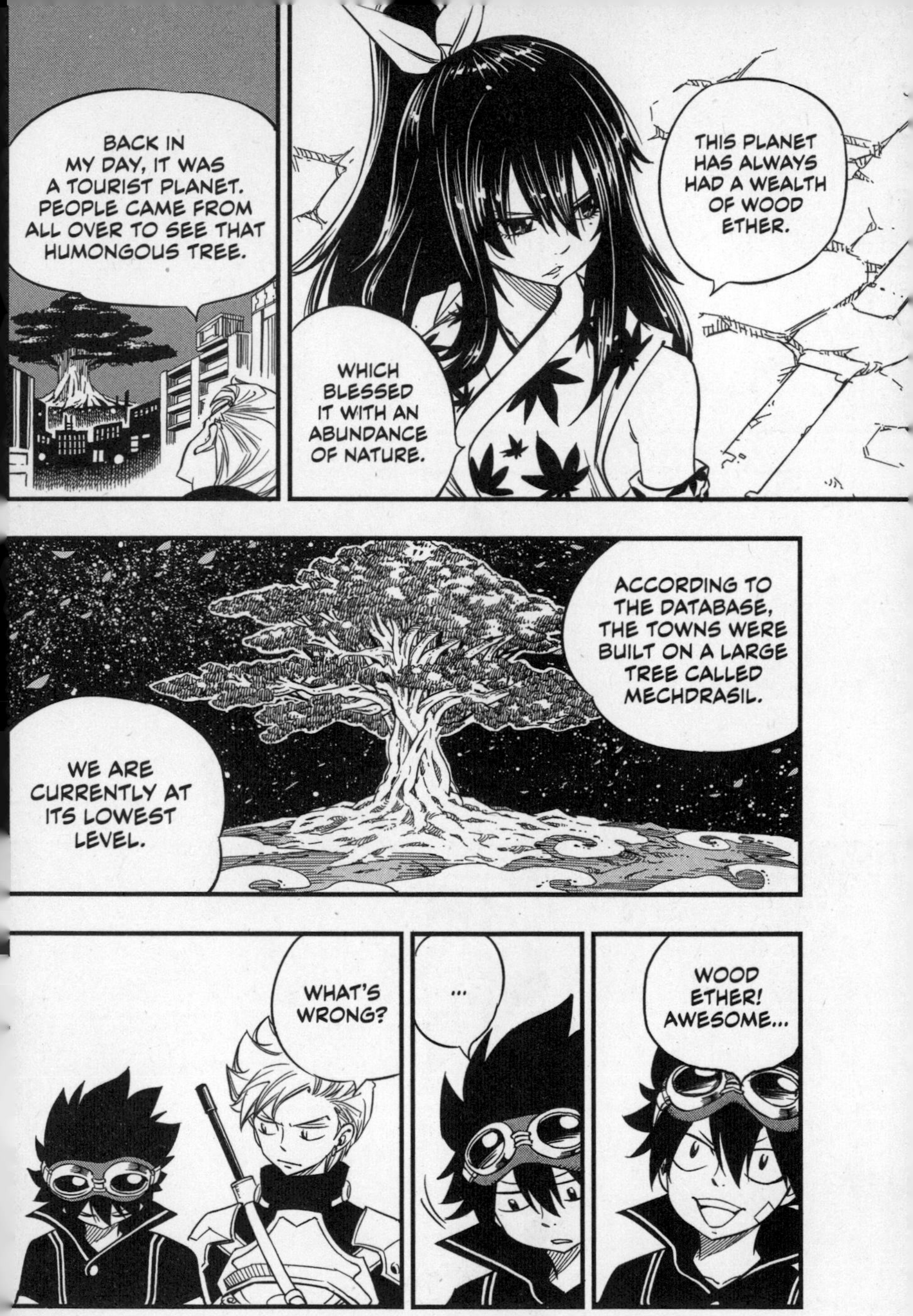
THIS PLANET HAS ALWAYS HAD A WEALTH OF WOOD ETHER.
WHICH BLESSED IT WITH AN ABUNDANCE OF NATURE.
BACK IN MY DAY, IT WAS A TOURIST PLANET. PEOPLE CAME FROM ALL OVER TO SEE THAT HUMONGOUS TREE.
ACCORDING TO THE DATABASE, THE TOWNS WERE BUILT ON A LARGE TREE CALLED MECHDRASIL.
WE ARE CURRENTLY AT ITS LOWEST LEVEL.
WOOD ETHER! AWESOME...
...
WHAT'S WRONG?

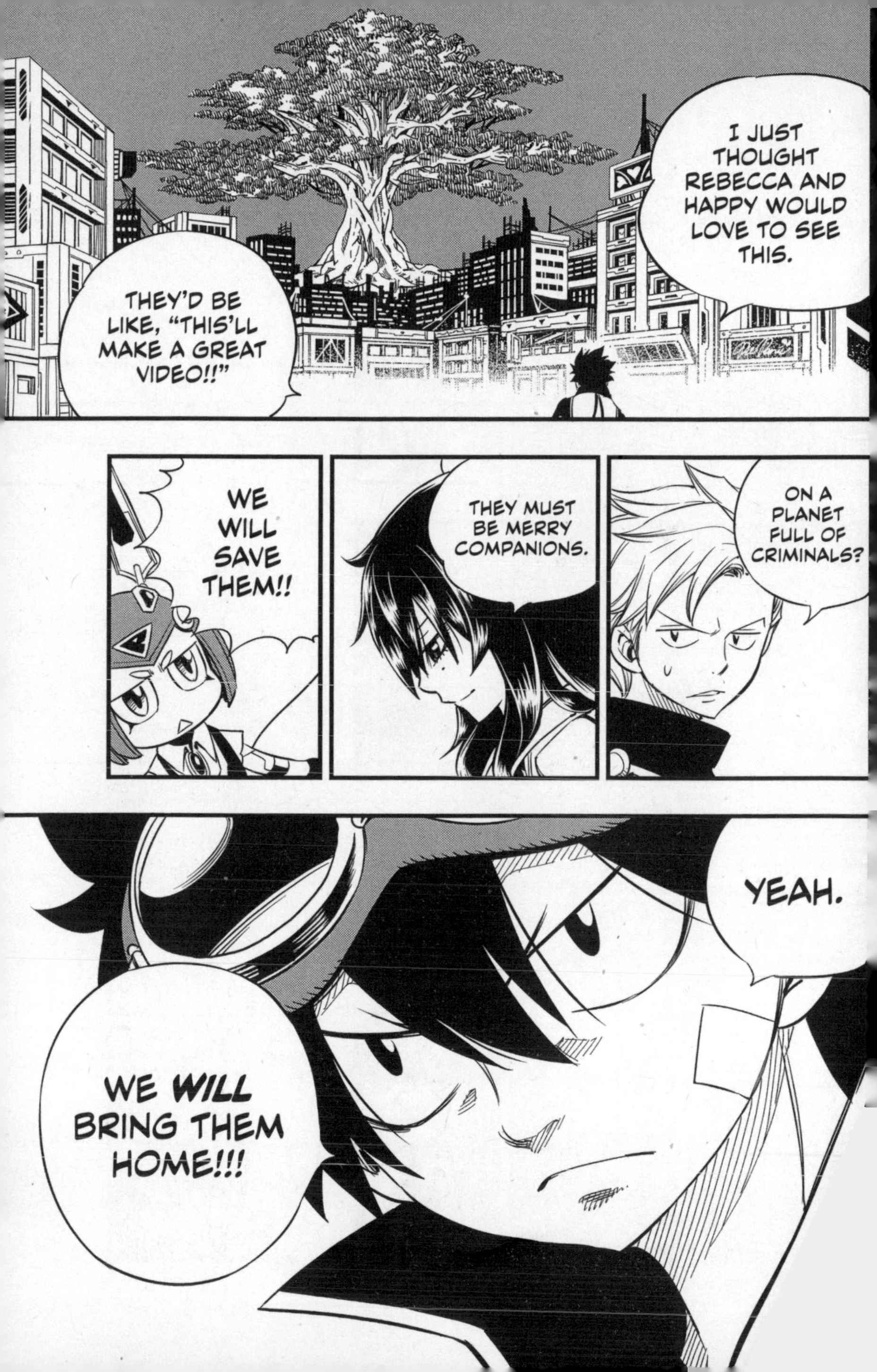
I JUST THOUGHT REBECCA AND HAPPY WOULD LOVE TO SEE THIS.
THEY'D BE LIKE, "THIS'LL MAKE A GREAT VIDEO!!"
ON A PLANET FULL OF CRIMINALS?
THEY MUST BE MERRY COMPANIONS.
WE WILL SAVE THEM!!
YEAH.
WE *WILL* BRING THEM HOME!!!

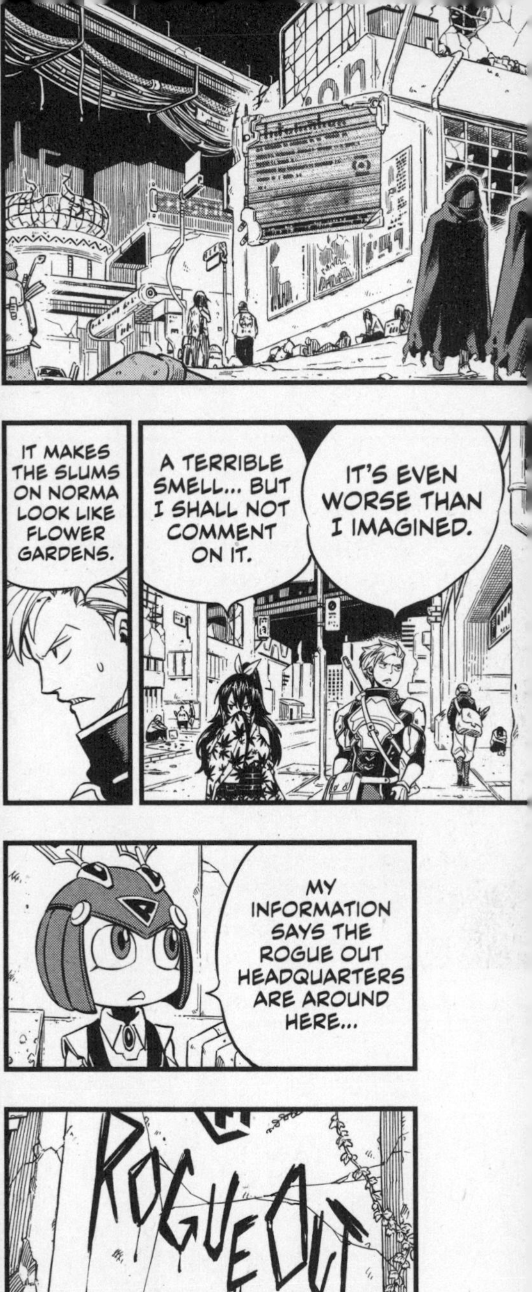
IT'S EVEN WORSE THAN I IMAGINED.
A TERRIBLE SMELL... BUT I SHALL NOT COMMENT ON IT.
IT MAKES THE SLUMS ON NORMA LOOK LIKE FLOWER GARDENS.
MY INFORMATION SAYS THE ROGUE OUT HEADQUARTERS ARE AROUND HERE...
ROGUE OUT
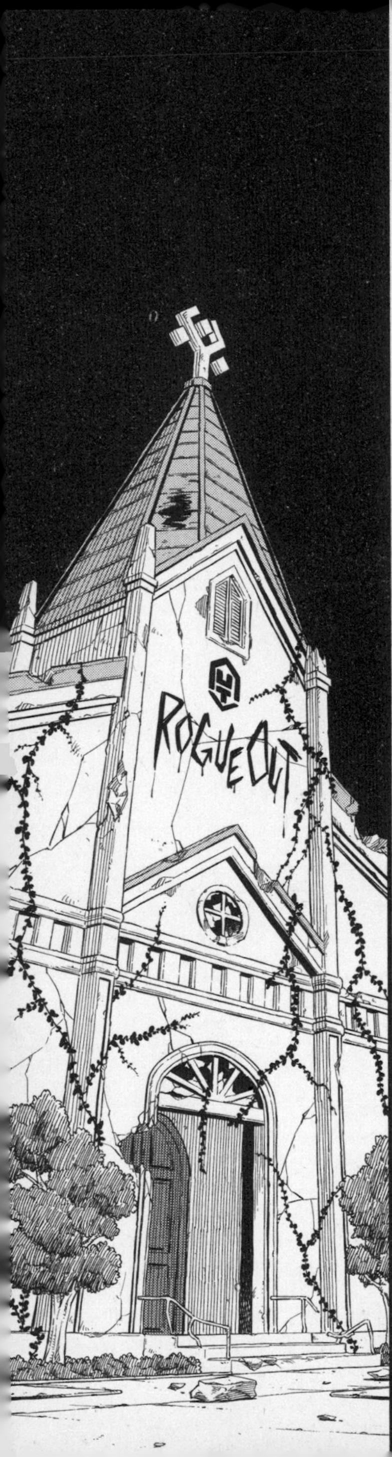
ROGUE OUT

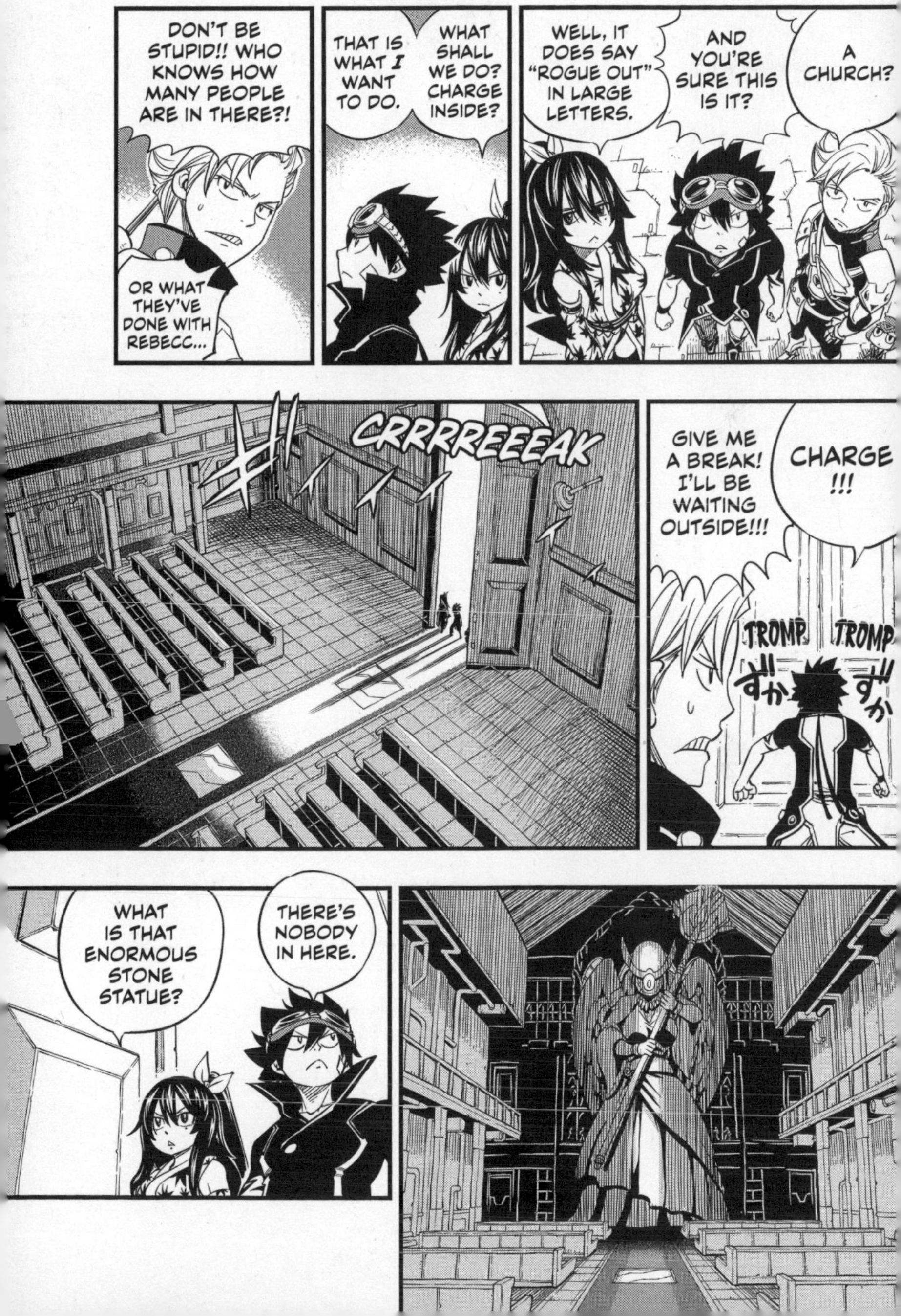
A CHURCH?
AND YOU'RE SURE THIS IS IT?
WELL, IT DOES SAY "ROGUE OUT" IN LARGE LETTERS.
WHAT SHALL WE DO? CHARGE INSIDE?
THAT IS WHAT *I* WANT TO DO.
DON'T BE STUPID!! WHO KNOWS HOW MANY PEOPLE ARE IN THERE?!
OR WHAT THEY'VE DONE WITH REBECC...
CHARGE!!!
GIVE ME A BREAK! I'LL BE WAITING OUTSIDE!!!
TROMP TROMP
ずかずか
CRRRREEEAK
THERE'S NOBODY IN HERE.
WHAT IS THAT ENORMOUS STONE STATUE?

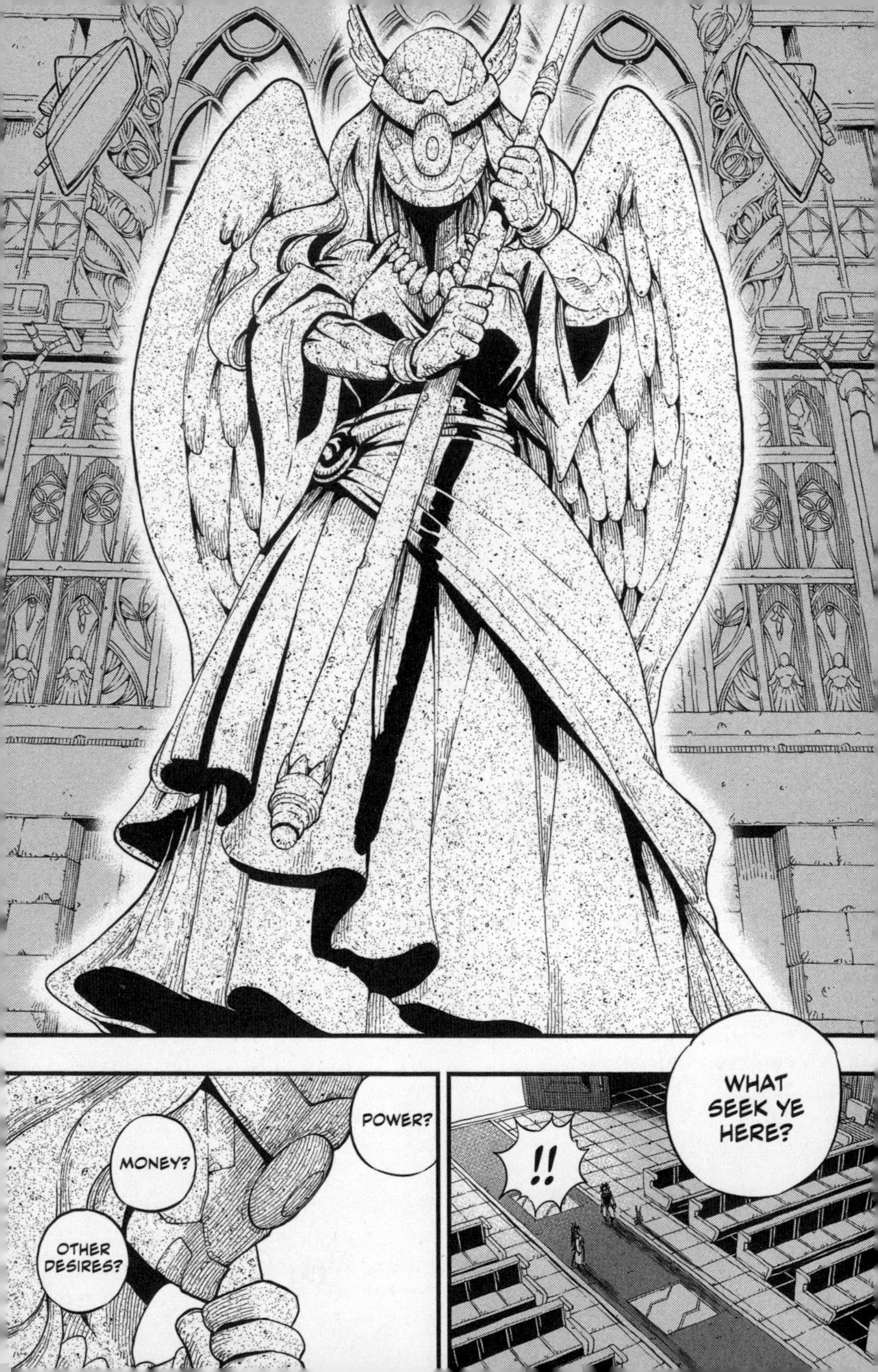
WHAT SEEK YE HERE?
!!
POWER?
MONEY?
OTHER DESIRES?

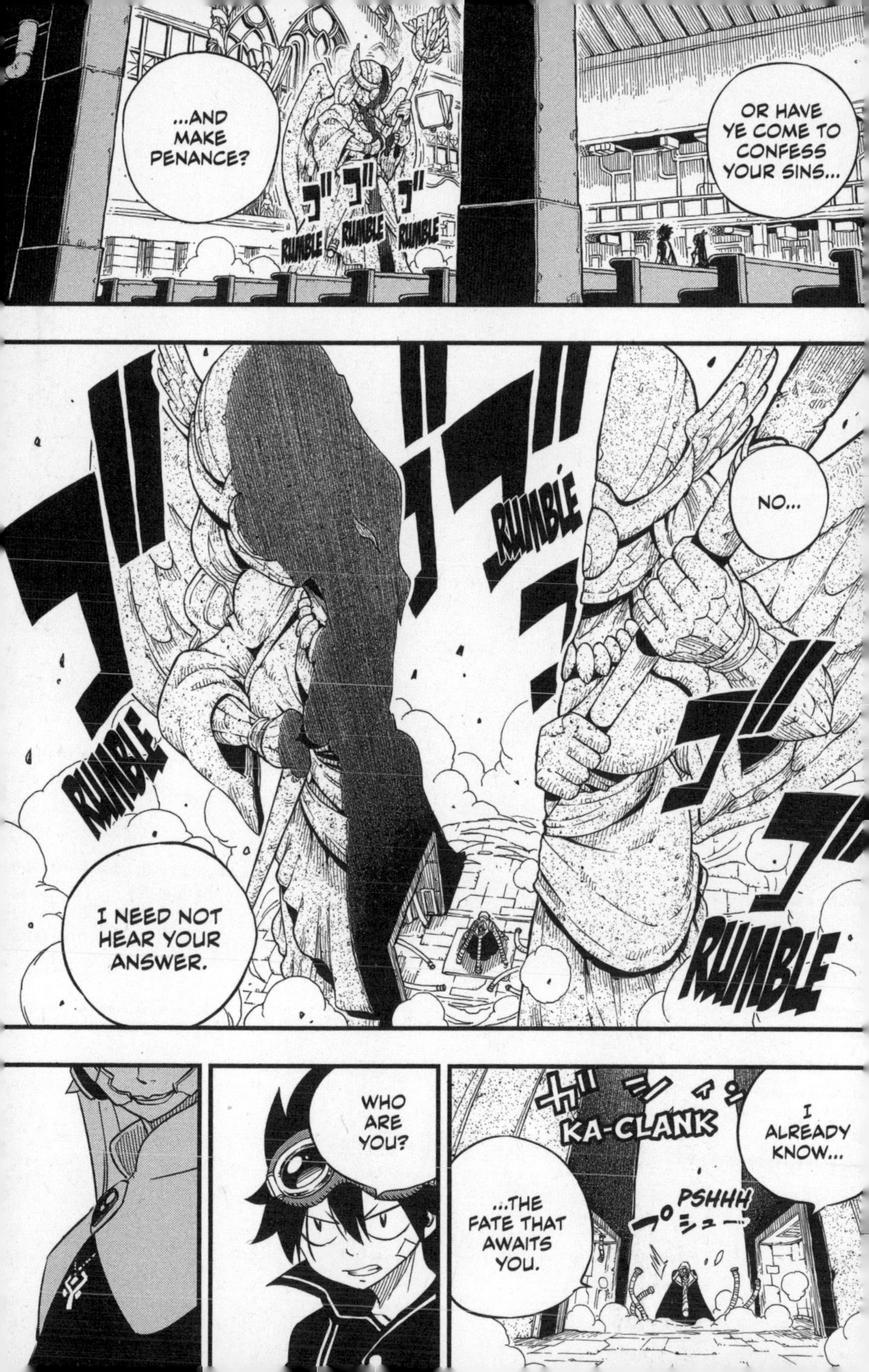
OR HAVE YE COME TO CONFESS YOUR SINS...
...AND MAKE PENANCE?
RUMBLE RUMBLE RUMBLE
NO...
RUMBLE
RUMBLE
RUMBLE
I NEED NOT HEAR YOUR ANSWER.
I ALREADY KNOW...
KA-CLANK
...THE FATE THAT AWAITS YOU.
PSHHH
WHO ARE YOU?

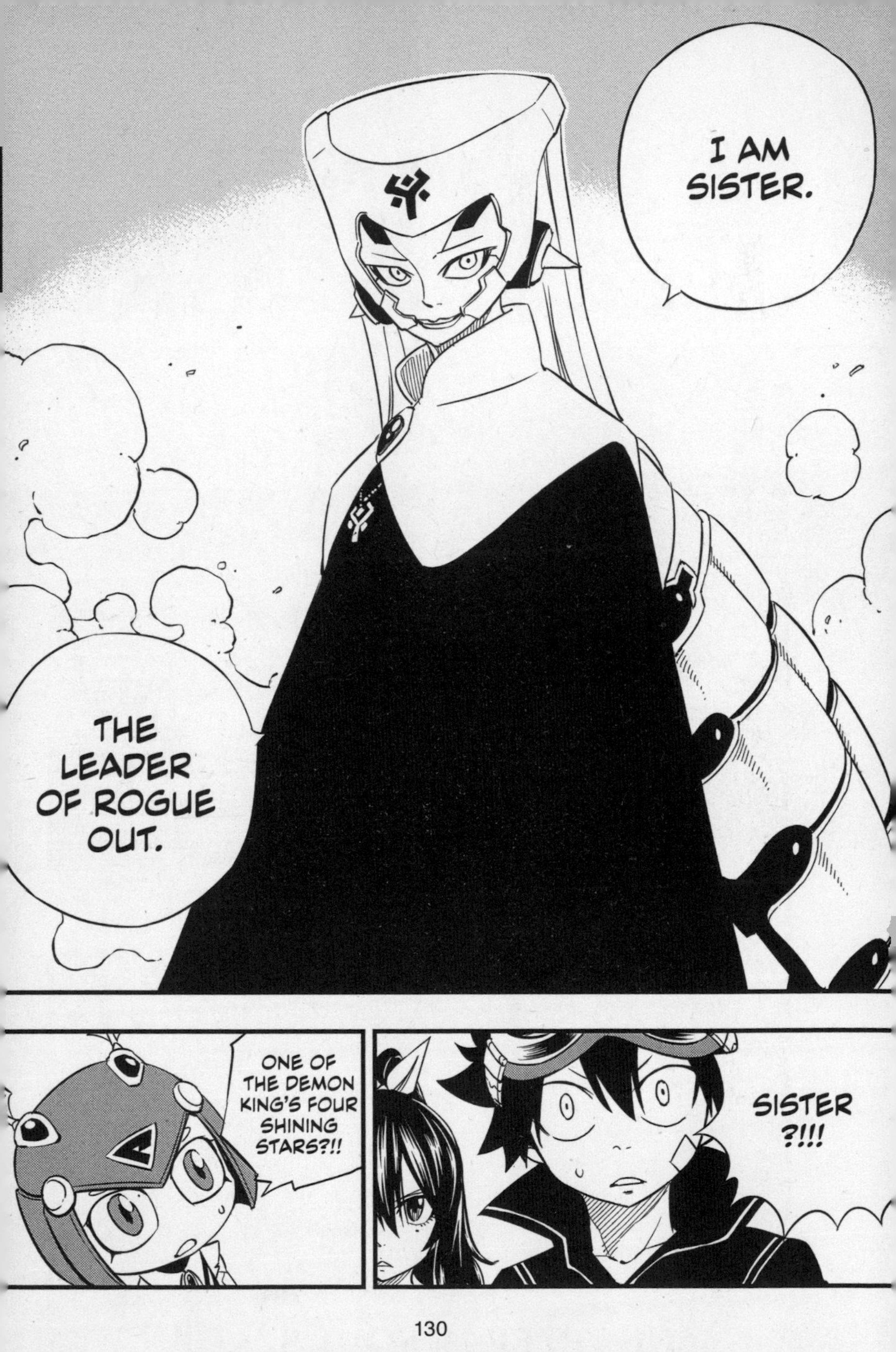
I AM SISTER.
THE LEADER OF ROGUE OUT.
SISTER ?!!!
ONE OF THE DEMON KING'S FOUR SHINING STARS?!!

EDENS ZERO

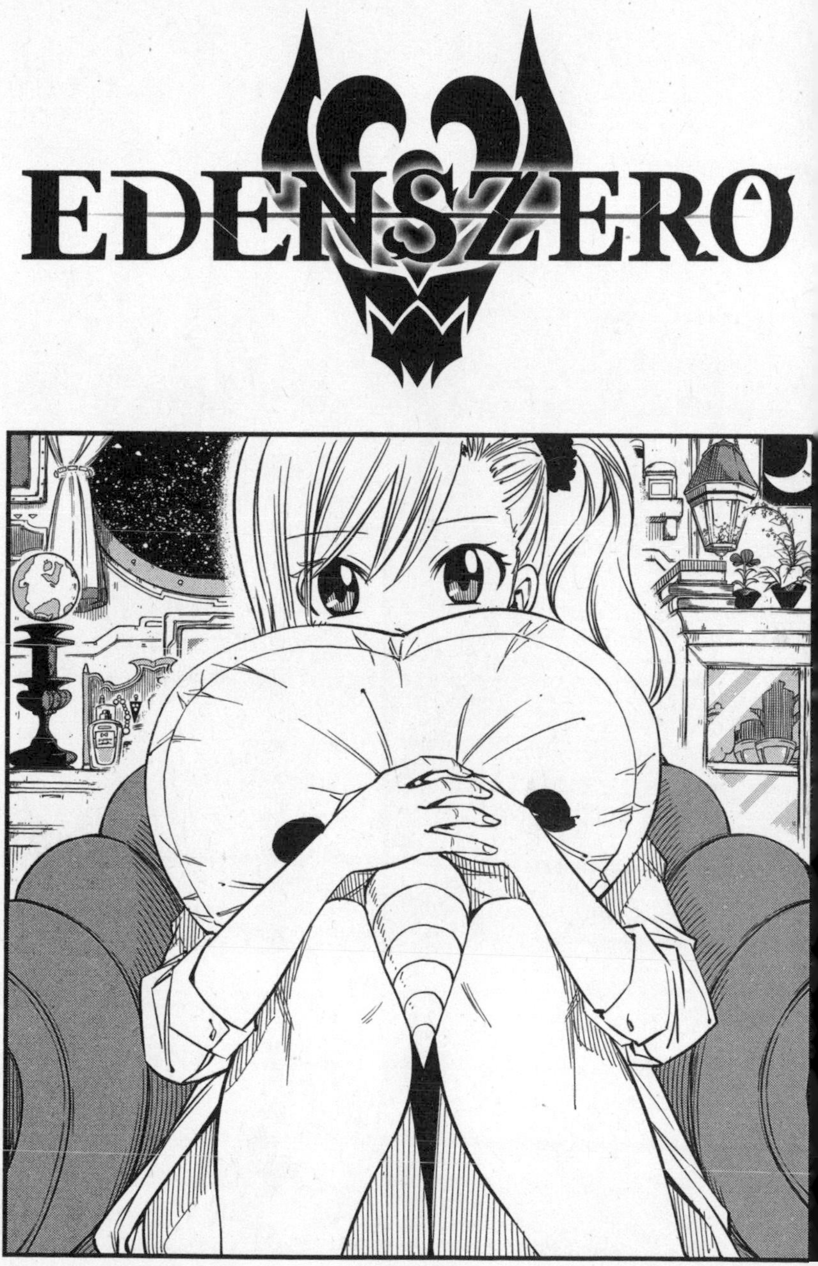

CHAPTER 21: SOUL BLADE

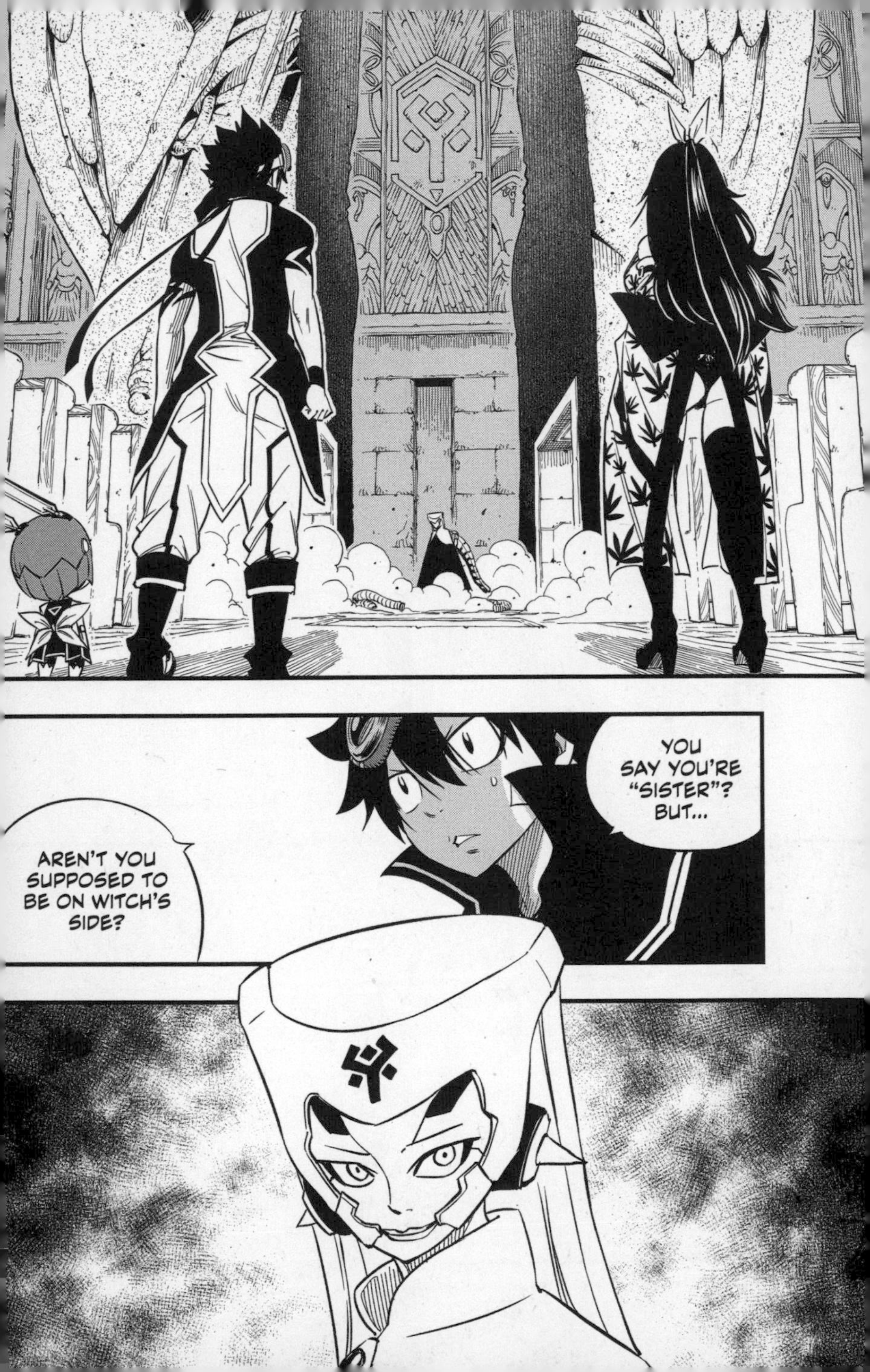
YOU SAY YOU'RE "SISTER"? BUT...
AREN'T YOU SUPPOSED TO BE ON WITCH'S SIDE?

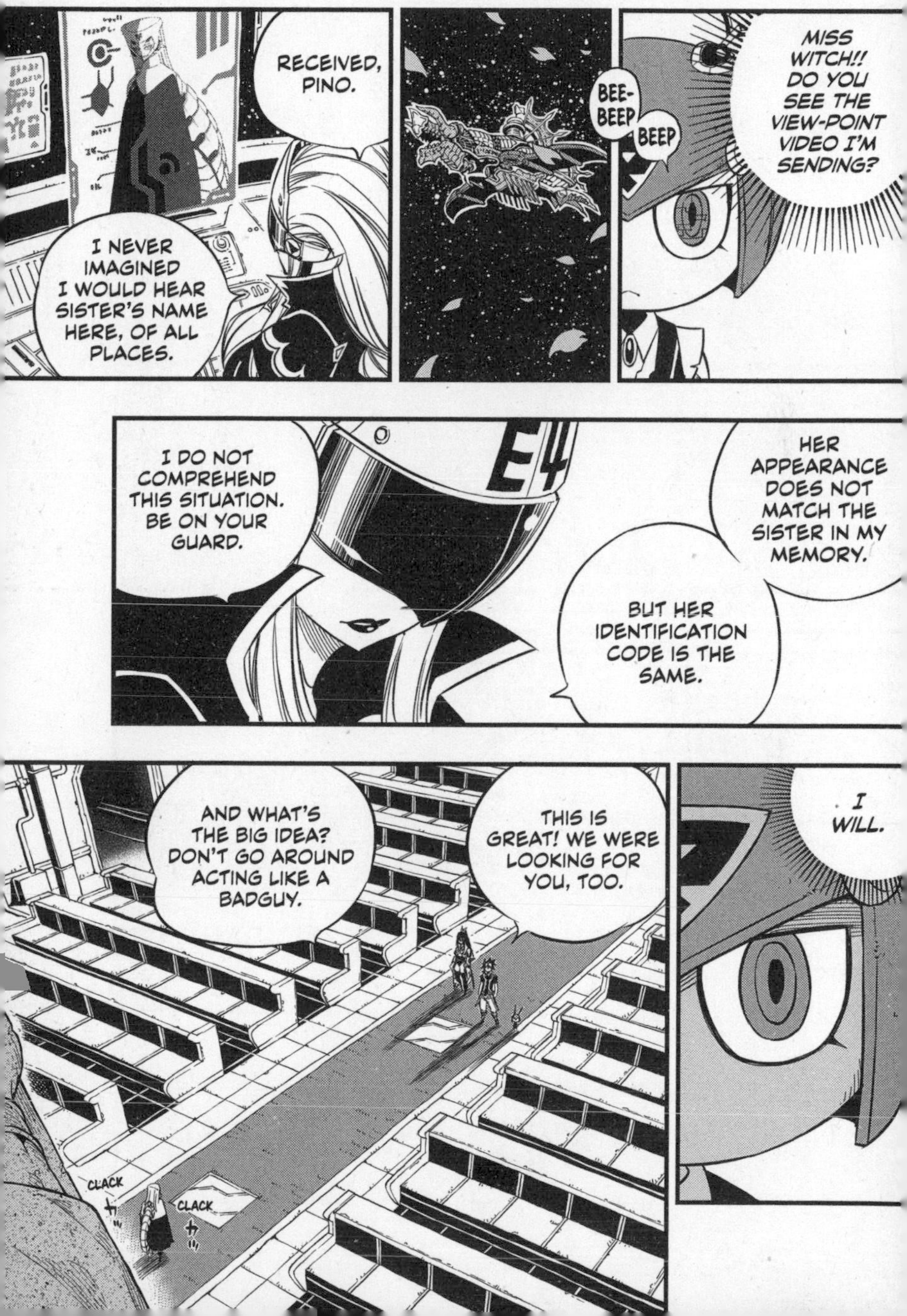
MISS WITCH!! DO YOU SEE THE VIEW-POINT VIDEO I'M SENDING?
BEE-BEEP
BEEP
RECEIVED, PINO.
I NEVER IMAGINED I WOULD HEAR SISTER'S NAME HERE, OF ALL PLACES.
HER APPEARANCE DOES NOT MATCH THE SISTER IN MY MEMORY.
BUT HER IDENTIFICATION CODE IS THE SAME.
I DO NOT COMPREHEND THIS SITUATION. BE ON YOUR GUARD.
I WILL.
THIS IS GREAT! WE WERE LOOKING FOR YOU, TOO.
AND WHAT'S THE BIG IDEA? DON'T GO AROUND ACTING LIKE A BADGUY.
CLACK
CLACK

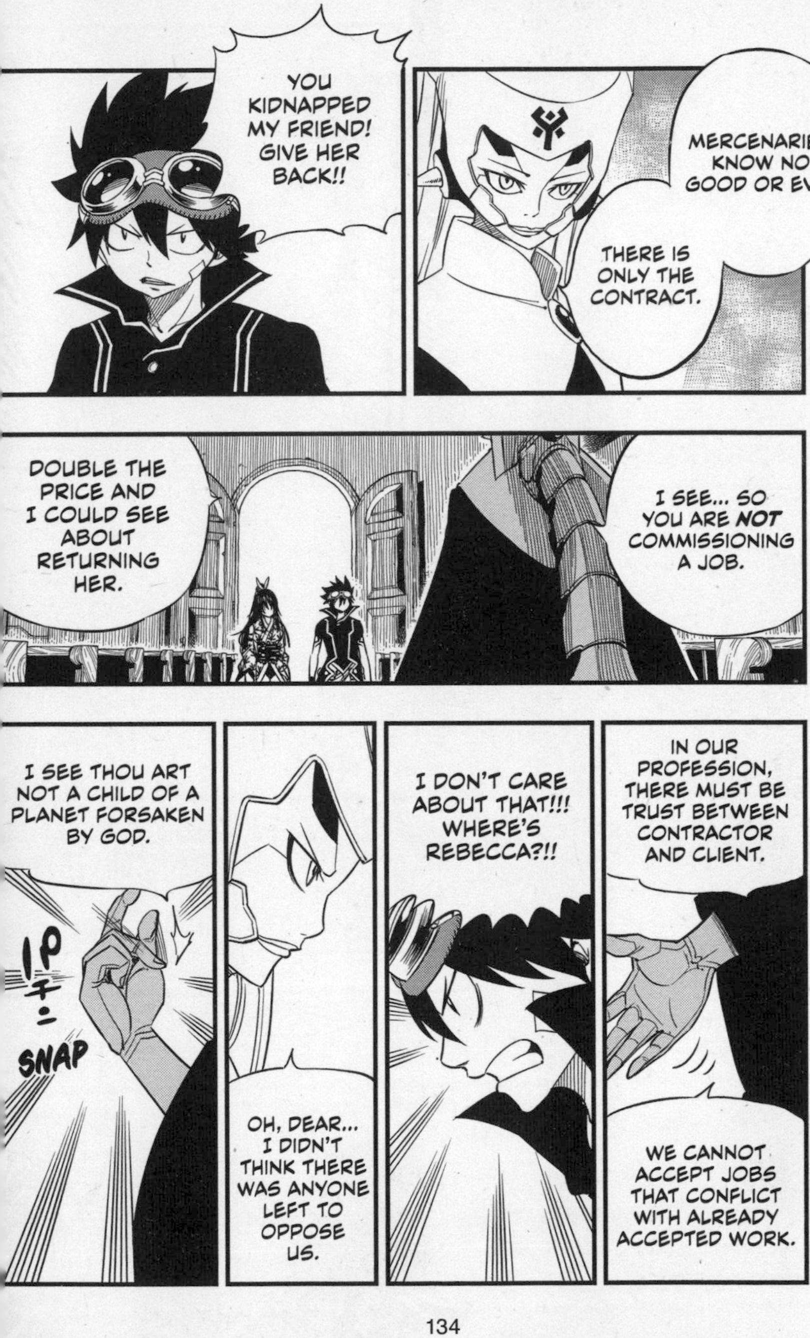
MERCENARIES KNOW NO GOOD OR EVIL.
THERE IS ONLY THE CONTRACT.
YOU KIDNAPPED MY FRIEND! GIVE HER BACK!!
I SEE... SO YOU ARE ***NOT*** COMMISSIONING A JOB.
DOUBLE THE PRICE AND I COULD SEE ABOUT RETURNING HER.
IN OUR PROFESSION, THERE MUST BE TRUST BETWEEN CONTRACTOR AND CLIENT.
WE CANNOT ACCEPT JOBS THAT CONFLICT WITH ALREADY ACCEPTED WORK.
I DON'T CARE ABOUT THAT!!! WHERE'S REBECCA?!!
OH, DEAR... I DIDN'T THINK THERE WAS ANYONE LEFT TO OPPOSE US.
I SEE THOU ART NOT A CHILD OF A PLANET FORSAKEN BY GOD.
SNAP

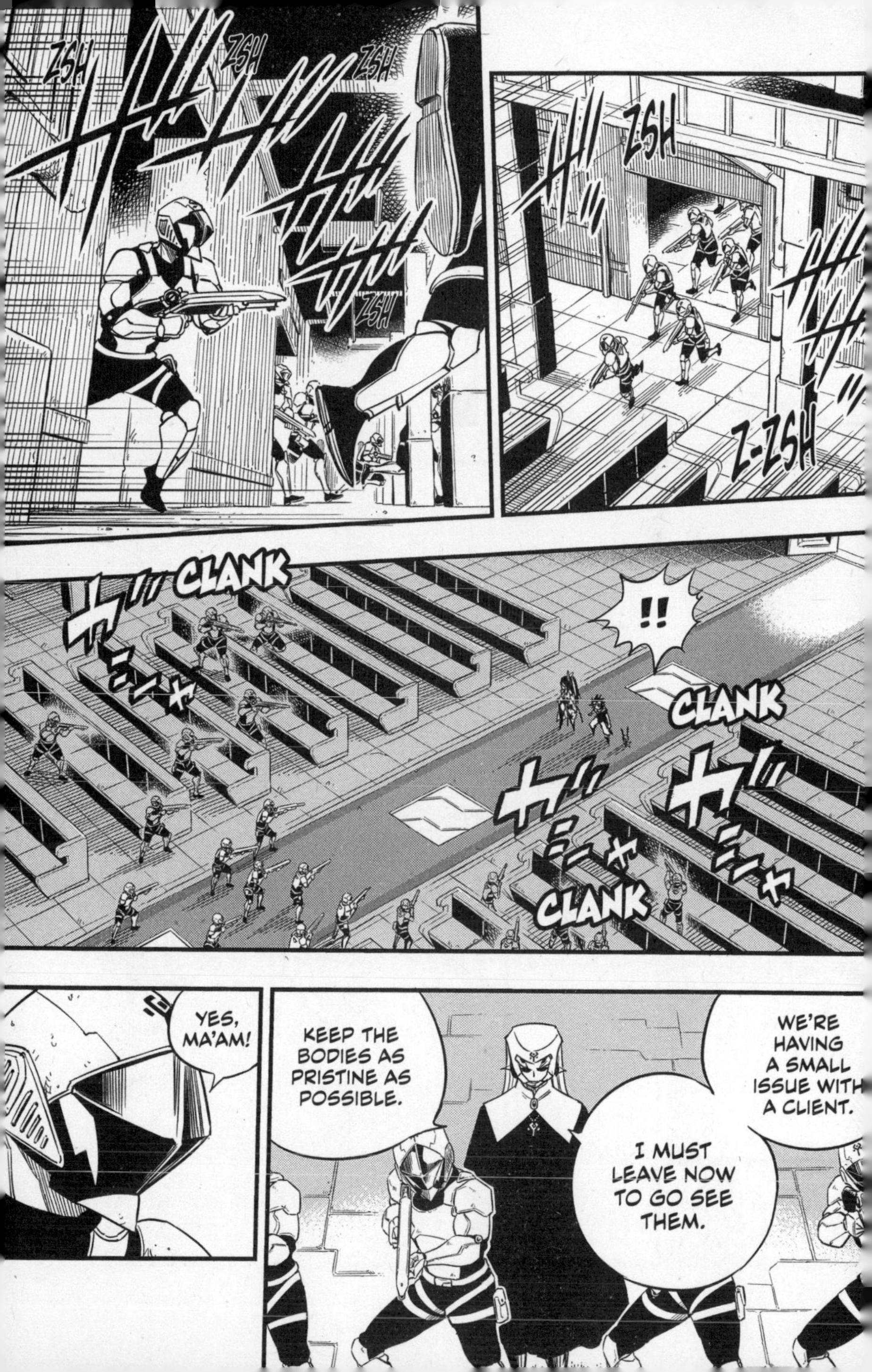
ZSH
Z-ZSH
ZSH
ZSH
ZSH
ZSH
ZSH
!!
CLANK
CLANK
CLANK
WE'RE HAVING A SMALL ISSUE WITH A CLIENT.
I MUST LEAVE NOW TO GO SEE THEM.
KEEP THE BODIES AS PRISTINE AS POSSIBLE.
YES, MA'AM!

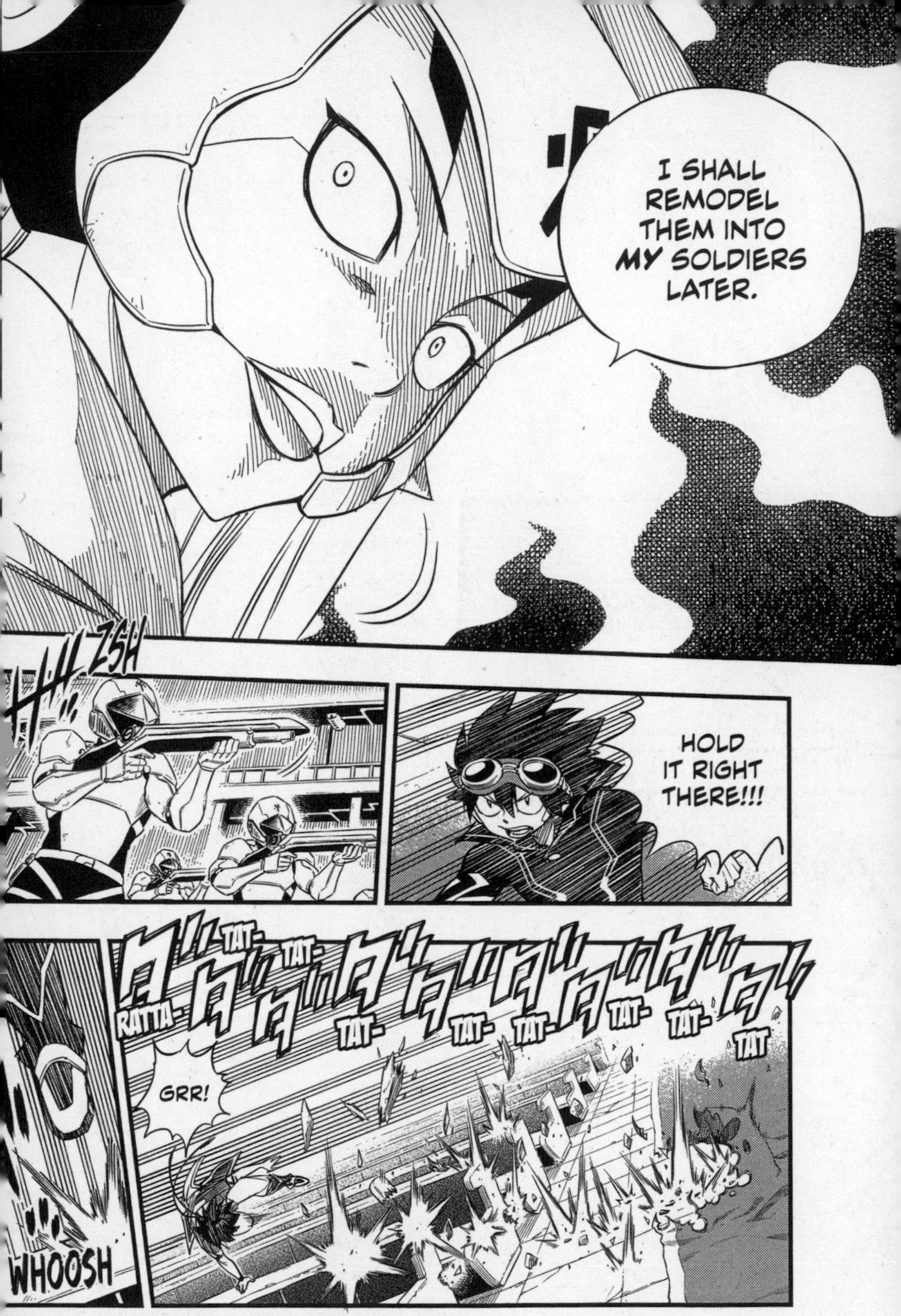
I SHALL REMODEL THEM INTO MY SOLDIERS LATER.
HOLD IT RIGHT THERE!!!
ZSH
RATTA-TAT-TAT-TAT-TAT-TAT-TAT-TAT-TAT
GRR!
WHOOSH

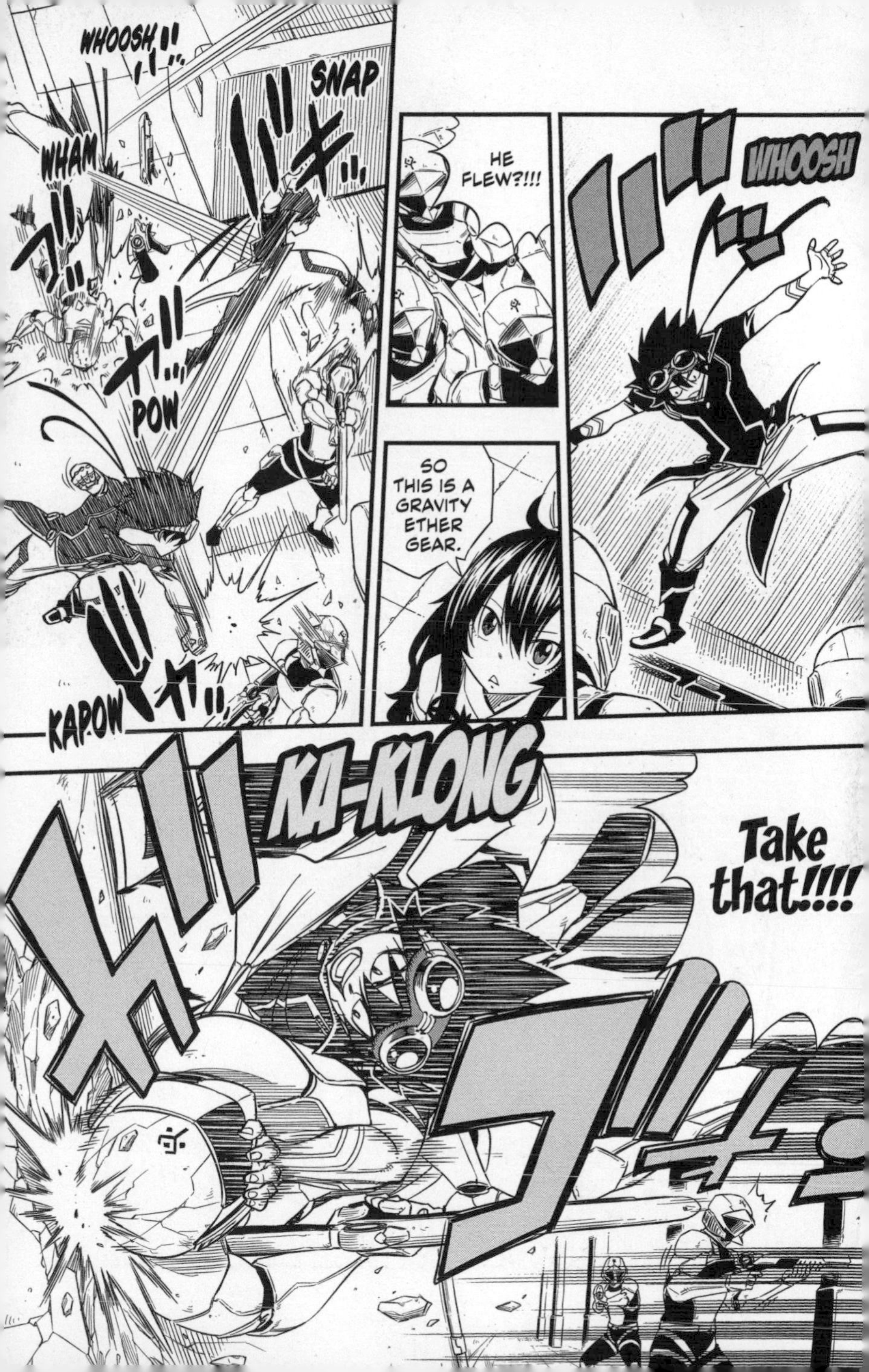
WHOOSH
HE FLEW?!!!
SO THIS IS A GRAVITY ETHER GEAR.
SNAP
WHOOSH
WHAM
POW
KAPOW
Take that!!!!
KA-KLONG

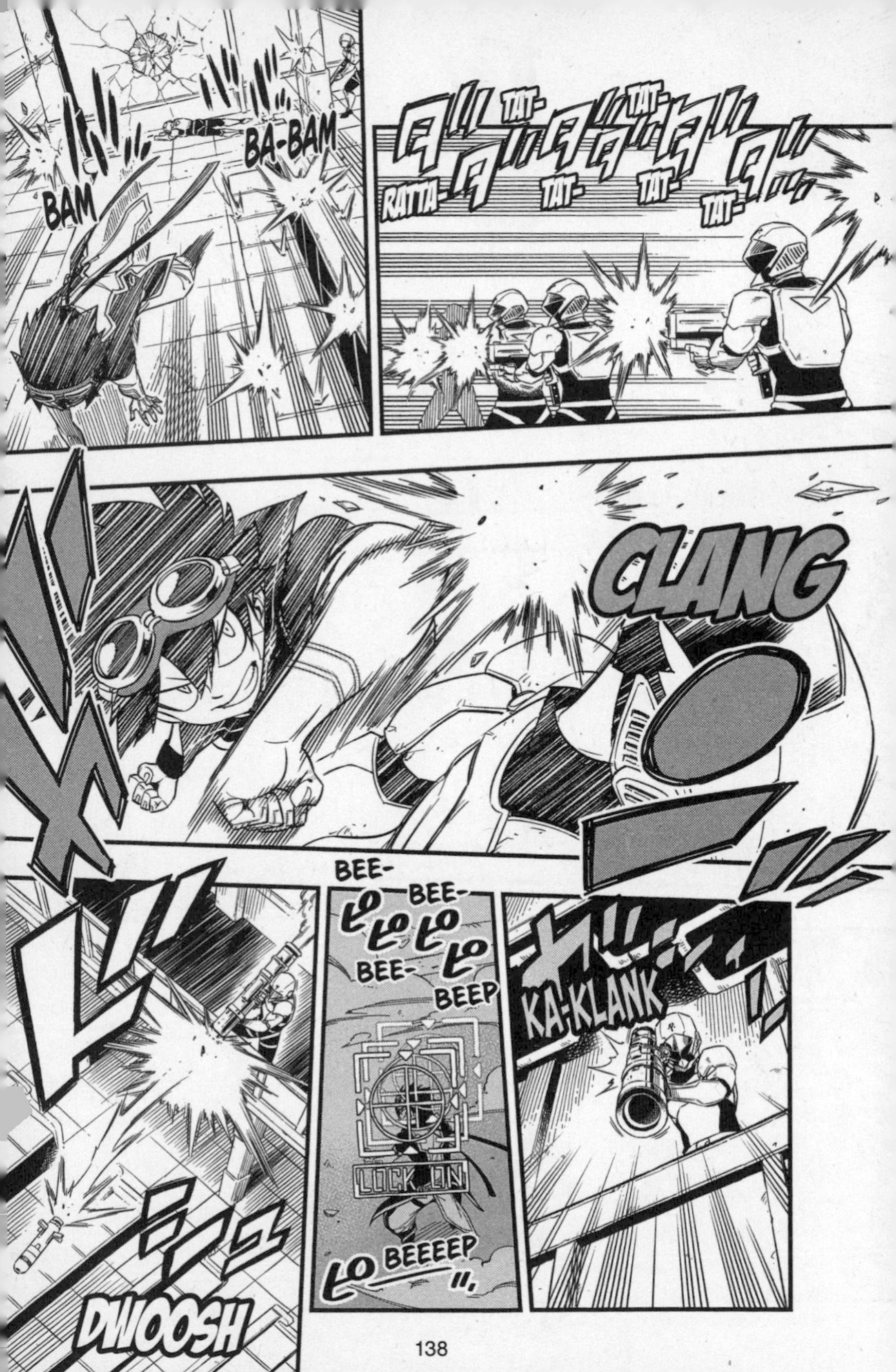
RATTA-TAT-TAT-TAT-TAT-TAT-
BA-BAM
BAM
CLANG
KA-KLANK
BEE-BEE-BEE-BEEP
LOCK ON
BEEEEP
DWOOSH

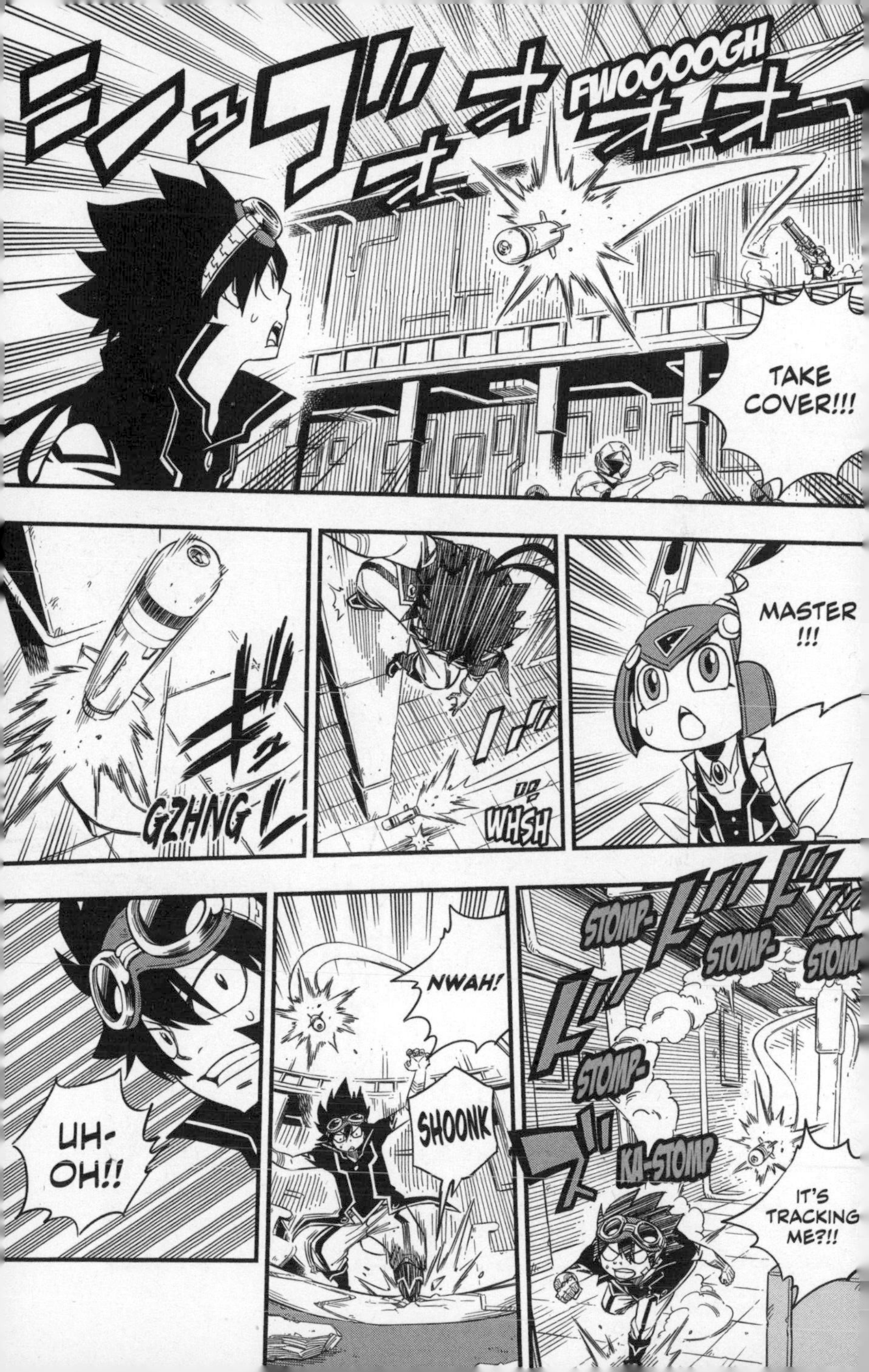
FWOOOOGH
TAKE COVER!!!
MASTER !!!
WHSH
GZHNG
STOMP-
STOMP-
STOMP-
STOMP-
KA-STOMP
IT'S TRACKING ME?!!
NWAH!
SHOONK
UH-OH!!

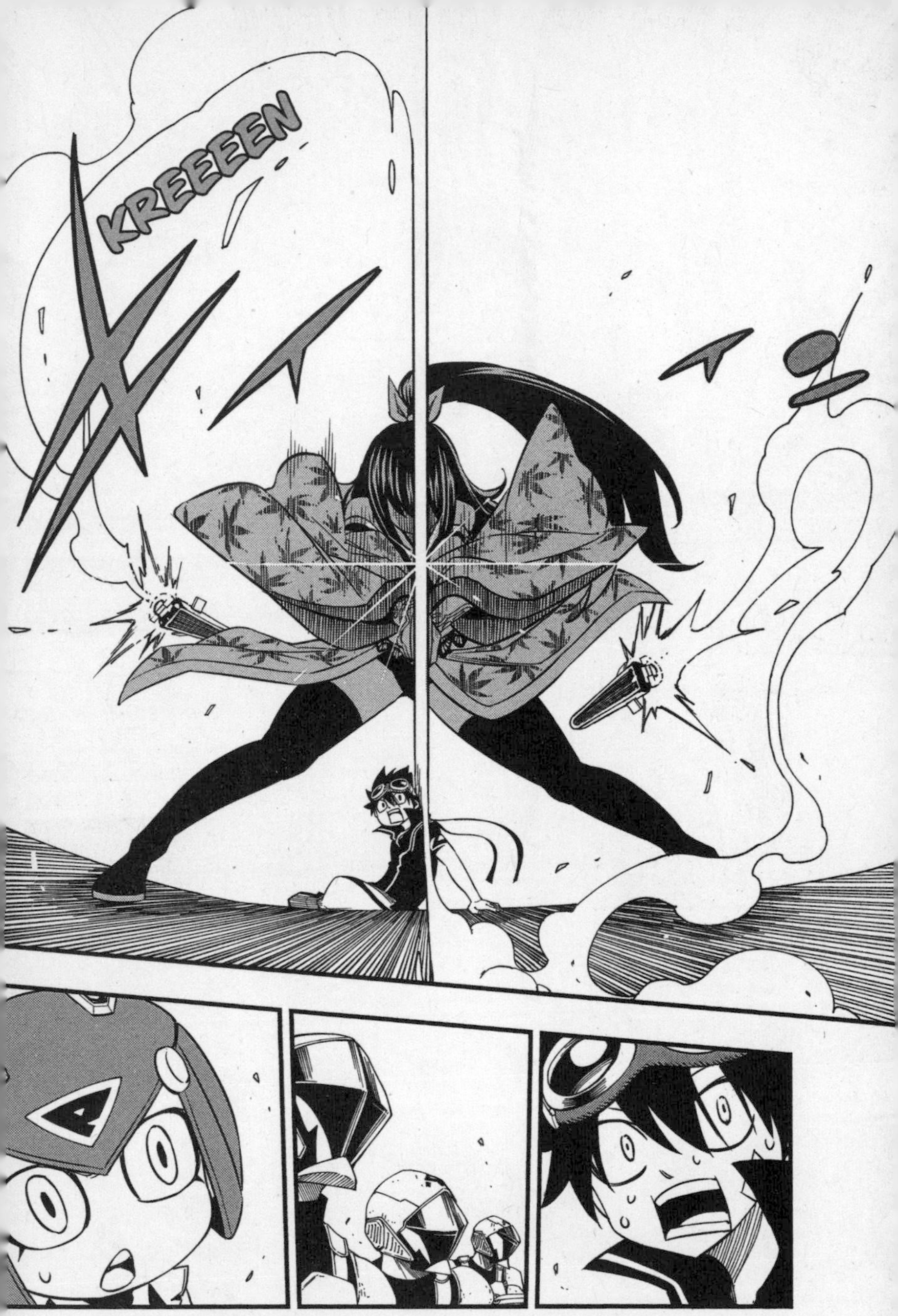
KREEEEN

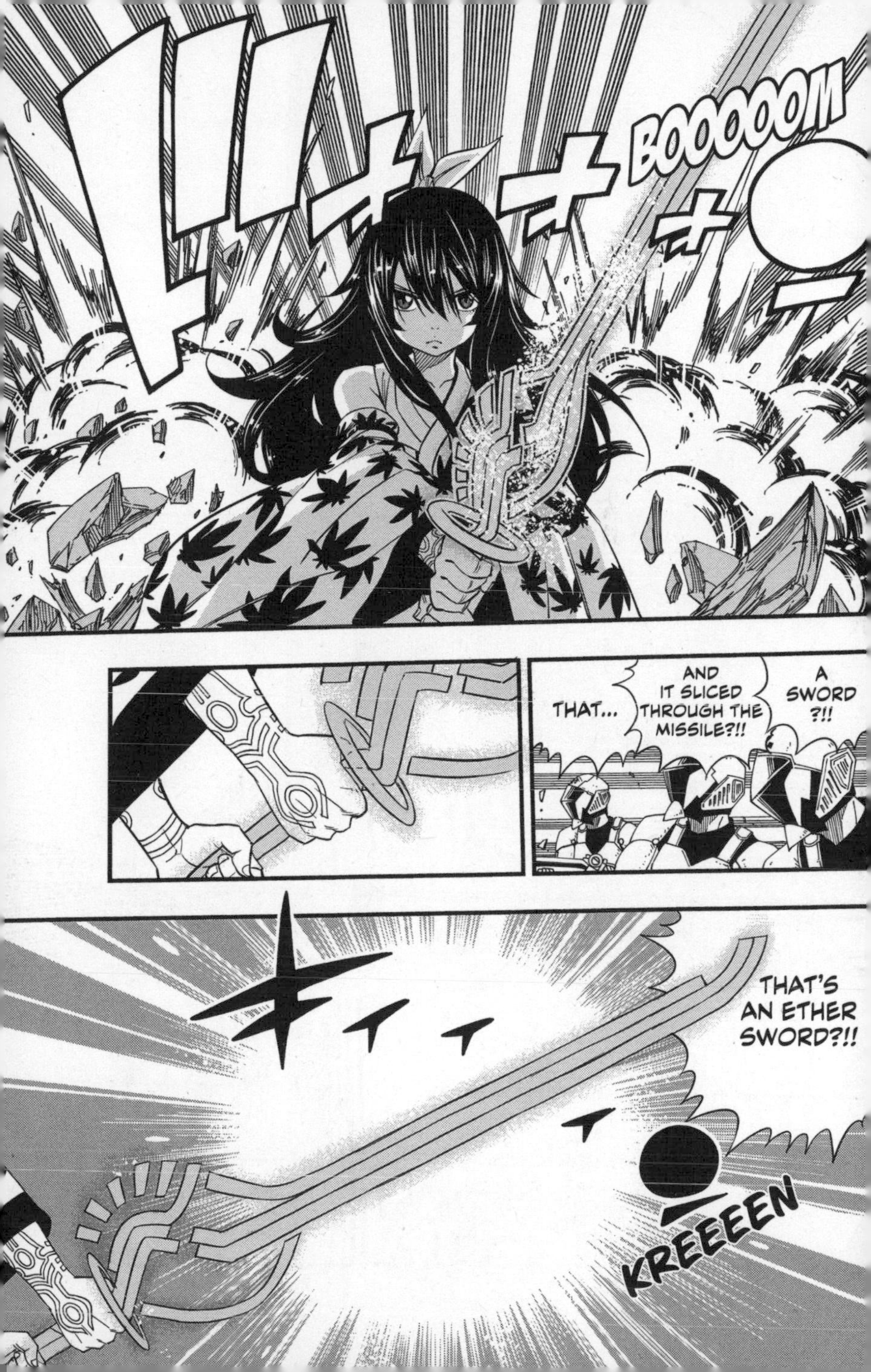
BOOOOOM
A SWORD?!!
AND IT SLICED THROUGH THE MISSILE?!!
THAT...
THAT'S AN ETHER SWORD?!!
KREEEEN

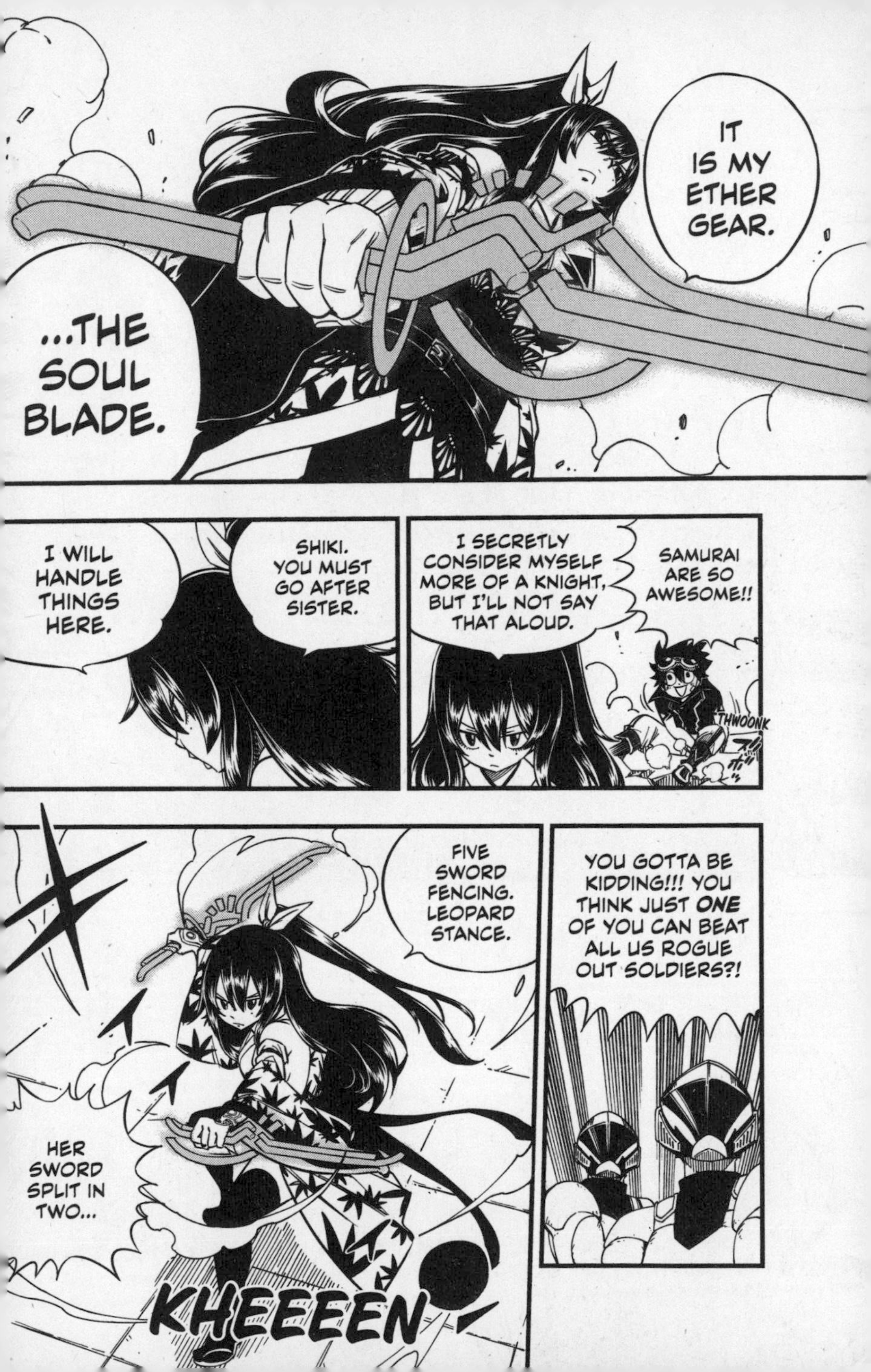
IT IS MY ETHER GEAR.
...THE SOUL BLADE.
SAMURAI ARE SO AWESOME!!
I SECRETLY CONSIDER MYSELF MORE OF A KNIGHT, BUT I'LL NOT SAY THAT ALOUD.
THWOONK
SHIKI. YOU MUST GO AFTER SISTER.
I WILL HANDLE THINGS HERE.
YOU GOTTA BE KIDDING!!! YOU THINK JUST **ONE** OF YOU CAN BEAT ALL US ROGUE OUT SOLDIERS?!
FIVE SWORD FENCING. LEOPARD STANCE.
HER SWORD SPLIT IN TWO...
KHEEEEN

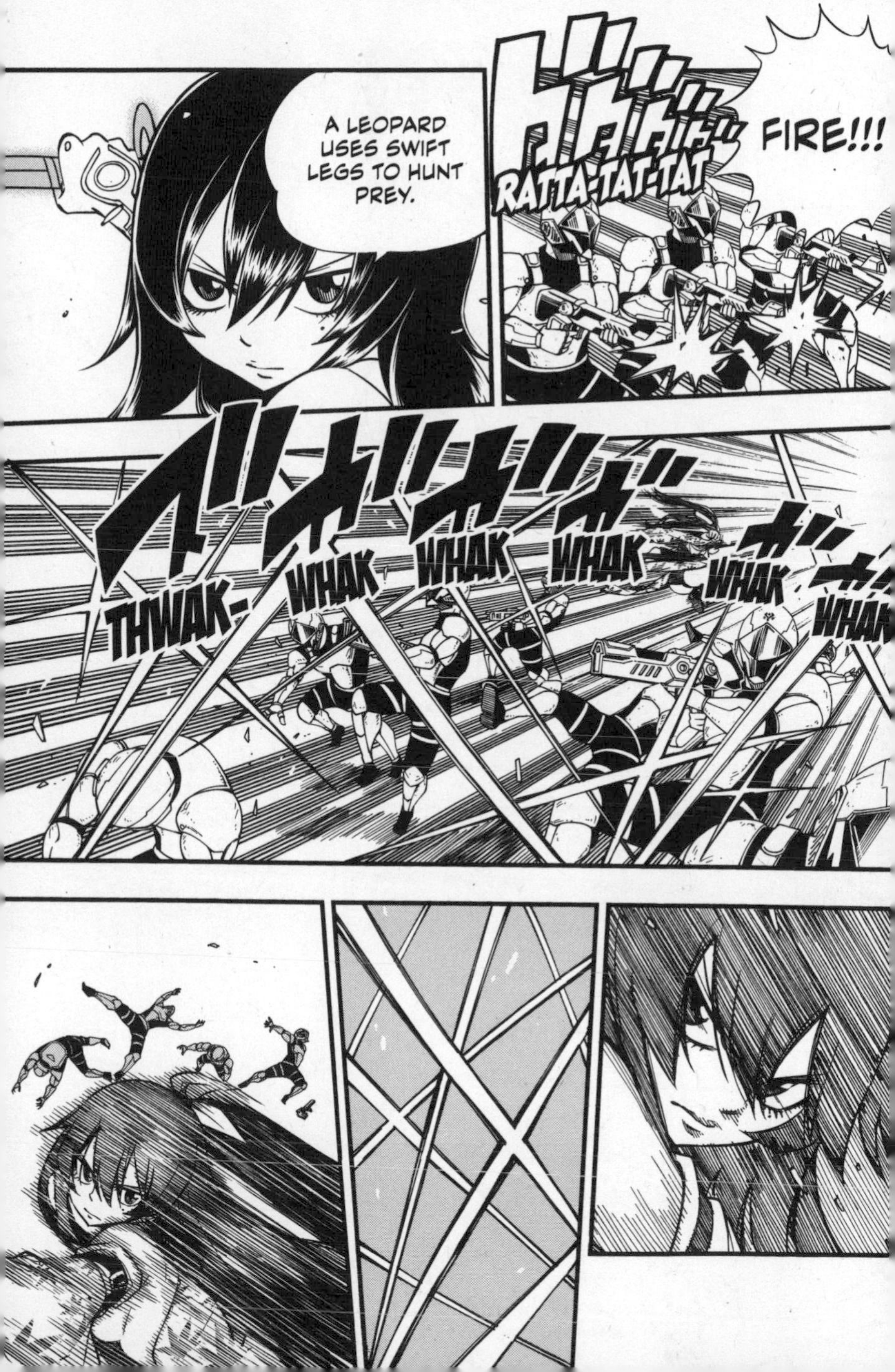
FIRE!!!
RATTA-TAT-TAT
A LEOPARD USES SWIFT LEGS TO HUNT PREY.
WHAK
WHAK
WHAK
WHAK
WHAK
THWAK-

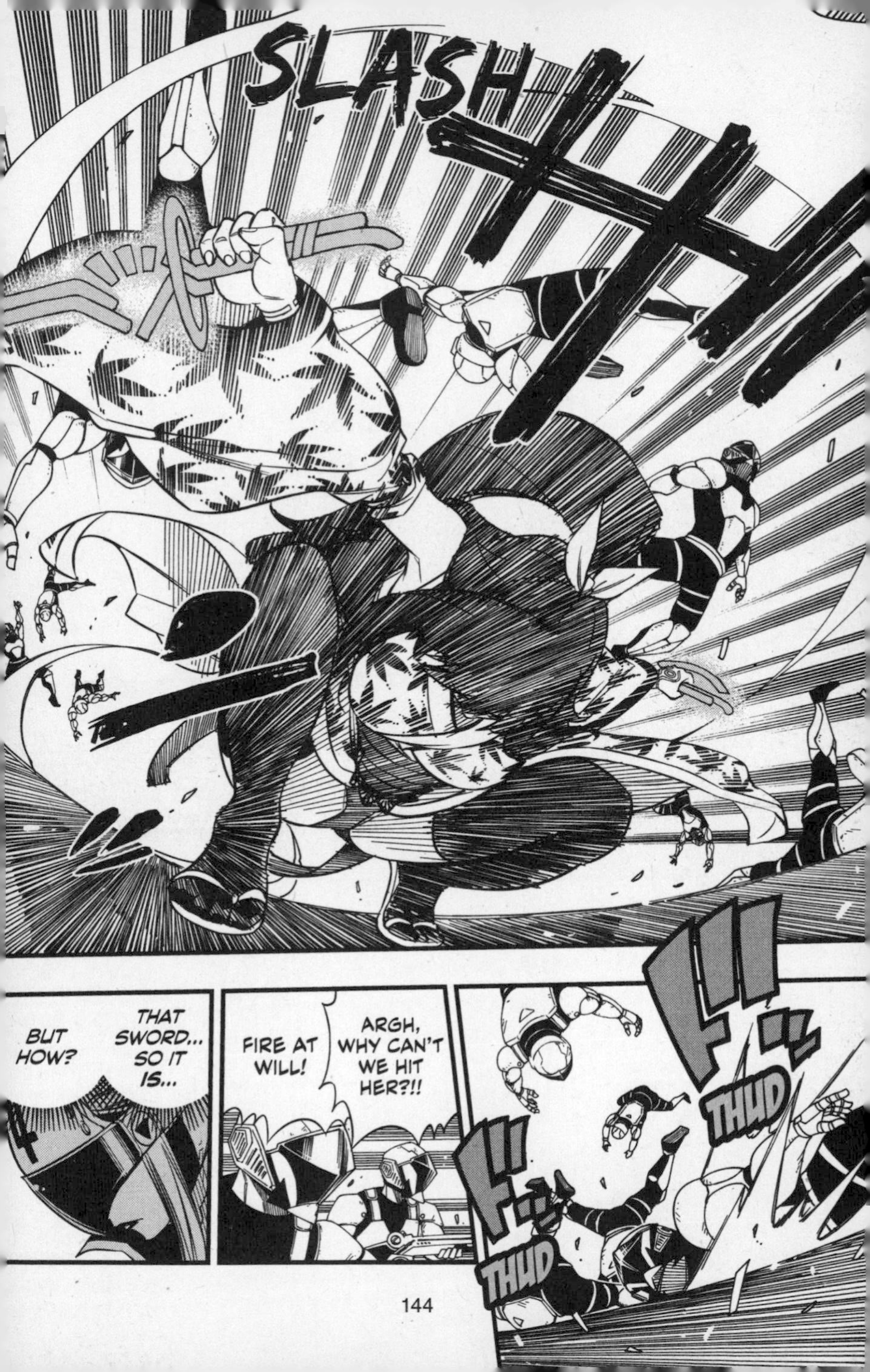
SLASH
F!!
THUD
F!!
THUD
ARGH, WHY CAN'T WE HIT HER?!!
FIRE AT WILL!
THAT SWORD... SO IT IS...
BUT HOW?

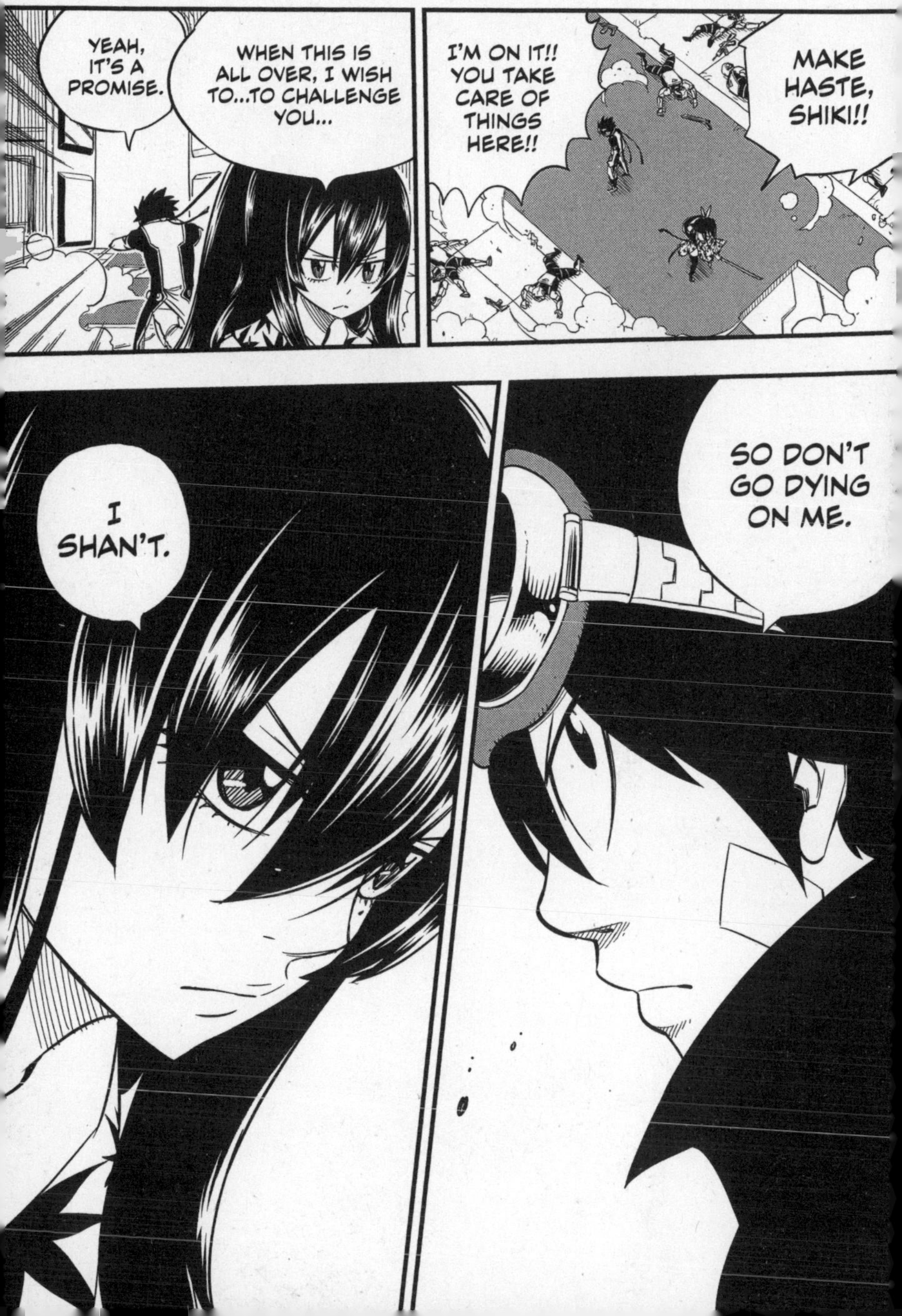
MAKE HASTE, SHIKI!!
I'M ON IT!! YOU TAKE CARE OF THINGS HERE!!
WHEN THIS IS ALL OVER, I WISH TO...TO CHALLENGE YOU...
YEAH, IT'S A PROMISE.
SO DON'T GO DYING ON ME.
I SHAN'T.

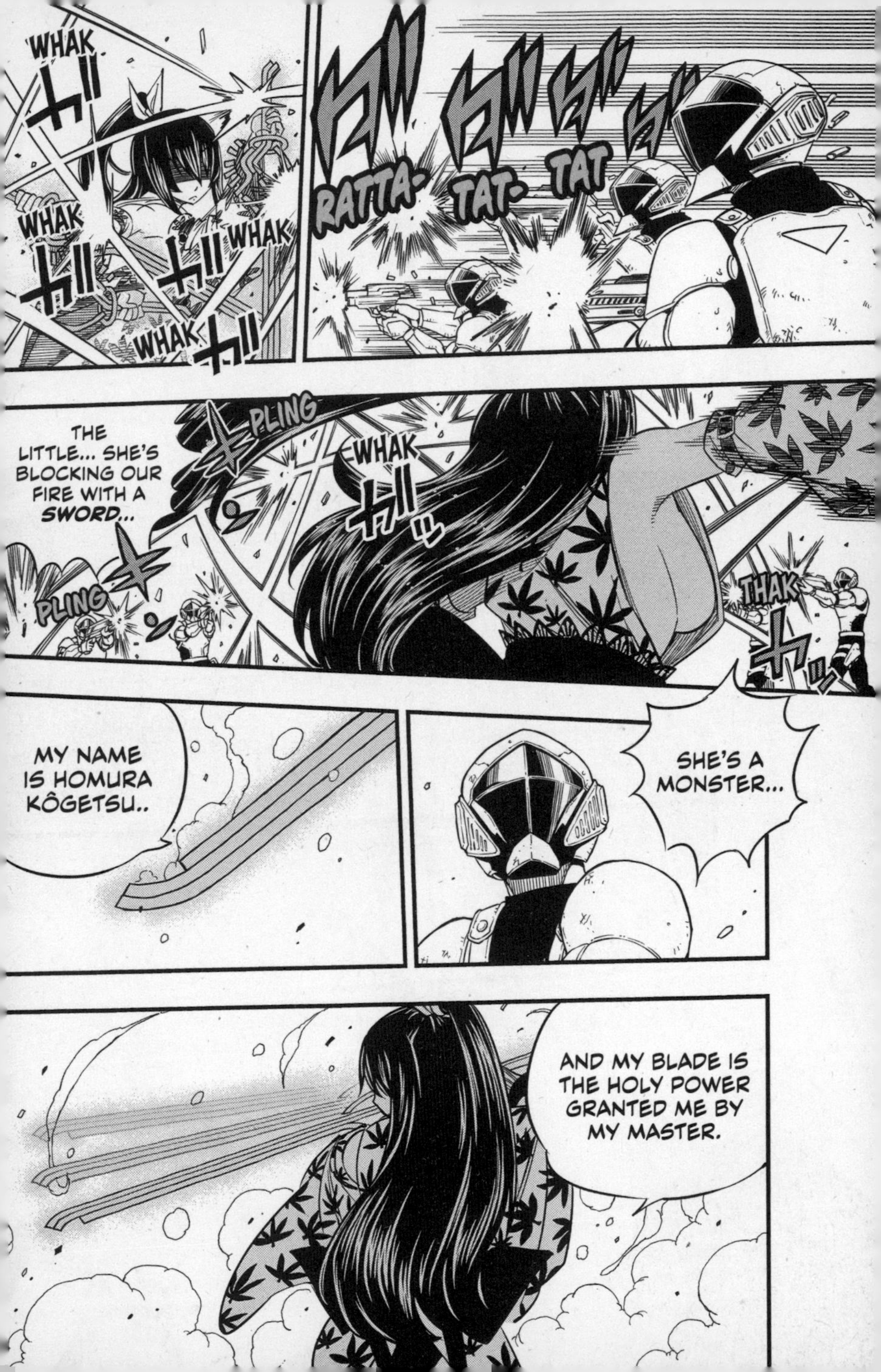
RATTA- TAT- TAT
WHAK
WHAK
WHAK
WHAK
THAK
PLING
WHAK
THE LITTLE... SHE'S BLOCKING OUR FIRE WITH A *SWORD*...
PLING
SHE'S A MONSTER...
MY NAME IS HOMURA KÔGETSU..
AND MY BLADE IS THE HOLY POWER GRANTED ME BY MY MASTER.

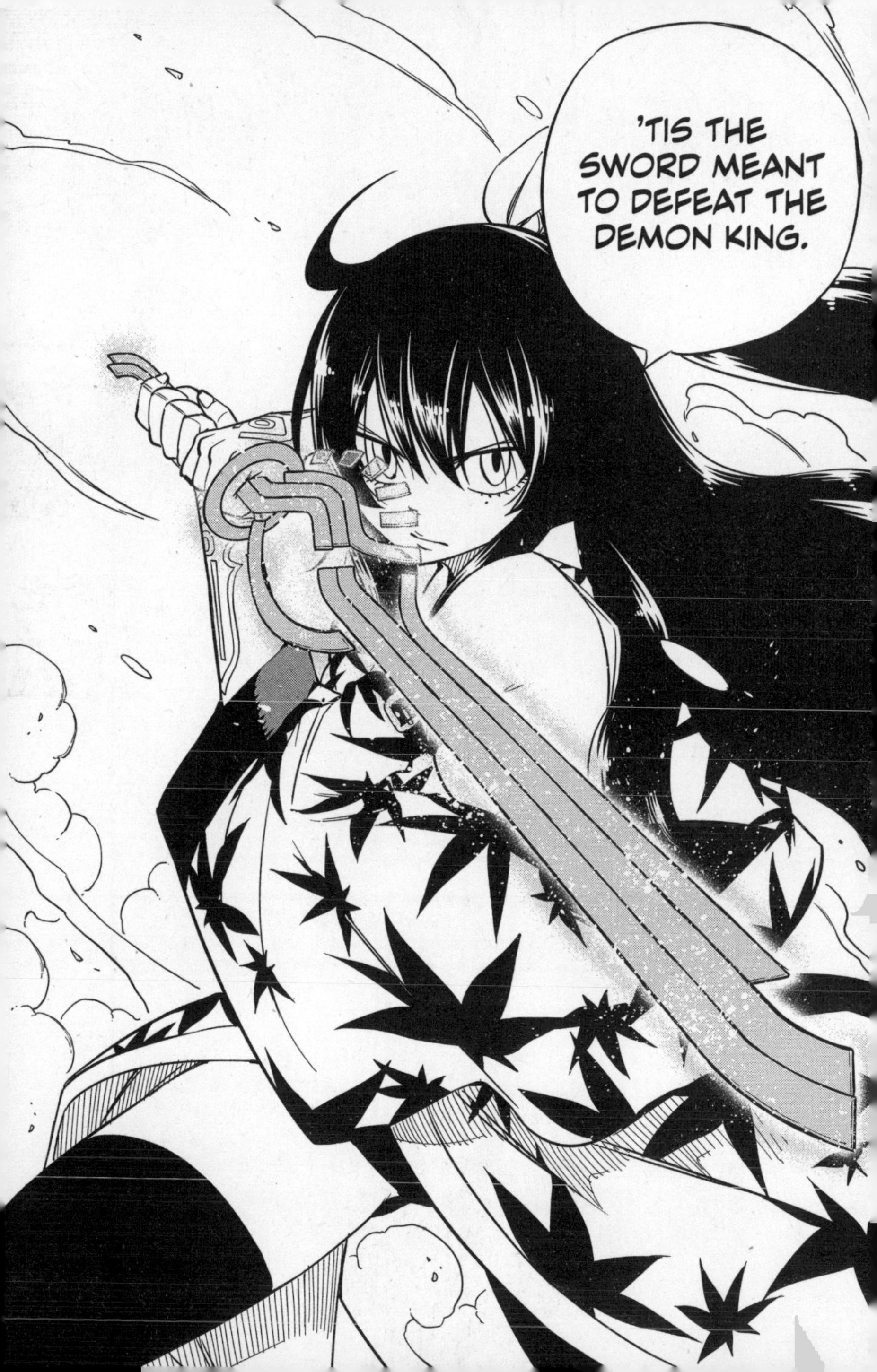
'TIS THE SWORD MEANT TO DEFEAT THE DEMON KING.

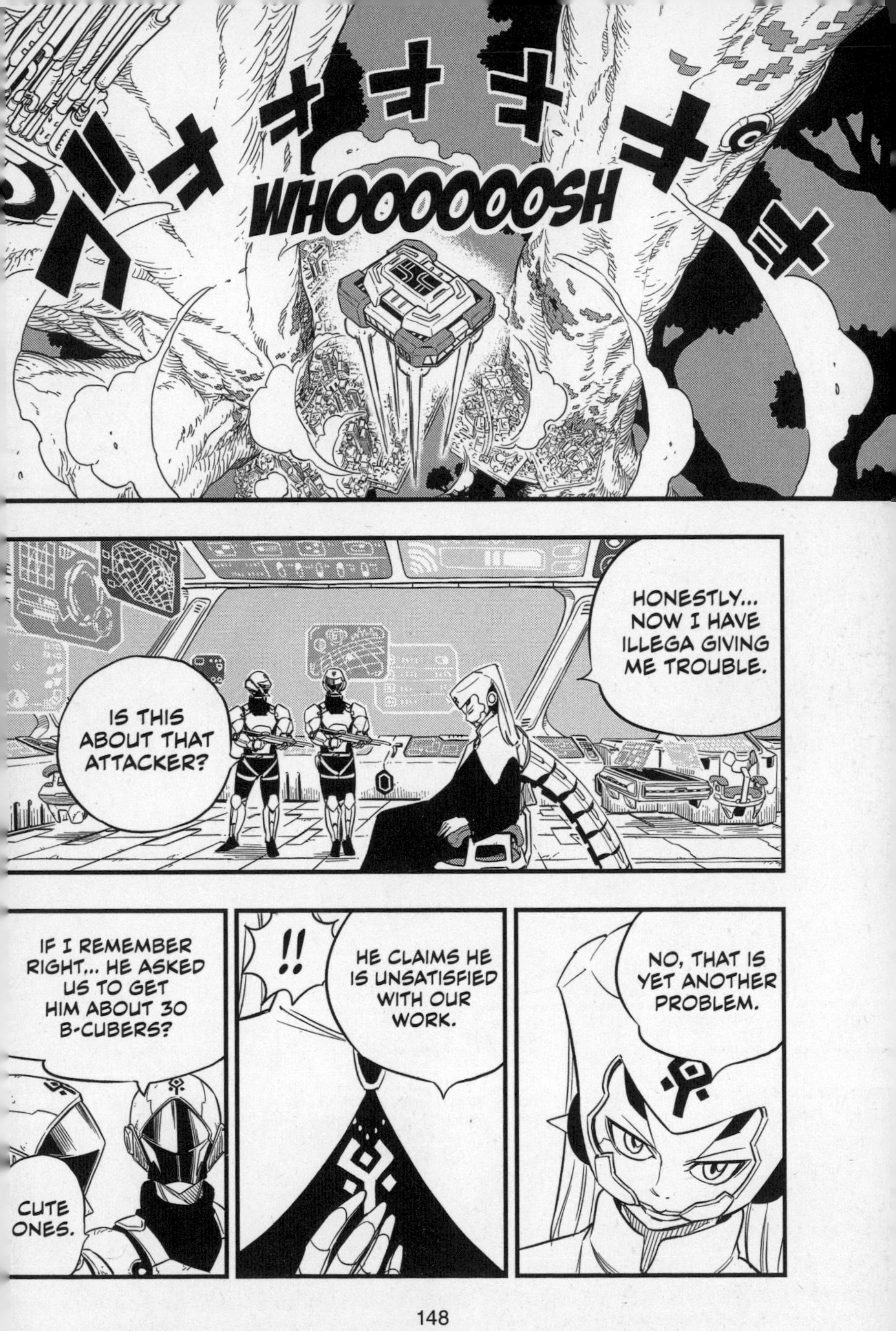
WHOOOOOOOSH
HONESTLY... NOW I HAVE ILLEGA GIVING ME TROUBLE.
IS THIS ABOUT THAT ATTACKER?
NO, THAT IS YET ANOTHER PROBLEM.
HE CLAIMS HE IS UNSATISFIED WITH OUR WORK.
!!
IF I REMEMBER RIGHT... HE ASKED US TO GET HIM ABOUT 30 B-CUBERS?
CUTE ONES.

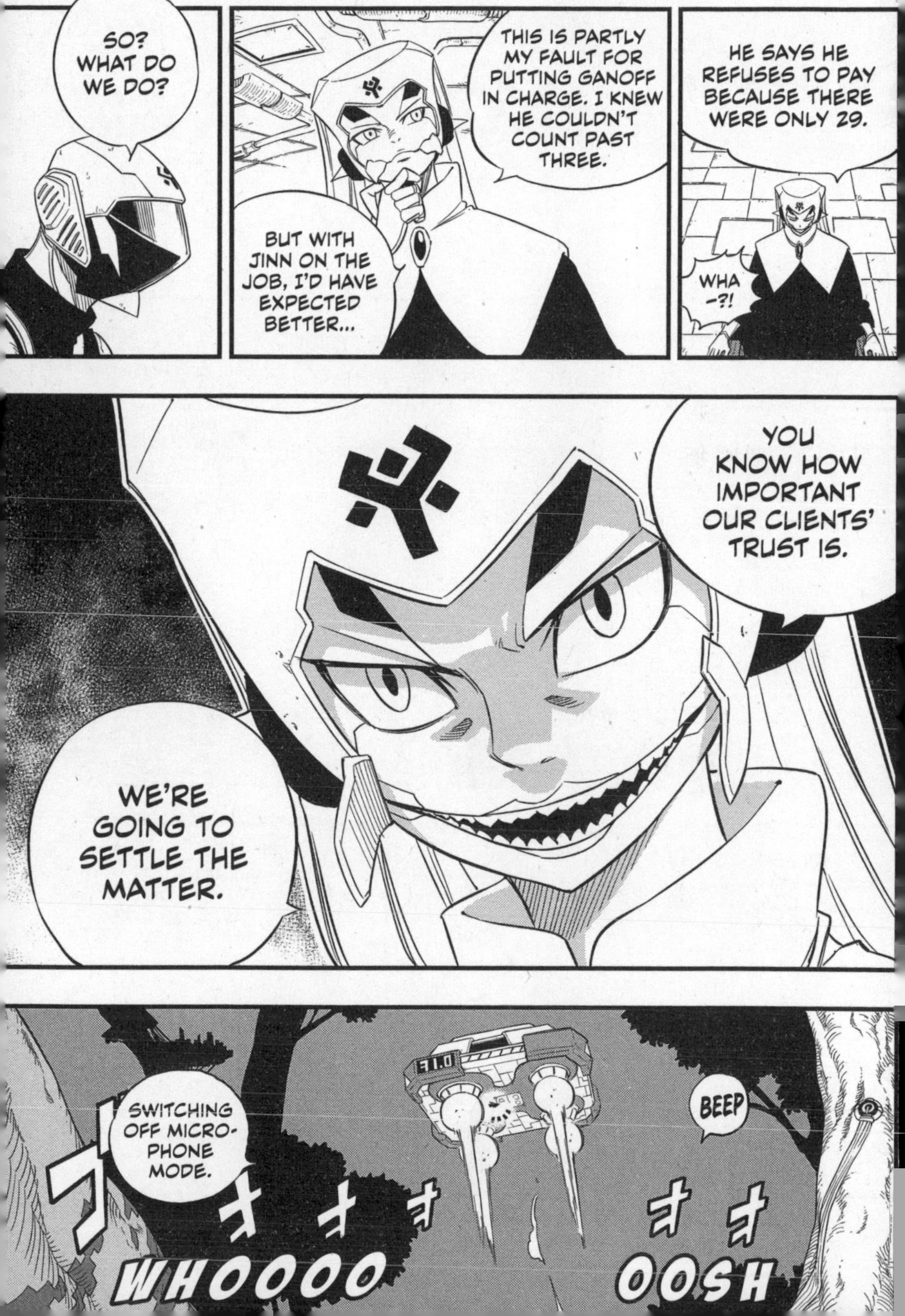
HE SAYS HE REFUSES TO PAY BECAUSE THERE WERE ONLY 29.
WHA-?!
THIS IS PARTLY MY FAULT FOR PUTTING GANOFF IN CHARGE. I KNEW HE COULDN'T COUNT PAST THREE.
BUT WITH JINN ON THE JOB, I'D HAVE EXPECTED BETTER...
SO? WHAT DO WE DO?
YOU KNOW HOW IMPORTANT OUR CLIENTS' TRUST IS.
WE'RE GOING TO SETTLE THE MATTER.
BEEP
SWITCHING OFF MICRO-PHONE MODE.
WHOOOO OOSH

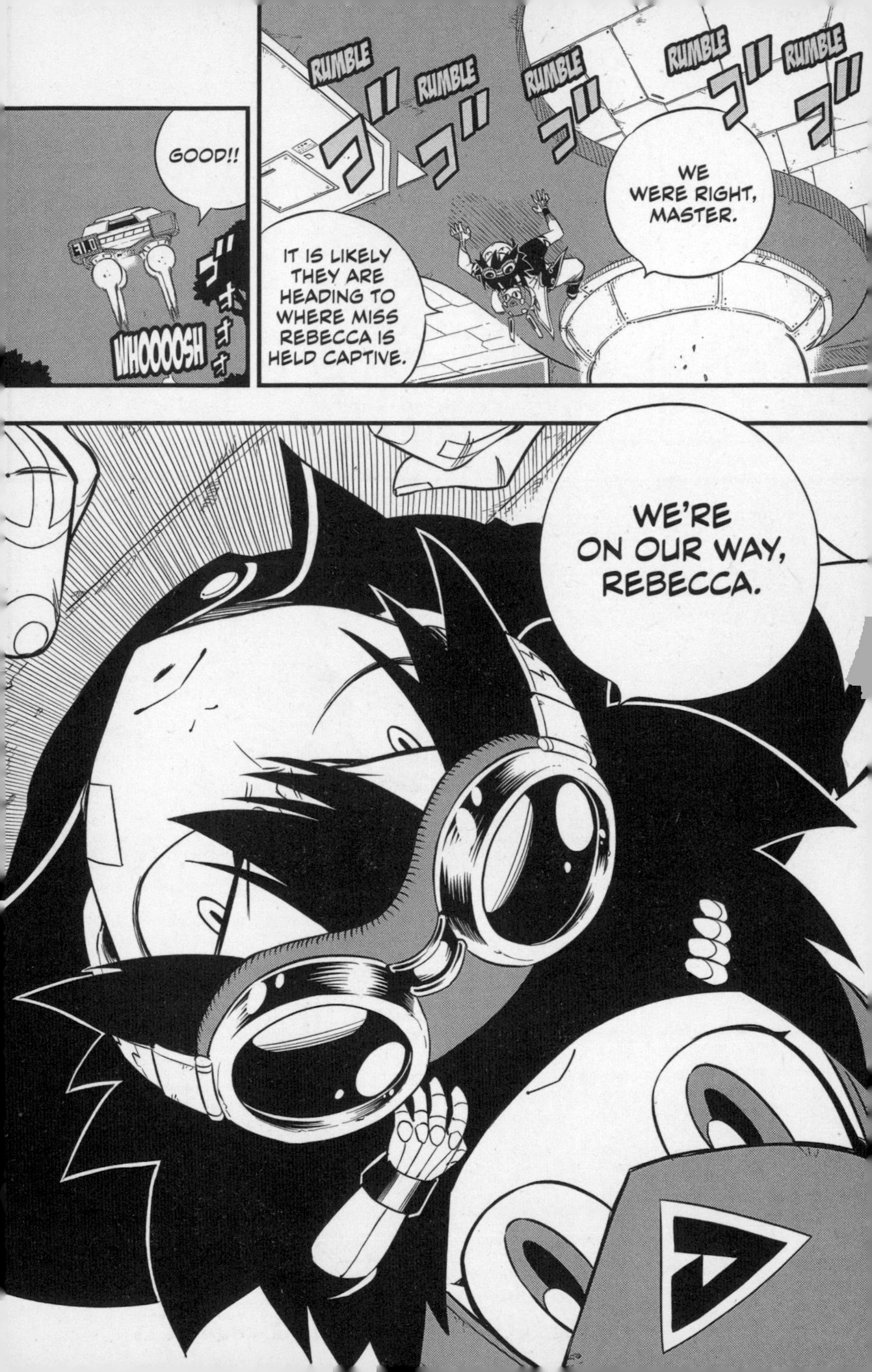
RUMBLE RUMBLE RUMBLE RUMBLE RUMBLE
WE WERE RIGHT, MASTER.
IT IS LIKELY THEY ARE HEADING TO WHERE MISS REBECCA IS HELD CAPTIVE.
GOOD!!
WHOOOOSH
WE'RE ON OUR WAY, REBECCA.

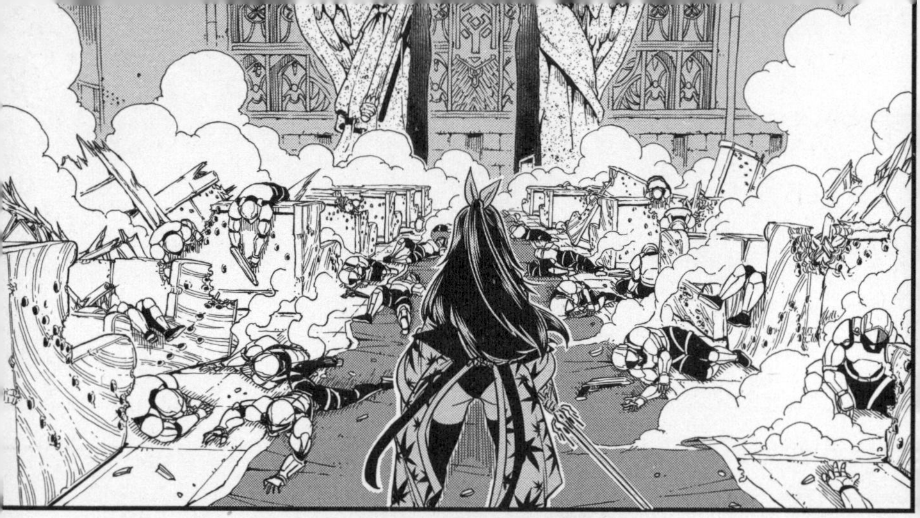

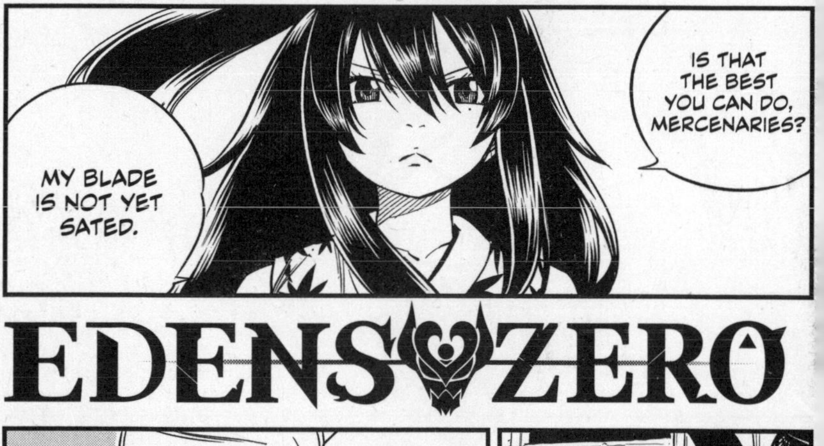
IS THAT THE BEST YOU CAN DO, MERCENARIES?
MY BLADE IS NOT YET SATED.

EDENS ZERO

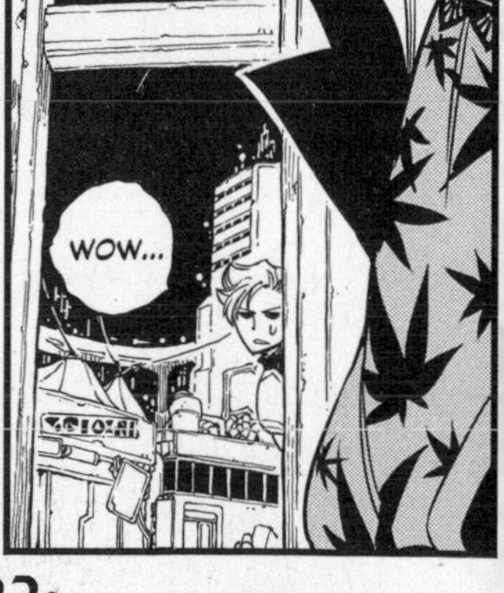
WOW...

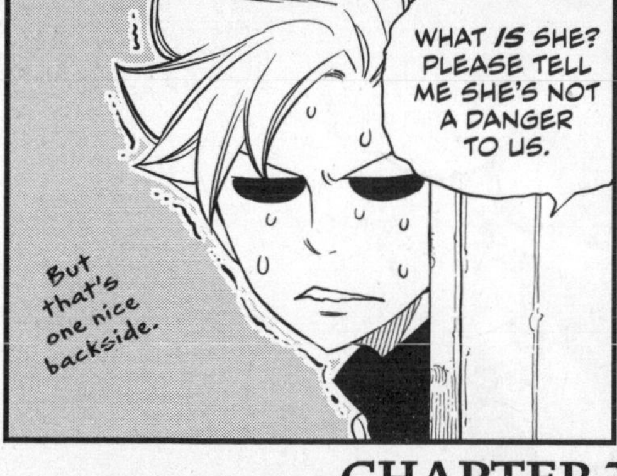
...
WHAT *IS* SHE? PLEASE TELL ME SHE'S NOT A DANGER TO US.
But that's one nice backside.

CHAPTER 22: THE GREAT NAKED ESCAPE

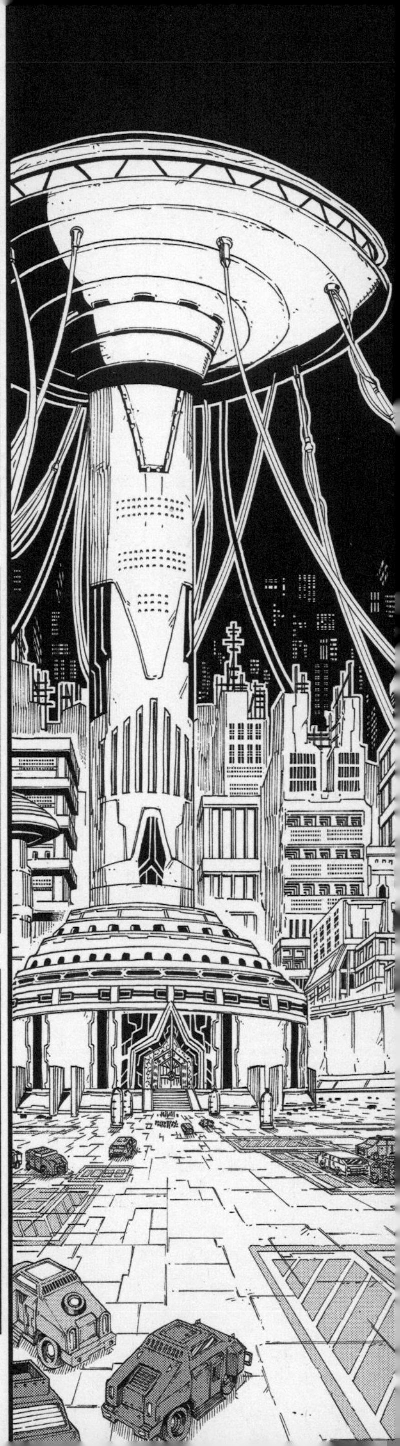

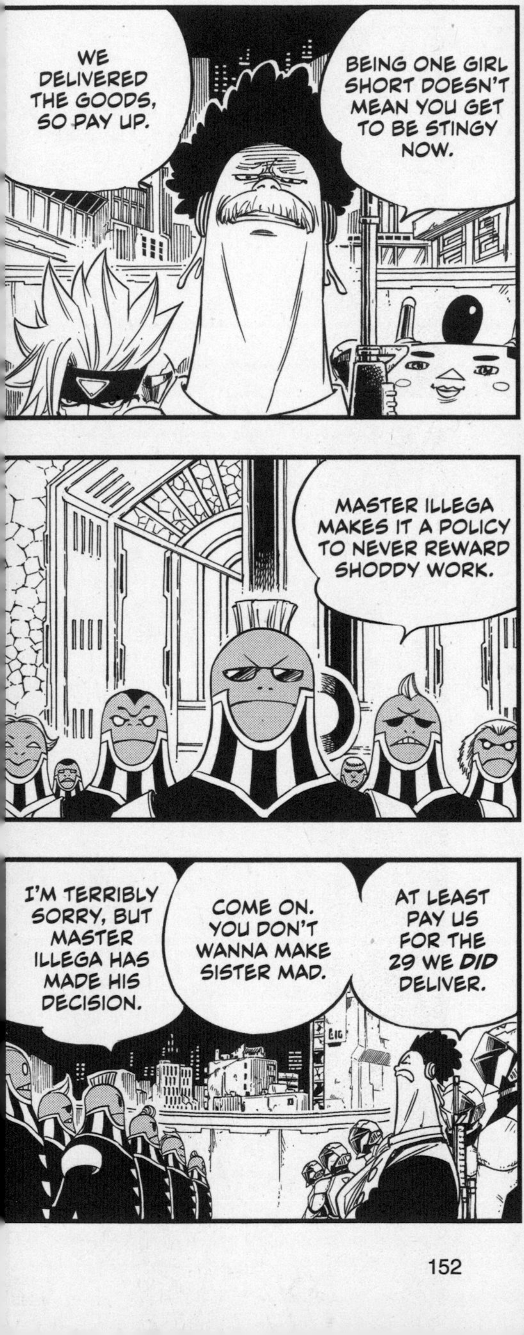
BEING ONE GIRL SHORT DOESN'T MEAN YOU GET TO BE STINGY NOW.
WE DELIVERED THE GOODS, SO PAY UP.
MASTER ILLEGA MAKES IT A POLICY TO NEVER REWARD SHODDY WORK.
AT LEAST PAY US FOR THE 29 WE *DID* DELIVER.
COME ON. YOU DON'T WANNA MAKE SISTER MAD.
I'M TERRIBLY SORRY, BUT MASTER ILLEGA HAS MADE HIS DECISION.

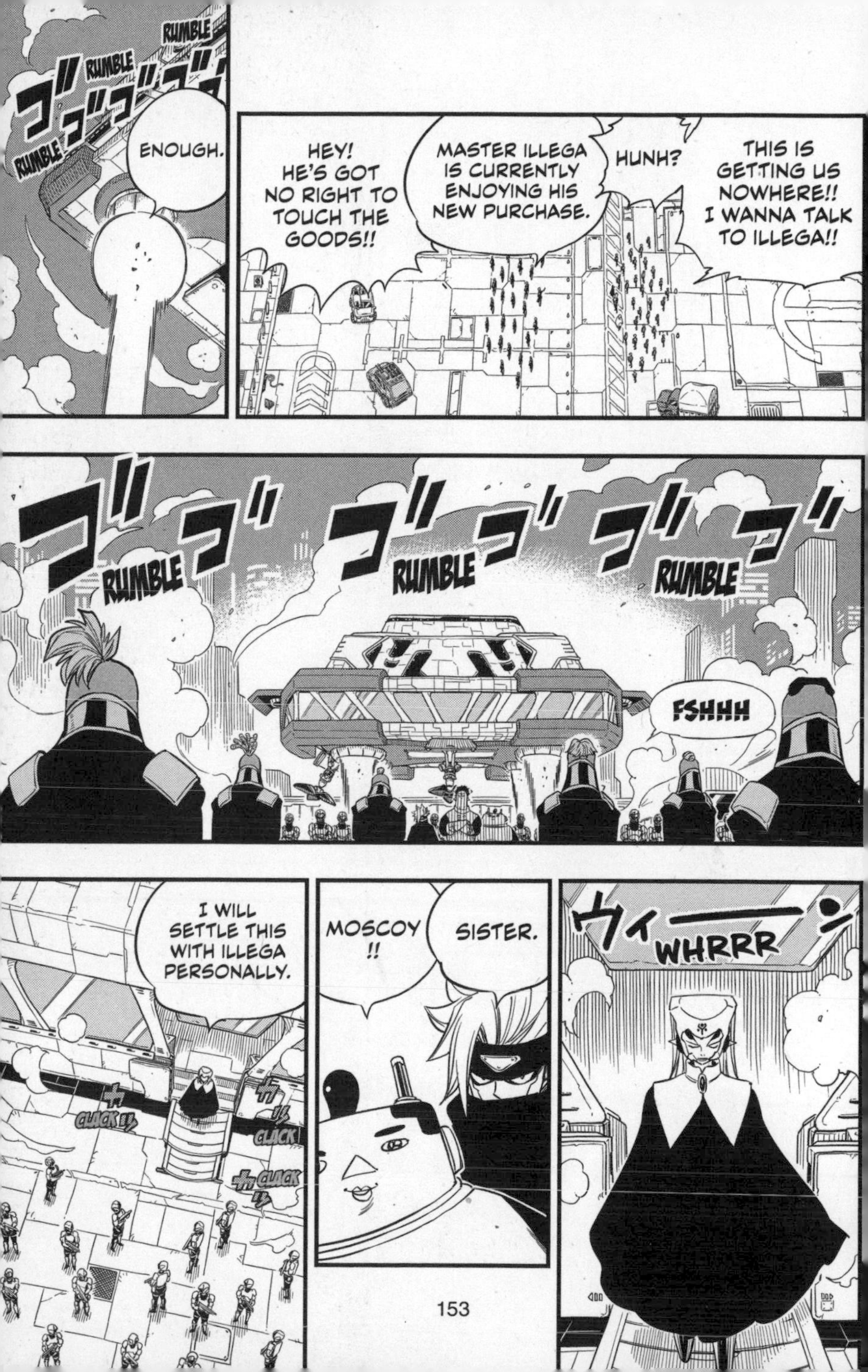
THIS IS GETTING US NOWHERE!! I WANNA TALK TO ILLEGA!!
HUNH?
MASTER ILLEGA IS CURRENTLY ENJOYING HIS NEW PURCHASE.
HEY! HE'S GOT NO RIGHT TO TOUCH THE GOODS!!
RUMBLE
RUMBLE
RUMBLE
ENOUGH.
RUMBLE
RUMBLE
RUMBLE
FSHHH
WHRRR
SISTER.
MOSCOY !!
I WILL SETTLE THIS WITH ILLEGA PERSONALLY.
CLACK
CLACK
CLACK

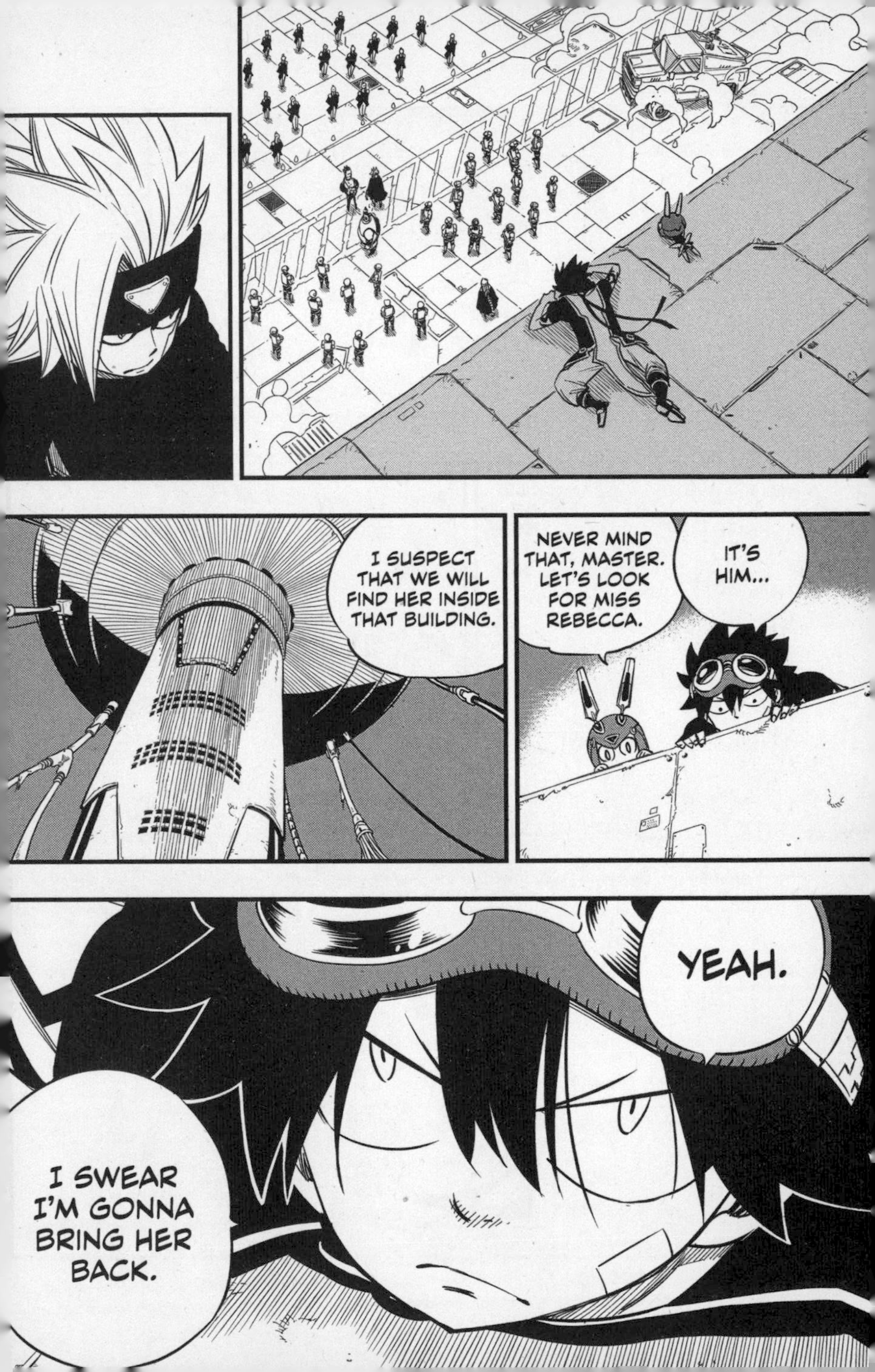
IT'S HIM...
NEVER MIND THAT, MASTER. LET'S LOOK FOR MISS REBECCA.
I SUSPECT THAT WE WILL FIND HER INSIDE THAT BUILDING.
YEAH.
I SWEAR I'M GONNA BRING HER BACK.

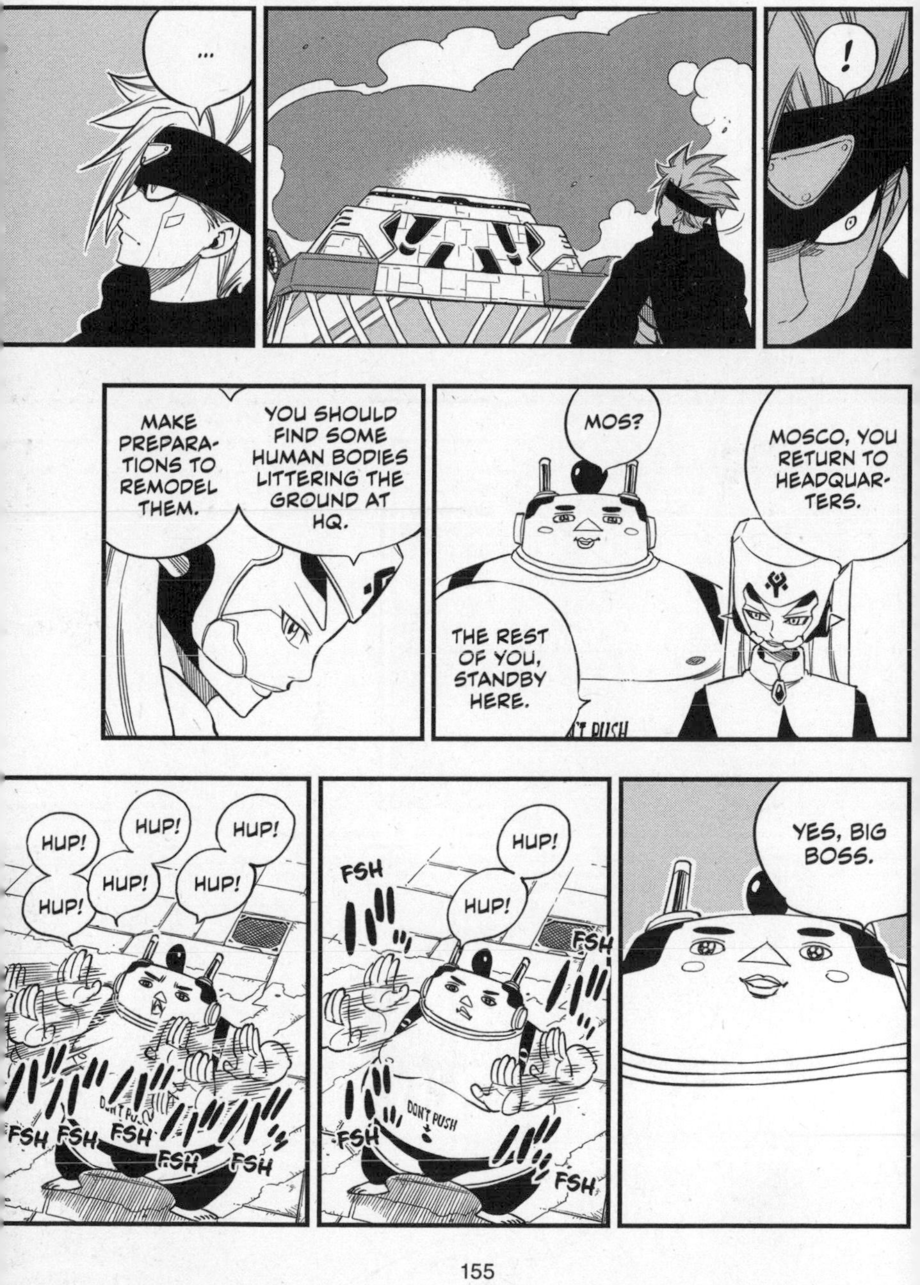
!
...
MOSCO, YOU RETURN TO HEADQUAR-TERS.
MOS?
THE REST OF YOU, STANDBY HERE.
YOU SHOULD FIND SOME HUMAN BODIES LITTERING THE GROUND AT HQ.
MAKE PREPARA-TIONS TO REMODEL THEM.
YES, BIG BOSS.
HUP!
HUP!
FSH
FSH
DON'T PUSH
FSH
FSH
HUP!
HUP!
HUP!
HUP!
HUP!
HUP!
FSH
FSH
FSH
FSH
FSH

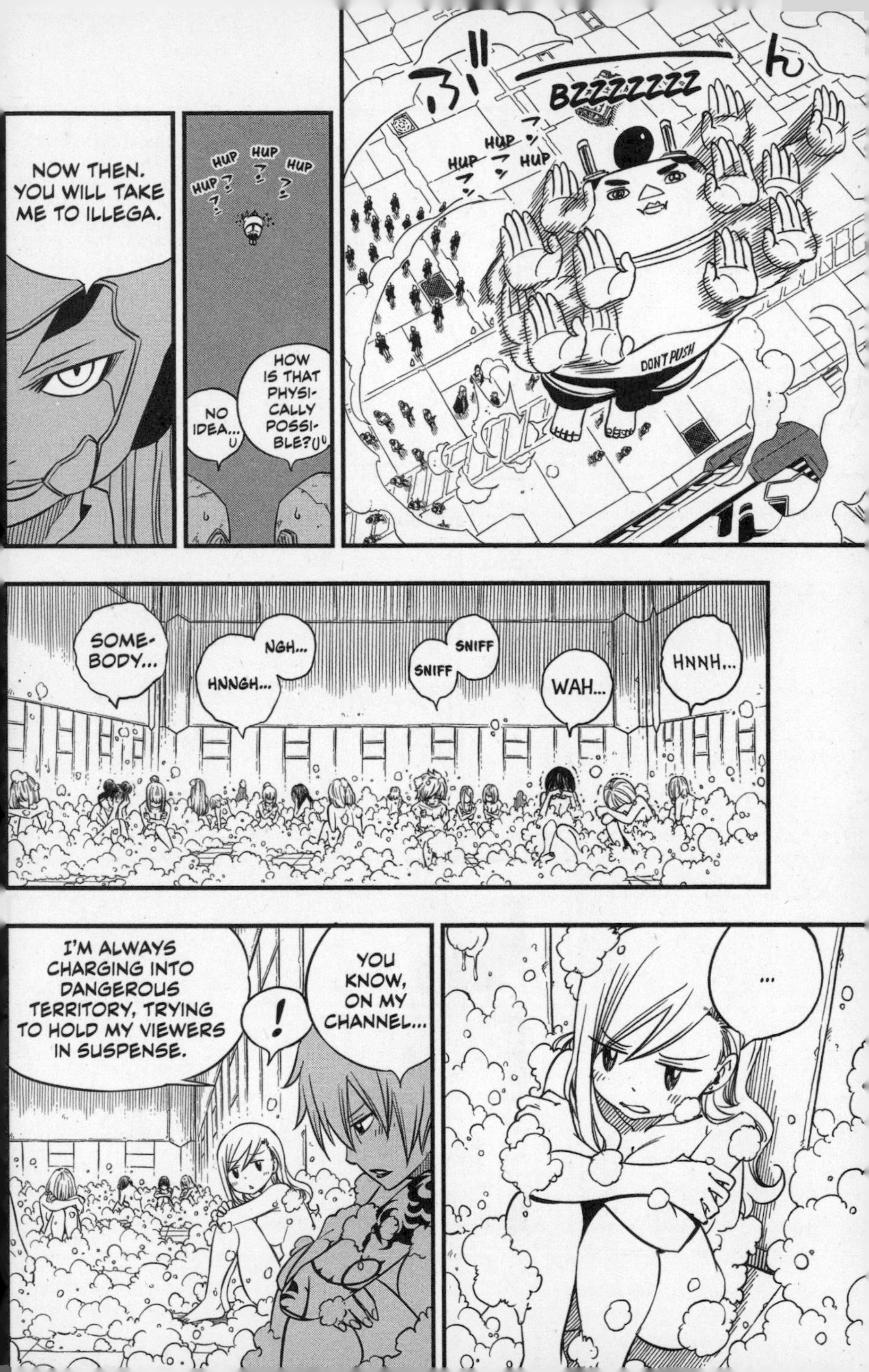
ぶ
ん
BZZZZZZZ
HUP HUP HUP
DON'T PUSH
HUP HUP HUP HUP
HOW IS THAT PHYSICALLY POSSIBLE?
NO IDEA...
NOW THEN. YOU WILL TAKE ME TO ILLEGA.
HNNH...
WAH...
SNIFF
SNIFF
NGH...
HNNGH...
SOME-BODY...
...
YOU KNOW, ON MY CHANNEL...
!
I'M ALWAYS CHARGING INTO DANGEROUS TERRITORY, TRYING TO HOLD MY VIEWERS IN SUSPENSE.

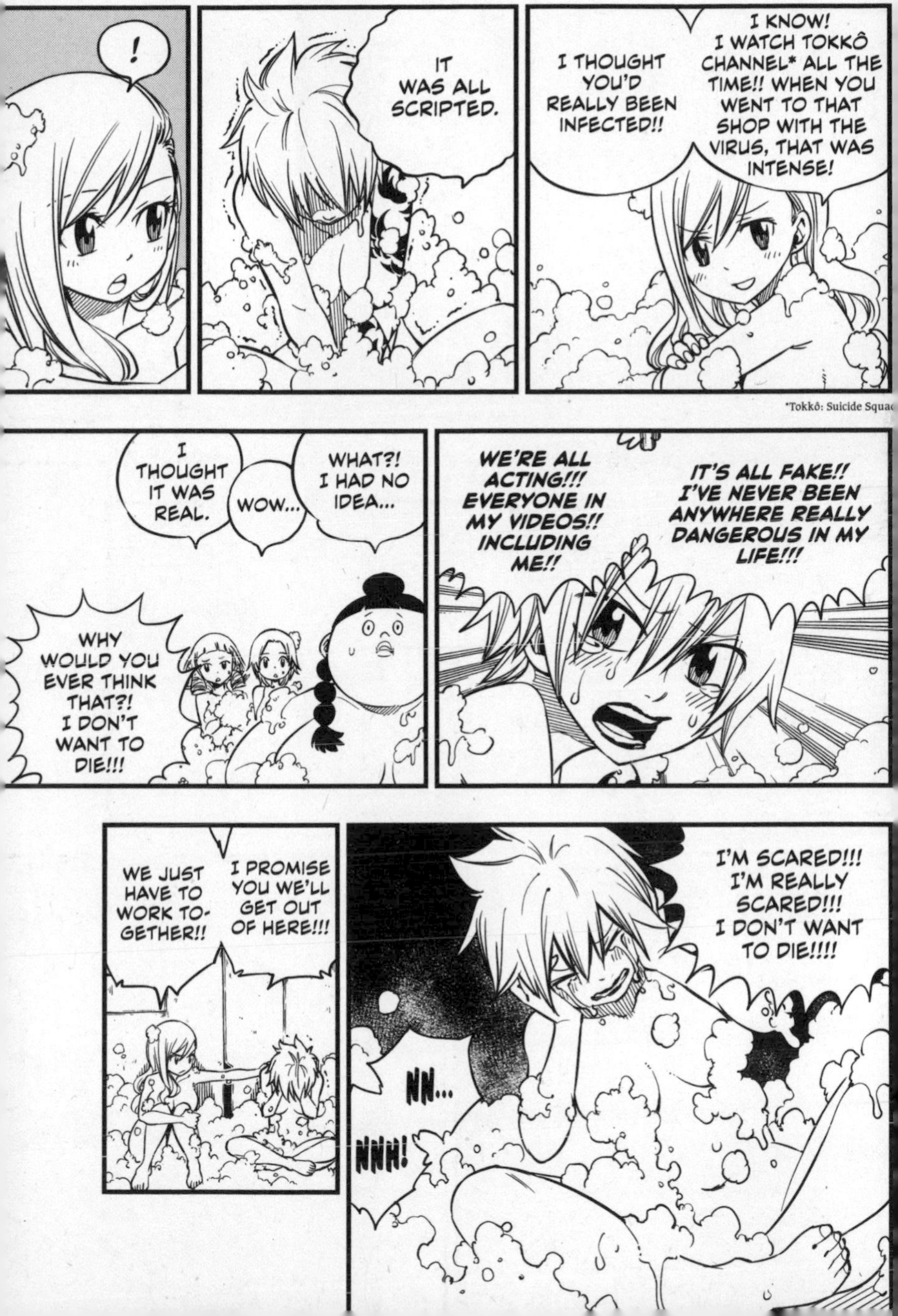
I KNOW! I WATCH TOKKÔ CHANNEL* ALL THE TIME!! WHEN YOU WENT TO THAT SHOP WITH THE VIRUS, THAT WAS INTENSE!
I THOUGHT YOU'D REALLY BEEN INFECTED!!
IT WAS ALL SCRIPTED.
!
IT'S ALL FAKE!! I'VE NEVER BEEN ANYWHERE REALLY DANGEROUS IN MY LIFE!!!
WE'RE ALL ACTING!!! EVERYONE IN MY VIDEOS!! INCLUDING ME!!
WHAT?! I HAD NO IDEA...
WOW...
I THOUGHT IT WAS REAL.
WHY WOULD YOU EVER THINK THAT?! I DON'T WANT TO DIE!!!
I'M SCARED!!! I'M REALLY SCARED!!! I DON'T WANT TO DIE!!!!
NN...
NNH!
I PROMISE YOU WE'LL GET OUT OF HERE!!!
WE JUST HAVE TO WORK TO-GETHER!!

*Tokkô: Suicide Squad

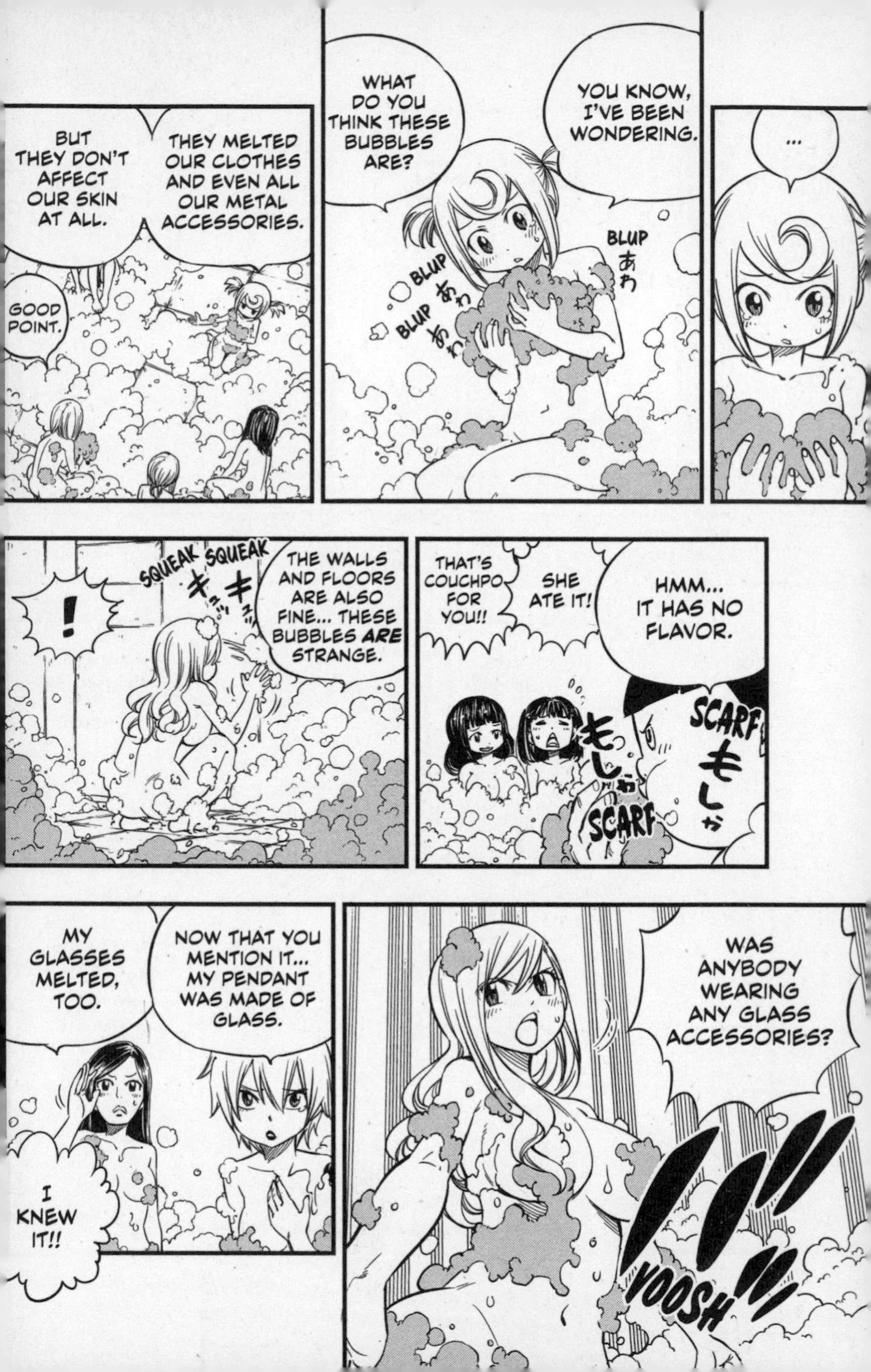
...
YOU KNOW, I'VE BEEN WONDERING.
WHAT DO YOU THINK THESE BUBBLES ARE?
BLUP あわ
BLUP あわ
BLUP あわ
THEY MELTED OUR CLOTHES AND EVEN ALL OUR METAL ACCESSORIES.
BUT THEY DON'T AFFECT OUR SKIN AT ALL.
GOOD POINT.
HMM... IT HAS NO FLAVOR.
SHE ATE IT!
THAT'S COUCHPO FOR YOU!!
SCARF もしゃ
SCARF もしゃ
THE WALLS AND FLOORS ARE ALSO FINE... THESE BUBBLES *ARE* STRANGE.
SQUEAK キュ
SQUEAK キュ
!
WAS ANYBODY WEARING ANY GLASS ACCESSORIES?
VOOSH
NOW THAT YOU MENTION IT... MY PENDANT WAS MADE OF GLASS.
MY GLASSES MELTED, TOO.
I KNEW IT!!

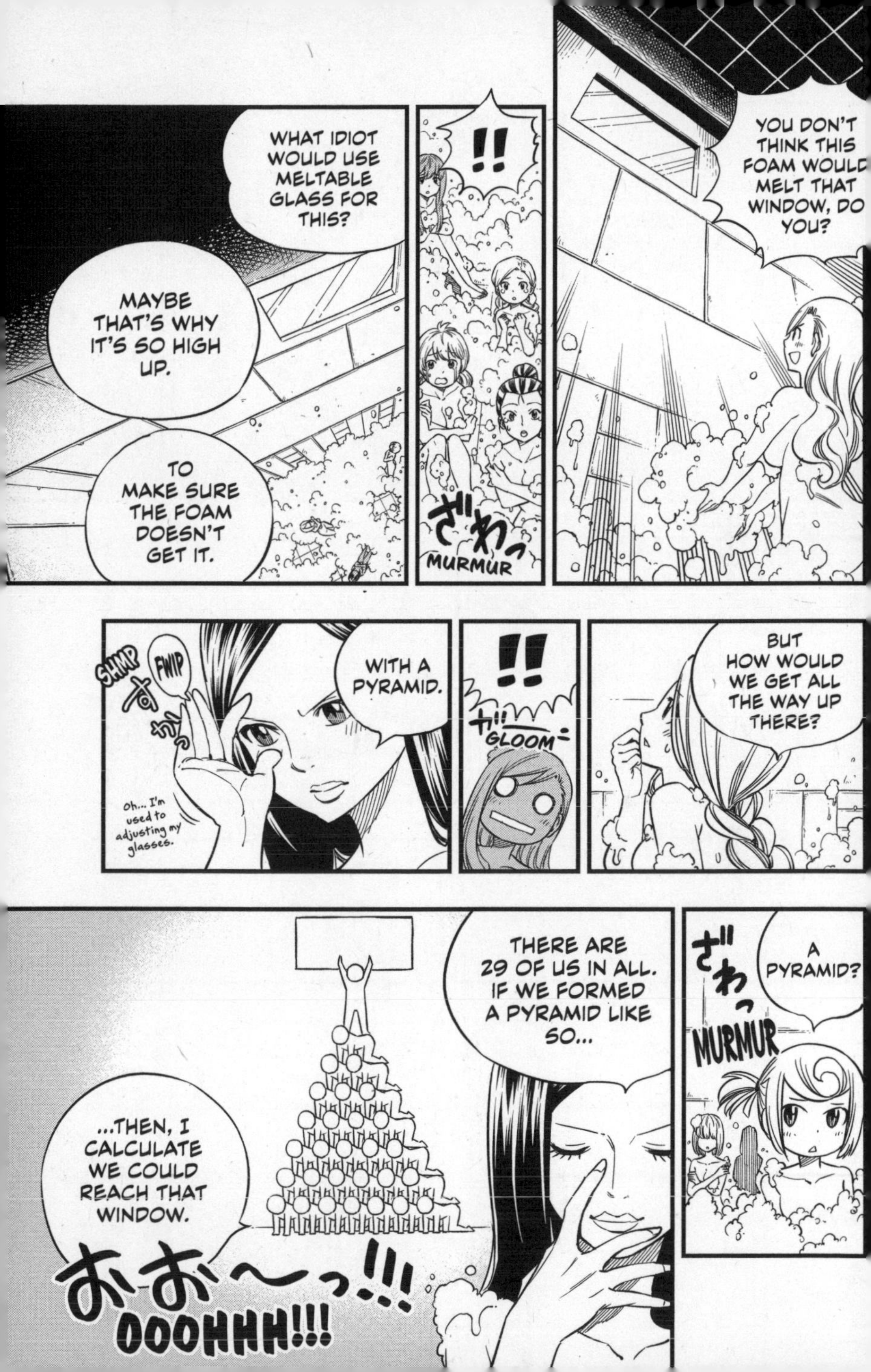
YOU DON'T THINK THIS FOAM WOULD MELT THAT WINDOW, DO YOU?
!!
ざわっ
MURMUR
WHAT IDIOT WOULD USE MELTABLE GLASS FOR THIS?
MAYBE THAT'S WHY IT'S SO HIGH UP.
TO MAKE SURE THE FOAM DOESN'T GET IT.
BUT HOW WOULD WE GET ALL THE WAY UP THERE?
!!
GLOOM
WITH A PYRAMID.
SHMP
FWIP
Oh... I'm used to adjusting my glasses.
A PYRAMID?
ざわっ
MURMUR
THERE ARE 29 OF US IN ALL. IF WE FORMED A PYRAMID LIKE SO...
...THEN, I CALCULATE WE COULD REACH THAT WINDOW.
おお〜っ!!!
OOOHHH!!!

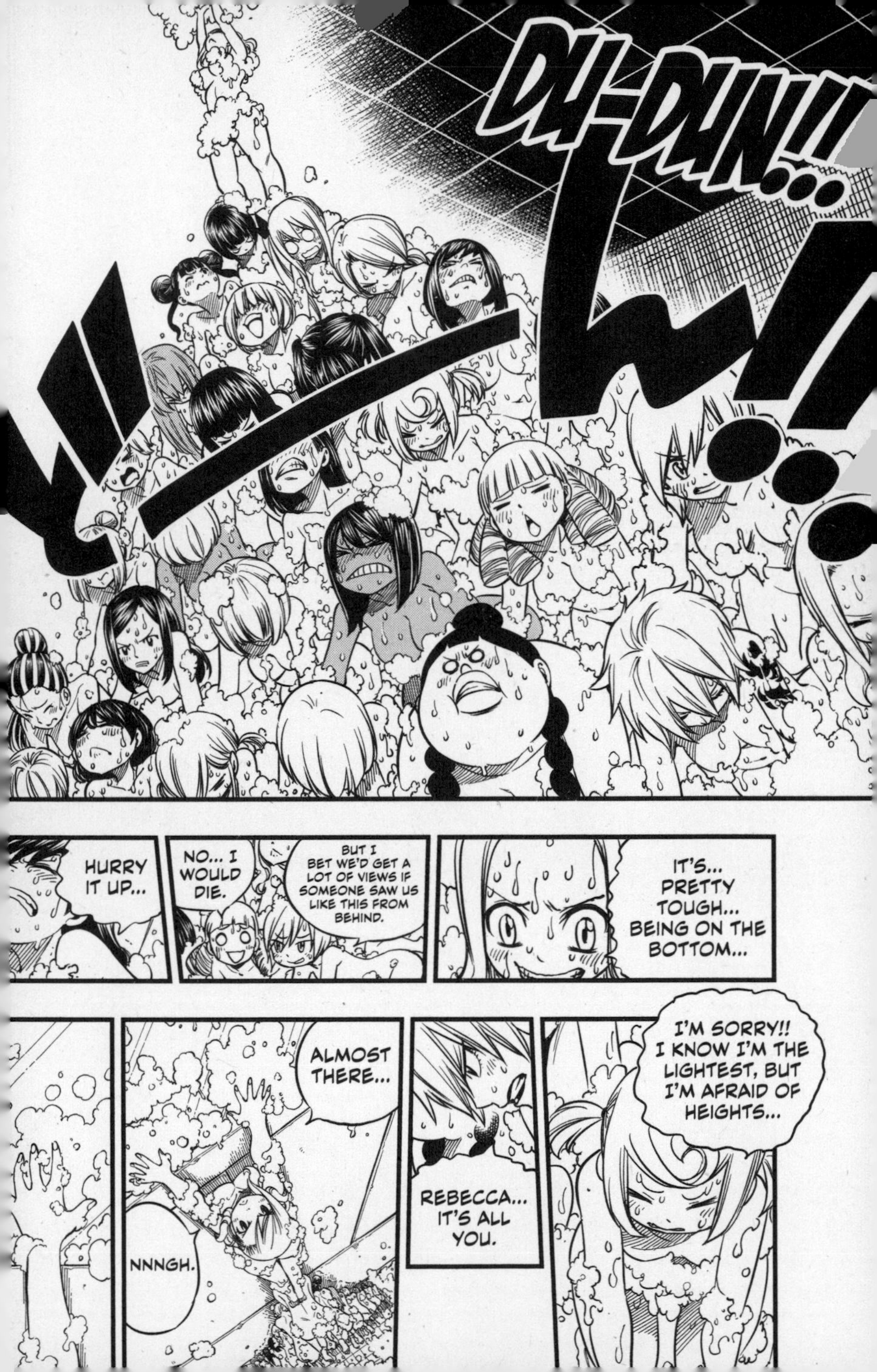
DU-DUN!!...
IT'S... PRETTY TOUGH... BEING ON THE BOTTOM...
BUT I BET WE'D GET A LOT OF VIEWS IF SOMEONE SAW US LIKE THIS FROM BEHIND.
NO... I WOULD DIE.
HURRY IT UP...
I'M SORRY!! I KNOW I'M THE LIGHTEST, BUT I'M AFRAID OF HEIGHTS...
REBECCA... IT'S ALL YOU.
ALMOST THERE...
NNNGH.

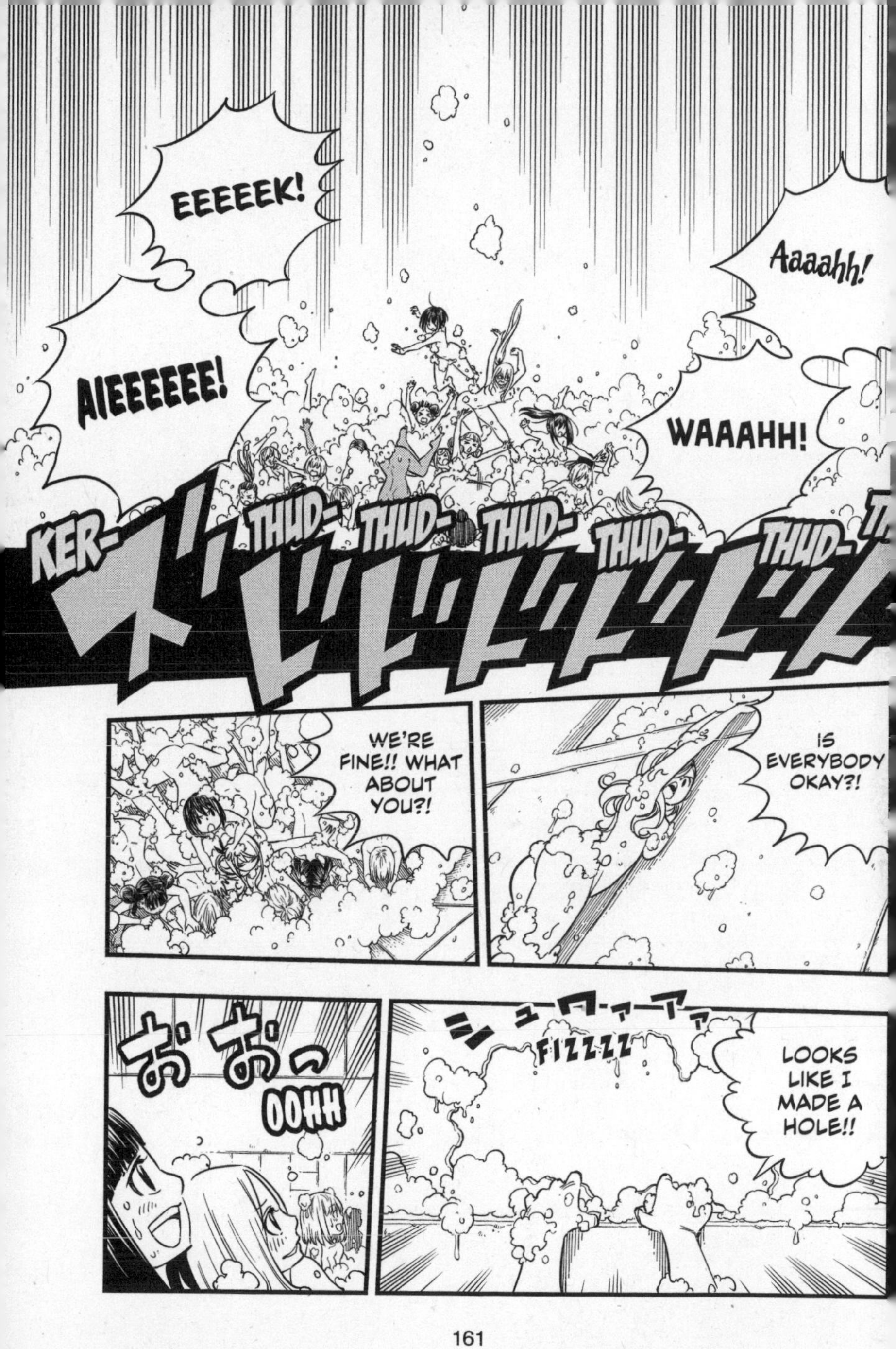
Aaaahh!
EEEEEK!
WAAAHH!
AIEEEEEE!
KER-THUD-THUD-THUD-THUD-THUD-
IS EVERYBODY OKAY?!
WE'RE FINE!! WHAT ABOUT YOU?!
FIZZZZ
LOOKS LIKE I MADE A HOLE!!
おおっ
OOHH

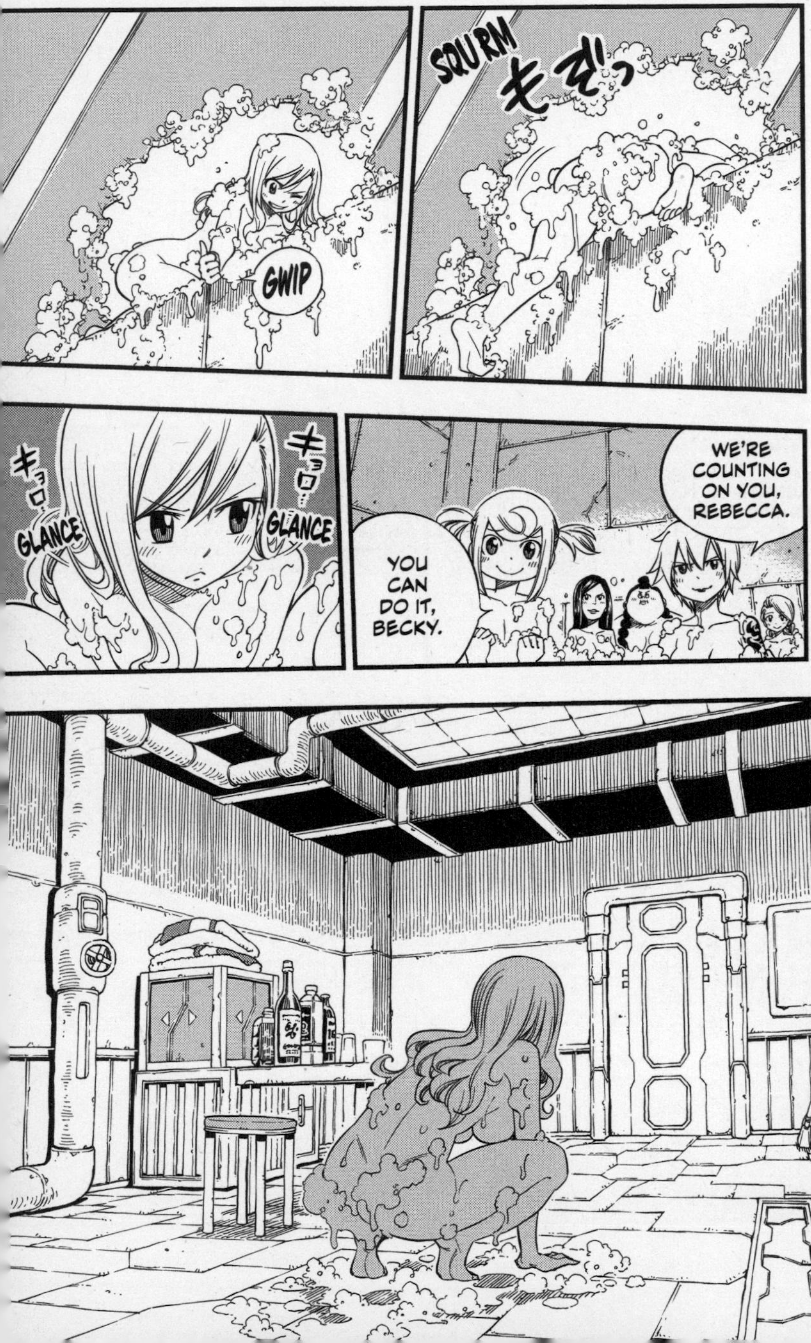
SQURM
もぞっ
GWIP
WE'RE COUNTING ON YOU, REBECCA.
YOU CAN DO IT, BECKY.
キョロ…
GLANCE
キョロ
GLANCE

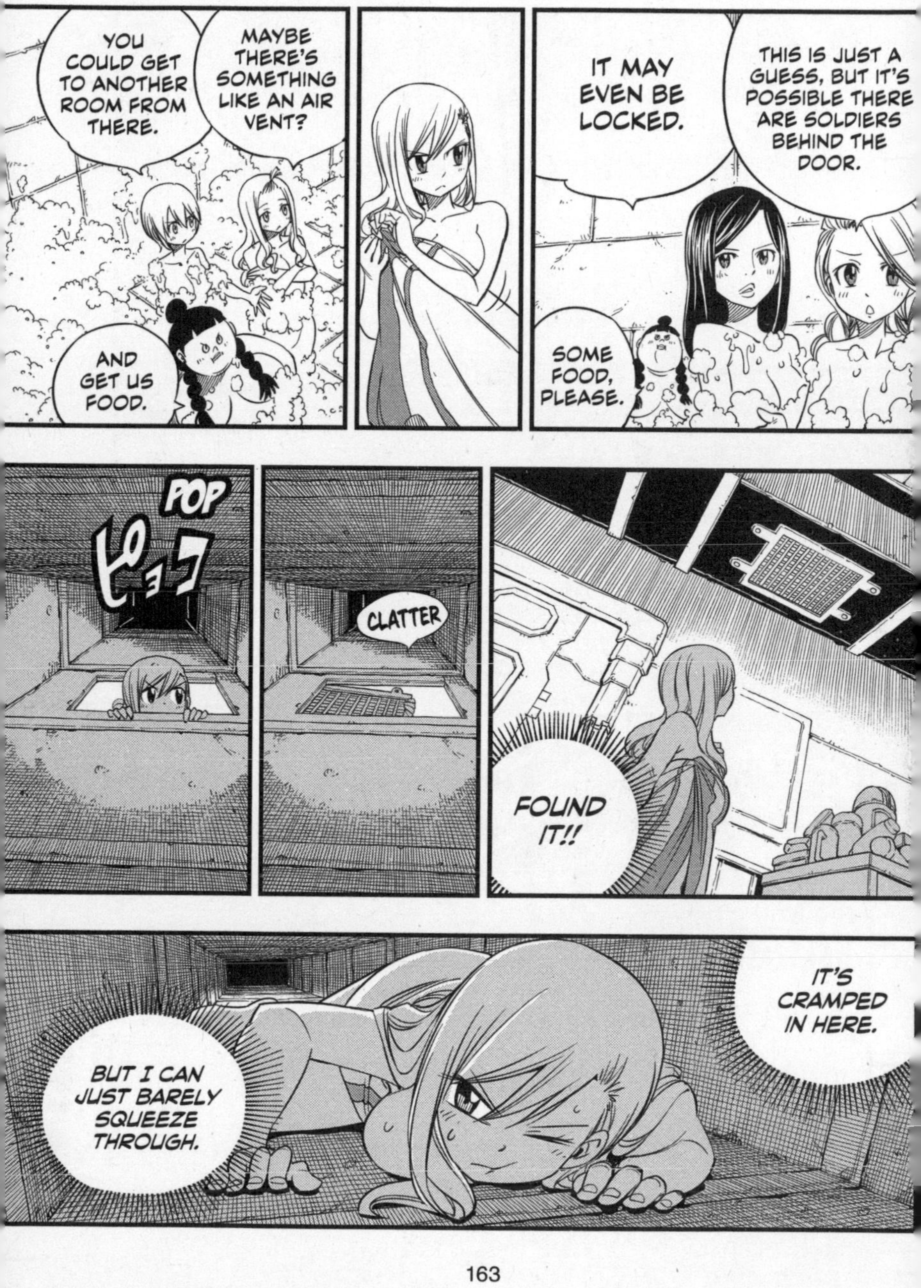
THIS IS JUST A GUESS, BUT IT'S POSSIBLE THERE ARE SOLDIERS BEHIND THE DOOR.
IT MAY EVEN BE LOCKED.
SOME FOOD, PLEASE.
MAYBE THERE'S SOMETHING LIKE AN AIR VENT?
YOU COULD GET TO ANOTHER ROOM FROM THERE.
AND GET US FOOD.
FOUND IT!!
CLATTER
POP
ピョコ
IT'S CRAMPED IN HERE.
BUT I CAN JUST BARELY SQUEEZE THROUGH.

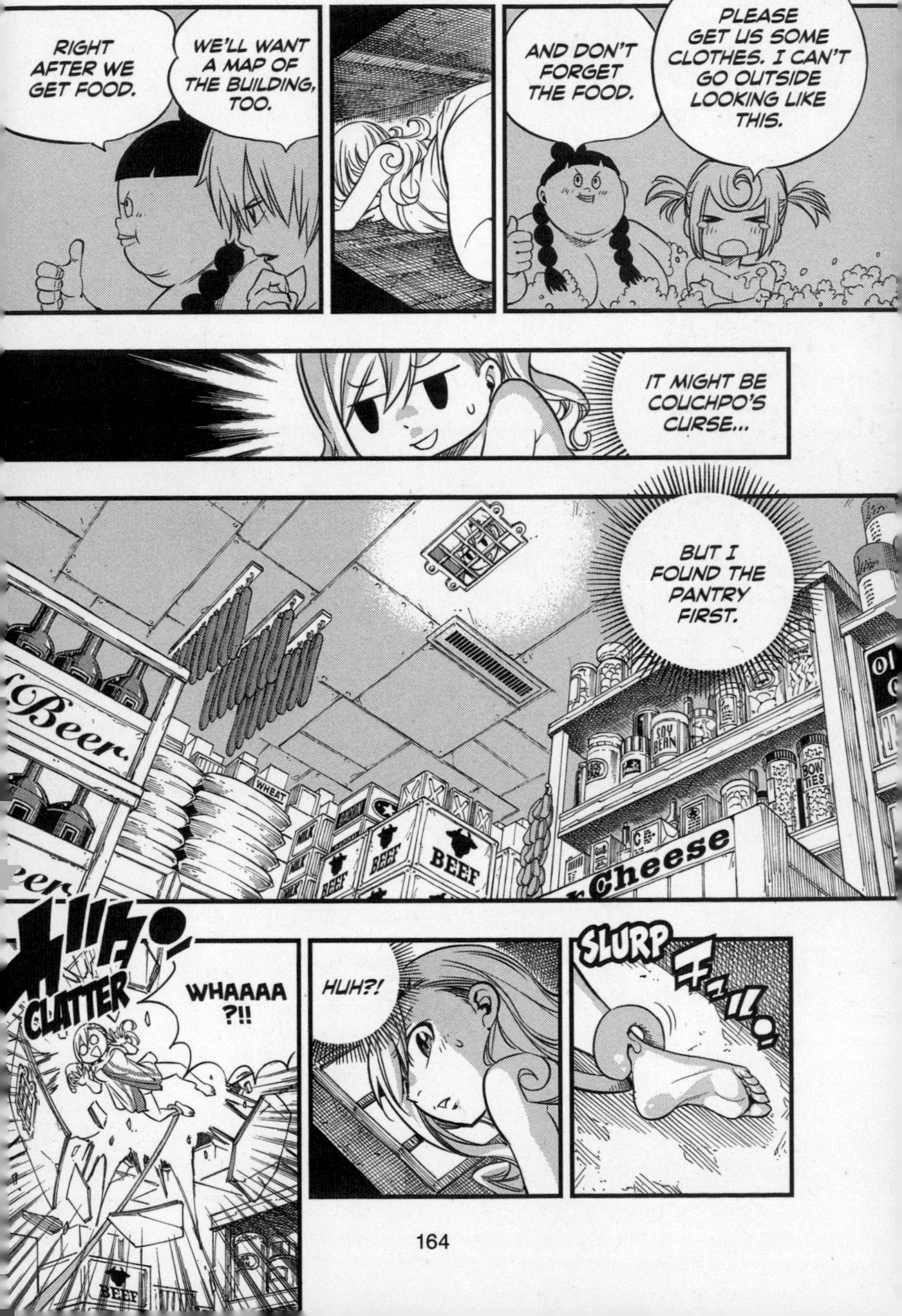

PLEASE GET US SOME CLOTHES. I CAN'T GO OUTSIDE LOOKING LIKE THIS.
AND DON'T FORGET THE FOOD.
WE'LL WANT A MAP OF THE BUILDING, TOO.
RIGHT AFTER WE GET FOOD.
IT MIGHT BE COUCHPO'S CURSE...
BUT I FOUND THE PANTRY FIRST.
Beer
WHEAT
MILK
BEEF
SOY BEAN
BOW TIES
Cheese
SLURP
HUH?!
WHAAAA ?!!
CLATTER
BEEF

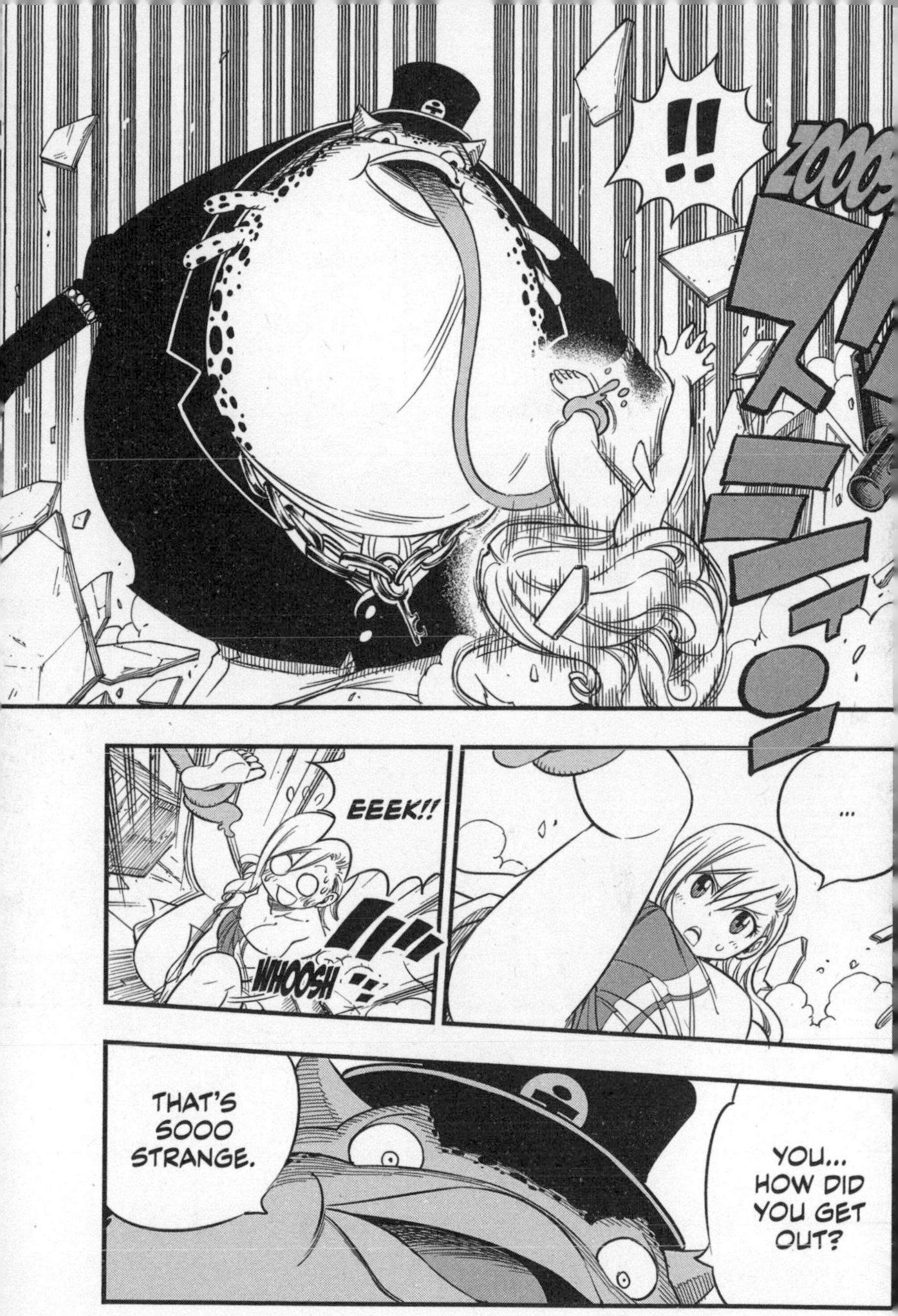
!!
ZOOO-
...
EEEK!!
WHOOSH
YOU... HOW DID YOU GET OUT?
THAT'S SOOO STRANGE.

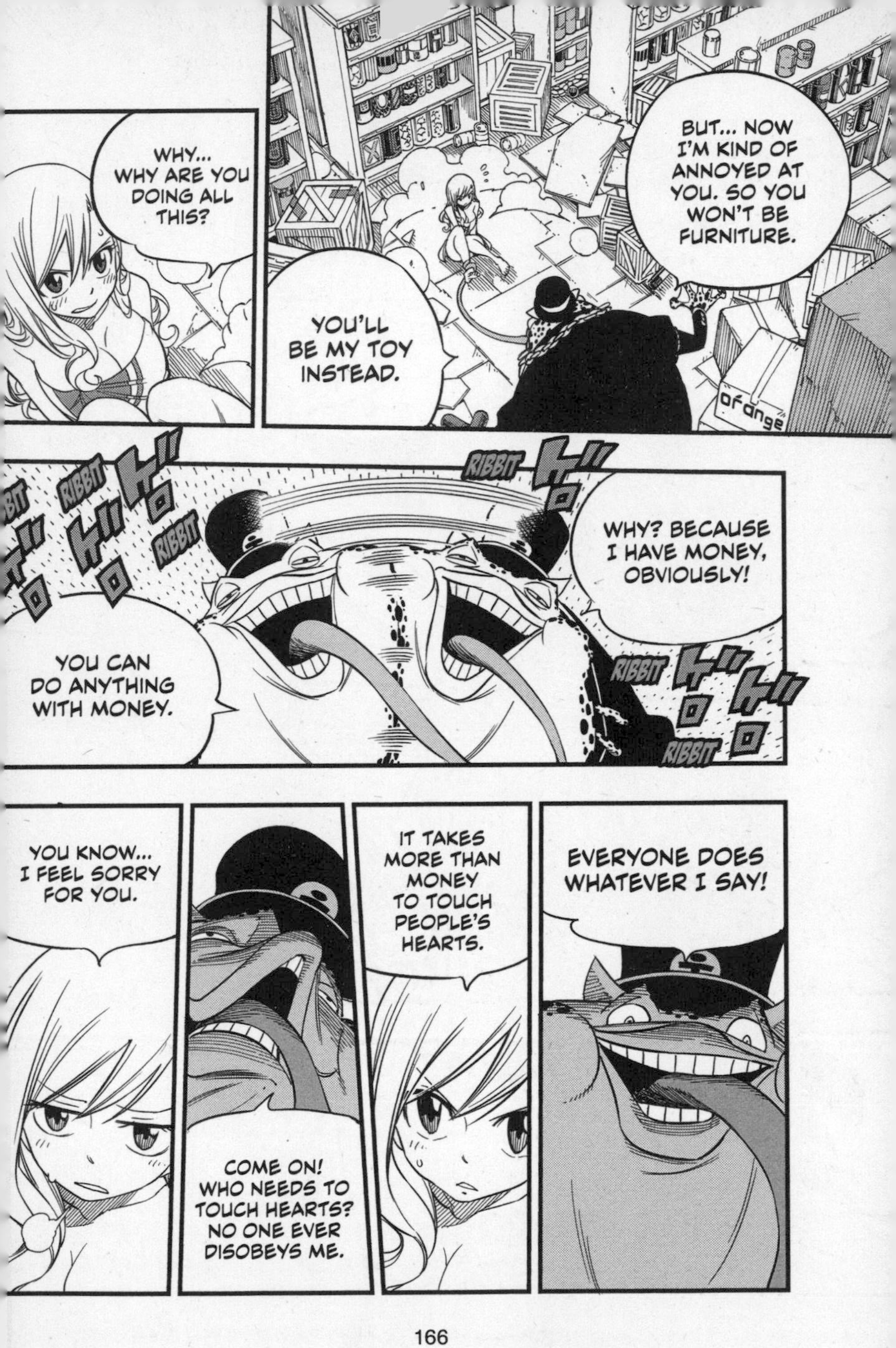
BUT... NOW I'M KIND OF ANNOYED AT YOU. SO YOU WON'T BE FURNITURE.
YOU'LL BE MY TOY INSTEAD.
orange
WHY... WHY ARE YOU DOING ALL THIS?
RIBBIT
WHY? BECAUSE I HAVE MONEY, OBVIOUSLY!
RIBBIT
RIBBIT
RIBBIT
RIBBIT
YOU CAN DO ANYTHING WITH MONEY.
RIBBIT
EVERYONE DOES WHATEVER I SAY!
IT TAKES MORE THAN MONEY TO TOUCH PEOPLE'S HEARTS.
COME ON! WHO NEEDS TO TOUCH HEARTS? NO ONE EVER DISOBEYS ME.
YOU KNOW... I FEEL SORRY FOR YOU.

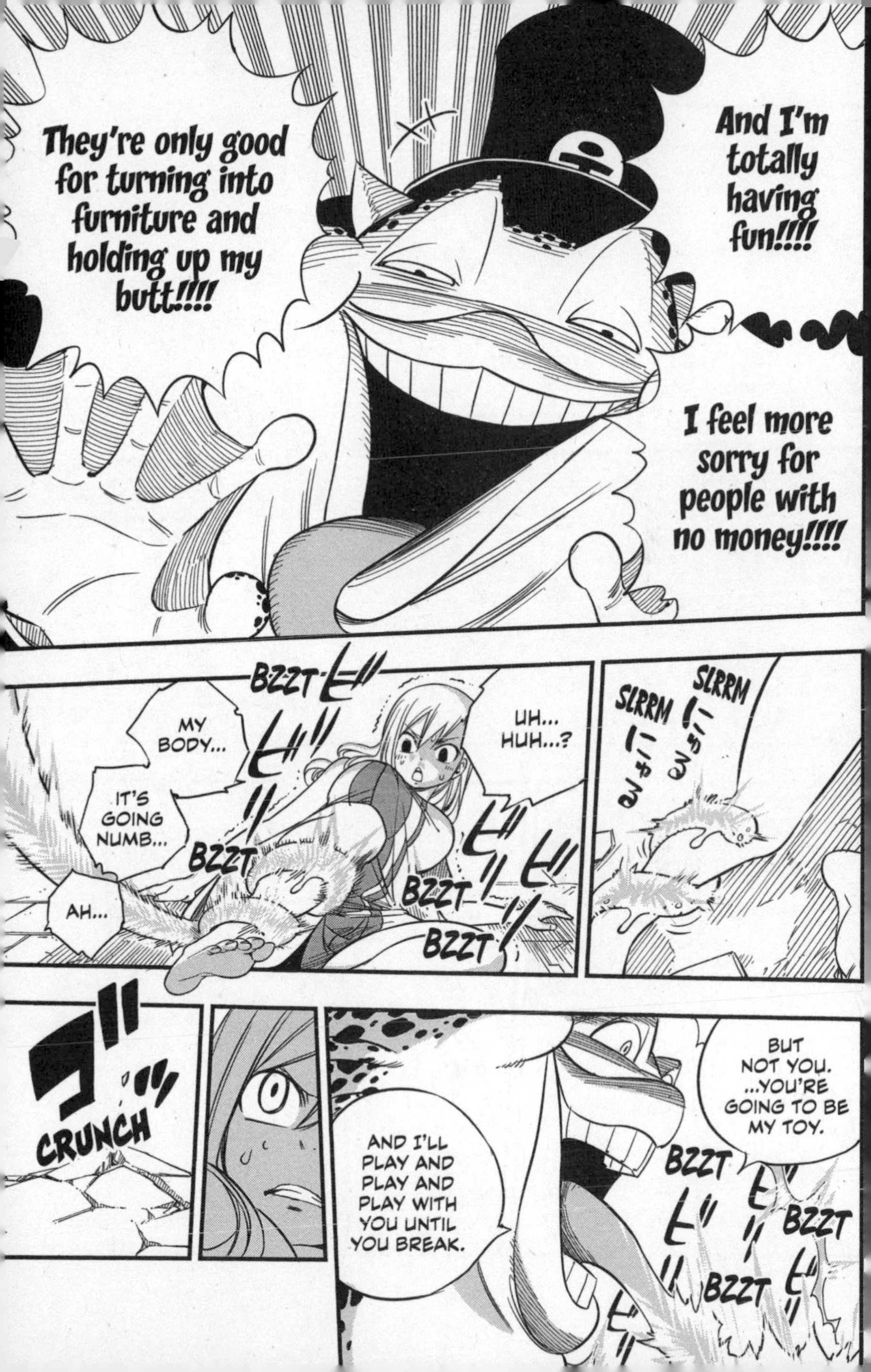
And I'm totally having fun!!!!
I feel more sorry for people with no money!!!!
They're only good for turning into furniture and holding up my butt!!!!
SLRRM
SLRRM
BZZT
UH... HUH...?
MY BODY...
IT'S GOING NUMB...
BZZT
BZZT
BZZT
AH...
BUT NOT YOU. ...YOU'RE GOING TO BE MY TOY.
BZZT
BZZT
BZZT
AND I'LL PLAY AND PLAY AND PLAY WITH YOU UNTIL YOU BREAK.
CRUNCH

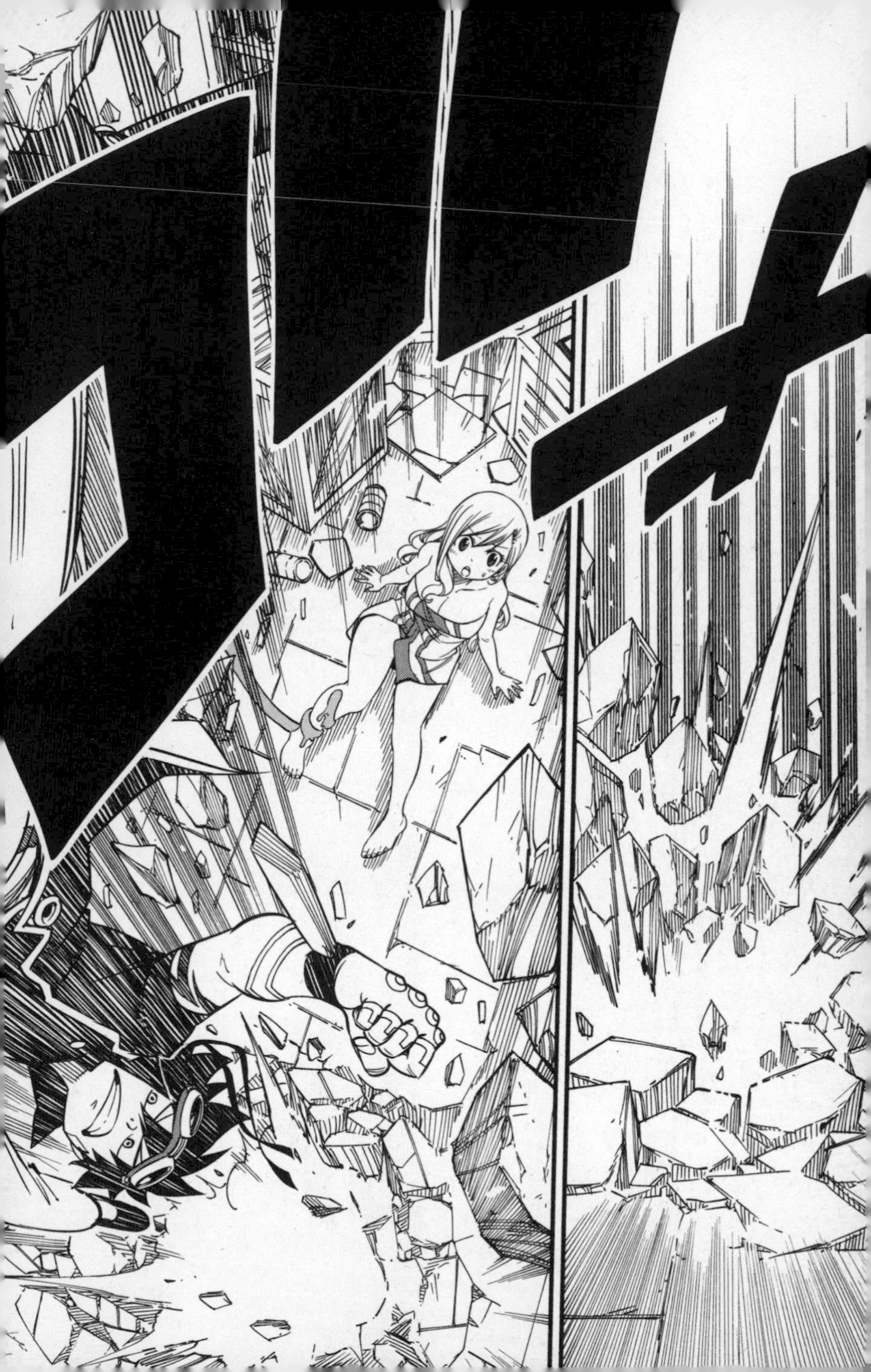

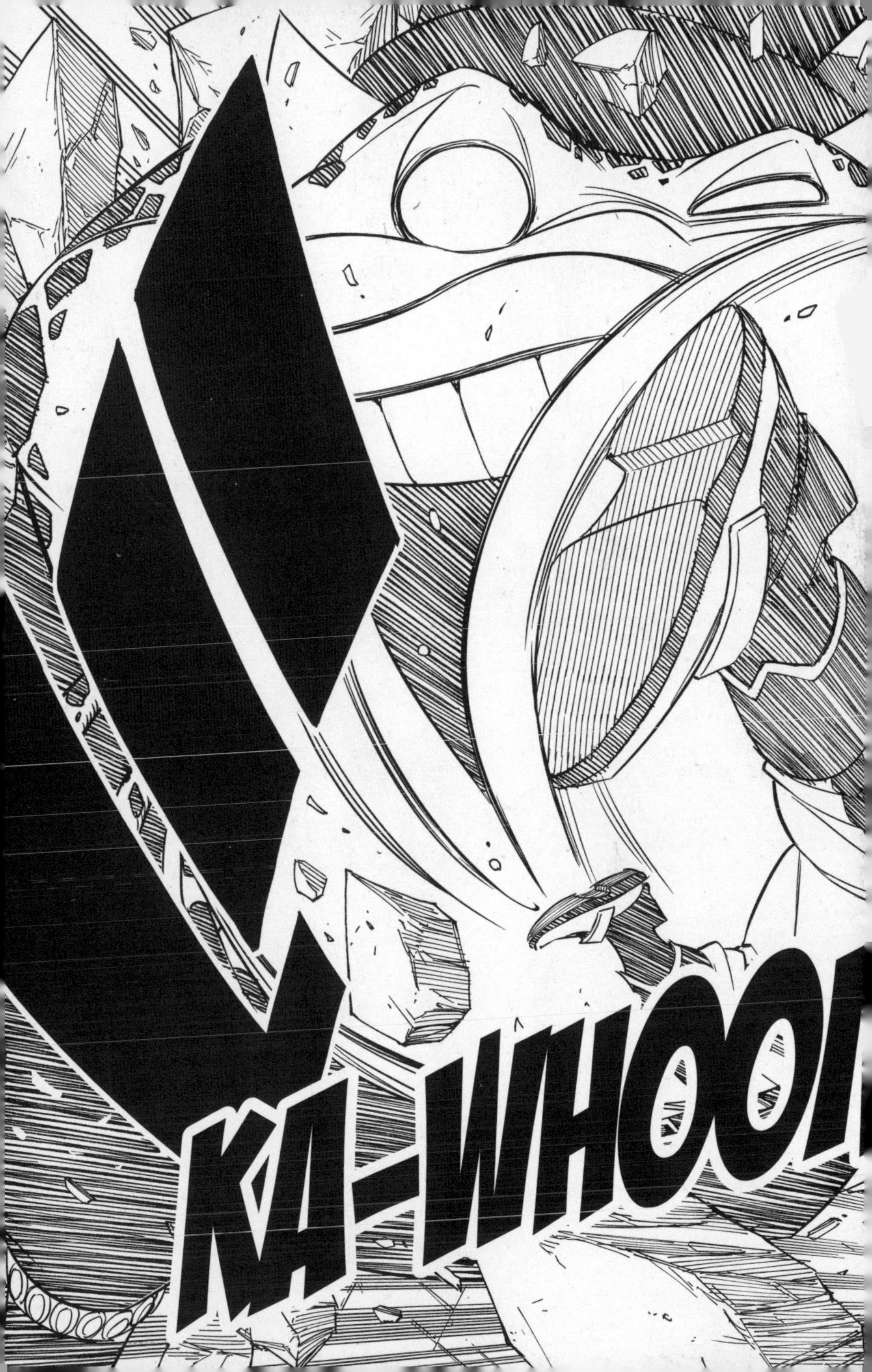
KA-WHOO!

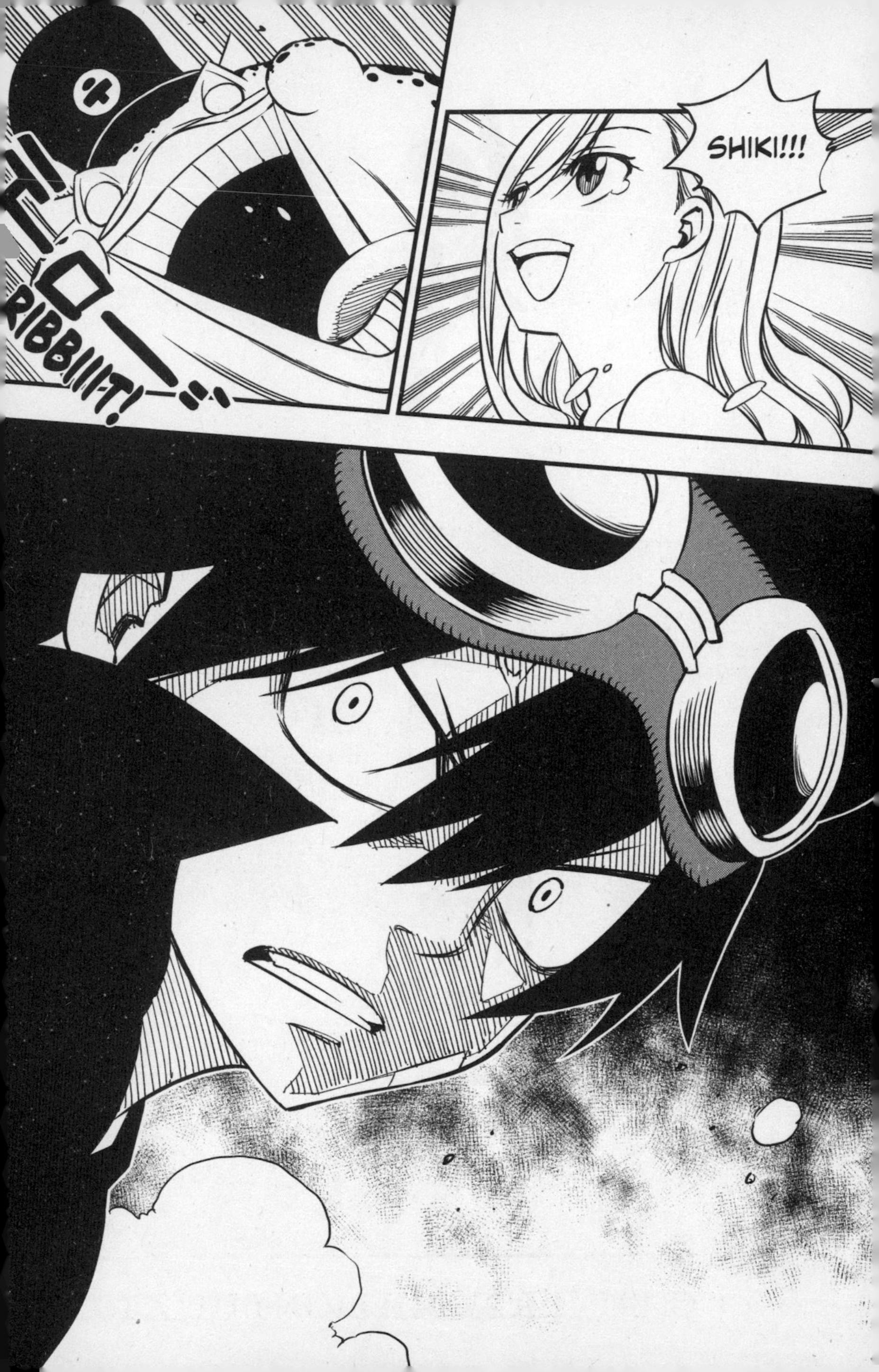
SHIKI!!!
RIBBIIIT!

EDENS ZERO

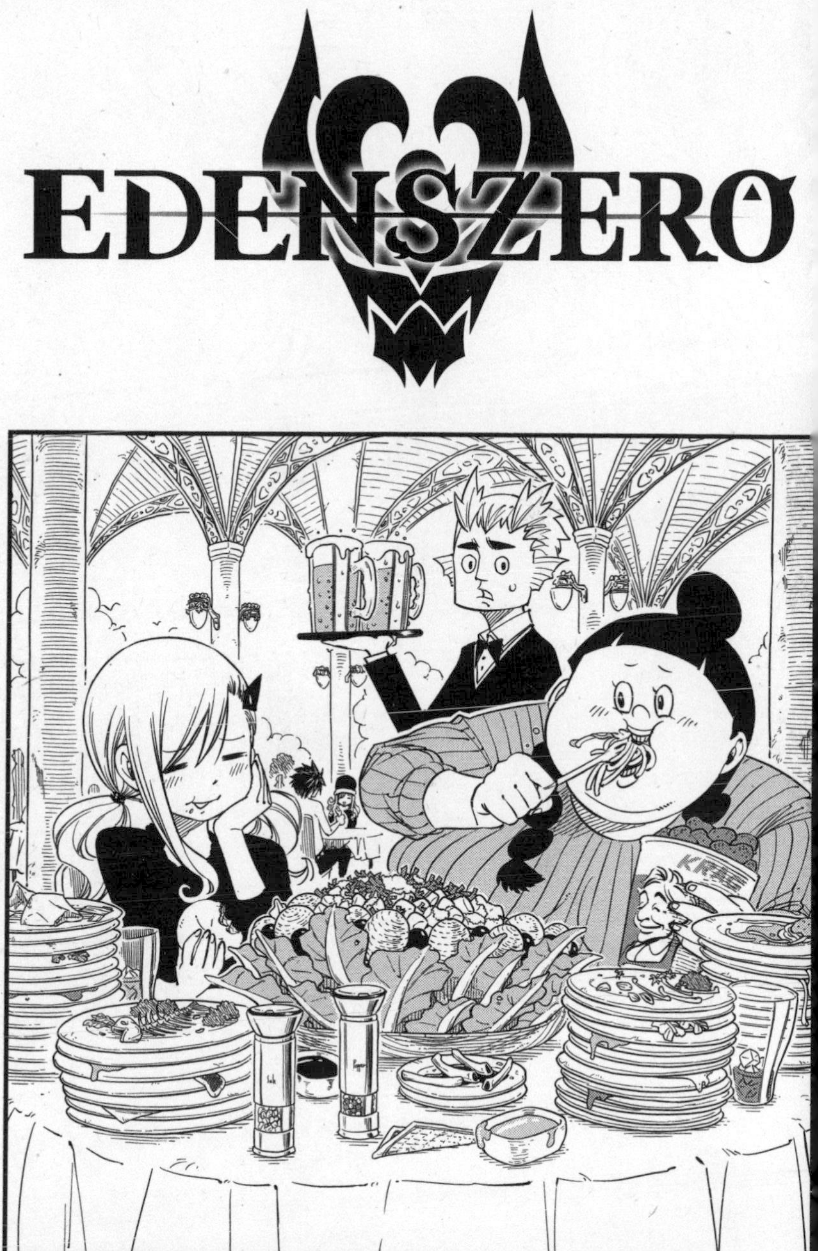

CHAPTER 23: MILLION BULLETS

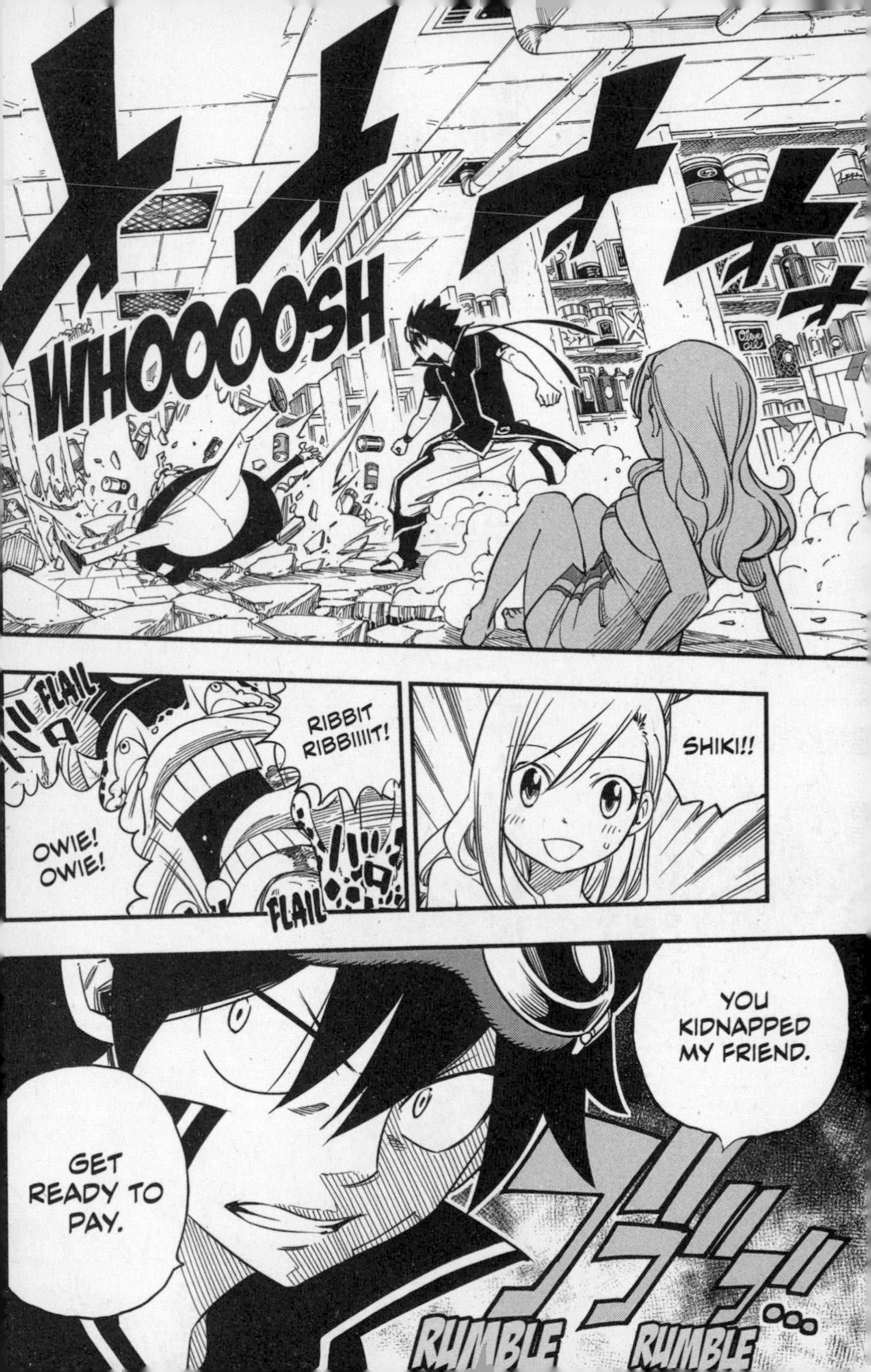
WHOOOOSH
SHIKI!!
RIBBIT RIBBIIIIT!
FLAIL
OWIE! OWIE!
FLAIL
YOU KIDNAPPED MY FRIEND.
GET READY TO PAY.
RUMBLE RUMBLE

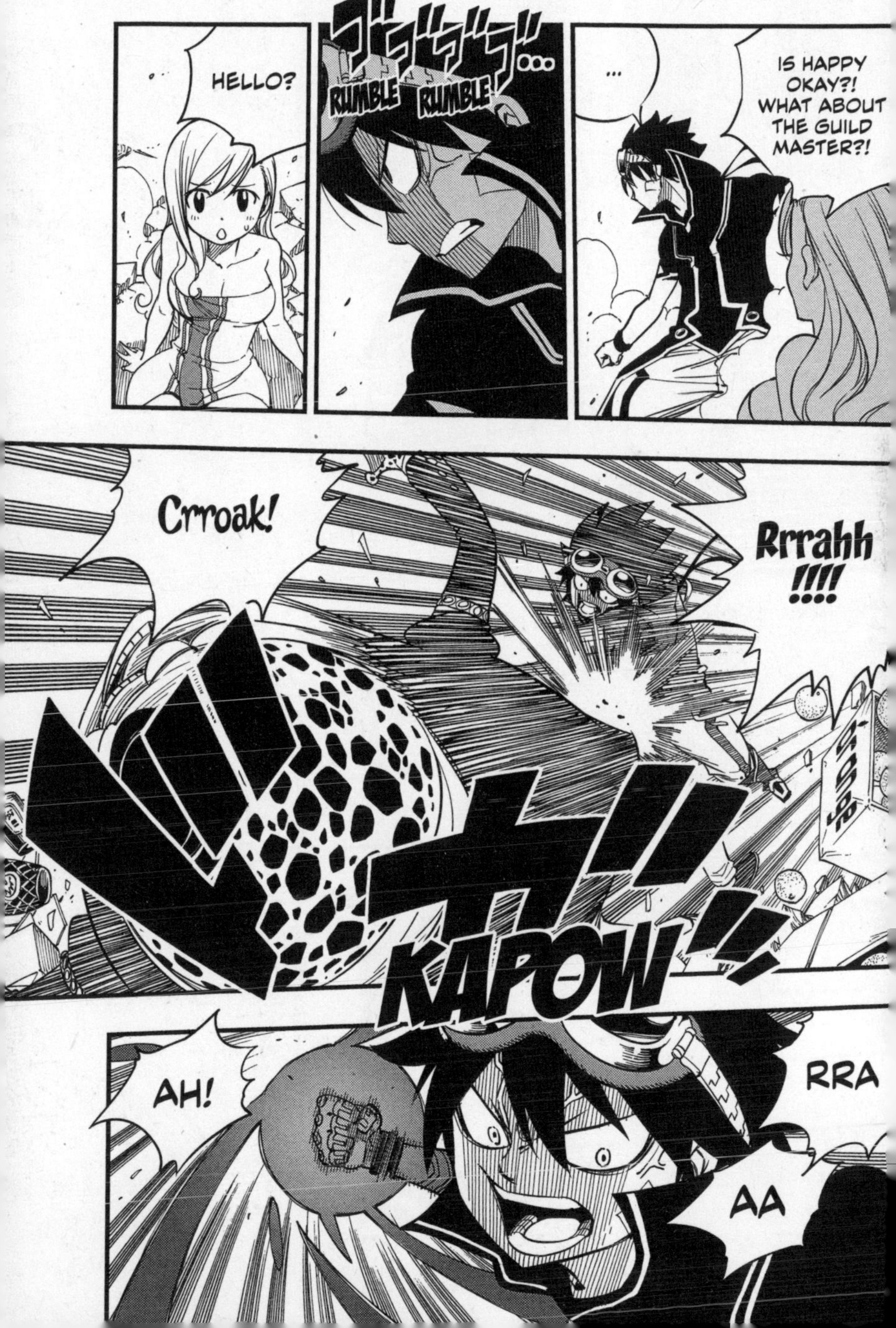
...
IS HAPPY OKAY?! WHAT ABOUT THE GUILD MASTER?!
RUMBLE RUMBLE
...
HELLO?
Rrrahh !!!!
Crrroak!
KAPOW
RRA AA
AH!

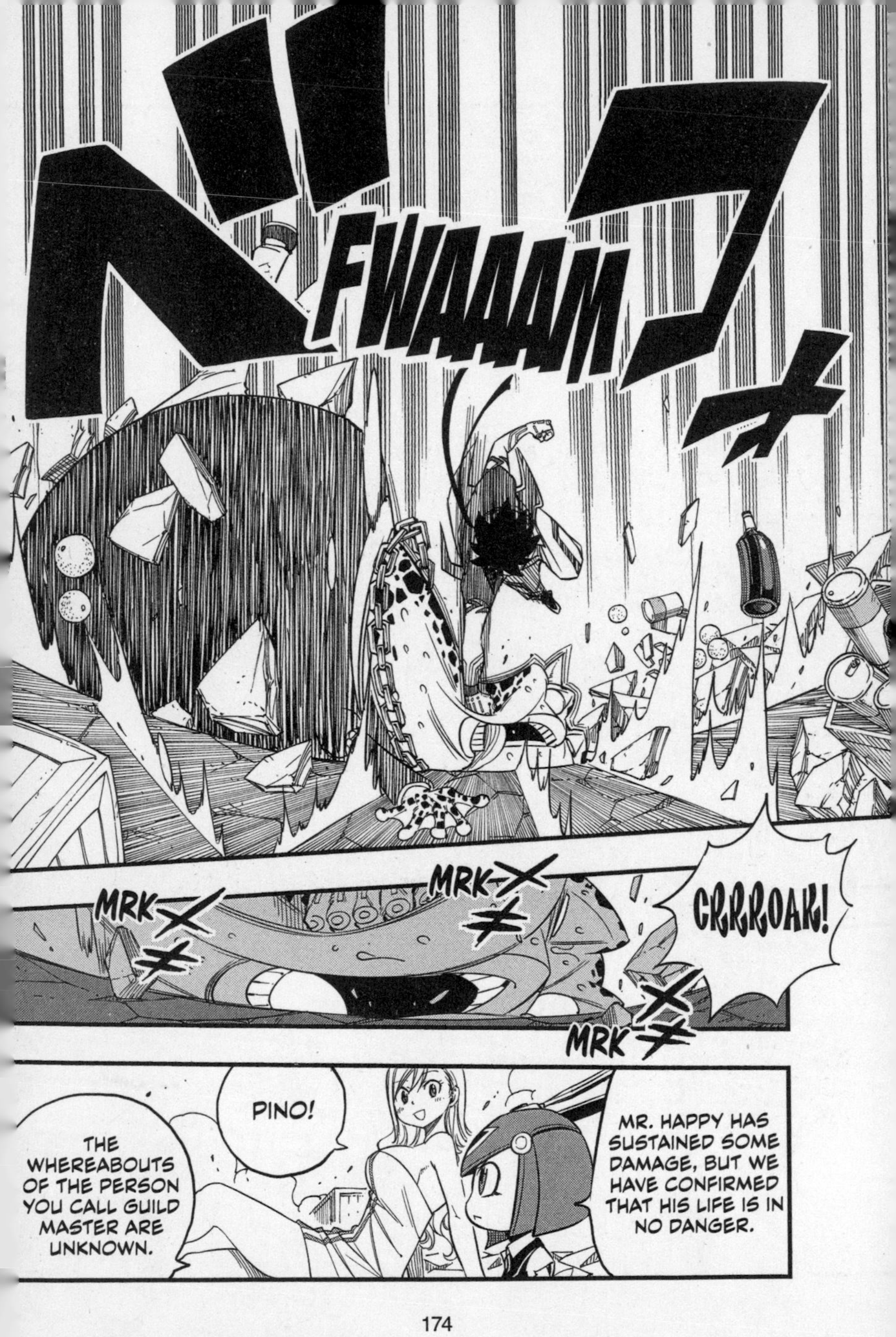
FWAAAM
CRRROAK!
MRK
MRK
MRK
MR. HAPPY HAS SUSTAINED SOME DAMAGE, BUT WE HAVE CONFIRMED THAT HIS LIFE IS IN NO DANGER.
PINO!
THE WHEREABOUTS OF THE PERSON YOU CALL GUILD MASTER ARE UNKNOWN.

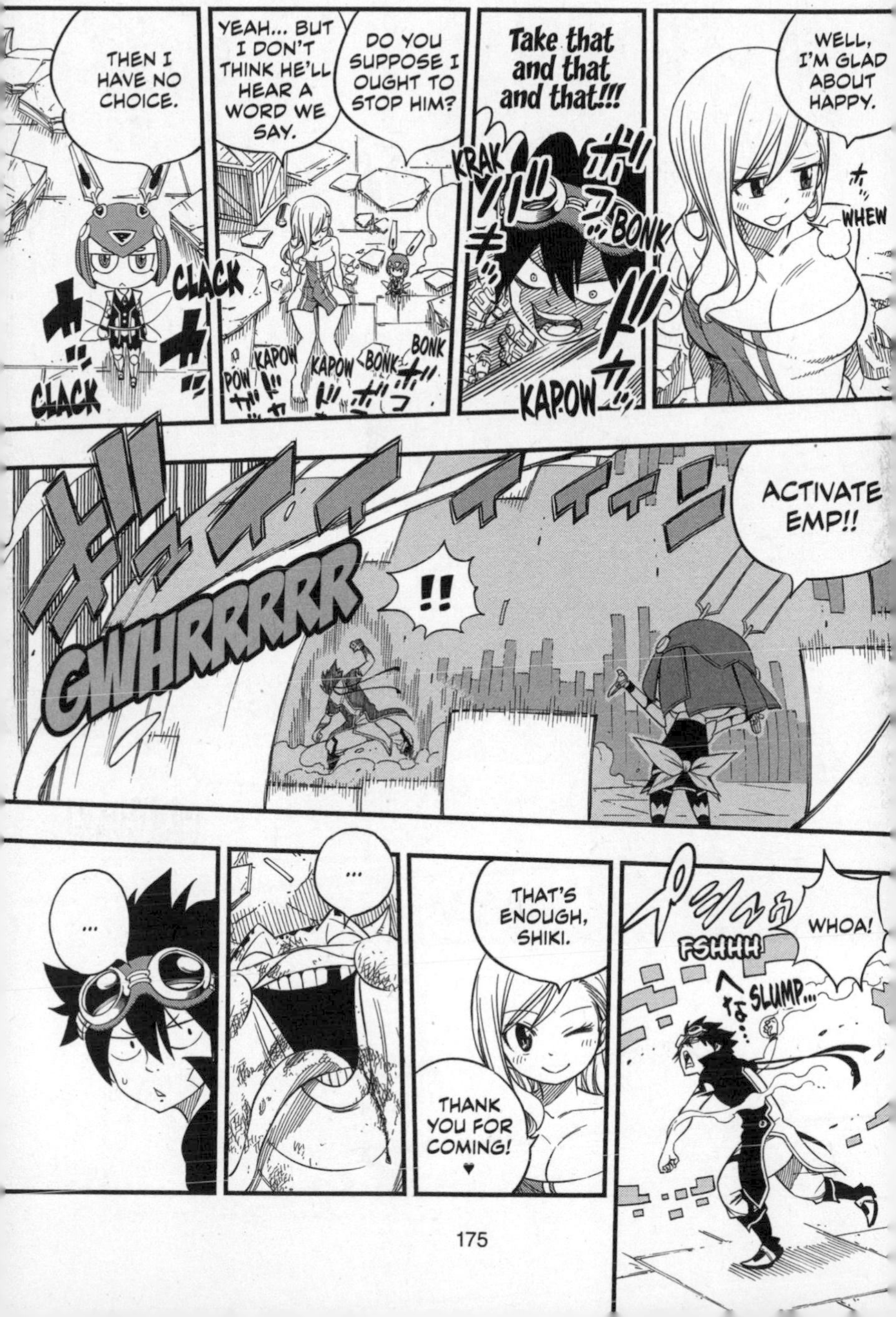
WELL, I'M GLAD ABOUT HAPPY.
WHEW
Take that and that and that!!!
KRAK
BONK
KAPOW
DO YOU SUPPOSE I OUGHT TO STOP HIM?
YEAH... BUT I DON'T THINK HE'LL HEAR A WORD WE SAY.
BONK
BONK
KAPOW
KAPOW
POW
THEN I HAVE NO CHOICE.
CLACK
CLACK
ACTIVATE EMP!!
!!
GWHRRRRR
WHOA!
FSHHH
SLUMP...
THAT'S ENOUGH, SHIKI.
THANK YOU FOR COMING! ♥
...
...

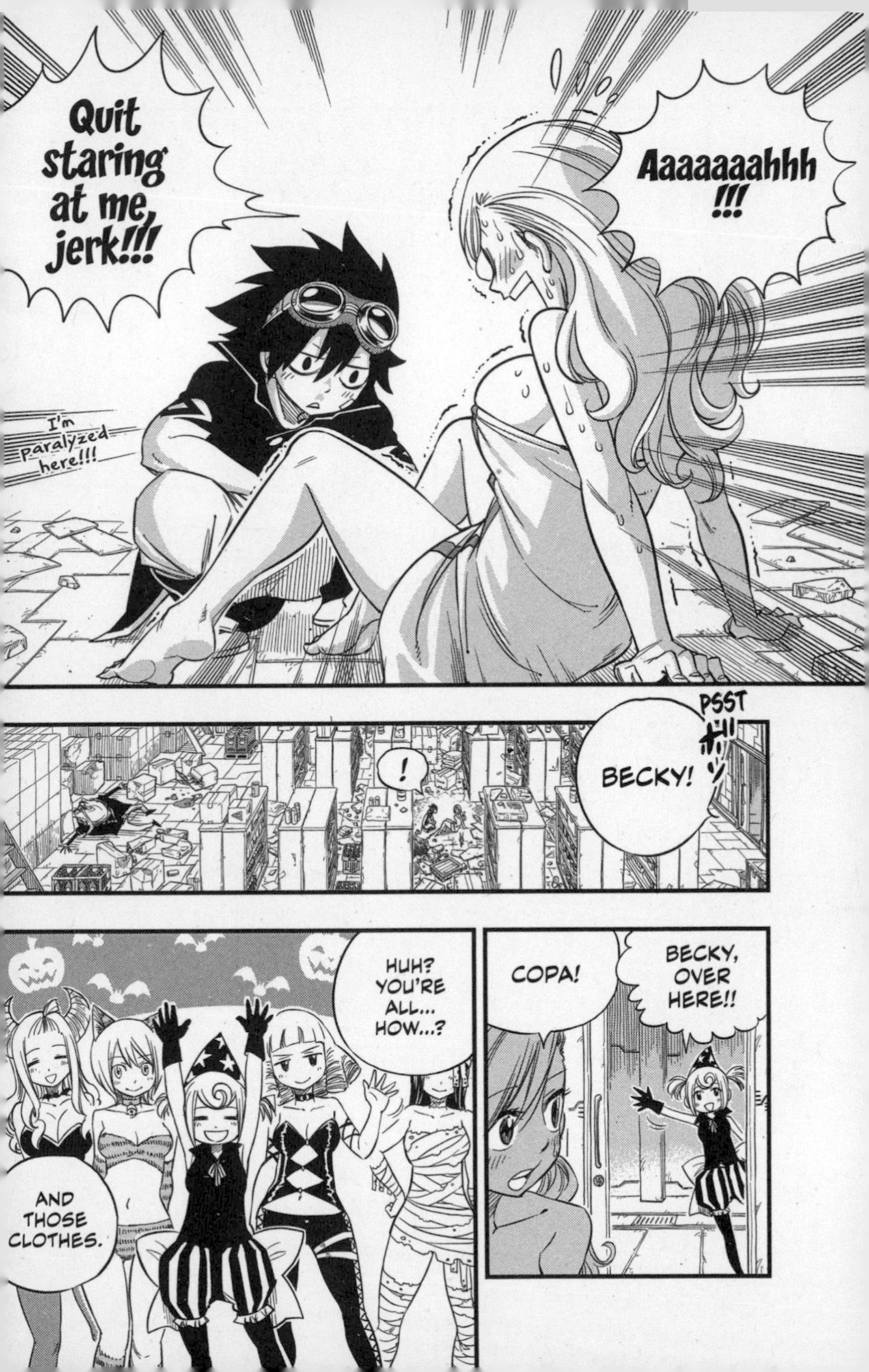
Aaaaaaahhh!!!
Quit staring at me, jerk!!!
I'm paralyzed here!!!
PSST
BECKY!
!
BECKY, OVER HERE!!
COPA!
HUH? YOU'RE ALL... HOW...?
AND THOSE CLOTHES.

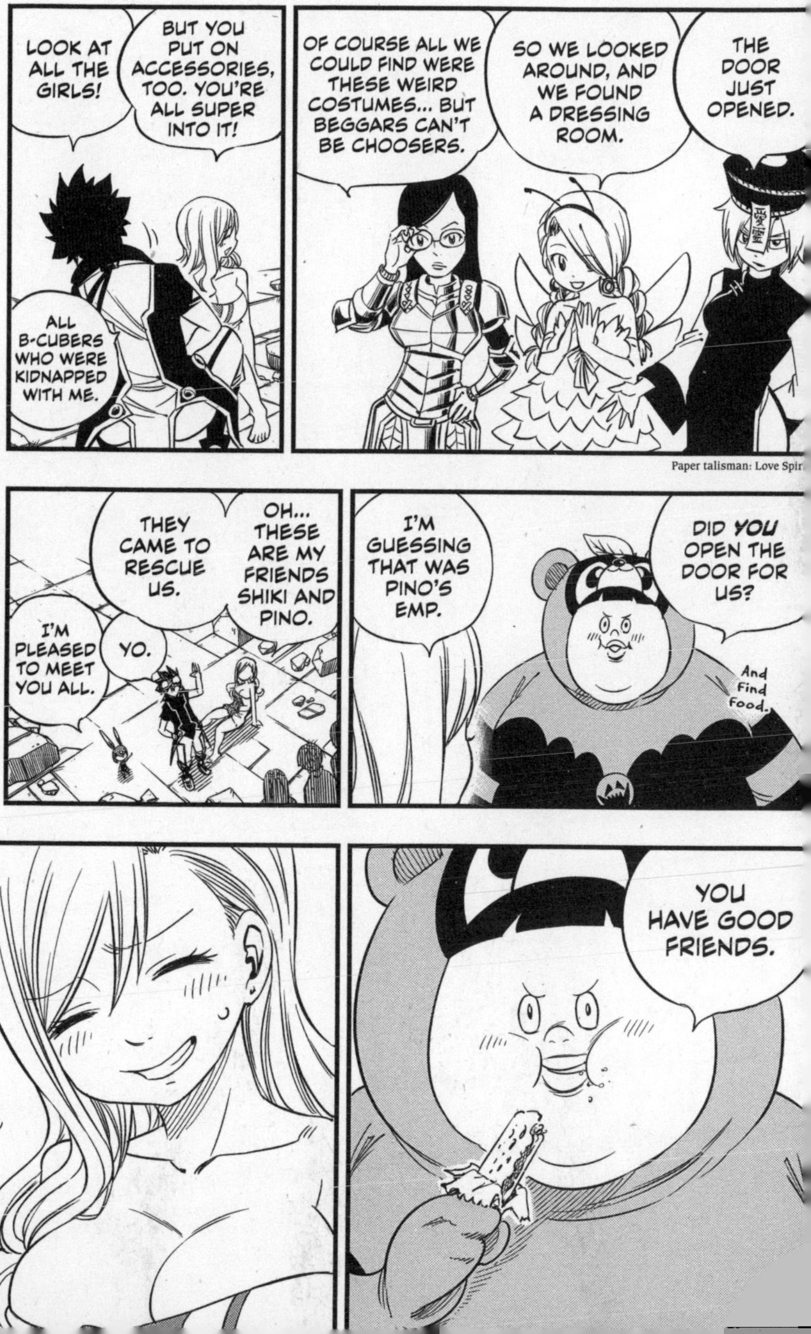
THE DOOR JUST OPENED.
SO WE LOOKED AROUND, AND WE FOUND A DRESSING ROOM.
OF COURSE ALL WE COULD FIND WERE THESE WEIRD COSTUMES... BUT BEGGARS CAN'T BE CHOOSERS.
BUT YOU PUT ON ACCESSORIES, TOO. YOU'RE ALL SUPER INTO IT!
LOOK AT ALL THE GIRLS!
ALL B-CUBERS WHO WERE KIDNAPPED WITH ME.
Paper talisman: Love Spir
DID *YOU* OPEN THE DOOR FOR US?
And Find Food.
I'M GUESSING THAT WAS PINO'S EMP.
OH... THESE ARE MY FRIENDS SHIKI AND PINO.
THEY CAME TO RESCUE US.
YO.
I'M PLEASED TO MEET YOU ALL.
YOU HAVE GOOD FRIENDS.

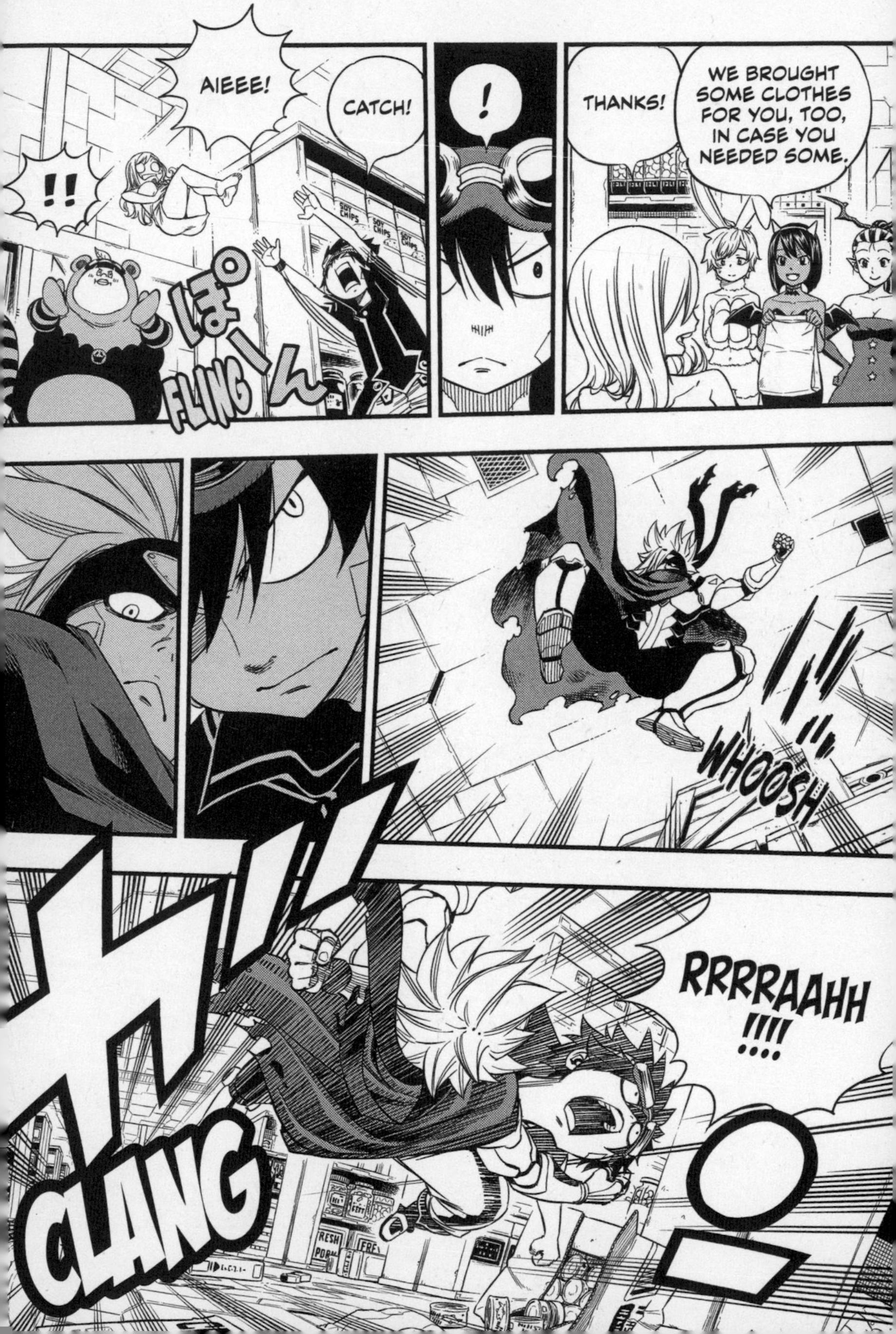
WE BROUGHT SOME CLOTHES FOR YOU, TOO, IN CASE YOU NEEDED SOME.
THANKS!
!
CATCH!
AIEEE!
!!
ぽ〜ん
FLING
WHOOSH
RRRRAAHH!!!!....
CLANG

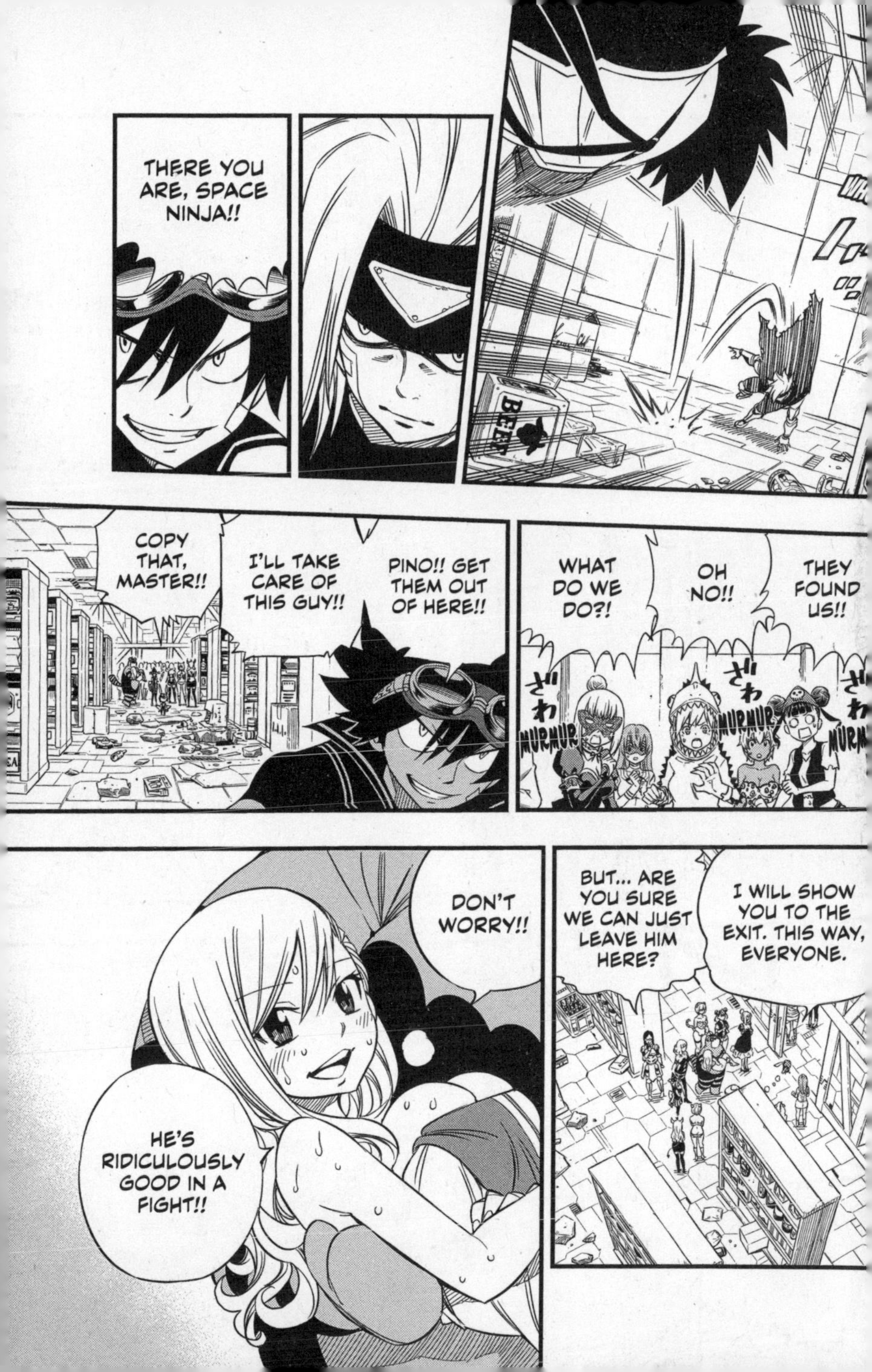
BEER
THERE YOU ARE, SPACE NINJA!!
THEY FOUND US!!
OH NO!!
WHAT DO WE DO?!
ざわ
MURMUR
PINO!! GET THEM OUT OF HERE!!
I'LL TAKE CARE OF THIS GUY!!
COPY THAT, MASTER!!
I WILL SHOW YOU TO THE EXIT. THIS WAY, EVERYONE.
BUT... ARE YOU SURE WE CAN JUST LEAVE HIM HERE?
DON'T WORRY!!
HE'S RIDICULOUSLY GOOD IN A FIGHT!!

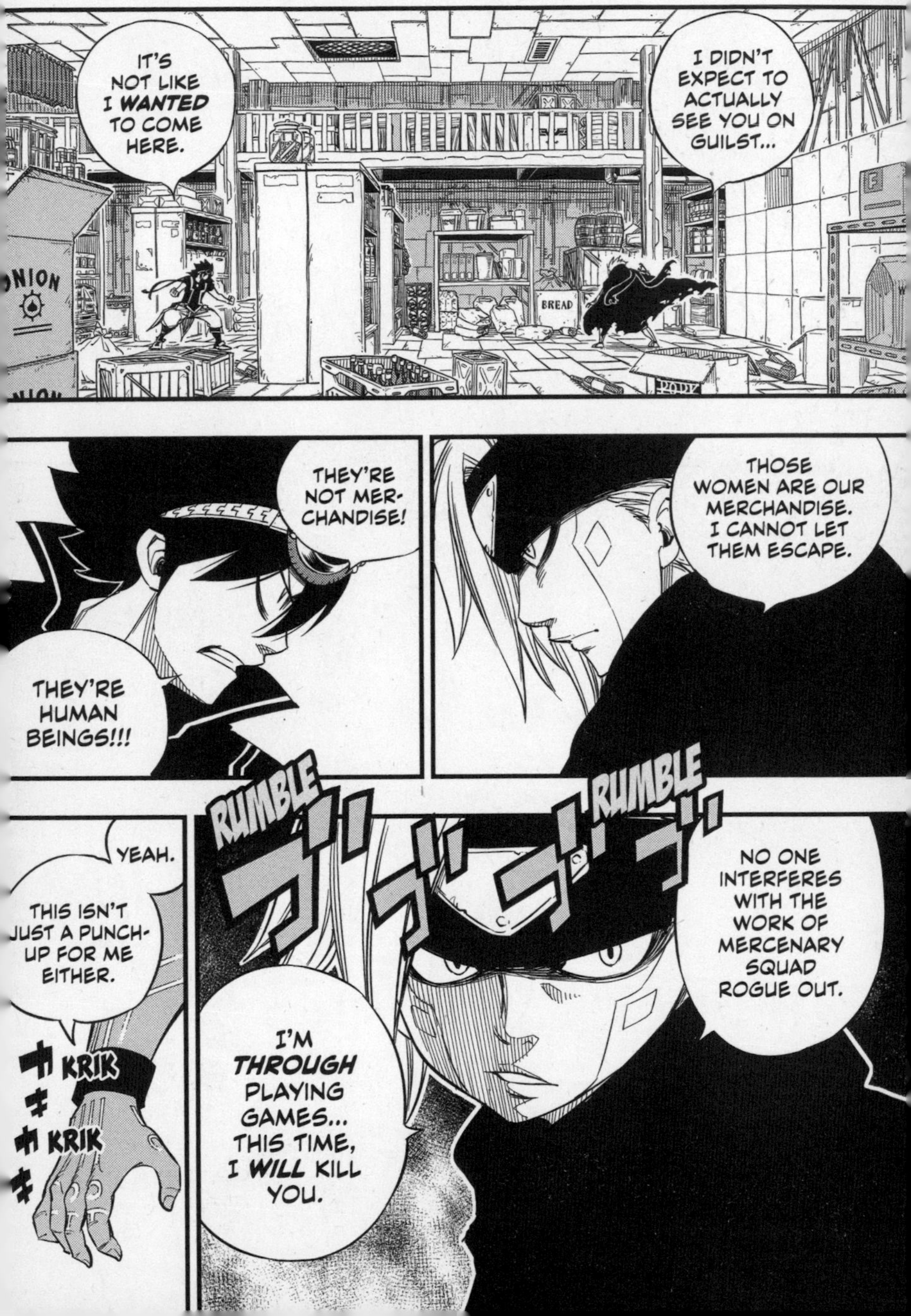
I DIDN'T EXPECT TO ACTUALLY SEE YOU ON GUILST...
IT'S NOT LIKE I WANTED TO COME HERE.
BREAD
ONION
THOSE WOMEN ARE OUR MERCHANDISE. I CANNOT LET THEM ESCAPE.
THEY'RE NOT MER-CHANDISE!
THEY'RE HUMAN BEINGS!!!
RUMBLE
RUMBLE
ゴゴ
ゴゴ
NO ONE INTERFERES WITH THE WORK OF MERCENARY SQUAD ROGUE OUT.
I'M THROUGH PLAYING GAMES... THIS TIME, I WILL KILL YOU.
YEAH.
THIS ISN'T JUST A PUNCH-UP FOR ME EITHER.
KRIK
KRIK

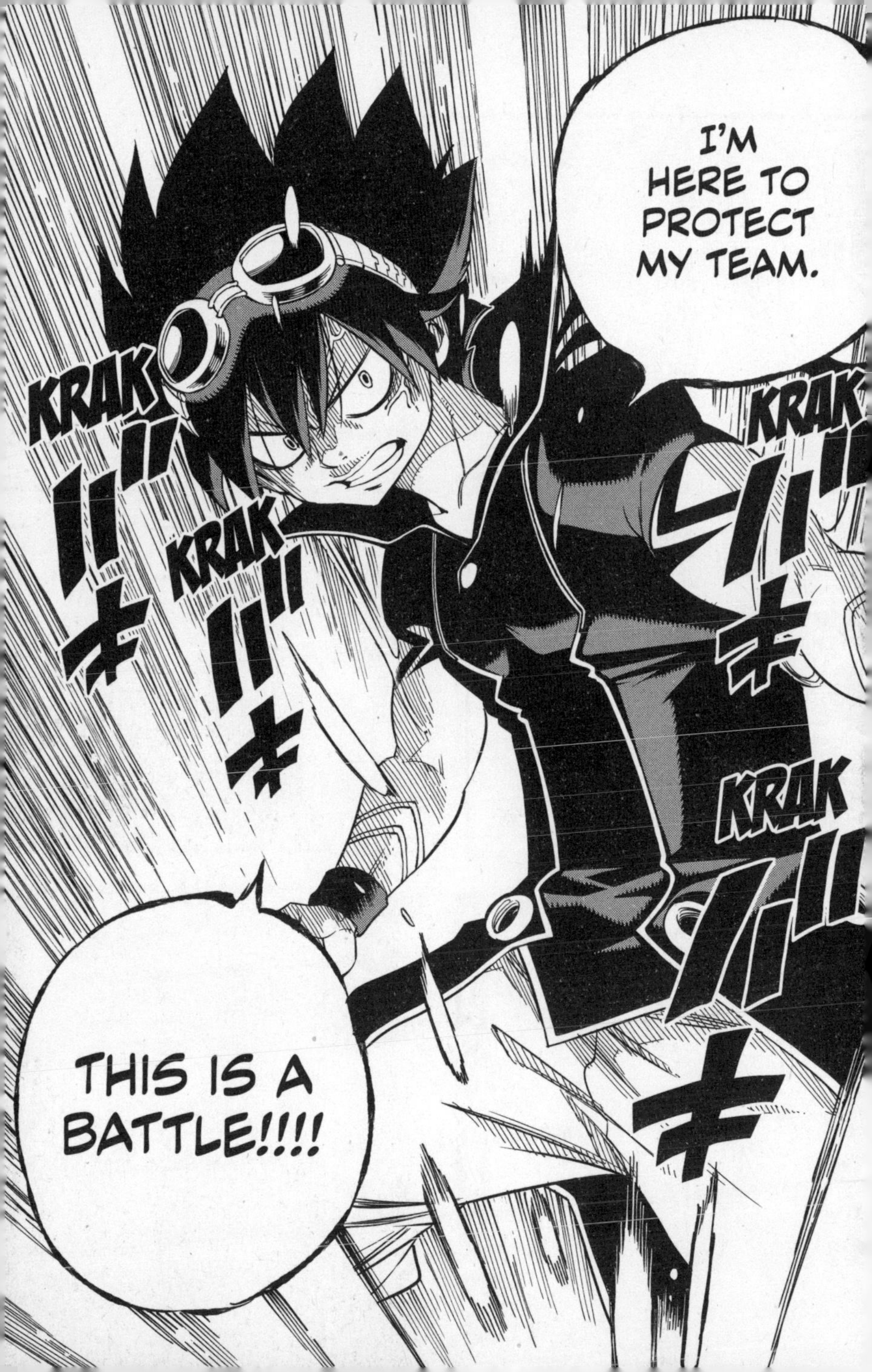
I'M HERE TO PROTECT MY TEAM.
KRAK
KRAK
KRAK
KRAK
THIS IS A BATTLE!!!!

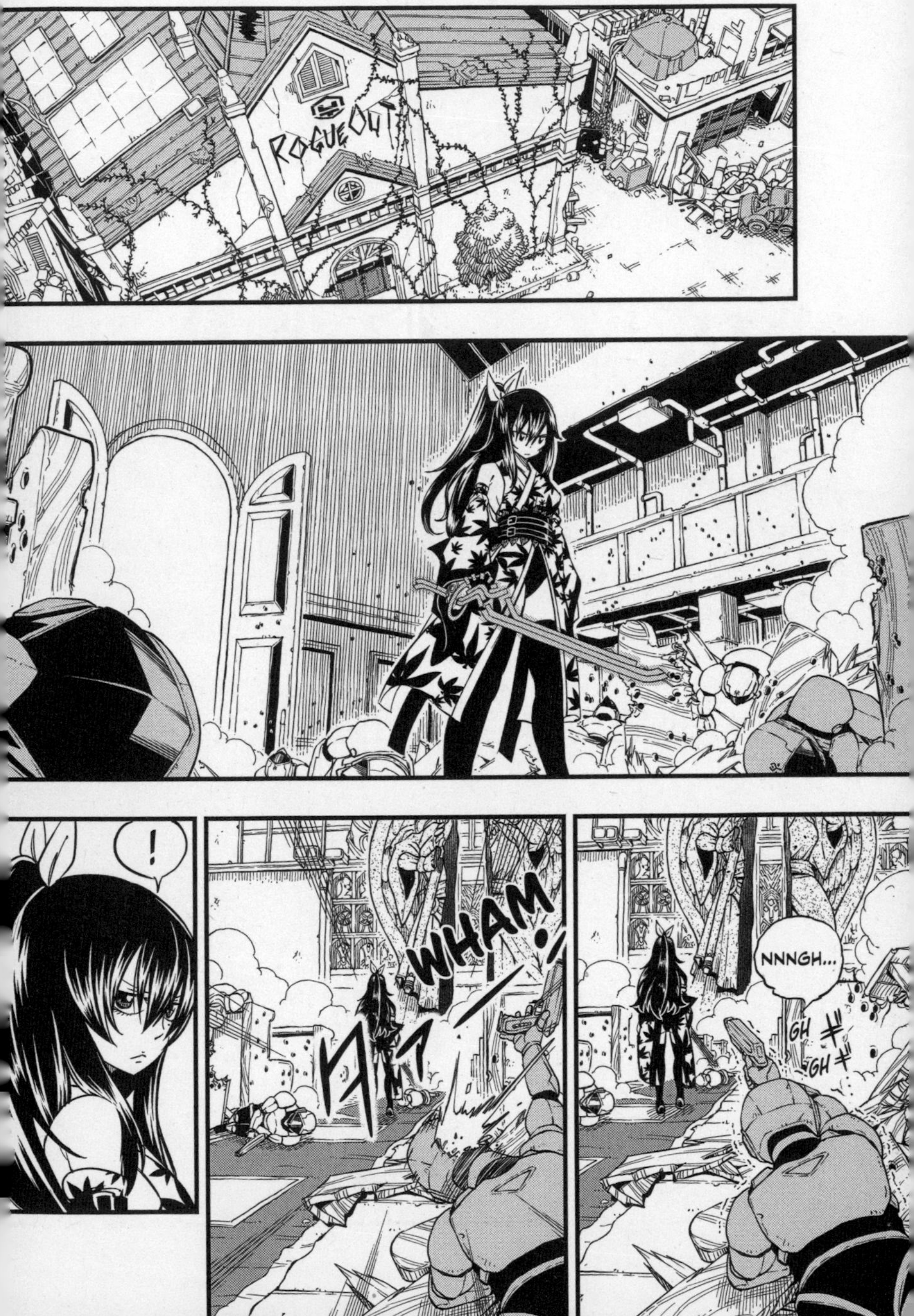
ROGUE OUT
NNNGH...
GH ギ
GH ギ
WHAM
!

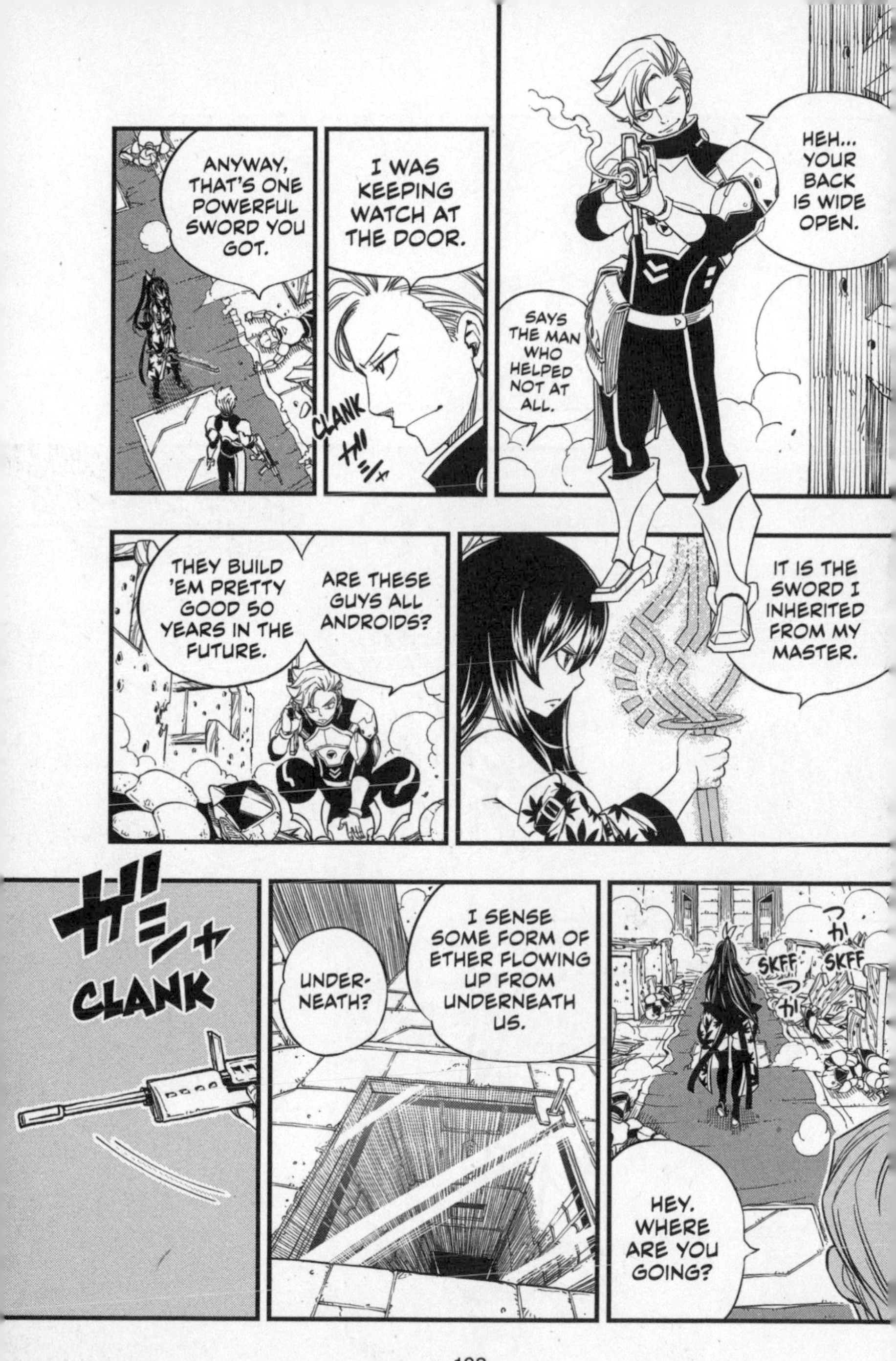
HEH... YOUR BACK IS WIDE OPEN.
SAYS THE MAN WHO HELPED NOT AT ALL.
I WAS KEEPING WATCH AT THE DOOR.
CLANK
ANYWAY, THAT'S ONE POWERFUL SWORD YOU GOT.
IT IS THE SWORD I INHERITED FROM MY MASTER.
ARE THESE GUYS ALL ANDROIDS?
THEY BUILD 'EM PRETTY GOOD 50 YEARS IN THE FUTURE.
SKFF
SKFF
HEY. WHERE ARE YOU GOING?
I SENSE SOME FORM OF ETHER FLOWING UP FROM UNDERNEATH US.
UNDER-NEATH?
CLANK

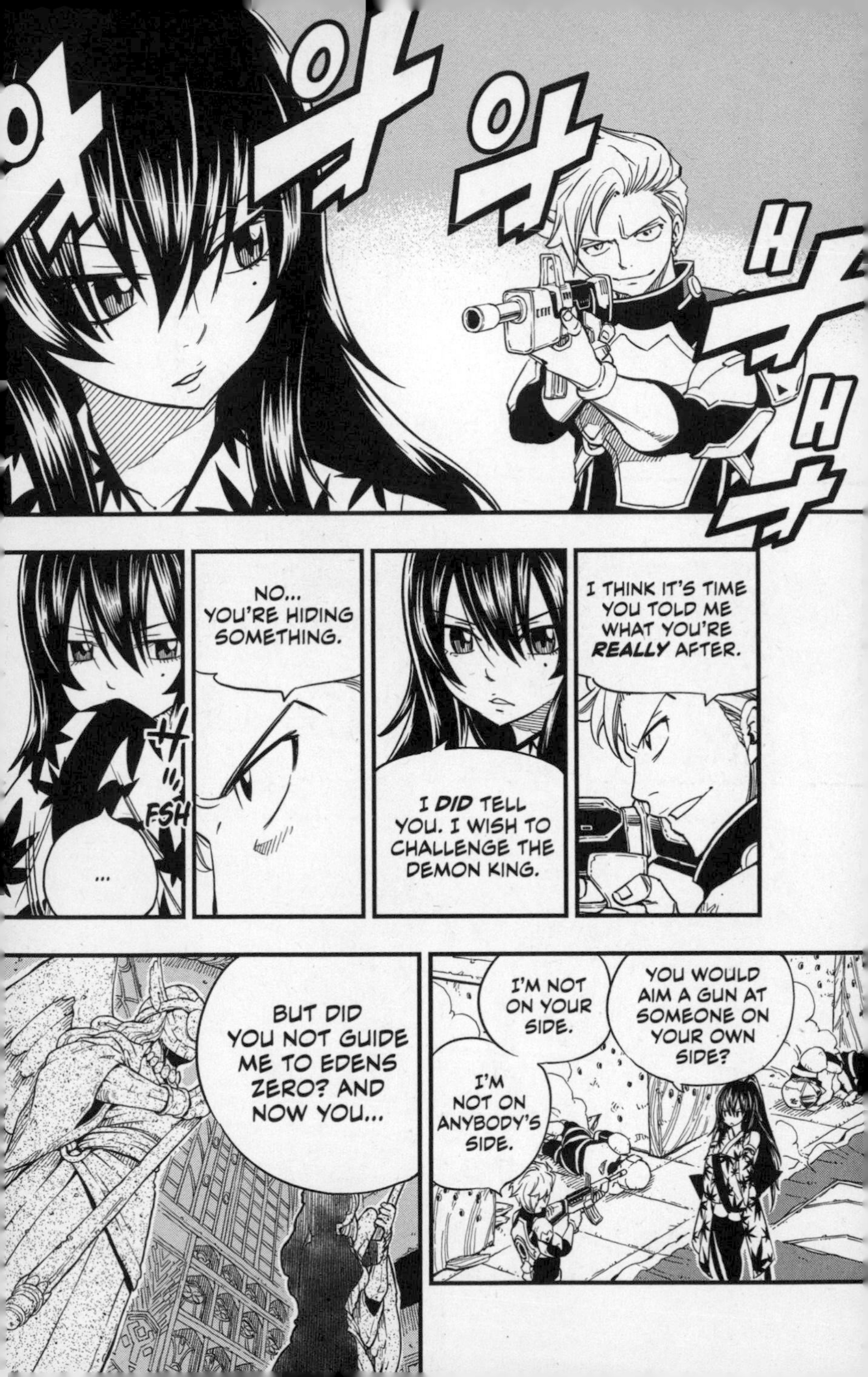
I THINK IT'S TIME YOU TOLD ME WHAT YOU'RE *REALLY* AFTER.
I *DID* TELL YOU. I WISH TO CHALLENGE THE DEMON KING.
NO... YOU'RE HIDING SOMETHING.
FSH
...
YOU WOULD AIM A GUN AT SOMEONE ON YOUR OWN SIDE?
I'M NOT ON YOUR SIDE.
I'M NOT ON ANYBODY'S SIDE.
BUT DID YOU NOT GUIDE ME TO EDENS ZERO? AND NOW YOU...

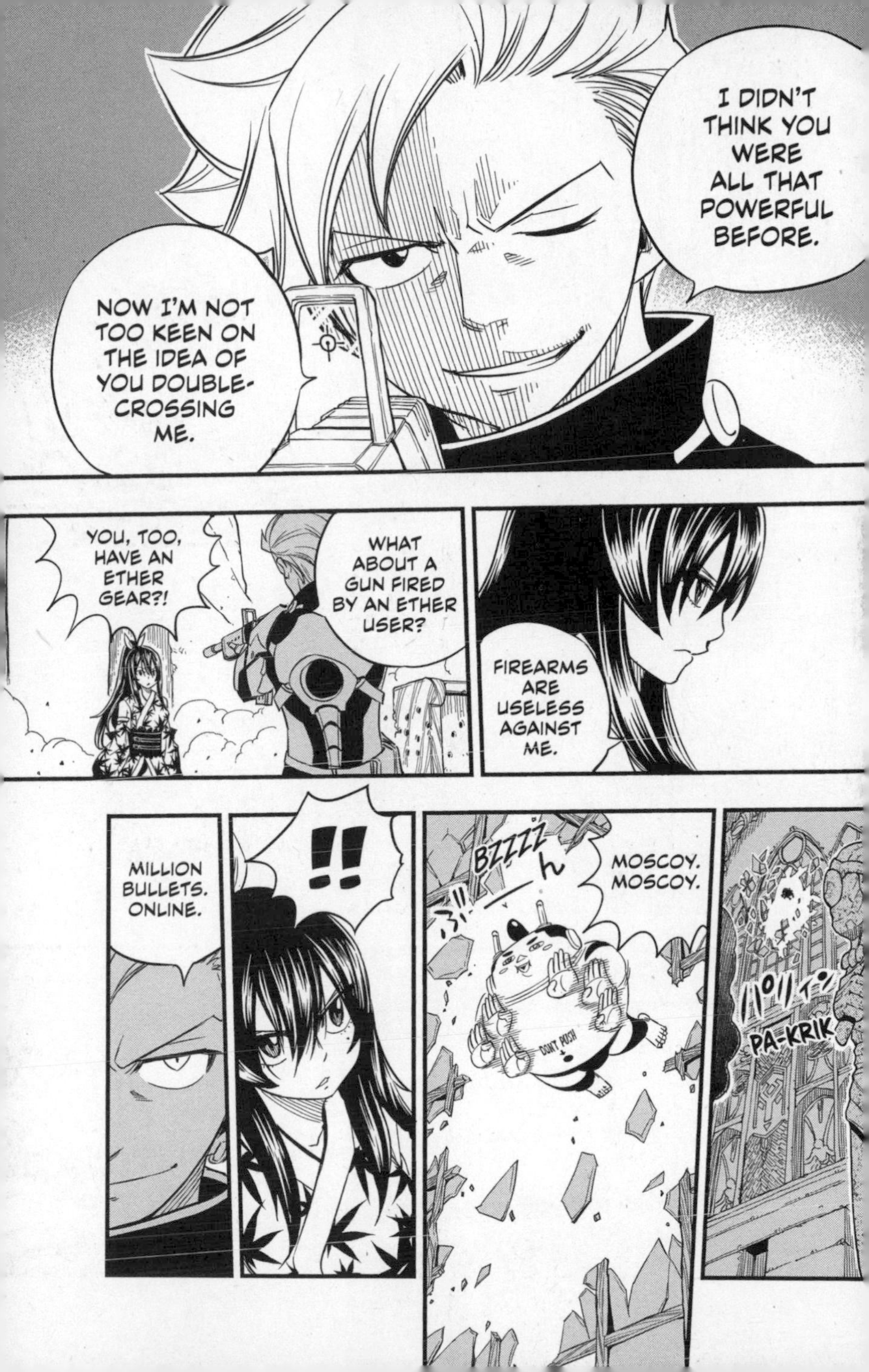
I DIDN'T THINK YOU WERE ALL THAT POWERFUL BEFORE.
NOW I'M NOT TOO KEEN ON THE IDEA OF YOU DOUBLE-CROSSING ME.
FIREARMS ARE USELESS AGAINST ME.
WHAT ABOUT A GUN FIRED BY AN ETHER USER?
YOU, TOO, HAVE AN ETHER GEAR?!
PA-KRIK
MOSCOY. MOSCOY.
BZZZZ
DON'T PUSH
!!
MILLION BULLETS. ONLINE.

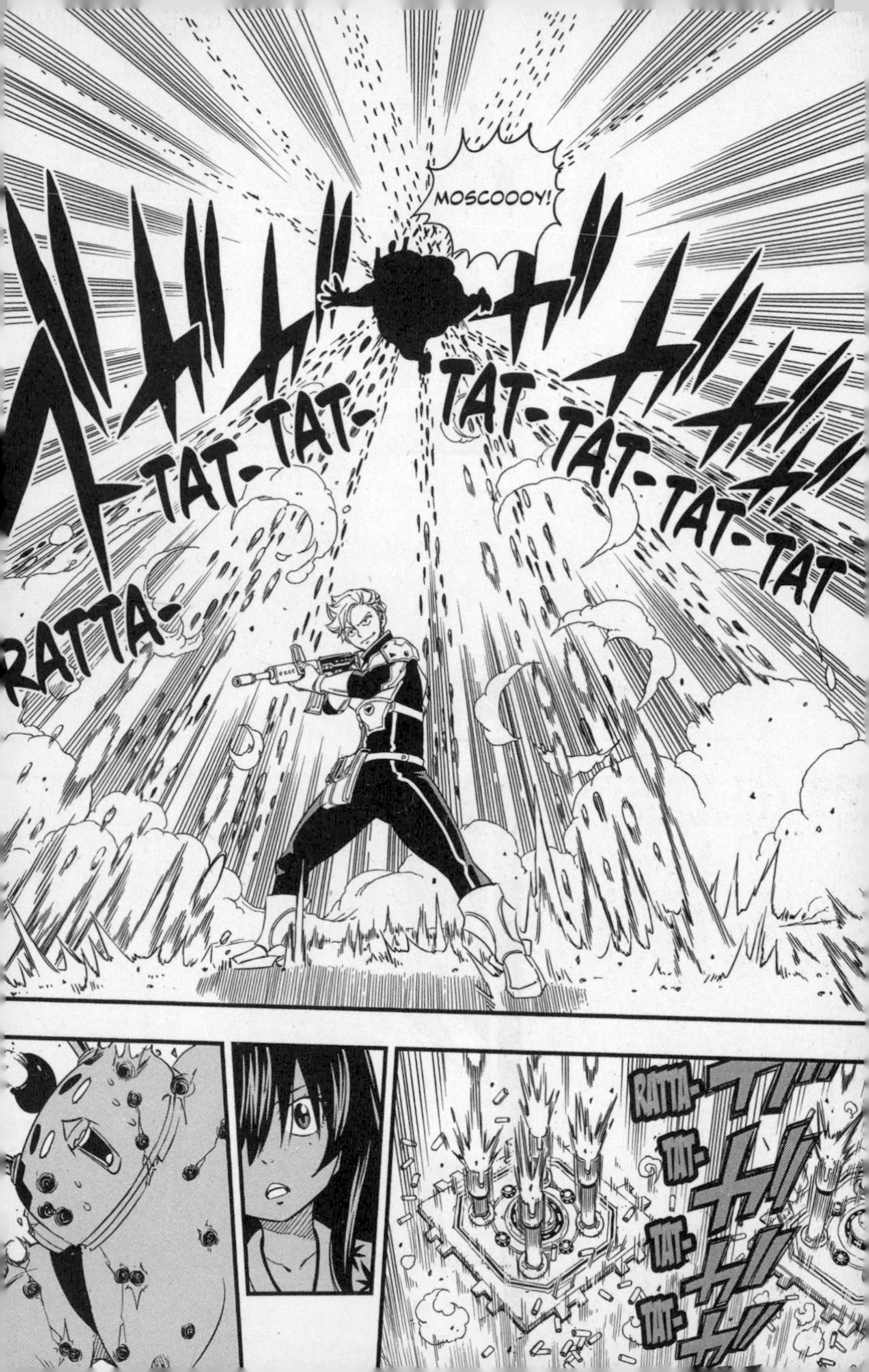
MOSCOOOY!
RATTA-TAT-TAT-TAT-TAT-TAT-TAT-TAT
RATTA-TAT-TAT-TAT-

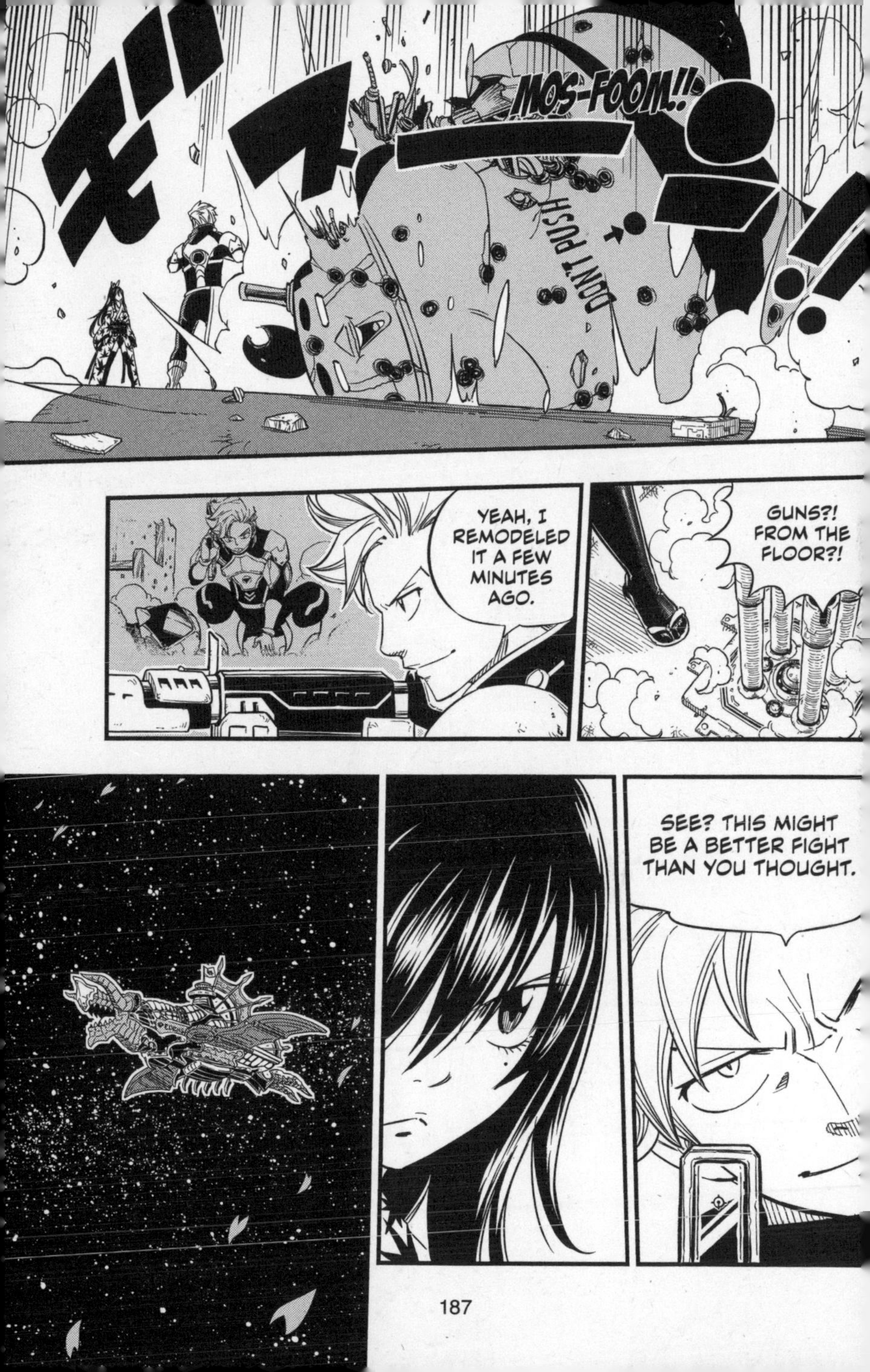
MOS-FOOM!!
DON'T PUSH
GUNS?! FROM THE FLOOR?!
YEAH, I REMODELED IT A FEW MINUTES AGO.
SEE? THIS MIGHT BE A BETTER FIGHT THAN YOU THOUGHT.

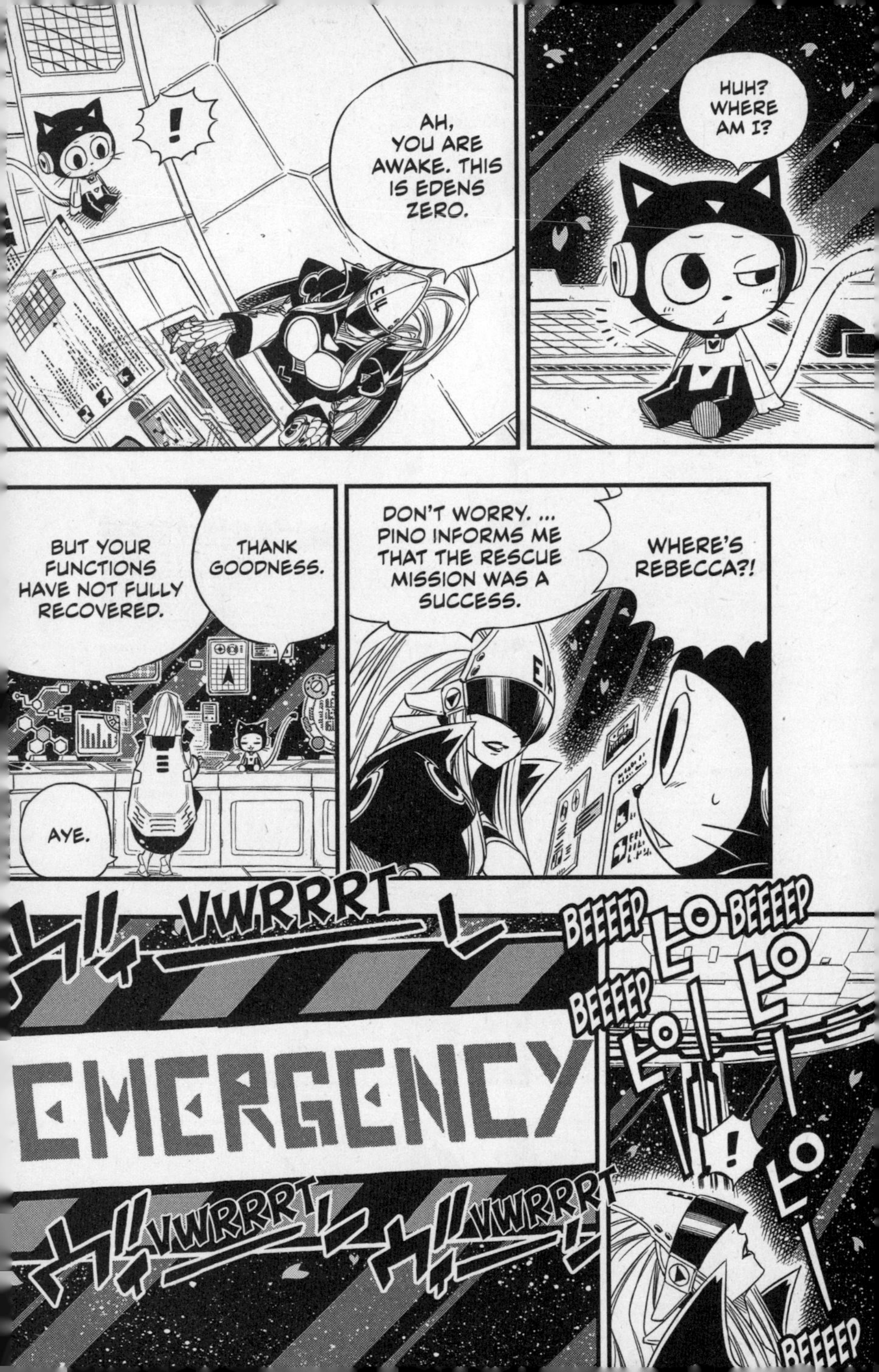
HUH? WHERE AM I?
!
AH, YOU ARE AWAKE. THIS IS EDENS ZERO.
WHERE'S REBECCA?!
DON'T WORRY. ... PINO INFORMS ME THAT THE RESCUE MISSION WAS A SUCCESS.
THANK GOODNESS.
BUT YOUR FUNCTIONS HAVE NOT FULLY RECOVERED.
AYE.
BEEEEP
BEEEEP
BEEEEP
!
BEEEEP
VWRRRT
EMERGENCY
VWRRRT
VWRRRT

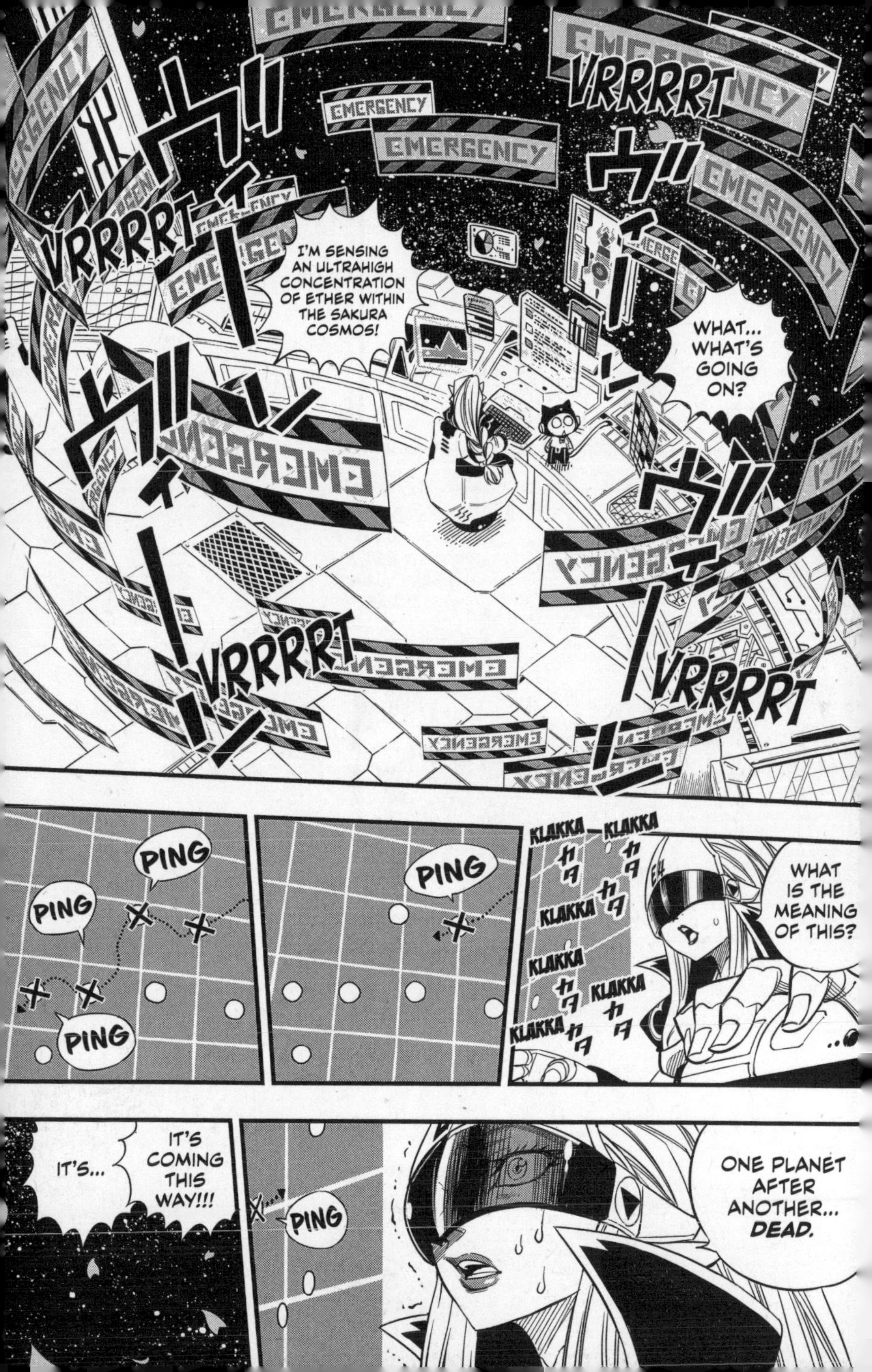
EMERGENCY
VRRRRT
WHAT... WHAT'S GOING ON?
I'M SENSING AN ULTRAHIGH CONCENTRATION OF ETHER WITHIN THE SAKURA COSMOS!
VRRRRT
VRRRRT
VRRRRT
KLAKKA KLAKKA
WHAT IS THE MEANING OF THIS?
KLAKKA
KLAKKA
KLAKKA
KLAKKA
PING
PING
PING
PING
ONE PLANET AFTER ANOTHER... DEAD.
PING
IT'S...
IT'S COMING THIS WAY!!!

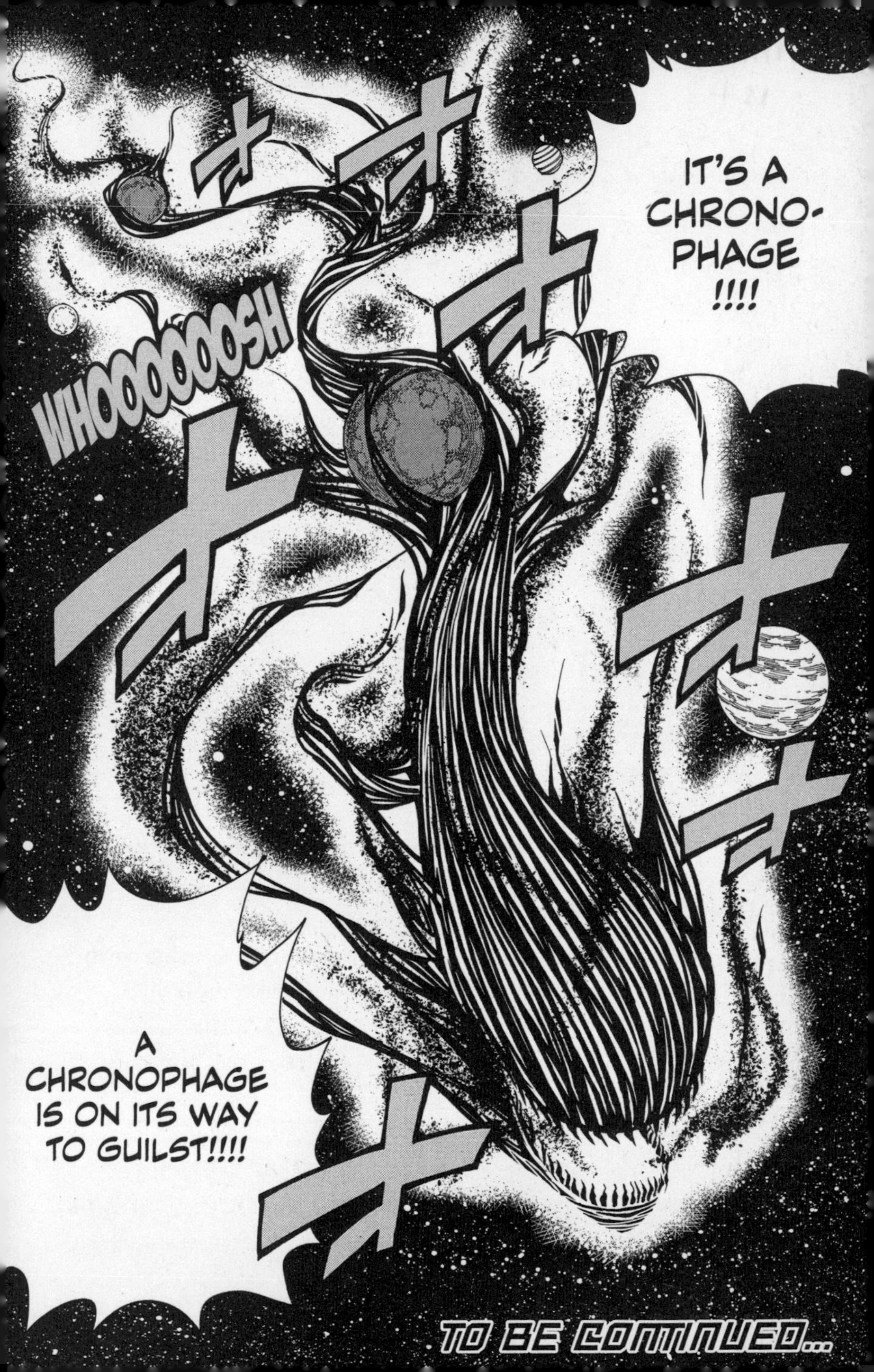
IT'S A CHRONO-PHAGE!!!!
WHOOOOOOSH
A CHRONOPHAGE IS ON ITS WAY TO GUILST!!!!
TO BE CONTINUED...

AFTERWORD

I finally managed to tie the title into the story. Really, I wanted to do it at the end of volume one, but after a lot of thought, it got moved to the beginning of volume three. As a matter of fact, it may or may not have a deeper meaning—I have technically thought of one, but whether or not it actually fits, I think is going to depend on future developments.

Now, you may not care about this, but I've used a different approach for each of my series, and I'd like to tell you about them.

For my debut series, *Rave Master*, I'd actually worked out the whole series from start to finish by the time I finished the first half. Of course, there were some details that got added in later, but the storyline was pretty solidly in place.

On the other hand, for my second series *Fairy Tail*, I went the opposite direction, and had pretty much nothing decided at all. The only thing that was predetermined was the hero's backstory, so from week to week, even I didn't know what was going to happen next.

And this series, *EDENS ZERO*, falls somewhere in between. The story elements that are set in stone are all jumbled together with elements that I've put on hold, and I'm really appreciating the "real time" feeling that comes from a weekly series.

That being the case, every week I end up drawing something just from momentum, and I can already see myself hanging my head in despair in the future, but I think I'll take that and turn it into even better and more exciting plot twists, so I hope you enjoy it.

MRYA
4-21

A Kodansha Comics Trade Paperback Original.

EDENS ZERO volume 3 copyright © 2019 Hiro Mashima
English translation copyright © 2019 Hiro Mashima

All rights reserved.

Published in the United States by Kodansha Comics,
an imprint of Kodansha USA Publishing, LLC, New York.

Publication rights for this English edition arranged through
Kodansha Ltd., Tokyo.

First published in Japan in 2019 by Kodansha Ltd., Tokyo.

ISBN 978-1-63236-758-7

Original cover design by
Atsushi Kudo, Erisa Maruyama (G x complex).

Printed in the United States of America.

www.kodanshacomics.com

9 8 7 6 5 4 3 2 1

Translation: Alethea and Athena Nibley
Lettering: AndWorld Design
Editing: Haruko Hashimoto
Kodansha Comics edition cover design by Phil Balsman